The Changing Faces of Ireland

Exploring the Lives of Immigrant and Ethnic Minority Children

Edited by

Merike Darmody
Economic and Social Research Institute, Dublin, Ireland

Naomi Tyrrell
University of Plymouth, UK

Steve Song
George Fox University, Oregon, USA

SENSE PUBLISHERS
ROTTERDAM/BOSTON/TAIPEI

A C.I.P. record for this book is available from the Library of Congress.

ISBN: 978-94-6091-473-7 (paperback)
ISBN: 978-94-6091-474-4 (hardback)
ISBN: 978-94-6091-475-1 (e-book)

Published by: Sense Publishers,
P.O. Box 21858,
3001 AW Rotterdam,
The Netherlands
www.sensepublishers.com

Printed on acid-free paper

The  and

TABLE OF CONTENTS

ACKNOWLEDGEMENTS

This book would not have been possible without the support and hard work of a number of people. We would like to thank all of the contributors to the volume for providing valuable insights into the experiences of immigrant and ethnic minority children in Ireland, and for their good-natured responses to various deadlines. We are very grateful to the external reviewers of the chapters for their detailed and perceptive comments. We would also like to thank our colleagues for providing the necessary time and space for us to see the book through to completion: Delma Byrne, Fran McGinnity and Emer Smyth (co-authors of the 'Adapting to Diversity' study at the Economic and Social Research Institute, Dublin); Caitríona Ní Laoire and Allen White ('Migrant Children Project' Marie Curie Excellence Grant, University College Cork) and Dorren McMahon ('Youth Inequalities Project' Marie Curie Excellence Grant, University College Dublin). Our heartfelt thanks go to our families for their support of this endeavour and their patience. Finally, we would like to thank Peter de Lifde from Sense Publishing for his interest in this volume and his encouragement.

Merike Darmody, Naomi Tyrrell and Steve Song
October 2010

FOREWORD

This is a very timely publication, coming as it does during a period of considerable economic and social challenge in Ireland. It is at such times that the perspectives and voices of those who are most 'othered' or at risk of marginalisation need to be heard. This is especially the case with children. We know of course that not all children are the same and there are many different childhoods, influenced by the social, familial and cultural context in which children live their everyday lives. Yet there are also commonalities across children, in terms of the importance of family and friends and the key role of identities and belonging in shaping their well-being. By focusing on the experiences and perspectives of immigrant children and young people, this publication provides rich insights into their lives across a range of social and institutional contexts in Ireland. Migrant children as a group come from a variety of social and cultural backgrounds but have a shared sense of dislocation and unsettling of the 'known' that is embedded in the experience of migration itself. This brings with it considerable challenges as they bridge 'home' and host society through their activities in school, as well as through their involvement in work and play in the local community. For some the transition is relatively seamless - supported by clear kinship relationships and valued social, material and cultural capital that facilitates entry into Irish life and society. For others, considerable resilience and initiative is required, as they seek to overcome stereotyping, racism and resistance to social and cultural change. These contrasting strands in migrant children's experiences are eloquently outlined in this book – the struggles over identity formation and meaning making through language acquisition, religious formation and recognition, the significant role of schools and schooling in shaping opportunities and belonging, the experience of racism and discrimination, the particularistic experiences of asylum seeker, trafficked children and unaccompanied minors and the contrasting experiences of health and overall well-being among immigrant children and young people. Key questions are raised about structurally embedded patterns of inequality in Irish society, about social and educational policies, as well as legislative provisions in shaping inclusionary/exclusionary dynamics in the lives of immigrant children and young people. They are underpinned by both quantitative and qualitative accounts that provide a succinct and critical overview of how these dynamics are played out for different groups of immigrant children across different contexts. This comprehensive collection is of relevance to those working with children in Ireland but also internationally to those with an interest in the experiences of first/second generation migrant children and how societies of relatively rapid in-migration have adapted (or not) to the pace of change. It is a wonderful resource for researchers, policy makers and practitioners and a welcome addition to the emerging literature in this important field.

Dympna Devine
School of Education
University College Dublin

NAOMI TYRRELL, MERIKE DARMODY AND STEVE SONG

INTRODUCTION

Exploring the Lives of Immigrant and Ethnic Minority Children in Ireland

'The circumstances and future prospects of children in immigrant families are important not only to the children themselves and to their parents, but also to the nations in which the families have settled, and where the children will live for years and decades to come.' (UNICEF, 2009: vii).

The Republic of Ireland (hereafter Ireland) is a country that has undergone rapid economic and population change since the mid-1990s. The period of economic boom between 1995 and 2007 transformed Ireland's global profile, changing it from a nation in economic hardship, necessitating emigration, to a country of prosperity and immigration. In public discourse, the years of successful economic development attracted the moniker 'Celtic Tiger', reflecting Ireland's place in, and embrace of, the competitive global marketplace. In 2002, the first year that the Census of Population included a question on nationality, just below six per cent of the total population usually resident in Ireland had non-Irish nationality (Ruhs, 2006). By 2006, the Census indicated that share had increased to just over ten per cent, with immigrants originating from more than 188 different countries (CSO, 2008). The sudden increase in immigration to Ireland is mirrored in broader migration trends in Europe, for example net immigration accounted for 81 per cent of the population growth experienced by all EU member states in 2004[1].

However, Ireland's experience differs from that of traditional immigration-receiving countries in Europe, such as the UK and France post-World War II, because of its long history of emigration: 'there are more people who identify themselves as Irish outside the country than within it' (Castles and Miller, 2009: 290). Added to this, the scale and speed of recent immigration flows to Ireland were unprecedented and this makes the immigration context quite different from other European countries. It is because of these differences that the ways in which Ireland has reacted to rapid immigration, and the government policies that have been put in place, may have more in common with other 'newer' immigration countries in Europe such as Italy, Greece and Portugal.

The increased population diversity resulting from increased immigration to Ireland over recent years, in the context of increased global population movement, leads us to consider the ways in which Ireland has dealt with immigration as well as the experiences of immigrants themselves. Until quite recently the majority of the research on the experiences of immigrants and ethnic minorities living in Ireland focused on the adult population[2]. To address this gap in the literature, this book contributes to a steadily growing body of work that explores the ways in which immigrant and ethnic minority children live their everyday lives in Ireland, as well as the ways in which they are positioned in Irish society (see Bushin and White, 2010; Devine, forthcoming; Devine, Kelly and MacNeela, 2004; Gilligan et al., 2010; Ní Laoire et al., 2009; Ní Laoire et al., in press; Smyth et al., 2009).

Although Ireland was not a mono-ethnic nation prior to the Celtic Tiger era, the diversity of the population has increased substantially in recent years, with immigrants coming from a range of national, social, cultural, linguistic and ethnic backgrounds. Unlike countries that have a long-standing history of immigration, Ireland does not yet have a substantial second (or subsequent) immigrant generation (Taguma et al., 2009). Therefore the majority of children with an ethnic minority background are also first generation immigrants[3] and have first-hand experience of immigrating to Ireland with parents, other adults or on their own.[4] These are the children whose lives are explored throughout this book.

The book is sectioned into three main parts, focusing on: Immigration, Identities and Language; Immigration, Education and Schooling; Immigration, Well-being and Risk. In this introductory chapter, we first define some key terms used throughout the book. We then describe the profile of the immigrant and ethnic minority population in Ireland, paying particular attention to children and young people. The chapter provides some broad contextual material which we hope will provide a useful background for the chapters that follow. Since national statistical offices seldom calculate the number or share of children in immigrant families, public discourse and policy deliberations do not fully recognise how many of these children live in the countries under study (UNICEF, 2009). Given the scale of immigration to Ireland over the last fifteen years, and the uncertainty over the future of Ireland's immigrant populations, we feel that it is timely to explore the experiences of immigrant and ethnic minority children from different disciplinary perspectives.

DEFINITIONS

At this point it is important to define some of the terms used throughout the chapters. The book focuses on the experiences and situations of immigrant children in Ireland. The authors use the term 'child', 'children' or 'young people' to refer to those aged below 18 years of age. When authors refer to 'Ireland', it is the Republic of Ireland.

We use the term 'immigrant' to describe individuals (or a population group) who have moved to Ireland from another country, i.e. they have migrated across the national border of the Republic of Ireland. We recognise that the term 'immigrant' is problematic, although it is in common usage in European and national policy documents. We prefer it to other terms that are also in common parlance in Ireland, such as 'newcomer' or 'non-national'. The vast majority of the children whose experiences are included in the book are first generation immigrants, i.e. they themselves migrated to Ireland either with or without family members. However, when children are described as being from an immigrant background or in an immigrant family, this means that they did not necessarily experience immigration themselves and that at least one of their parents does not have Irish citizenship.

Based on Finney and Simpson (2009), throughout this book the term ethnic minority is used to encompass a broad idea of difference and as a self-adopted identity based on a mixture of the following: physical attributes, birthplace, legal status (nationality), family origins, beliefs (including religion) and practices of language and culture. A question on ethnicity appeared in the Census of Ireland for the first time in 2006 (see King-O'Riain, 2007) but its ethnic categories are quite limited. We use the term ethnic minority to refer to individuals whose identity and attributes differ from the majority of the population in Ireland.

RECENT IMMIGRATION TO IRELAND

In the past decade, immigrants of non-European background have entered Ireland in larger and more visible numbers. This has challenged existing frameworks of racial and ethnic understanding (King-O'Riain, 2007). What Mac Gréil (1996) has defined as Ireland's 'defensive ethnocentrism', which is based on resistance to imposition from the 'outside', has been challenged by increased immigration. The Census of Ireland conducted in 2006 indicated that there were 420,000 non-Irish nationals living in Ireland – ten per cent of the total population (see Table 1). Although the full range of origin countries of this immigrant and ethnic minority population is diverse, 82 per cent were from just ten countries (CSO, 2008). Countries with over 10,000 nationals living in Ireland were: China, Germany, Latvia, Lithuania, Nigeria, Poland, the UK and the USA (CSO, 2008). British nationals have been living in Ireland for longer than the other national groups, with large numbers arriving in the 1970s and 1980s. Nationals from EU 15 states[5] (excluding Ireland and the UK) mainly migrated to Ireland between 2001 and 2006 but a substantial number had been in Ireland since the early 1990s. The majority of nationals from states that acceded to the EU in 2004[6] migrated to Ireland between 2002 and 2006, with more than 44 per cent migrating to Ireland in 2005 or later.

Table 1. Number of immigrants from each region/country in Ireland in 2006[7]

Region/Country	Number of immigrants
EU12	121,000
UK	113,000
Asia	47,000
EU15	43,000
Africa	35,000

A first phase of immigration to Ireland, from the mid-1990s onwards, saw an increase in Irish return migration and also an increase in the number of people claiming asylum. There were several reasons for this including EU migration policy, freedom of movement and labour shortages. Immigration rates increased rapidly after 2004, with the expansion of the EU and the Irish government's decision not to place restrictions on migrant workers from these countries (a decision replicated by the UK and Sweden). Between 2004 and 2007 inclusive, net inward migration amounted to over 225,000, equivalent to more than five per cent of the resident population (Barrett and Bergin, 2009). An influx of immigrants was expected but such large numbers exceeded all expectations (Barrett, 2009).

In addition to an increase in employment-led or economic-led migration, during the 1990s and into the early 2000s, higher numbers of people were claiming asylum in Ireland, particularly from African countries. It has been considered that this sudden increase in the number of asylum-seekers was the result of children being born in Ireland being entitled to Irish citizenship and thus the right to remain residing in Ireland (along with a parent who could apply for citizenship on the basis of an Irish-born child). However, in 2004, the government initiated a Citizenship Referendum, the results of which ended the right to citizenship on the basis of location of birth – *jus soli* – with citizenship being granted on the basis of bloodline – *jus sanguinis* (MacEínri and White, 2008). The number of people applying for refugee status in Ireland has fallen since the introduction of this policy, which coincided with the expansion of the EU, and is now at similar levels to the late 1990s – 2689 applications in 2009 (ORAC, 2009).

Research from more traditional immigration countries has explored issues of geographical and social segregation (e.g. Ellis, 2001; Finney and Simpson, 2009; Goodwin-White, 2008; Peach, 1996). In Ireland, immigrants' locations often reflect affordable housing options hence, in general, immigrants are found in areas with a supply of private rented housing close to places of employment. However, there were immigrants living in every town across Ireland at the time of the Census in 2006 (CSO, 2008), and one in seven non-Irish nationals (excluding UK nationals) were living in rural areas. This pattern of settlement likely reflects the policy of dispersing asylum seekers within the Direct Provision system in Ireland[8] and the employment sectors of migrant workers – predominantly in agriculture, construction and hospitality.

The economic decline and rising unemployment in Ireland since 2008 has resulted in a decline in the number of people migrating to Ireland, as well as an increase in out-migration. Between 2008 and 2009, out-migration increased from 45,300 people to 65,100 people and remained at around this level between 2009 and 2010 (CSO, 2009; 2010). Immigration has been decreasing since 2008 and this has resulted in Ireland's return to net outward migration for the first time since 1995 (CSO, 2009). The highest number of out-migrants between 2008 and 2009 were nationals of new EU accession states (CSO, 2009), however, between 2009 and 2010 the highest number of out-migrants were Irish nationals (CSO, 2010). In-migration of all non-Irish national groups has been declining (CSO, 2009; 2010), although it is important to note that immigration is still occurring (albeit on a much smaller scale). These figures undoubtedly reflect the economic recession and associated unemployment in Ireland. However, as yet, there is little substantial evidence that immigrant families with children are out-migrating in high numbers; their situations are discussed in detail in the following section.

IMMIGRANT AND ETHNIC MINORITY CHILDREN
AND YOUNG PEOPLE IN IRELAND

Child immigrant populations frequently exceed adult immigrant populations because immigrants are often in a family-building stage of life (UNICEF, 2009).

However, there are difficulties in estimating the number of child migrants globally, as well as child movements between and within individual countries or regions (see White et al., in press). Sometimes, children's migrations are not recorded at the time of migration (as is the case when children move between member states of the EU, for example), and/or data are collated into age group categories that span a large number of years. This has obvious implications for states' planning and provision for children in areas such as health and education, particularly as migration is a dynamic process which often involves a series of moves rather than a singular move from 'Place A' to 'Place B' (see Heckmann, 2008). Some recent research illustrates the difficulty in gaining comprehensive immigration data for child age groups: Taguma et al. (2009) estimate that approximately 10 per cent of children in primary schools and 8 per cent of children in secondary schools in Ireland are from immigrant backgrounds; however, Smyth et al. (2009) estimate the secondary school immigrant population to be lower, at 6 per cent. Ní Laoire et al. (2009) have used the information that is available in the most recent population census in Ireland (carried out in 2006) to highlight several relevant points concerning immigrant children in Ireland. For example, just over 10 per cent of the total childhood population of Ireland was born in countries other than Ireland – mainly in European countries; children make up almost 20 per cent of the total immigrant population of Ireland (as defined by country of birth); just over seven per cent of all children living in Ireland do not have Irish nationality; and the most common nationality of immigrant children living in Ireland is British (22,157 children), followed by EU15-25 (13,828 children) and Africa (9,788) (Ní Laoire et al., 2009). However, Census 2006 does not record the nationality of 13,000 children because their nationality was not stated. Again, this exemplifies some of the difficulties associated with collecting and collating accurate data on immigrant children.

Studies of immigrant children tend to focus on 'child-specific' aspects of their lives, or their immediate needs, such as education and schooling. Research that has been carried out into immigrant children's experiences in Ireland often has been focused in these areas, for example: Bryan (2009), Byrne et al. (2010), Deegan, Devine and Lodge (2004), Devine (2005), Devine and Kelly (2006), Devine, Kenny and MacNeela (2004), Keogh and White (2006), McGovern, 1995; McGorman and Sugrue (2007), Nowlan (2008), Smyth et al. (2009) and Taguma et al. (2009). However, for an exception see Ní Laoire et al. (2009; in press). Given the rapid increase in the number of immigrant children in Ireland, and the issues involved in providing education to children whose first language often is not English (or Irish), it is understandable that the majority of research has focused on education and schooling. Studies have shown the difficulties that some immigrant children face when attending school in Ireland and the need for more support for them in school contexts. Early indications suggest that, unlike other countries, the attainment gap between immigrant and Irish-born children is minimal (apart from for children who do not speak English at home) (Taguma et al., 2009). This may be because of the similar socio-economic backgrounds of immigrant and non-immigrant children in Ireland (Taguma et al., 2009), although there is evidence that immigrants to Ireland possess higher levels of human capital than the majority Irish population

(Barrett, Bergin and Duffy, 2006) but they earn considerably less (Barrett, 2009). Further studies of educational attainment are required, preferably on a longitudinal basis, to address this issue at a more nuanced level. The need for immigrant children to have language and intercultural support in school settings in Ireland is evident from the body of work in this area, and these issues are explored in some of the chapters in this volume.

Overall, in many countries, including Ireland, many aspects of immigrant children's lives have been largely missing from migration debates (White et al., in press) and from related efforts in data collection and analysis (UNICEF, 2009). Economic perspectives tended to overshadow children and young people's experiences of migration because, unlike adults, they are not active in the labour market and tend to be 'tied' migrants, i.e. they migrate with one or more adults, usually a parent (Bushin, 2009). This neglect of children's experiences of migration and their lives in their migration destinations is short-sighted and problematic.

As the quotation that we chose to begin this chapter with suggests, the circumstances and future prospects of children in immigrant families are important not only to the children and their families, but also to the wider societies of which they are a part. The ways in which immigrant children may (or may not) feel part of communities, or may (or may not) develop attachments to places in their migration destinations, are important to consider. This is particularly important in a country like Ireland, where it has been argued that state policy on immigration is highly racialised (Loyal, Coulter and Coleman, 2003; Garner, 2004), and where debates about the 'integration' of recent immigrants into what has been traditionally been classified as 'white, sedentary and Roman Catholic' (Devine, 2005: 50) require further attention.

Recently, increased interest has focused on immigrant children and young people's broader experiences of living in Ireland, moving beyond studies focused solely on education and schooling. Studies have begun to disaggregate the term 'immigrant children', and examine themes such as identity, belonging and friendships (Ní Laoire et al., 2009; Ní Laoire et al., in press), children's experiences of the asylum system (Charles, 2009; Mooten, 2006; Ní Raghallaigh and Gilligan, 2010; Fanning, Veale and O'Connor, 2002; White and Bushin, 2010), the ways in which immigration politics affect young people (Bushin and White, 2010) and social integration (Gilligan et al., 2010). The analyses in this book contribute to furthering this shift from research on the immigrant/non-immigrant boundary, thus exploring the similarities and differences in and across immigrant children's experiences.

The context for this edited volume on immigrant and ethnic minority children and young people in Ireland is one of economic and social change. Indeed, the situation in Ireland is somewhat different now to what it was to when the editors started working on their ideas for the book! Ireland has been designated as one of the European countries most affected by the economic recession and has suffered significant economic decline, a very different scenario to the 'Celtic Tiger' economic boom period. In overall terms, the number of immigrants moving to Ireland since 2008 has begun to fall quite substantially and the numbers of emigrants has increased. However, although the economic landscape in Ireland has changed, with a resultant impact on in-migration and out-migration flows, examining the experiences of immigrant children and young people in Ireland over the last ten years is still highly important. Data from the 2006 Census show that although high numbers of young, single people migrated to Ireland during the economic boom period, the household type 'couples with children' was a common household type among non-Irish nationals (Ní Laoire et al., 2009). This was particularly the case for immigrants from EU Accession states (CSO, 2008), who moved to Ireland in high numbers. Arguably, the immigrants who are most likely to remain in Ireland following the economic recession are family groups, particularly those with children of school age because of the disruption that migration means for children's education. In addition, although emigration now outweighs immigration, it is likely that emigration is highest among migrants who do not have children living with them in Ireland because of the connections that families with children have to their local communities.

The out-migration rate of families has yet to be calculated and perhaps will be revealed more comprehensively in the Census of Population, due to take place in April 2011, than annual statistical snapshots may reveal. Calculating and forecasting migration is not an exact science and it is important to note that although emigration has increased substantially, immigration to Ireland is still occurring. Research has shown that Ireland was (and perhaps still is) perceived as offering a good quality of life for children and their parents, with immigrant parents and children themselves often referring to a healthy and safe living environment for children (Gilligan et al., 2010; Ní Laoire et al., 2009). Although the recent economic downturn has been accompanied by a reduction in immigration and an increase in emigration, including onward migration of some of those who had immigrated during the 2000s, many immigrants have stayed in Ireland and are building their lives here. In this 'age of migration' (Castles and Miller, 2009), where goods, capital and people are increasingly mobile, Ireland's history of sustained emigration may not be the best indicator of its future.

AIM OF THE BOOK

Ireland is now a multi-ethnic society, with all of the opportunities and challenges that this presents. The veneer associated with the notion of Ireland as 'the land of a thousand welcomes' – of friendliness, community spirit, treating immigrants better than Irish emigrants were treated on their travels – has begun to be unraveled with some incidences of racial abuse and racially-motivated crimes being reported. Equally worrying is the signal that the closure of the National Consultative Committee on Racism and Interculturalism (NCCRI) in December 2008 (due to government spending cuts) sends to immigrant and wider populations. The aim of this book is not to provide definitive insights and answers to all of the issues and challenges that immigrant children and young people face in Ireland. However, given the current economic and population context, we feel that it is timely to critique, discuss and begin to learn from the recent experiences of immigrant and ethnic minority children and young people living in Ireland.

The following chapters draw on a range of themes pertinent to immigrant and ethnic minority children's lives, often including research carried out with children themselves, and/or incorporating the views of parents, teachers and/or community representatives, and/or relevant statistics. We have sectioned the book according to the main themes that the chapters embrace: identity and language (La Morgia; McDaid; Nestor and Regan; Veale), education and schooling (Devine; Kitching; Bryan and Bracken; Smyth and Darmody; McCoy and Darmody), and well-being and risk (Fanning, Haase and O'Boyle; Molcho, Kelly and Nic Gabhainn; Horgan, Martin and O'Riordan; Ní Raghallaigh; Joyce and Quinn). However, these broad themes are not exhaustive and chapters also explore issues such as faith, religion, health, exclusion and inclusion, amongst others. Some chapters provide overviews of the current policies affecting particular groups of immigrant children, such as unaccompanied minors or trafficked children, whilst other chapters offer in-depth exploration of the lives of particular groups of immigrant children in particular contexts. The research presented in the chapters varies in terms methodology and scope, and the authors are from a wide range of disciplinary backgrounds. It was our intent that this plurality of perspectives would strengthen the book and we hope that you will find this to be the case. All of the chapters retain one central focus: elucidating the experiences of immigrant and ethnic minority children and young people in Ireland.

The research findings that are discussed in the following chapters offer deep insights into the contexts, backgrounds and experiences of immigrant and ethnic minority children and young people who lived in Ireland during the years of the 'Celtic Tiger'. The chapters are not mere snapshots of immigrant children's lives, the relevance of which may be diminished due to the changed socio-economic situation. Indeed, as has been discussed, although the rate of immigration has slowed, immigrants are still moving to Ireland, including children, and there is still a size-able immigrant population. Moreover, the existing population of ethnic minority children may well be added to in the coming years because a high proportion of immigrants were of childbearing age and have contributed to Ireland's high birth rate – 74,500 births between April 2008 and April 2009, not seen since 1896 (CSO, 2009).

We hope that you will find this book informative and useful in furthering your understanding of the lives of children from immigrant and ethnic minority back-grounds who are living in contemporary Ireland, whether you are a researcher, teacher, practitioner, policymaker, student and/or of course, a child or parent. As is often the case with edited collections, the themes and topics covered are not exhaustive and we do not claim that the findings and discussion presented here represent the lives and experiences of all immigrant and ethnic minority children in Ireland. The book is intended to be a springboard for further discussion, discussion which we hope may be influential in shaping children and young people's lives for the better in 'post-Celtic Tiger 'Ireland. In addition, many of the topics explored in this volume are relevant to other 'new' immigration countries as well. As Smyth et al. (2009) optimistically suggest, effective support for children in the present may well help to avoid the sorts of social segregation experienced by immigrant and ethnic minority children and young people in other countries. The socio-economic contexts for children in Ireland and other countries may have changed as a result of the 'global' economic recession but as the following chapters demonstrate, the needs of immigrant and ethnic minority children living in the here-and-now are very real, as are their hopes for the future.

NOTES

[1] United Nations Human Rights Council, Report of the Special Rapporteur on the Human Rights of Migrants, Jorge Bustamante, document no. A/HRC/11/7, 14 May 2009, presented to the UN Human Rights Council, 11th session, 2 June 2009.
[2] See the early work of Devine and her colleagues in the References.
[3] Please note that the experiences of Traveller children and youth are not included in this book because of our simultaneous focus on immigration and citizenship. Travellers have lobbied for ethnic minority status in recent years and although this has not been granted fully, their cultural difference is being acknowledged. The experiences of children in Irish return-migrant families also are not included because of the dual focus on immigration and citizenship.
[4] As separated children.
[5] Austria, Belgium, Denmark, Finland, France, Germany, Greece, Italy, Luxembourg, Netherlands, Portugal, Spain and Sweden.
[6] Cyprus, Czech Republic, Estonia, Hungary, Latvia, Lithuania, Malta, Poland, Slovakia and Slovenia.
[7] Based on figures from Census 2006; Barrett and Bergin, 2009.
[8] The Direct Provision system, as it is implemented in Ireland, often involves asylum seekers moving to accommodation centres in different parts of the country.

REFERENCES

Barrett, A. (2009). *EU enlargement and Ireland's labour market.* IZA Discussion Paper No. 4260. Germany: IZA.

Barrett, A., Bergin, A., & Duffy, D. (2006). *The labour market characteristics and labour market impacts of immigrants in Ireland.* Dublin: ESRI.

Barrett, A., & Bergin, A. (2009). Estimating the impact of immigration in Ireland. *Nordic Journal of Political Economy, 35*(2), 1–15.

Bryan, A. (2009). The intersectionality of nationalism and multiculturalism in the Irish curriculum: Teaching against racism? *Race, Ethnicity and Education, 12*(3), 297–317.

Byrne, D., McGinnity, F., Smyth, E., & Darmody, M. (2010). Immigration and school composition in Ireland. *Irish Educational Studies, 29*(3), 271–288.

Bushin, N. (2009). Researching family migration decision-making: A children-in-families approach. *Population, Space and Place, 15,* 429–443.

Bushin, N., & White, A. (2010). Migration politics in Ireland: Exploring the impacts on young people's geographies. *Area, 42*(2), 170–180.

Castles, S., & Miller, M. (2009). *The age of migration: International population movements in the modern world.* Basingstoke: Palgrave Macmillan.

Charles, K. (2009). *Separated children living in Ireland: A report by the Ombudsman for Children's Office.* Dublin: Ombudsman for Children's Office.

CSO. (2007). *Census 2006: Volume 4 – Usual residence, migration, birthplaces and nationalities.* Dublin: Stationary Office.

CSO. (2008). *Census 2006: Non-Irish nationals living in Ireland.* Dublin: Stationary Office.

CSO. (2009). *Population and migration estimates - April 2009.* Cork; Dublin: Author.

CSO. (2010). *Population and migration estimates - April 2010.* Cork; Dublin: Author.

Deegan, J., Devine, D., & Lodge, A. (2004). *Primary voices' equality, diversity and childhood in Irish primary schools*. Dublin: Institute of Public Administration.

Devine, D. (2005). Welcome to the Celtic Tiger? Teacher responses to immigration and increasing ethnic diversity in Irish schools. *International Studies in Sociology of Education, 15*(1), 49–70.

Devine, D. (forthcoming). *Making a difference? Immigration and schooling in Ireland*. Manchester: Manchester University Press.

Devine, D., & Kelly, M (2006). 'I just don't want to get picked on by anybody' - Dynamics of inclusion and exclusion in a newly multi-ethnic Irish primary school. *Children and Society, 20*(2), 128–139.

Devine, D., with Kenny, N., & MacNeela, E. (2004). Experiencing racism in the primary school – Children's perspectives. In J. Deegan, D. Devine, & A. Lodge (Eds.), *Primary voices – Equality, diversity and childhood in Irish primary schools*. Dublin: Institute of Public Administration.

Ellis, M. (2001). What future for whites? Population projections and racial imaginaries in the US. *International Journal of Population Geography, 7*, 213–229.

Fanning, B., Veale, A., & O'Connor, D. (2001). *Beyond the pale: Asylum seeking children and social exclusion in Ireland*. Dublin: Irish Refugee Council and the Combat Poverty Agency.

Finney, N., & Simpson, L. (2009). *Sleepwalking to segregation? Challenging myths about race and immigration*. Bristol: Policy Press.

Garner, S. (2004). *Racism in the Irish experience*. Dublin: Pluto Press.

Gilligan, R., Curry, P., McGrath, J., Murphy, D., Ní Raghallaigh, M., Rogers, M., et al. (2010). *In the front line of integration: Young people managing migration to Ireland*. Dublin: Trinity College Dublin.

Goodwin-White, J. (2008). Placing progress: Contextual inequality and immigrant incorporation in the United States. *Economic Geography, 84*(3), 303–332.

Heckmann, F. (2008). *Education and migration, strategies for integrating migrant children in European schools and societies*. Brussels: European Commission.

Keogh, A., & Whyte, J. (2006). *Getting on*. Dublin: Children's Research Centre, Trinity College.

King-O'Riain, R. (2007). Counting on the 'Celtic Tiger': Adding ethnic census categories in the Republic of Ireland. *Ethnicities, 7*, 516–542.

Loyal, S., Coulter, C., & Coleman, S. (Eds.). (2003). *The end of Irish history? Critical reflections on the Celtic Tiger*. Manchester: Manchester University Press.

Mac Éinrí, P., & White, A. (2008). Immigration into the Republic of Ireland: A bibliography of recent research. *Irish Geography, 41*(2), 151–179. http://www.informaworld.com/smpp/title~db=all~content=t791546828~tab=issueslist~branches=41-v41.

Mac Gréil, M. (1996). *Prejudice in Ireland revisited*. Maynooth: Survey and Research Unit, St Patrick's College.

McGorman, E., & Sugrue, C. (2007). *Intercultural education: Primary challenges in Dublin 15*. Dublin: Social Inclusion Unit, Department of Education and Science.

McGovern, F. (1995). The education of refugee children in Ireland. *Oideas, 43*, 82–94.

Mooten, N. (2006). *Making separated children visible: The need for a child-centred approach*. Dublin: Irish Refugee Council.

Ní Laoire, C., Bushin, N., Carpena-Méndez, F., & White, A. (2009). *Tell me about yourself: Migrant children's experiences of moving to and living in Ireland*. Cork, Ireland: University College Cork.

Ní Laoire, C., Carpena-Mendez, F., Tyrrell, N., & White, A. (in press). *Childhood and migration in Europe: Portraits of mobility, identity and belonging in contemporary Ireland*. Farnham: Ashgate.

Ní Raghallaigh, M., & Gilligan, R. (2010). Active survival in the lives of unaccompanied minors: Coping strategies, resilience, and the relevance of religion. *Child and Family Social Work*. Online early version available.

Nowlan, E. (2008). Underneath the band-aid: Supporting bilingual students in Irish schools. *Irish Educational Studies. 27*(3), 253–266.

Office of the Refugee Applications Commissioner. (2009). *Office of the refugee applications commissioner monthly statistics December 200*. Retrieved September 14, 2010, from http://www.orac.ie/pages/Stats/2009.htm

Peach, C. (1996). Does Britain have ghettos? *Transactions of the Institute of British Geographers, 22*(1), 216–235.

Ruhs, M. (2006). *A report by the International Organization for Migration for the National Economic and Social Council of Ireland, No. 116.* Ireland: A Social and Economic Analysis.

Smyth, E., Darmody, M., McGinnity, F., & Byrne, D. (2009). *Adapting to diversity: Irish schools and newcomer students.* Dublin: ESRI.

Taguma, M., Kim, M., Wurzburg, G., & Kelly, F. (2009). *OECD reviews of migrant education.* Ireland: OECD.

UNICEF. (2009). *Children in immigrant families in eight affluent countries: Their family, national and international context* [Online: UNICEF Inocenti Insight Series]. Retrieved April, 2010, from http://www.unicef-irc.org/cgi-bin/unicef/research/main.sql?file=scheda_projects.sql&key=193#Project_ publications

White, A., & Bushin, N. (2010). More-Than-Methods: Learning from research with children in the Irish Asylum System. *Population, Space and Place*, Online early version available.

White, A., Ní Laoire, C., Tyrrell, N., & Carpena-Mendez, F. (in press). Children's roles in transnational migration. *Journal of Ethnic and Migration Studies.*

Merike Darmody
Economic and Social Research Institute
Dublin

Naomi Tyrrell
School of Geography, Earth and Environmental Sciences
University of Plymouth

Steve Song
George Fox University
Oregon

PART 1: IMMIGRATION, IDENTITIES AND LANGUAGE

FRANCESCA LA MORGIA

1. WHO IS AFRAID OF MULTILINGUALISM?

Evaluating the Linguistic Impact of Migration in Ireland

INTRODUCTION

The face of Europe is constantly changing, as a result of mobility, migration and globalisation. It is estimated that today there are at least 175 nationalities within the EU borders (Eurostat, 2007). Migration and mobility have brought about changes in the linguistic landscape of Europe, making multilingualism an increasingly common reality, and highlighting the need for new policies and projects that take into account linguistic diversity (European Commission, 2004)[1].

Ireland represents an interesting case of co-existence of bilingual and multilingual realities, which include the autochthonous Irish-English bilingual population and many ethnic minority groups whose first language is not English. Many of these groups have migrated to Ireland during the economic boom of the 1990s and according to the latest Census more than 100 languages are spoken in the country alongside Irish and English (CSO, 2006). Since immigration is a relatively new phenomenon in Ireland, issues related to language learning, multilingualism, cultural and linguistic diversity have only recently started to be addressed (Ní Laoire, 2007; 2008; McFayden, 2008; Carson and Extra, 2010).

In recent years, both government policies and independent projects have been implemented for the multilingual population in Ireland: the government has been promoting the revival of the Irish language and has been providing supplementary English language classes for non-native speakers in primary and secondary schools; meanwhile, new projects have emerged with the aim of supporting minority languages, to promote awareness of linguistic diversity and to understand the benefits of multilingualism. These independent initiatives[2] are often run by individuals, community groups and non-governmental organisations.

As this chapter shows, many of these projects aim to develop awareness of linguistic diversity among children, and they demonstrate that the new generation plays a significant role in the transmission and maintenance of different languages and cultures. This chapter provides an overview of how multilingualism develops within the family and the educational context and examines some of the policies and projects that have recently been implemented in Ireland in order to promote awareness of linguistic diversity and multilingualism among children.

Darmody, Tyrrell, Song (eds.), The Changing Faces of Ireland: Exploring the Lives of Immigrant and Ethnic Minority Children, 3–16.
© *2011 Sense Publishers. All rights reserved.*

MULTILINGUAL FAMILIES

In order to understand how multilingualism[3] develops within the family, it is necessary to examine the parents' and the child's background, their attitudes towards their own mother tongue and towards the country's language(s). It is possible to identify many different family contexts in which children acquire two or more languages. In multilingual families in Ireland we can find some of the following situations: both parents[4] are native speakers of a language other than English; the parents are native speakers of two different languages other than English; one parent is a native speaker of English and the other of another language; in single parent families the mother or the father is not a native speaker of English (see Carson and Extra, 2010). In each of these contexts the parents may have different levels of proficiency in two or more languages, different expectations regarding their child's linguistic skills and different attitudes towards multilingualism. Moreover, the fact that parents are native speakers of a language does not necessarily imply that they use it to communicate with the child (or to each other) and therefore that the child will speak it. Some parents decide to use the language(s) they are more comfortable with, others select strategies to adopt on the basis of what they think would be the most suitable linguistic upbringing. In addition, linguistic input coupled with the attitude of parents, siblings and family members towards multilingualism and their native language(s) can play an important role in the child's linguistic development both in the early phases and in the successive stages of language maintenance. It also has to be considered that multilingual families can be autochthonous or they may have migrated to Ireland before or after the child's birth. We talk of simultaneous plurilingualism when the child is exposed to two or more languages from birth, and of successive plurilingualism when the child acquires one language after the other. Both types of development allow the child to become a native speaker of both languages. However, the later the second language is introduced, the harder it may be to acquire it. For this reason, parents who are native speakers of a minority language[5] are generally advised to use their own mother tongue with their children from birth if they want them to acquire it spontaneously (Baker, 2000b).

Several studies have shown that multilingualism has a positive effect on many aspects of a child's development. Firstly, plurilingual children have enhanced cognitive functions due to the fact that both languages are active in their brain. The cognitive benefits concern the areas of memory and attention span. It has also been found that plurilingualism can delay the onset of dementia in later life (Bialystok, 2009; Stern et al., 2005; Bialystok, Craik and Freedman, 2007). Moreover, many plurilingual children are precocious readers, they are tolerant and aware of other people's perspectives, and they have an enhanced ability to learn foreign languages and to multitask. Other benefits include the expanded opportunities for communication, the development of literacy in two languages, and more possibilities of employment in the future (Baker, 2000b).

Parents who are faced with the reality of raising a multilingual family are often unaware of the short-term and long-term benefits that plurilingualism brings to the child throughout life. In addition, there are widespread myths about multilingualism which might have a negative impact on the choices that parents make for their children.

Parents may also be influenced by the opinion of other people, such as extended family, teachers, neighbours and friends (Baker, 2000a). Some people believe that speaking two or more languages might cause slow linguistic development, as well as difficulties in the achievement of integration and academic success (De Hower, 2009). While multilingualism is becoming increasingly common in Ireland, such beliefs remain quite widespread[6]. For this reason, parents often seek advice on how to raise plurilingual children. The issues raised by parents are different depending on their experience, beliefs and expectations and on the age of the child. The three stages described below represent an overview of different factors affecting the linguistic development of a plurilingual child. In the first stage, which generally starts before or soon after the child is born, parents are responsible for the decision of the strategy to adopt; in the second stage the parents and their child establish the languages spoken at home; the third stage starts when the child enters the education system and begins to interact more regularly with peers and adults.

In the first stage, parents decide on the linguistic strategy to use. Initially, the most common issues concern the selection of languages spoken at home. Parents often have expectations about their child's linguistic attainment, and they are eager to find the best strategy to achieve the expected outcome. In Ireland, some parents may worry that their child is not exposed to enough English at home[7], others may fear that since English is the dominant language in the external environment, the child will start forgetting the minority language and will ultimately lose it. It is also common for parents to wonder whether it is better to introduce the other language(s) at a later stage rather than raising a child with two languages from the start. Unfortunately, there is no single formula that can ensure success[8]. Every family context has its unique characteristics, and there are so many linguistic, emotional, social and environmental factors which come into play that each case should be examined individually to gain a full understanding of what strategies could be applied. In Ireland, as in other migratory contexts, there is a wide variety of families coming from many different countries, with their own cultural background, beliefs and expectations for their children's linguistic attainment. The situations described below show some of the choices made by families where at least one parent is a native speaker of Italian[9]. Even though they don't cover the whole range of contexts, they can help to understand some of the reasons behind parents' decisions.

Family I – Italian-Irish couple. The Italian parent speaks English to his spouse and has decided not to use his mother tongue on a daily basis with the child. The couple made their decision based on their view that Italian would not be useful to the child, they have few links with Italy, and they don't have time to teach Italian to the child. These parents are not completely against their child being exposed to Italian, but they believe that if the he visits his grandparents once a year and watches some cartoons in the language, he will learn enough Italian to "get by".

Family II – Italian-Irish couple. The couple decided to adopt the "one-parent-one-language" strategy, consisting of each parent addressing the child in their own mother tongue. The parents made their choice after reading books that suggested that this strategy is quite effective in early bilingual development.

Family III – Italian couple. The Italian couple speak only Italian to the child because they feel it is the most natural approach. They also believe that the child should acquire English only by interacting with native speakers.

Family IV – Italian couple. The parents speak Italian to each other but one of them decided to use English when addressing the child. The purpose of this strategy was to expose the child to both English and Italian in the early stages of linguistic development, when he was mostly spending time at home with his parents and getting little interaction with people outside the family environment.

Family V – Italian-French couple. When the couple met, English was their *lingua franca*. Since then, they have always been speaking English to each other, but they decided to speak their own mother tongue when addressing the child, so he would be exposed daily to three languages.

Family VI – One parent family – Italian mother. When the child was 3 months old, the mother decided to leave Italy and move to Ireland. She speaks only Italian to her child, but she wants her to attend a crèche so that she is exposed to English on a daily basis.

These examples are only a small range of possible linguistic situations that can be found in multilingual families and they refer only to contexts in which the child is raised in Ireland from birth or from a very young age. The scenarios outlined show that parents' linguistic choice can vary according to what they believe to be the most appropriate or the most natural strategy to use. Parents' choices are often determined by their own experiences and their attitude and feelings towards the language(s). In addition, parents who are uncertain about what strategy to adopt might look for information by talking to other families, contacting experts or seeking advice from books and online resources. This phase is very important, because the choice made by the parents will influence the child's own linguistic attitudes and future linguistic attainment.

Many multilingual families in Ireland have started to express the need for information and support in raising plurilingual children. The first organisations providing this service were Cuidiú, Comhluadar and the Health Service Executive (HSE), which have been involved in projects to help parents make an informed choice on how to raise plurilingual children by providing talks and publication of materials that parents could freely access[10]. The success of these initiatives highlighted the need for more information on raising plurilingual children[11]. In an effort to fill this gap, a group of researchers, community workers, speech and language therapists and teachers founded Bilingual Forum Ireland (BFI) in 2007 with the aim of providing information on multilingualism. BFI volunteers have been working with families and teachers to develop awareness of the benefits of multilingualism and also to support local projects and initiatives which promote minority languages, as well as the understanding of the value of linguistic diversity. The events run by BFI aim to provide parents with the information they need to make an informed choice on the basis of research findings and also through interaction with other families. Through a website[12], parents can access different resources and use a forum to interact with families in similar situations. This online forum represents an opportunity for parents from different parts of Ireland to share experiences on raising plurilingual children and to ask for the help of experts. The examples below show some of the experiences parents have shared on the forum, which are a window into the different realities of multilingual families in Ireland[13].

> [...] me - Polish, my husband Irish - we met in Germany and [German] remains our language. We have two children (4 and 2 years) and they have three languages on a daily basis, as I would speak to them Polish, my husband and his relatives plus the whole outer world (as we are living in Ireland) English but they listen to us speaking German to each other all the time. I have noticed recently - while visiting my friends in Germany - that my kids do understand a lot German and after only few days were able to pick some new words. I don't see any confusion, delays in speech development or other negative aspects of this situation.

> [...] I am originally from Flanders (Belgium), so my mother tongue is Flemish (Dutch). My now 3-year old daughter was born in Ireland and has been going to crèche and pre-school in English. From when she was born, I have made a conscious effort to speak to her in Flemish only, even in the presence of people who don't understand Flemish. At the beginning I used to worry about whether or not this was appropriate or polite, but I don't really care anymore at this stage, as it's become entirely natural to me and my daughter. Her dad is Polish, so she has a good understanding of that language as well. It's a pity that he hasn't been more consistent in speaking only Polish to her, as her Polish is significantly less developed than her English and Flemish. 1 parent, 1 language is the best strategy, in my opinion!

> [...] I have a child of 4 who is just starting school this week. I am French and speak French to him, and his father is Irish and speaks English. He understands both languages, but he mixes his speech and does not have the fluency other children seem to have. Should I worry? He has been assessed by a speech therapist who thinks he is speech delayed, but at the same time admits not having experience with bilingual/multilingual children. Is there any way to find someone who can help?

These extracts show the type of linguistic experience shared by parents on the online forum. As well as providing detailed information on the family's linguistic behaviour, they can be useful for finding out what strategies are being used among different families and what results they have achieved. A resource such as the forum can be exceptionally valuable because it allows parents to be aware of how other people deal with similar issues and to interact with other families as well as experts in different areas of multilingualism. The increase in the demand for information sessions on multilingualism reflects the growing interest in child language development and in the different ways of raising a multilingual family.

The second stage in the building of a multilingual family begins when the child starts to talk. In the first year of life, a normally developing child learns to distinguish the sounds of different languages and to produce the first sounds or words; in the second year, they start producing short sentences, often made of two or three words; between the age of 3 and 4 they construct more complex sentences and the vocabulary rapidly expands (Guasti, 2004). These milestones are common to the vast majority of monolingual and plurilingual children. Plurilingual children are also able to switch from one language to the other within the same sentence or between sentences. This is sometimes regarded by parents as a sign of confusion. However, as many studies have shown, code-switching is a communicative strategy used by many plurilingual children (and adults), and it is more common among those who are immersed in an environment where code-switching is used frequently (Cantone, 2007; De Houwer, 2009). Another important element that characterises bilingual speech is the possibility to choose which language to speak depending on the situation, the interlocutors and the topic. It is important to consider that the more children are exposed to a language and have the opportunity to use it, the more chances they have of developing the necessary lexical, grammatical and phonological skills in that language. In addition, the change of circumstances in a child's life, such as moving to a new country, separating from the extended family, losing a parent, or starting school may have an impact on the child's linguistic behaviour, which may result in the rejection (and sometimes the loss) of one of the languages. Language loss can happen at different stages during childhood, but it is not necessarily a permanent condition. Just as there are many factors which may cause it, there are also many ways to avoid it (Priven, 2008; Park, 2008). As much research has shown, bilingualism is not hereditary, but it needs to be transmitted from the parents to the child. This process may require time and effort from parents both at the initial stages and throughout the child's development.

Many parents in Ireland have a positive attitude towards the transmission of their native language to their children. They also seem to find it easy to expose them to the family language(s) before they start school. This is mostly due to the fact that in the first years of life children interact mostly with their parents, and they can easily engage in language games and activities. The following extracts from McFayden (2008: 139) show that at this stage parents' choices, attitudes and beliefs can strongly affect the experience of children.

> I try to talk to her in English but she won't answer in English; maybe wait. I want her to learn culture but see what she wants. I'm not forcing her. If she wants to know, I'm not going to push her.

> [The children] speak English because I think they can handle English better but, if I insist, they will speak Cantonese.

> About three years ago, I invited somebody to do special lessons for my kids to learn how to speak Mandarin. I think it's important to know the official language of China.

The second stage is characterised by the interaction between the parents' strategies and expectations and the child's behaviour. Children start to understand what languages are spoken around them, which language to choose according to the interlocutor, the situation and the topic, and which is the majority language of the environment external to the family.

In Ireland, the need for accessing information and for interaction among multilingual families has resulted in initiatives such as Multilingual Family Support Groups. The aim of these groups is for parents to discuss issues concerning multilingualism, share experiences, create links and form friendship among multilingual families and children. This type of experience can be very beneficial for parents who can meet other families in similar situations, as well as for children, who start to encounter realities that are similar to their own and therefore grow up seeing multilingualism as the norm. At the moment, there are groups that offer multilingual family support in Cork, Dublin and Belfast. These meetings also provide the opportunity for children to hear stories in different languages, play and interact in a multilingual environment, and learn about other languages and cultures.

Reflecting on her own experience, Natalia Kublova, the organiser of the Multilingual Family Support Group in Dublin, says:

> Only when I became a parent myself, I started questioning myself how to give him another language, what is the best strategy, when to start, which language to support. [...] It became clear that in Ireland there is not enough support for bilinguals.

Talking about the group's activities, she adds:

> We [...] also have meetings where parents could come with their children, to show them that we are different but it's great. Unfortunately some kids become embarrassed with their mother tongue at some stage in their life. Especially if they go to monolingual schools. Meeting other international children can really help to be proud of being Chinese, Spanish, German, Norwegian, Russian.

The experience of Natalia Kublova shows the difficulty parents start encountering when they raise a plurilingual child, and it highlights the benefits of these support groups for the whole family.

Another initiative which has become very popular in Ireland in recent years is the language playgroup. The aim of language playgroups is to allow children to be exposed to a language (other than English) by being in contact with their peers. These meetings take place in libraries, community centres or other public or private premises. At the moment, there are playgroups organised by ethnic minority community groups including German, Italian, Polish, Russian, Latvian, Spanish, Czech, Slovak, Estonian and French. The long-term purpose of language playgroups is to preserve languages across generations. The success of these initiatives lies in the fact that there are more and more families interested in transmitting their mother tongue to their children, which shows an increasing awareness and acceptance of child plurilingualism. The activities run during playgroups also help children to be in touch with their heritage and aware of the fact that there are other children who speak the same minority language. Some of the benefits of language playgroups are highlighted by Alessandra Di Claudio, the coordinator of Playgroup Italiano:

> By meeting other children and their families in the same situation, I think the kids realise that they are not the only ones who speak "the funny language" and that helps to accept Italian as a language alongside English. They also

gradually understand the notion that language is very much linked to the culture of a country[14].

As Alessandra Di Claudio points out, it is important for children to be aware that the "funny language" is not only spoken by their parents but also by other adults and children. Language playgroups often represent the only opportunity for children to interact in a minority language outside their home.

Language playgroups constitute an initial step towards the establishment of community activities that promote the use of minority languages among children. As much as playgroups help children acquire and maintain the minority language, the school plays a very important role in the child's linguistic development and evolving language preference.

The third stage in the establishment of multilingualism in the family starts when the child begins to attend pre-school and school. Parents may find this stage the most complex to deal with because the child is immersed in a new environment and starts communicating with peers. In the first and second stage parents play a major role in decision making and in the child's attitude towards the language(s) spoken at home. However, in the third stage the child's linguistic behaviour may shift, and parents often report sudden changes, such as increase in the use of English, refusal to speak one language, or loss of interest in activities in the minority language[15].

While there are many sources of information about the first stages of language acquisition, the role of the school environment in the development of two (or more) languages has not yet been extensively researched. As in the second stage, the support of other families and the sharing of experiences is a good way to understand what behaviours are common and to find out about the ways for further supporting the language through new activities that are suitable for the developing child. In this phase, the school also plays a major role in developing children's awareness and acceptance of linguistic diversity.

MULTILINGUAL EDUCATION

The pre-school and school environment has a great impact on the child's awareness of linguistic diversity and on the perception of the status of the majority language and of the language(s) spoken at home. Childcare workers and teachers are responsible for the transition into this new phase in the child's life and they can play a major role in the development of awareness of linguistic diversity in the classroom environment.

In 2006 the Office of the Minister for Children published guidelines for childcare providers, which included recommendations for the support of children's identity and sense of belonging by encouraging pedagogical strategies that would take account of linguistic diversity[16], as the following extract shows.

Be aware of the cultural and educational significance of the child's first language. For example, while assisting the children in acquiring English/ Irish as a second language, encourage parents to use their family language with children. Also encourage parents to support the child in the learning of the second language. [...] Display tapes of children's songs in a variety of languages, including the Irish and English language. Play tapes with music from different cultures to the children (p. 10 and 36).

Other important recommendations concern the benefits of having bilingual staff:

Fluency in a child's home language can facilitate communication with children and families. A bilingual staff member can help to foster a child's home language. [...] Find out if there are any bilingual staff or families willing to help to develop materials in different home languages e.g. a recording of a story, song or rhyme in a different language so children can listen to the tape while looking at the book, or words in other languages pasted into scrapbooks (p. 35).

These guidelines are an important step towards the development of awareness of linguistic diversity in the childcare environment, and their implementation should allow children to learn about diversity from a very young age.

While there is not yet an indication on how these guidelines are being used in pre-school settings around the country, more data is available on the situation of primary schools. Many primary schools have a high number of children who speak languages other than English and Irish at home. In a recent study, Carson and Extra (2010) collected data from two primary schools in Dublin and found that the most widely spoken languages other than English and Irish in these schools were Tagalog and Yoruba. This study showed that 1 in 3 children was born outside Ireland, and that 63% of their fathers and the 60% of their mothers were also born outside Ireland, mostly in the Philippines, Nigeria and Poland. It emerged from this study that there were 33 different languages being spoken among the families of the 191 children who participated in the study.

Linguistic diversity is a relatively new reality in schools, and teachers and policy makers are facing new challenges posed by multilingualism in the classroom. The two main challenges concern the English proficiency of non-native speakers and the introduction of activities that promote the awareness of multilingualism and linguistic diversity. The first issue has been addressed by the Irish Department of Education and Science since 1999, when English language support teaching was introduced. This system is mostly based on the withdrawal of children from their class to participate in a language support class. Some schools have also put in place independent support initiatives for pupils who need to learn English as a second language, based on activities run by their staff on a voluntary basis (Smyth et al., 2009). As Smyth et al. (2009) argue, the system put in place by the Department of Education could be improved by combining withdrawal and within-class support and by providing more training and more specific materials for support and also mainstream teachers[17].

While provisions are in place for English language support, there are no policies that concern the maintenance of minority languages within the school context. As O'Rourke (2010) points out, many teachers understand the importance of including language awareness activities in the curriculum, but they are uncertain on how to run them. She also reports the case of a principal in a Dublin school who was concerned that newcomers, while learning English, were losing their mother tongue. It is therefore clear that minority language support within the classroom environ-ment is becoming a necessity. An initial step towards the introduction of minority language activities in the curriculum can be achieved by running language awareness activities in the classroom. These activities are relatively new to the Irish education system, and most of the projects are run independently by the teachers. Language awareness projects are beneficial for the whole classroom because they allow all children to be proud of their linguistic identity, to get to know more about each other's background and to develop awareness of linguistic diversity. Examples of good practice in this area are emerging in schools with high percentages of students who speak languages other than English at home. One example is a language awareness project which offered multilingual activities in one class in Lane Street Primary school in Dublin (O'Rourke, 2010). The class had 13 children, of which 3 were of Irish origin, while the others were of Bulgarian, Polish, Indian, Philippine, Vietnamese and Albanian origin. The project started as a weekly stand-alone activity, but it was later integrated in a science project that was part of the curriculum. The students found out more about the different languages spoken by their classmates and they learned new words and phrases. The activities also required the contribution of parents, who helped with the pronunciation and spelling of words, and became part of their children's learning experience.

Availing of linguistic diversity as a pedagogical resource in the classroom presents a positive message to children, showing them that all languages are valuable. In cases where parents are also involved, both the children and the parents benefit from feeling that their home language is being recognised and valued. The main problem in running these activities is the deficit of specific teacher training, of appropriate materials and of economic resources. However, the emergence of a number of initiatives that support both the learning of English and the awareness of linguistic diversity represents a positive trend in education and show that teachers and principals are increasingly sensitive to language related issues.

Just as linguistic diversity is starting to be acknowledged and celebrated in the classroom, many immigrant communities have started to provide independent minority language courses for children. In the last few years, we have seen a rapid increase in the number of language classes and Saturday schools, with the purpose of transmitting the linguistic and cultural heritage to the new generations. Now children can attend classes through Russian, Polish, Lithuanian, Hungarian, Italian, Arabic, Chinese, Japanese, Edo, as well as other languages. These classes take place in different premises, including schools, libraries and community centres[18] and provide the opportunity to study the language and the culture, learn to read and write, and in some cases to follow the curriculum of the country where the language is spoken.These independent initiatives constitute a first important step towards the promotion and maintenance of minority languages, the creation of links among multilingual families and the transmission of a sense of belonging to a culture that should not be left behind. The presence of minority language classes shows that several communities are interested in encouraging their children to integrate in Ireland while learning about their own cultural and linguistic heritage. At the same time, language awareness activities run in schools have two major benefits: firstly, they make children aware of the importance of their own heritage within the classroom; secondly they show children who speak other languages at home that their language is not only confined to the home or to weekend activities, but also has a place in the school they attend and in the society they live in.

MULTILINGUAL IRELAND

A few important steps have been made towards the promotion and awareness of linguistic diversity in Irish society, and some of them have been extremely beneficial to both families and children alike.

A recent report of the Immigrant Council of Ireland (ICI) encourages the understanding of multilingualism and the promotion of linguistic diversity. It also emerges from this report that while the knowledge of English is considered a basic requirement for living in Ireland, it is also important to support minority languages:

> It is time to initiate a debate on linguistic diversity and on the positive effects of such diversity if it is well managed. Language is a core element in the expression and preservation of cultural identity. The ICI welcomes and supports a policy of encouraging migrants to learn English as the *lingua franca* and second official language of the country, provided the means for acquiring an adequate knowledge of the language are made available. However, there also needs to be a recognition and positive validation of multilingualism, including the special place of the Irish language, in all sectors of life including the workplace and the community.

(McFadyen, 2008: 37)

The *Diversity and Equality Guidelines for Childcare Providers* (2006) also highlight the influence society has on children's perception of diversity:

> Children are growing up in a diverse society. Research reveals they are aware, at three and four years and sometimes earlier, of ethnic, 'racial', gender, language and physical differences. They notice differences and similarities as part of their natural developmental process and assimilate positive and negative, spoken and unspoken messages about difference. These influences are part of the child's development of self-identity and self-esteem. Children learn and have their views reinforced by attitudes they experience primarily through relationships with adults and the broader community.

(Office of the Minister for Children, 2006: 2)

According to this statement, the experience of children is affected by the adults and also by the community they live in. Therefore, the process of awareness of linguistic diversity should start from the child's home, develop in the school, and be acknowledged in the society. In recent years, different projects and events have contributed to the development of the awareness of linguistic and cultural diversity in Ireland. *Kids' Own Publishing* recently started promoting the introduction of books in different languages, by getting children and teachers involved in the creation of books that celebrate linguistic diversity in schools and in the community. In February 2010, Bilingual Forum Ireland, the Dodder Valley Partnership, the CPLN Partnership[19] and South Dublin County Council joined together in the organisation of *International Mother Language Day*, a family event that celebrated linguistic diversity and multilingualism. In 2008 the Metro Éireann Media and Multicultural Awards (MAMA) recognised a number of initiatives that promoted cultural diversity. One of these projects was *Many Faces Many Places*, organised by Dublin City Libraries, which offered an intercultural programme including over 90 events aimed to inform children about ethnic diversity and to allow them to learn about other cultures and languages. Also in 2008, on the occasion of the EU Year of Intercultural Dialogue, several events were organised to promote interaction between different communities and to celebrate diversity by involving children in activities such as storytelling, drama, music, and different types of workshops.

These initiatives show that there is a growing awareness of the importance of supporting and celebrating cultural and linguistic diversity within society with the involvement and joint efforts of families, educators, community workers and policy makers.

Although some progress has been made towards the acknowledgment of the importance of linguistic diversity in Ireland, more effort is needed in order to start developing innovative projects that meet the growing need for specific activities for children, more specialised training for educators, and more accessible information and support for multilingual families. These improvements will bring about benefits for monolingual and plurilingual children and for the communities they live in. The acceptance and appreciation of multilingualism, which can start from learning to say a few words in the language spoken by a neighbour or a classmate, can help the development of children's sense of identity, tolerance, and openness towards diversity in all its forms. The joint efforts of families, educators and policy makers in nurturing linguistic diversity among children will allow the future generations to grow up in a country where multilingualism is not feared, but respected, valued and celebrated.

NOTES

[1] More information can be found in a recent publication of the European Commission entitled *Multilingualism: an asset for Europe and a shared commitment* - SEC(2008) 2443-2444-2445.

[2] These initiatives include language playgroups, meet-ups, courses for children and adults, language awareness activities and intercultural events.

[3] Following the terminology established by the EU, the term *multilingual* is used to refer to a group of people, while *plurilingual* refers to an individual.

[4] Throughout this chapter, the term parent refers to any carer or guardian.

[5] A minority language is a language spoken by a minority of the population in the country.

[6] Data on attitudes towards multilingualism have been obtained by Bilingual Forum Ireland.

[7] This is mostly the case of families where both parents speak other languages (other than Irish or English).

[8] For more details on strategies of linguistic upbringing see De Houwer (2009).

[9] These families were interviewed as part of a research on Italian-English bilingual children (La Morgia 2010).

[10] In 2001 Máiréad Ní Chinnéide published *Ag Tógáil Clainne Le Gaeilge - Speaking Irish at home*, a bilingual guide for parents published by Foras na Gaeilge for Comhluadar. Although it focuses on Irish, most of the information contained in the booklet can be applied to any bilingual context. In 2008 the

Speech and Language Therapy Department, Community Services Dublin West published a leaflet entitled *Do you speak more than one language at home? A guide for parents/carers of multilingual children*. This leaflet is a very useful and reader-friendly resource for parents.
[11] Information on raising plurilingual children will also be included in a toolkit that will be compiled by the Immigrant Council of Ireland and distributed in schools from September 2011.
[12] www.bilingualforumireland.com.
[13] The answers given by the experts on the forum, as well as the other resources can be accessed by visiting www.bilingualforumireland.com. The quotes are in verbatim.
[14] The full interview with Alessandra Di Claudio can be found in *The BFI Bulletin*, Issue 1, 2009.
[15] See Baker (2000a) for a discussion of these issues.
[16] These guidelines refer also to the "promotion of awareness of cultures and languages indigenous to Ireland as part of Irish cultural identity".
[17] The English Language Support Teacher Association (ELSTA) have recently started running Saturday morning sessions for teachers, some of which explore different issues related to multilingualism, including the use of different languages in the classroom.
[18] Information on international and ethnic minority schools and educational centres can be found in *Find Your Way. A guide to key services in Dublin City Centre*. Published in 2009 by Dublin City Centre Citizens Information Service, in association with Dublin City Public Libraries and North West Inner City Network. More information can be found by contacting the relevant ethnic minority organisations, which are listed in the guide or the Immigrant Council of Ireland.
[19] Clondalkin, Palmerstown, Lucan and Newcastle Partnership.

REFERENCES

Alton-Lee, A. (2003). *Quality teaching for diverse students in schooling. Best evidence synthesis.* New Zealand: ministry of education.

Baker, C. (2000a). *A parents and teachers guide to bilingualism* (2nd ed.). Multilingual Matters.

Baker, C. (2000b). *The care and education of young bilinguals.* Multilingual Matters.

Bialystok, E. (2009). Bilingualism: The good, the bad and the indifferent. *Bilingualism: Language and Cognition, 12*(1), 3–11.

Bialystok, E., Craik, F. I. M., & Freedman, M. (2007). Bilingualism as a protection against the onset of symptoms of dementia. *Neuropsychologia, 45*, 459–464.

Cantone, K. F. (2007). *Code-switching in bilingual children.* Springer.

Carson, L., & Extra, G. (2010). *Multilingualism in Dublin. Home language use among primary school children.* Centre for Language and Communication Studies. Trinity College Dublin.

De Hower, A. (2009). *An introduction to bilingual development.* Multilingual Matters.

Edwards, V. (1998). *The power of Babel: Teaching and learning in multilingual classrooms.* Stoke-on-Trent: Trentham Books.

European Commission. (2004). *Promoting language learning and linguistic diversity.* Luxembourg: Office for Official Publications of the European Communities.

Eurostat. (2007). *Europe in figures: Eurostat yearbook 2006–2007.* Luxembourg.

Guasti, M. T. (2004). *Language acquisition. The growth of grammar.* Cambridge: MIT Press.

La Morgia, F. (2010). *Input and dominance in bilingual first language acquisition.* Unpublished PhD thesis. Dublin City University.

McFadyen, C. (Ed.). (2008). *Getting on: from migration to integration. Chinese, Indian, Lithuanian, and Nigerian migrants' experiences in Ireland.* Immigrant council of Ireland.

Ó Laoire, M. (2008). Education for participation in a bilingual or multilingual society? Challenging the power balance between English and Irish (Gaelic) and other minority languages in Ireland. In C. Hélot, & A. M. de Mejía (Eds.), *Forging multilingual spaces. Integrated perspectives on majority and minority bilingual education* (pp. 256–264). Clevedon: Multilingual Matters.

Ó Laoire, M. (2007). Language use and language attitudes in Ireland. In D. Lasagabaster, & A. Huguet (Eds.). *Language use and attitudes* (pp. 164–184). Clevedon: Multilingual Matters.

O'Rourke, B. (forthcoming 2010). Negotiating multilingualism in an Irish primary school context. In C. Hélot, & M. Ó Laoire (Eds.), *Teaching in the multilingual classroom: Policies for pedagogy.* Multilingual Matters.

Office of the Minister for Children. (2006). *Diversity and equality guidelines for childcare providers.*

Park, H.-Y. (2008). *Raising ambi-lingual children: Linguistic minority children's heritage language learning and identity struggle.* Berlin: VDM-VerLag.

Priven, D. (2008). Grievability of first language loss: Towards a reconceptualisation of European minority language education practices. *International Journal of Bilingual Education and Bilingualism, 11*(1), 95–106.

Smyth, E., Darmody, M., McGinnity, F., & Byrne, D. (2009). *Adapting to diversity: Irish schools and newcomer students.* The Economic and Social Research Institute. Research Series, n.8.

Stern, Y., Habeck, C., Moeller, J., Scarmeas, N., Anderson, K. N., Hilton, H. J., et al. (2005). Brain networks associated with cognitive reserve in healthy young and old adults. *Cerebral Cortex, 15*, 394–402.

Francesca La Morgia
School of Applied Languages and Intercultural Studies
Dublin City University

RORY MC DAID

2. GŁOS, VOCE, VOICE

Minority Language Children Reflect on the Recognition of their First Languages in Irish Primary Schools

INTRODUCTION

"My grandmother would kill me!" announced Laima, a Lithuanian student, one day during an English language support class. We had just been discussing some vocabulary. I asked her for a certain word in English and she did not know the answer. I asked her for the word in Lithuanian and noticed immediately the look of shock as she realised that the word, previously well-known to her, had disappeared from her repertoire. Earlier, at the start of the lesson, she had told me about how happy she felt that her grandmother had come to visit from Lithuania. It was this previous conversation which now prompted the revelation of a murderous matriarch! Laima's comment, while made in half-jest, suggested a deeper issue with regard to her language, identity and family relations. It was this comment, this interaction, which drove me to examine further this area of first languages and minority language students in Irish schools.

At the time, I was employed as an English Language Support teacher in a Dublin primary school with a high proportion of minority language students. My job was to work with these children to improve their English language proficiency with the aim of helping them to fully participate in their mainstream class. The importance of a child's first language was of secondary concern to their development of a good level of English, quickly. As I read myself deeper into this literature I began to realise how fundamentally vital the issue of first language could be to minority language students. Wong Fillmore (1991; 2000) enlightened me as to the implications on family relations of losing a child's first language, Cummins (1981; 1986; 2001a) highlighted the positive implications of maintaining and developing first language in terms of learning a second and subsequent languages (contradicting the common-sense approach that it actually works as a barrier), while Ruiz (1984) outlined the benefits of multilingualism, that it was something to encourage rather than frustrate and block.

In addition to the teaching position, I was also enrolled on a taught Ed.D programme at the time of this interaction with Laima, and decided to avail of the opportunity to further investigate this issue from the perspective of some minority language children. More specifically, I set out to investigate what the feelings, experiences and understandings were of a selection of minority language children in some Irish primary schools with regard to the non-recognition of their first languages in those schools. This chapter outlines some of the answers that I unearthed.

Darmody, Tyrrell, Song (eds.), The Changing Faces of Ireland: Exploring the Lives of Immigrant and Ethnic Minority Children, 17–33.

Moving forward from this introduction, I will outline some of the most important theoretical, pedagogical and policy literature of interest to the study. Following this, I will briefly outline the methodological approach that I undertook in order to obtain fruitfully those feelings, experiences and understandings of the minority language children involved. The main body of the chapter makes judicious use of the children's words to elucidate those feelings, experiences and understandings. I conclude the chapter by recommending some developments which would arrest many of the more negative experiences of the children who worked with me during this study.

MULTILINGUAL IRELAND: SOCIETY AND SCHOOLS

Ireland's ethnic profile has altered dramatically over the last fifteen years. This is predominantly as a result of significant inward migration following overwhelmingly increased economic prosperity, European Union developments – namely expansion and freedom to travel – and the positioning of Ireland as one of the most globalised countries in the world.[1] These changing demographics have resulted in a substantial increase in the number of languages being spoken in Ireland (Cronin, 2004), although there are no definitive data on the number of languages being spoken in Ireland at present. The Valeur Report identified 158 languages, placing Ireland third behind the United Kingdom (288) and Spain (198) in the number of additional language spoken in their survey of 21 European states (Mc Pake and Tinsley, 2007). Research carried out by the Language Centre at the National University of Ireland, Maynooth, which found that there were 167 languages being spoken in Ireland, confirms this increase (O' Brien, 2006).

In the context of the expansion discussed above, it must be understood that the ethnic and linguistic profile of many Irish schools has altered quite dramatically over this period also. While there are limited comprehensive national data available, some research evidence is emerging as to the nature and extent of this ethnic expansion and concomitant linguistic explosion. Certain individual studies on the area have extrapolated relevant numbers from Census data (Smyth et al., 2009; Wallen and Kelly-Holmes, 2006; Mc Daid, 2007; Quinn et al., 2007; Nowlan, 2008). Other studies have also included more focused examination on the particular geographical area concerned in their work (McGorman and Sugrue, 2007; Mc Daid, 2008). On a national level, Smyth et al. (2009) estimate that in spring 2007, there were approximately 18,000 "newcomer" students in Irish post-primary schools[2], or six per cent of the total post-primary population of 327,000. This compares with around 10 per cent of the primary school population, or 45,700 out of 476,600 students. Not all of these "newcomer" children can accurately be classified as minority language students, in that they may speak a version of English as a first language. Furthermore, these figures are in constant flux with children and their families moving from school to school, or in and out of the country. Hence, ascertaining the precise number of minority language students in Irish schools is a fraught exercise. This confusion notwithstanding, it is clear that linguistic diversity is a key feature of many Irish primary and post-primary classrooms.

The multifarious potential contained within this linguistic diversity on a personal, pedagogical and social level, is well understood (Cummins, 2000; Kharkhurin, 2007; Ruiz, 1984). Yet this change also poses significant challenges for the Irish school system, one which was, itself, already, a dual language system, in that both Irish and English are compulsory subjects at primary and post-primary level. The Department of Education and Skills (DES) has reacted to these linguistic challenges by providing a system of English language support, based on the allocation of English language support teachers, and through funding the development of resource materials (DES, 2005; 2007; 2009). This model of provision is in keeping with OECD (2006) findings that the most widely used approach to supporting minority language students was through immersion education supplemented with systematic language support. This approach in Ireland has been described previously as a monolingual English-only system of language support (Mc Daid, 2007) in that there is no systematic provision for the teaching of the minority language child's first language. It is rooted in a wider public discourse that identifies lack of English proficiency as the premier barrier to social integration (Department of Justice, Equality and Law Reform (DJELR), 2008). This discourse has permeated the scholastic arena with one public commentator arguing that "[t]here is good reason to outlaw foreign languages being spoken in the playground because the playground is the primary vector for children to learn about the culture of the school and the society they are in" (Meyers, 2007). Such discourse echoes those in other jurisdictions which have cited the use of languages other than English with lack of integration and even civil disorder (Blackledge, 2005).

The literature is clear about the importance of learning the majority language with regard to pedagogical success and social integration (Ip et al., 1998; Ip et al., 2007; Lidgard et al., 1998; Smyth et al., 2009; Valdés, 1998; Winkleman and Winkleman, 1998). However, the literature also highlights that this focus becomes problematic when it is enacted without recognising the importance of those other languages spoken as first languages by these minority language children (Wong-Filmore, 1991; 2000). This approach is rightly understood as linguistic assimilation. Yet, there is plenty of international evidence to refute this course of action. Data from the United States, for instance, illustrate that Cuban-Americans have attained significant economic success without linguistic assimilation (García, 1995). Furthermore we understand from pronouncements by African migrants themselves that it is their ethnic background or perceived racial identity that is their biggest obstacle when trying to secure employment, not their linguistic proficiency (Dunbar, 2008: 58). The ongoing marginalization and ghettoisation of Irish Travellers speaks further to the complicated and multifactorial aspect of integration issues in Ireland.

First Languages in Irish Schools

There are limited empirical data on the topic of first language recognition in schools in Ireland. No previous studies have focused specifically on the issue of recognition of first languages, or indeed, the linguistic patterns of Irish multilingual class-rooms. There are some studies, however, which highlight the issue of recognition as a component of wider research findings: Post-primary teachers' and principals' perceptions of English language support in 11 schools in an urban centre (Nowlan, 2008); policy and practice of teaching English as an additional language in ten primary schools in Galway (Wallen and Kelly-Holmes, 2006); and teacher responses to immigration and increasing ethnic diversity in eight primary and post-primary schools (Devine, 2005). These research data are unambiguous about the absence of any positive focus on children's first languages. While Nowlan (2008) identifies one example of a school hiring a part-time bilingual teacher who taught both Romanian and Russian, she outlines that this type of initiative was absent in the vast majority of schools within her study. Devine (2005) asserts that at no point in any of the interviews conducted in her research did the teachers mention the multilingual capacities which many of the children had, while Wallen and Kelly-Holmes (2006) failed to observe any similar activities in their study and argued for this as an area requiring further study in the Irish educational context.

Yet we must also be aware this is not a completely new field in Irish educational discourse. Fifteen years have passed since McGovern, writing in the context of the support provided for Vietnamese refugee children in Irish schools, called for a policy based on the principles of equality and anti-racism (McGovern, 1995). Such a policy would involve language support for children from linguistic and cultural minority backgrounds. She cautioned, however, that this support should not be viewed in the assimilationist perspective but should ensure affirmation and status for their first languages. Thus, this important issue of recognition of first languages has been brought to our attention in the past. This present study intended to address, in some way, the research gap in this area as articulated by Wallen and Kelly-Holmes (2006).

FIRST LANGUAGE RECOGNITION AS AN ISSUE OF EQUALITY

Recognition has been established as one of the five dimensions of equality which underpin the theoretical construct of 'Equality of Condition' (Baker et al., 2004 Lynch and Lodge, 2002; Lynch and Baker, 2005). Equality of Condition has been described as being about "enabling and empowering people to exercise what might be called real choices among real options" (Baker et al., 2004: 34). It is a far more radical egalitarian approach than liberal egalitarianism which can promote the toleration of difference, while still retaining a position of superiority. Hence, liberal egalitarians often leave dominant views unquestioned. Taylor (1994) bases his critique of procedural liberalism on the point that it is unable to accommodate people of different cultural backgrounds. As an alternative, Taylor (ibid.) proposes a politics of recognition, which will promote the recognition and survival of minority cultures within majority culture societies. Such recognition must originate in respect for difference rather than emerge from an obligatory act of recognition. This approach necessitates a politics of equal respect – an approach rooted in a presumption of cultural equality. Such an understanding of cultural equality promotes the concept that all cultures have something important to impart to all human beings.

Recognition is understood as important for the development of positive self-image. As humans, we internalise the messages we receive from those around us regarding our identity. When these messages render as illegitimate those aspects of our identity, which we view as foundational, these messages can work to injure our perception of our own worth. Thus, according to Taylor:

> [T]he thesis is that our identity is partly shaped by recognition or its absence, often by misrecognition of others, and so a person or group of people can suffer real damage, real distortion, if the people or society around them mirror back to them a confining or demeaning or contemptible picture of themselves. (Taylor, 1994: 25).

Hence, positive self-image is constructed through the receipt of positive messages about foundational aspects of our identity. Honneth (1992: 188) explains that "[w]e owe our integrity, in a subliminal way, to the receipt of approval or recognition from other persons". According to Taylor (op cit.), the crucial feature of human life is that it is fundamentally dialogical in character; humans self-define through interaction with others who matter to us. This is an enduring process so that even after we outgrow some of these others or they disappear from our lives in that "the conversation with them continues within us as long as we live" (Taylor, 1994: 33). When one of the interlocutors within this conversation experiences the "subtle humiliation that accompanies public statements as to the failings of a given person" (Honneth, 1992: 189) the results can be quite deleterious. Honneth (1992: 191) argues that "[t]he individual who experiences this type of social devaluation typically falls prey to a loss of self-esteem … [and may] no longer [be] in a position to conceive of himself as a being whose characteristic traits and abilities are worthy of esteem." Fraser (2000: 113–114) conceptualises recognition as a matter of status and contends that to be misrecognised is "to be denied the status of a full partner in social interaction, as a consequence of institutionalised patterns of cultural value that constitute one as comparatively unworthy of respect of esteem."

Misrecognition, Inequality and Schooling

Highlighting that misrecognition or "inequality of recognition" runs deeply in many familiar settings, Lynch et al. (2004: 6) outline that "it is an everyday practice to describe some students as 'smart' or 'brainy' and others as 'slow', 'weak', 'stupid' or 'duds'" and contend that this is a "pervasive inequality of recognition in the educational system." It is well-established that schools very often reproduce inequalities rather than challenge them (Baker and Lynch, 2005; Bourdieu, 1990; and Bourdieu and Passeron, 1977; Lynch and Lodge, 2002). Lynch and Lodge (2002) reveal that assumptions of homogeneity tended to prevail among both teachers and students within the schools in their study. Concomitant domination and misrecognition of diversity with respect to race, gender, ability, sexuality and social class, for instance, are thus fundamental to the identity and lived experience of children in Irish schools. The suppression of different identities becomes problematic for the children involved in that these differences often become devalued and condemned (Baker and Lynch, 2005).

According to Bourdieu (1990) struggles for recognition are a fundamental dimension of social life and that what is at stake in these struggles is the accumulation of a particular form of capital. Giroux (1983) articulates that Bourdieu's theory of cultural reproduction highlights that dominant groups orchestrate symbolic violence to mediate and reproduce class-divided societies. In the context of education, this is achieved through the transmission of a selection of meanings which objectively defines a group's or a class's culture as a symbolic system. This selection of meanings is not neutral, however, rather it is:

> arbitrary insofar as the structure and functions of that culture cannot be deduced from any universal principle, whether physical, biological or spiritual, not being linked by any sort of internal relation to 'the nature of things' or any 'human nature' (Bourdieu and Passeron, 1977: 8).

As pedagogic agents, teachers engage in pedagogic work based on pedagogic authority, which is given institutional legitimacy as school authority. The status authority conveyed upon the teacher by the school by virtue of the teacher's appointment tends "to rule out the question of the informative efficiency of the communication" (Bourdieu and Passeron, 1977: 108). Teachers can impose the reception of the selection of meanings by virtue of this status authority. This pedagogical work produces a legitimacy of what it transmits "by designating what it transmits – by mere fact of transmitting it legitimately – as worthy of transmission, as opposed to what it does not transmit" (Bourdieu and Passeron, 1977: 22). In so doing, it also seeks to impose on the dominated groups "recognition of the illegitimacy of their own cultural arbitrary" (Bourdieu and Passeron, 1977: 41). With regard to minority language children, there is misrecognition of the "arbitrary nature of the legitimacy of the dominant language" (Blackledge, 2002: 68). This then "tends to reproduce, both in the dominant and in the dominated classes, misrecognition of the truth of the legitimate culture as the dominant cultural arbitrary, whose reproduction contributes towards reproducing the power relations (Bourdieu and Passeron, 1977).

Misrecognition, Self-identity and Family Relations

When this selection of meanings imposed by teachers excludes first languages it can have significant long-term effects for minority language children. Messages which exclude a child's first language can hurt deeply, as Anzaldúa (1987: 59) eloquently elaborates when she declares "[s]o, if you want to really hurt me, talk badly about my language. Ethnic identity is twin skin to linguistic identity – I am my language". This pain emerges beautifully from the pen of John Montague (1982: 110) when he writes:

> [T]o stray sadly home
> And find
> the turf-cured width
> of your parent's hearth
> growing slowly alien:
> … To grow
> a second tongue, as
> harsh a humiliation
> as twice to be born.

In addition to the impact on self-identity, failure to recognise and provide support for first languages within the education system can have significant implications for relations within minority language families and communities. Minority language children who experience language loss can no longer communicate freely with members of their family and communities. In losing this social and cultural capital, there exists the potential for rifts to develop and families to lose the intimacy that comes from shared beliefs and understandings. As Wong-Fillmore points out "[w]hat is lost is no less than the means by which parents socialize their children" (Wong-Fillmore, 1991: 343 as cited in Kouritzin, 1999: 16). Similar findings have been outlined elsewhere. Tseng and Fuligni (2000) found that adolescents that spoke the home language with their parents had emotionally closer relations with their parents than those who spoke English with their parents. These adolescents also indicated that they had less conflict with their parents than those who spoke English. Problems with parent-adolescent relationships can be a precursor to problematic behaviour. In this context then, it is important to understand the advice of Mouw and Xie (1999) who, while recognising the importance of developing second language proficiency in English for academic success, asserted that we must remain aware of the social and interpersonal dangers of rapid linguistic assimilation in order to ensure effective communication between parents and children.

Pedagogical Importance of First Languages

There is clear pedagogical evidence for the importance of recognition of first languages in education. Students who feel that their language is important in school feel that they belong in the school. According to Cummins (1997), the message is not just about bilingualism and language learning as linguistic and educational phenomena; more fundamentally it is a message about what kinds of identity are acceptable in the classroom and society. The literature also highlights the importance to first languages to the development of proficiency in second and subsequent languages. Of most immediate relevance here is the work of Cummins (1986; 2000; 2001a; 2001b) which offers a framework for empowering minority students through preventing school failure. This framework is underpinned by a commitment to transformative pedagogy based on the creation of collaborative rather than coercive relations of power. A central tenet of this theoretical framework is that students from 'dominated' societal groups are 'empowered' or 'disabled' as a direct result of their interactions with educators in the schools. Cummins explains that these "interactions are mediated by the implicit or explicit role definitions that educators assume in relation to four institutional characteristics of schools" (Cummins, 1986: 22). One of these characteristics is the extent to which minority students' *languages* and cultures are incorporated into the school program.

Within Cummins' framework, teachers empower their students by adding to their linguistic and cultural repertoire. This is achieved through incorporation of first language and culture within their pedagogy rather than pursuing a pedagogy that seeks to replace first languages and culture with that which is dominant in the society. Teachers who positively recognise the importance of children's first languages, and thus infuse their pedagogy with such understanding, convey a message to their minority language children that their language is important, and hence that what they bring with them to school is valued within the school setting. In this way they show respect for the student's language (Lucas *et al.*, 1990). These teachers advocate for such students to feel proud of their linguistic identity and help to empower them to sculpt a society that appreciates multilingualism as a resource and opportunity rather than treat it as a problem in need of solution.

Linguistic Interdependence Principle

In order to substantiate the above framework, from a pedagogical perspective a consideration of the interaction between first and second languages is necessary. Cummins (1981) has theorised this as the Linguistic Interdependence Principle. Cummins' articulation of the importance of incorporation of the first language of minority language students emerges from analysis of research data into the effectiveness of bilingual education. The Stanford Working Group (1993), Ramírez (1992) and Thomas and Collier (1997) all argue that first language use is one of the most important indicators of educational success for minority language children. Genesse et al. (2005) point out that bilingual proficiency and biliteracy are positively related to academic achievement in both languages. They highlight that bilingual Hispanic students had higher educational expectations and achievement scores than their monolingual English-speaking Hispanic peers and conclude that educational programs for English Language Learners should seek to develop their full bilingual competencies. Moll and Diaz (1985) illustrate that Spanish speaking English Language Learners who read a story in English, discussed the story in Spanish and delivered their answers to set comprehension questions in English, demonstrated higher levels of comprehension than a control group which discussed the story in English. Research has shown that language recognition and use is of importance for those students who Suárez-Orozco (2001) identify as tending to achieve below their native born peers. In this instance it is more important that socio-economic background.

To explain the success of this counter-intuitive approach to teaching minority language children, Cummins (1981) has advanced a theory of "interdependence". This theory holds that:

> To the extent that instruction in Lx is effective in promoting proficiency in Lx, transfer of this proficiency to Ly will occur provided there is adequate exposure to Ly (either in school or environment) and adequate motivation to learn Ly (Cummins, 1981: 20).[3]

In essence, Cummins (ibid.) argues that given adequate exposure to a second language, and adequate motivation to learn that language, learning in the first language will transfer to the second language. Thus if a child is taught the processes involved with multiplication or an explanation of the water cycle in their first language, they can transfer this learning into their second language given adequate motivation and exposure. Cummins (ibid.) clarifies the Interdependence Principle by highlighting the difference between two alternative conceptualisations of bilingual proficiency, which he refers to as the Separate Underlying Proficiency (SUP) and Common Underlying Proficiency (CUP). The SUP Model of Bilingual Education implies that the proficiency of the minority language child in their first language is separate from their proficiency in English, thus content and skills learned through L1 cannot be transferred to L2 or vice versa. The research evidence would argue that this is not the case, however, finding that content and skills can be transferred from one language to the other.

Thus I have established that the issue of minority language recognition is fundamentally an issue of inequality within the Irish education system. I have further outlined the potential deleterious impact of misrecognition for minority language children with regard to self-identity and family and community relations. In addition to this, I have provided clear evidence that first languages do not act as a barrier to pedagogical success, rather, when seized on as a resource, can actually facilitate second language learning. I proceed from this point to provide a brief outline of the methodology used in the study upon which this chapter is based and go on to examine the data which emerged from the research study.

METHODOLOGY

The data upon which this chapter is based were gathered during a Trilingual Literacy Camp (TLC), with 13 Polish and Romanian speaking children, a lead researcher, two interpreters and a teaching assistant held during the school Easter holidays in 2008. The central purpose of the TLC was to answer the question, "what are the feelings, experiences and understandings of minority language children in the Irish primary education system with regard to the non-recognition of their first languages in school?". During the TLC, the participants wrote a dual language text to the broad title of "Me, My School and My Languages". This text was used as a child-developed codification for further exploration of issues pertaining to the children's experience of language learning. In addition to the dual language books, I also facilitated a number of language specific focus groups, with the aid of an interpreter, while ongoing conversations were held with the children throughout the duration of the TLC. Return visits to some of the children were used to verify the accuracy of assertions being made, while a showcase event was held a number of months following the TLC where the children launched their dual language texts and watched short videos of their texts in a cinema-like setting.

LINGUISTIC OUTSIDERS

Drawing on the children's feelings, understandings and experiences as enunciated through the focus groups, and in reaction to their dual language texts, the argument is made that the minority language children who participated in the TLC have been constructed as linguistic outsiders within their schools. None of the children involved in this research project had ever been asked directly by any of their teachers to talk with them about their languages. In addition to this, detailed evidence emerged of cases of actual repression of these languages. Many of the children have been explicitly told to desist from using their first languages in school. According to one child, Irenka, who is her friend Celina's teacher, "always tells me to talk to her in English, not in Polish". This occurs both in the classroom and at break times. Adrianna reveals that "we are not allowed to speak Romanian in class". This message is conveyed to the children new to the class, and the teachers expect their peers to help to enforce it, with Adrianna again revealing "when I first got here the teacher told the other kids not to speak to me in Romanian because I had to learn English very quickly". This message has also been conveyed into the children's social practices in the school, for example Gheorghe and Adrianna, have been instructed to speak only in English in the schoolyard.

Some of the children are afraid to use their own language in front of their teachers. Klaudia declared that her teachers "don't even know that I speak Polish". She has decided not to speak Polish in front of them as she "thought that they would be angry that I speak Polish". Some of the children resist the messages that they receive from their teachers with Stefan telling me "when the teacher cannot hear me and I want to say something to Gheorghe I say it in Romanian". If his teacher hears this use of Romanian "he shouts at me". Similarly Irenka outlined how "we still talk in Polish ... [because] it is our language so ...".

In this respect, these minority language children are given a clear message that their own first language is a barrier to succeeding in the Irish education system. Misrecognition of their linguistic capabilities by teachers is articulated through a pedagogical commitment to the acquisition of English, based on an approach rooted in the time-on-task argument (Imhoff, 1990). Other studies in Ireland reveal similar findings (McGorman and Sugrue, 2007; Nowlan, 2008; Wallen and Kelly-Holmes, 2006). Devine (2005) argues that this originates in a construction of children in deficit terms, and asserts that it is underpinned by a concern that the children could not integrate socially without the requisite proficiency in English. It is important to further understand this approach in the context of wider public discourse that establishes multilingualism as a barrier to integration, and an associated focus by the DES on the provision of monolingual English language support to minority language children to access the curriculum.

Minority language children's lack of proficiency in English is constructed as problematic. Messages to this effect amount to public statements of failings (Honneth, 1992) and constitute an institutionalised pattern (Fraser, 2000) that presents English language speakers as normative and minority language speakers as deficient or inferior. Proficiency in first languages is devalued and condemned (Lynch and Baker, 2005). Many of the children experience the message that the solution to these "failings" lies in successful acquisition of English. This is often pursued through quite detrimental pedagogical practices, including the repression of their own first language. Moreover, some of the children's classmates echo and enforce this prioritisation of English within the school.

According to the data, a number of the children experienced injury as a result. Stefan's displeasure resulting from his teacher shouting at him for speaking Romanian is important in this context, as is Adrianna's experience of her Romanian-speaking peer speaking with her only in Romanian, and Klaudia's account of feeling "stupid because I have to talk in English and I can't talk in my own language". The language that Klaudia uses echoes Baker et al. (2004: 6), and points to what they refer to as the "pervasive inequality of recognition in the education system". The link between self-image and identity emerges quite strongly at this point. In this context, then, it is insightful to reflect again on the words of Anzaldúa (1987: 59), "I am my language". While the effect of Klaudia's interaction might not exactly constitute what Honneth (1992: 189) characterises as "an injury that can cause the identity of the entire person to collapse", in that Klaudia did not seem decimated by the inter-action, it is important to reflect on Taylor's (1994) caution that the conversations with those who matter to us continues within us as long as we live. In this regard, then, it is difficult to foretell the longer-term consequences of the experiences of Klaudia, Adrianna and Stefan, though the potential for damage is quite significant.

When the children spoke of how their multilingualism was recognised in their schools, it was either quite instrumentalist or in an extremely peripheral fashion. The use of dictionaries is a very good pedagogical method for scaffolding learning. The children themselves see the merit in their usage in this regard and it is obvious that some teachers have grasped this potential. Nevertheless, such activity is similarly rooted in the need to learn English rather than any recognition of the importance of the children's linguistic capabilities. There is no sense in which the children's linguistic capabilities are showcased as something to be proud of (Cummins et al., 2005). Rather, a cultural arbitrary which aims at first language replacement in favour of English language proficiency is imposed by the teachers (Bourdieu and Passeron, 1977). Proficiency in English is legitimised while multilingualism is problematised and rendered illegitimate.

On other occasions when the children's linguistic capabilities are recognised, these once more emerge from the overall context of addressing the problematics of lack of English language proficiency on the part of minority language speakers within the school. The use of children as interpreters in school can be understood in this context. The literature highlights the difficulties teachers face in communicating with minority language parents (McGorman and Sugrue, 2007). In the absence of an available translation and interpretation service they are often faced with asking children to work as language brokers within their school. In many cases, this is seemingly unavoidable. While the literature is inconclusive as to the overall effect on parent/child relations, there is evidence that it can, for instance, challenge traditional intergenerational authority relationships within families (De Ment et al., 2005: 260). This emerged as an issue within the present study, with Sylwia reflecting that she felt like a teacher when she had to interpret for her mother. There is a very clear sense in which Sylwia has attained greater linguistic capital than her mother. Gheorghe's account of interpreting for his mother highlights the feelings of embarrass-ment which can emerge as a result of language brokering. He has had to do this in school because "she doesn't really speak any English, but she knows some English". He doesn't like doing this work for his mother because "she has four years here and she don't speak English". Importantly, he believes that his mother speaks "like a baby" when she tries to speak English and he feels "ashamed to do that" for her. This feeling of shame has also been found in other studies (Hall and Sham, 2007;

McQuillan and Tse, 1995). Gheorghe's mother's linguistic capital has no purchase within the institution. In this context, her proficiency in Romanian is problematic. In addition to the negative consequences for Gheorghe's mother in experiencing such infantilisation, this is also a potentially injurious activity for Gheorghe himself, the longer-term consequences of which might only be revealed well into the future (Taylor, 1994).

Some of the children have been asked to translate particular high profile phrases or words, for instance, 'Hello', 'Easter' or 'Happy Christmas'. Such activities reflect recommendations made in the Intercultural Guidelines for Primary Schools (NCCA, 2005a) that the children should be encouraged to take pride in using words from their own language. It is an important first step on the recognition ladder but it remains quite peripheral recognition, more fixed in the "Steel Bands, Saris and Samosas" (Troyna, 1983) approach to multicultural education, than one rooted in respect for, and recognition of, diversity. Such peripheral activity will not adequately address the fundamental issues of inequality of recognition that remain embedded within these children's schools.

There were some examples of the children experiencing more positive recognition of their linguistic status. Two teachers emerged as having grasped some of the significance of positive recognition of the linguistic identities of the minority language children in their schools. Elisabeta, Petru and Adrian revealed how their English language support teacher, Miss O'Reilly, used their first language to scaffold their learning in both oral language work and literacy activities. Adrian also revealed that his mainstream class teacher has made dual language books available to him. These teachers clearly understand the pedagogical implication of first language recognition, at the very least, and, perhaps, are in some way appreciative of the importance of the intersection between recognition of linguistic identity and self-image (Churchill, 2003). These two examples notwithstanding, however, the dominant experience has been misrecognition of the children's linguistic identity. There is very little evidence that their linguistic identity is either accepted or appreciated. Rather, it is seen as a barrier to be overcome or, at best, as a difference to be merely tolerated (Lynch and Baker, 2005).

It should also be noted that teacher influence is not confined within the school; rather it also extends into both family education and diffuse education (Bourdieu and Passeron, 1977). This is most clearly indicated through the experience of Adrianna. Not only has her teacher excluded her language within the institutionalised education setting of school, but also in the diffuse educational setting and the family educational setting. Adrianna's mother clearly accepted the status authority of the teacher who told her not to speak with Adrianna in Romanian at home. She proceeded to try to speak with her in English, and also to remove other vestiges of linguistic diversity, most obviously the access to Romanian television through the satellite dish. While she found that she could not sustain speaking only in English with Adrianna, the television situation remained unaltered. Adrianna, herself, has also now come to understand that the best way to learn English is through using it as much as possible. In addition to the family space, the teacher also influenced the social space, wherein one of Adrianna's Romanian speaking friends stopped speaking with her in Romanian after the teacher instructed her to so do. This introduced an unnecessary tension into the relationship between these two children, with Adrianna recalling that "I was upset with her at first but then I apologised when I knew what the situation was".

PEDAGOGUES, POWER AND PERPETUATION

It is evident that teachers exercise considerable power over the life experiences of the minority language children in this study. This can be understood through the ideas of Bourdieu and Passeron (1977) who argue that teachers are endowed with status authority by the school by virtue of their very appointment to the position of teacher. This status authority then empowers them to perpetuate a cultural arbitrary within the school system. Devine (2003a) highlights that children understand that power is exercised by teachers through this authority and that the teachers in her study regard their authority as sacrosanct. The cultural arbitrary transmitted to the children in this study legitimises monolingual English and renders the children's multilingualism as illegitimate.

Bourdieu and Passeron (1977) argue that pedagogic action may constitute a form of symbolic violence when the cultural values of the dominant are imposed on the less dominant group. The delegitimisation of the first languages of the children in this study constitutes a form of symbolic violence within the institutionalised educational setting of their schools. In the absence of evidence as to the motivation of the teacher in this regard it is possible to interpret the teacher's actions in light of Devine's (2005) findings that teachers are concerned with social integration. In not having had access to adequate pre-service or in-service training on this issue (McGorman and Sugrue, 2007; Smyth et al., 2008), it is probable that some of the teachers simply fail to understand the positive links between first language proficiency, self-identity and English language learning.

The origin of this perspective notwithstanding, as articulated quite eloquently by the children in this study, the result is in no doubt. There is clear misrecognition of them as multilingual children. There is very little evidence that these children's teachers understand the purpose of education as the empowerment of minority language children to challenge the *status quo* within wider Irish society (Cummins, 2001a). The data reveal that these children's teachers hold quite conservative identity options for their students and for the society that they hope their students will help to form. There is little respect for the students' language (Lucas et al., 1990). There is a very clear message that a public multilingual identity is not acceptable in the classroom and society (Cummins, 1997). To retain a public multilingual identity is to remain as a linguistic outsider. The perpetuation of the English language, to the exclusion of minority languages within the classroom replicates and reinforces the problematisation of multilingualism in wider Irish society. These pedagogues have failed to create "interpersonal spaces where students identities are validated" (Cummins, 2001b: 48) and in so doing miss the opportunity to challenge the under-standing of multilinglualism as a *problem* (Ruiz, 1984).

The data reveal that some of the children's majority language peers are interested in multilingualism, substantiating the findings of McGorman and Sugure (2007) that the Irish children in their study regretted that they only spoke English at home. This is a fertile base upon which to build a challenge to the wider societal problematisation of multilingualism. In neglecting to do so, however, these teachers legitimise interactions such as Gheorghe being subjected to jeering in the context of "blah, blah, blah" or Klaudia being told to not to speak Polish by some of her majority language friends.

I understand, as Lynch (1999) highlights, that teachers may have little control over the forms of knowledge that they teach. Lynch (1999) holds out the possibility of concerted action on the part of teachers to realise or resist change in Irish education. It must be also realised, however, that teachers do make choices within their classrooms as to their pedagogical practices. They can choose to recognise the importance of first languages through a whole range of pedagogical practices, what Cummins (2000) articulates as collaborative micro-level interactions. Such activities can include the use of dual language texts, the creation of dual language texts, organisation of multilingual projects and multilingual group work, all of which are rooted in solid pedagogical theory and are entirely consistent with the aims of the Revised Primary School Curriculum (Ireland, 1999). Support for teachers by way of informed in-service training, the development of dual language texts and the publication of a DES circular on the importance of first languages in education would help arrest the misrecognition of first languages as highlighted in this chapter. The provision of bilingual teaching assistants would greatly help with further highlighting the importance of children's first languages in the educational setting, as would the provision of optional first language lessons during the school day.

NOTES

[1] According to the ATKearney Globalisation index (2006), Ireland was the fourth most globalised country in the world in 2006, a slight fall from the premier position in 2001 and 2002.

[2] The term "post-primary" is used to denote the full range of second level school sector in Ireland. It includes community schools, comprehensive schools, voluntary secondary schools and vocational schools.

[3] Lx refers to Language "x". Ly refers to Language "y".

REFERENCES

Anzaldúa, G. (1987). *Borderlands/la frontera: The new mestiza*. San Fransisco: Spinsters.

Baker, J., Lynch, K., Cantillon, S., & Walsh, J. (2004). *Equality: From theory to action*. Basingstoke, Hampshire: Palgrave Macmillan/Houndmills.

Blackledge, A. (2002). The discursive construction of national identity in multilingual Britain. *Journal of Language, Identity, and Education, 1*(1), 67–87.

Blackledge, A. (2005). *Discourse and power in a multilingual world*. Amsterdam: John Benjamin.

Bourdieu, P. (1990). *In other words: Essays towards a reflexive sociology* (M. Adamson, Trans.). Stanford, CA: Stanford University Press.

Bourdieu, P., & Passeron, J. C. (1977). *Reproduction in education, society and culture* (R. Nice, Trans.). London: SAGE Publications.

Churchill, S. (2003). *Language education, Canadian civic identity and the identities of Canadians*. Strasbourg: Council of Europe.

Cronin, M. (2004). Babel Átha Cliath: The languages of Dublin. *New Hibernia Review, 8*(4), 9–22.

Cummins, J. (1981). The role of primary language development in promoting educational success for language minority students. In *Schooling and Language Minority Students* (pp. 3–49). Los Angeles: Evaluation, Dissemination and Assessment Center California State University.

Cummins, J. (1986). Empowering minority students: A framework for intervention. *Harvard Educational Review, 56*(1), 18–36.

Cummins, J. (1997). Cultural and linguistic diversity in education: A mainstream issue? *Educational Review, 49*(2), 105–114.

Cummins, J. (2000). This place nurtures my spirit: Creating contexts of empowerment in linguistically-diverse schools. In R. Phillipson (Ed.), *Rights to language: Equity, power and education* (pp. 249–258). London: Lawrence Erlbaum Associates, Publishers.

Cummins, J. (2001a). *Negotiating identities: Education for empowerment in a diverse society* (2nd ed.). Los Angeles: California Association for Bilingual Education.

Cummins, J. (2001b). *Language, power and pedagogy: Bilingual children in the crossfire*. Clevedon: Multilingual Matters.

Cummins, J. (2005). A proposal for action: Strategies for recognizing heritage language competence as a learning resource within the mainstream classroom. *The Modern Language Journal, 89*(4), 585–592.

De Ment T. L., Buriel, R., & Villanueva, C. M. (2005). Children as language brokers.

Department of Education and Science. (2009). *Circular 0015/2009: Meeting the needs of pupils for whom English is a second language*. Dublin: Department of Education and Science.

Department of Education and Science. (2007). *Circular 0053/2007: Meeting the needs of pupils for whom English is a second language*. Dublin: Department of Education and Science.

Department of Education and Science. (2005). *Educational provision for non-English speaking pupils*. Retrieved on September 19, 2006, from http://www.education.ie/servlet/blobservlet/padmin_lang_non_national.doc?language=EN

Department of Justice, Equality and Law Reform. (2008). *Immigration, residence and protection bill, 2008*. Dublin: The Stationery Office.

Devine, D. (2003a). *Children, power and schooling: How childhood is structured in the primary school*. Stoke-on-trent: Trentham Books.

Devine, D. (2003b). Voicing concerns about children's rights and status in school. In M. Shevlin, & R. Rose (Eds.), *Encouraging voices: Respecting the insights of young people who have been marginalised*. Dublin: The National Disability Authority.

Devine, D. (2005). Welcome to the celtic tiger? Teacher responses to immigration and increasing ethnic diversity in Irish schools. *International Studies in Sociology of Education, 15*(1), 49–70.

Dunbar, P. (2008). *Evaluating the barriers to employment and education for migrants in cork: Research report*. Cork: NASC.

Fraser, N. (2000). Rethinking recognition. *New Left Review, 3*(May/June), 107–120.

Garcia, O. (1995). Spanish language loss as a determinant of income among Latinos in the United States: Implications for language policy in schools. In J. Genesee, F., Lindholm-Leary, K., Saunders, W. & Christian, D. (2005). English language learners in U. S. schools: An overview of research findings. *Journal of Education for Students Placed at Risk (JESPAR), 10*(4), 363–386.

Giroux, H. A. (1983). *Theory and resistance: A pedagogy for the opposition*. South Hadley, MA: Bergin & Garvey.

Hall, N., & Sham, S. (2007). Language brokering as young people's work: Evidence from Chinese adolescents in England. *Language and Education, 21*(1), 16–30.

Harker, K. (2001). Immigrant generation, assimilation and adolescent psychological wellbeing. *Social Forces, 79*(3), 969–1004.

Honneth, A. (1992). Integrity and respect: Principles of a conception of morality based on the theory of recognition. *Political Theory, 20*(2), 187–201.

Imhoff, G. (1990). The position of U. S. English on bilingual education. In C. B. Cazden & C. E. Snow (Eds.), *English plus: Issues in bilingual education* (pp. 48–61). Newbury Park, CA: SAGE Publications.

Ip, D., Wu, C. T., & Inglis, C. (1998). Settlement experiences of Taiwanese immigrants in Australia. *Asian Studies Review, 22*(1), 79–97.

Ip, D., Lui, C. W., & Chui, W. H. (2007). Veiled entrapment: A study of social isolation of older Chinese migrants in Brisbane, Queensland. *Ageing and Society, 27*(5), 719–738.

Ireland, Government of. (1999). *Primary school curriculum.* Dublin: The Stationery Office.

Kharkhurin, A. V. (2007). The role of cross-linguistic and cross-cultural experiences in bilinguals' divergent thinking. In I. Kecskes, & L. Albertazzi (Eds.), *Cognitive aspects of bilingualism* (pp. 175–210). Dordrecht: Springer.

Kouritzin, S. (1999). *Face(t)s of first language loss.* Mahwah, NJ: Lawrence Erlbaum Associates, Publishers.

Lidgard, J. E., Ho, Y.-Y., Chen, J., Goodwin, P., & Bedford, R. (1998). Immigrants from Korea, Taiwan and Hong Kong in New Zealand in the mid-1990s: Macro and micro perspectives. In *Population studies centre discussion paper* (Vol. 29). Hamilton: University of Waikato.

Lynch, K. (1999). *Equality in education.* Dublin: Gill & Macmillan.

Lynch, K., & Baker, J. (2005). Equality in education: An equality of condition perspective. *Theory and Research in Education, 3*(2), 131–164.

Lynch, K., & Lodge, A. (2002). *Equality and power in schools: Redistribution, recognition and representation.* London: Routledge/Falmer.

Mc Daid, R. (2007). *New kids on the block.* In P. Downes & A. L. Gilligan (Eds.), *Beyond educational disadvantage* (pp. 268–280). Dublin: Institute of Public Administration.

Mc Daid, R. (2008, March). *'Tears, fears and transformation?' Facilitating cross language communication through the Dublin 7 school cultural mediation project.* Paper presented at the ESAI Annual Conference, Galway, Ireland.

Mc Pake, J., & Tinsley, T. (2007). *Valuing all languages in Europe.* Graz: European Centre for Modern Languages.

McGorman, E., & Sugrue, C. (2007). *Intercultural education: Primary challenges in Dublin* (Vol. 15). Dublin: Social Inclusion Unit of the Department of Education and Science.

McGovern, F. (1995, Summer). The education of refugee children in Ireland. *Oideas,* 82–93.

McQuillan, J., & Tse, L., (1995). Child language brokering in linguistic minority communities: Effects on cultural interaction, cognition and literacy. *Language and Education, 9*(3), 195–215.

Meyers, K. (2007, May 21). *Morning Ireland.* Dublin: Radio One, Radio Teilifís Éireann.

Moll, L. C., & Diaz, S. (1985). Ethnographic pedagogy: Promoting effective bilingual instruction. In E. García & R. Padilla (Eds.), *Advances in bilingual education research* (pp. 127–149). Tucson, AZ: University of Arizona Press.

Montague, J. (1982). *Selected poems.* Oxford: Oxford University Press.

Mouw, T., & Xie, Y. (1999). Bilingualism and the academic achievement of first- and second- generation Asian Americans: Accommodation with or without assimilation. *American Sociological Review, 64*(2), 232–252.

National Council for Curriculum and Assessment. (2005a). *Intercultural education in the primary school: Guidelines for schools. Enabling students to respect and celebrate diversity, to promote equality and to challenge discrimination.* Dublin: NCCA.

Nowlan, E. (2008). Underneath the band-aid: Supporting bilingual students in Irish schools. *Irish Educational Studies, 27*(3), 253–266.

O'Brien, C. (2006, March 25). From Acholi to Zulu, Ireland a land of over 167 languages, *The Irish Times,* p. 1.

Organisation for Economic Co-operation and Development. (2006). *Where immigrant students succeed: A comparative review of performance and engagement in PISA 2003.* Paris: Author.

Quinn, E., Stanley, J., Corona, J., & O'Connell, P. J. (2007). *Handbook on immigration and asylum in Ireland 2007.* Dublin: ESRI.

Ramírez, J. D. (1992). Executive Summary. *Bilingual Research Journal, 16*(1), 1–62.

Ruiz, R. (1984). Orientations in language planning. *NABE: The Journal for the National Association for Bilingual Education, 8*(2), 15–34.

Smyth, E., Darmody, M., McGinnity, F., & Byrne, D. (2009). *Adapting to diversity: Irish schools and newcomer students.* Dublin: ESRI.

Stanford Working Group. (1993) *Federal education programs for limited English proficiency students: A blueprint for the second generation.* Stanford, CA: School of Education, Stanford University.

Suárez-Orozco, C. (2001). Understanding and serving the children of immigrants. *Harvard Educational Review, 71*(3), 579–589.

Taylor, C. (1994). *Multiculturalism: Examining the politics of recognition.* Princeton NJ: Princeton University Press.

Thomas, W. P., & Collier, V. P. (1997). *School effectiveness for language minority students.* Washington, DC: National Clearinghouse for Bilingual Education.

Troyna, B. (1983). Multicultural education: Just another brick in the wall? *New Community, 10*, 424–428.

Tseng, V., & Fuligni, A. J. (2000). Parent-adolescent language use and relationships among immigrant families. *Journal of Marriage and the Family, 62*(2), 465–476.

Valdés, G. (1998). The world outside and inside schools: Language and immigrant children. *Educational Researcher, 27*(6), 4–18.

Wallen, M., & Kelly-Holmes, H. (2006) 'I think they just think it's going to go away at some stage': Policy and practice in teaching English as an additional language in Irish primary schools. *Language and Education, 20*(2), 141–161.

Winkelmann, L., & Winkleman, R., (1998). *Immigrants in New Zealand: A study of their labour market outcomes.* Wellington: New Zealand Department of Labour.

Wong Fillmore, L. (1991). When learning a second language means losing the first. *Early Childhood Research Quarterly, 6*, 323–346.

Wong-Fillmore, L. (2000). Loss of family languages: Should educators be concerned? *Theory Into Practice, 39*(4), 203–210.

Rory Mc Daid
Children's Research Centre
Trinity College Dublin

NIAMH NESTOR AND VERA REGAN

3. THE NEW KID ON THE BLOCK

A Case Study of Young Poles, Language and Identity[1]

INTRODUCTION

Ireland has experienced momentous change over the last 15 years, with a sharp reversal in its traditionally outward-migration patterns to a very rapid increase in inward-migration. Mac Éinrí and White have characterised Ireland's experiences of migration as 'unique, at least in European terms' (2008: 153). This came to the fore towards the mid 1990s onwards when increased economic prosperity led to a skills shortage on the labour market and the concomitant inward migration led to rapid population diversification. This was particularly noticeable after the accession of ten new EU Member States, including Poland, on May 1st 2004.

The impact of this population change has been particularly striking in the pupil profiles of Irish schools. At present, approximately 10% of primary school pupils and 8% of post-primary school students were born outside of Ireland (OECD, 2009). There is a growing body of scholarship on migration into Ireland, with a particular focus on integration and social cohesion. Within this work, there is a dearth of material on young people (Mac Éinrí & White, 2008; Ní Laoire, *et al.*, 2009; Smyth, *et al.*, 2009). While some research is available[2], e.g., on separated children (e.g., Ward, 2004), migrant children's experiences at school (e.g., Devine, 2009; Keogh & Whyte, 2003), immigration as understood by children from the host community (e.g., Devine & Kelly, 2006; Devine, *et al.*, 2008), the recognition of migrant children's first languages (e.g., McDaid, 2009), and the provision of English language support at school (e.g., Kirwan, 2009; Nowlan, 2008), there continues to be the need for improved policy-making to be better informed by more evidence-based academic research, with particular reference to enhanced social cohesion and inclusion policies.

The Department of Education and Skills (previously, the Department of Education and Science) published its Intercultural Education Strategy, 2010–2015 (IES) in September 2010 (www.education.ie/servlet/blobservlet/mig_intercultural_education_ strategy.pdf). The IES identifies ten key components and (based on these) five high level goals of intercultural education. Among these is the recognition that knowledge of the language(s) of instruction is crucial for academic success (2010: 46). The IES also acknowledges the importance of valuing the minority student's first language and of encouraging first language maintenance, noting that this will enhance second language acquisition and support identity development (ibid.: 40). We suggest that identity development is not only linked to first language development and

Darmody, Tyrrell, Song (eds.), The Changing Faces of Ireland: Exploring the Lives of Immigrant and Ethnic Minority Children, 35–52.

maintenance but is inextricably bound up with second, third, and further language learning as well. In this regard, we believe that a thorough understanding of the dynamics of language and identity is necessary to underpin the IES and it is with this in mind that this chapter has been written. Key questions that arise for consideration in this context are: How is identity constructed through the use of a second language? How does this play out in the daily interactions at school? And, finally, what implications, if any, does this have for policy development and implementation?

This chapter is divided into three parts. First, the authors will briefly review the literature on language and social identity. A description of the nature of Polish migration to Ireland and the doctoral study will follow. Finally, some case study data will be presented and conclusions will be drawn.

LANGUAGE AND SOCIAL IDENTITY

International research on language, language variation, and identity has undergone significant transformation in the last half-century. In the 1960s, researchers became increasingly interested in language variation in a social context.[3] Since Labov's famous studies in the 1960s (1963, 1966), many studies have been carried out on variation in (first) language (L1) speech (e.g., Labov, 1972a, 1972b). In this tradition, speech variables are the resources available to speakers to mark their place in society, to 'affirm membership in their own social group, or to claim membership in other groups to which they aspire' (Eckert & McConnell-Ginet, 1992: 468–469). Identity is seen as fixed and (relatively) stable and speakers use the linguistic repertoire at their disposal to mark their 'place in the social grid' (ibid.: 469). This approach to L1 speech was later applied to the variation found in second language (L2) speech (e.g., Schumann, 1978). From the mid 1990s, however, researchers began to conceive of the language learner as something other than the 'ahistorical "stick figure"' (McKay & Wong, 1996: 603) from previous L2 research and moved away from the essentialist treatment of identity to a view which perceived identity as fluid and multi-faceted (e.g. Miller, 1999; Norton, 2000; Norton Peirce, 1995; Pavlenko & Blackledge (Eds.), 2004; Rampton, 1995).

In order to learn an L2, learners must have sufficient opportunities to hear and practise the language, whether these are in the formal environment of the classroom (for example, English as an Additional Language (EAL) classes) or in the informal environment of interactions with friends, teachers, and so on. This 'input', as it is formally known in second language acquisition (SLA) research, is crucial as it makes the '"facts" [i.e. the grammar, phonology, etc.] of the L2 salient to the learner' (Ellis, 1994: 244).

A further concept which has been widely researched in the field of SLA is that of motivation (cf. Ellis, 1994), whereby a highly motivated learner will acquire a new language with ease. Taking a poststructuralist approach, Norton Peirce (1995) challenges the notion of motivation as overly simplistic in that it fails to 'capture the complex relationship between relations of power, identity, and language learning' (ibid.: 16–17). McKay and Wong (1996) suggest that motivation has connotations of some 'monolithic inner quality that a learner may summon in varying amounts' and leads one to the assumption that a lack of motivation is the root cause for unsuccessful learning (ibid.: 579). As an alternative to the concept of 'motivation', Norton Peirce developed the notion of 'investment' (1995: 17). She argues that a language learner will 'invest' in learning the L2 and will expect a return on his/her investment in the form of 'a wider range of symbolic and material resources' (ibid.). This return should be 'commensurate with the effort expended' (ibid., citing Ogbu, 1978). Thus, each interaction with a target language speaker (a speaker whose first language is the language being learned) will involve an investment in both the target language and the learner's social identity (ibid.: 18).

McKay and Wong (1996) develop Norton Peirce's theory of 'investment' to illustrate the interrelations of power, discourse and the language learner's social identity. Their work describes the various paths taken by the L2 learners in their study to negotiate their identities in the context of the various discourses at work in the school and the wider society. In McKay and Wong's study, parents and teachers positioned Asian students in a 'model-minority' discourse which views Asians and Asian Americans as 'hardworking, disciplined, [and] academically inclined' (ibid.: 586). In other words, the students were perceived as having the essential characteristics to help them succeed at school, simply because of where they (or their parents) were born. In the Irish context, Devine (2005) identifies certain discourses which educators use to position non-Irish-born pupils according to different stereotypical descriptions. For example, teachers described children from Eastern Europe using adjectives such as 'bright', 'diligent', and 'willing to learn' (ibid.: 62).

The authors suggest that the young Poles in this study were subjected to similar discourses and that this may have been reflective of a model-minority discourse at the wider societal level. A popular description of Polish migrants in Ireland is that they are 'hardworking'. This type of discourse may serve to create a stereotype of Polish people but it may also reinforce the view that, in contrast to Poles, other minorities may not be as hardworking. Conversely, this creates a situation whereby Poles may *only* be hardworking and not, for example, 'lazy'. Individuals may accommodate to (i.e., embrace) a positioning in a discourse or they may resist (i.e., reject) (Leki, 1995: 250, cited in McKay and Wong, 1996: 595).[4] Resistance occurs when an individual is subjected to an undesirable positioning in a discourse. As a result, he/she can engage in a counterdiscourse 'which positions the person in a powerful rather than marginalized subject position' (Norton Peirce, 1995: 16).

In the following discussion, the authors draw on Norton Peirce's notion of investment in language learning and McKay and Wong's discussions of discourse and power in order to illustrate the fluid and multi-faceted social identities of one young Polish woman living in Ireland who, on arrival, spoke little English.

POLISH MIGRATION TO IRELAND

There have been previous migration waves to Ireland from Poland, but not by any means as great as that during the Celtic Tiger years. Grabowska (2005: 32) summarises these waves as follows:

(i) Post World War II migration. The Irish government offered approximately 1,000 third-level scholarships to Polish people who had been forced to leave Poland.

(ii) 'Solidarity migration' in the early 1980s. In the aftermath of the imposition of martial law in Poland (1981–1983), the ruling Communist Party only allowed one-way cross-border movement (Regan and Nestor, 2010: 146).

(iii) 'Migration of hearts' in the mid 1980s. This wave was made up mostly of young Polish women who emigrated to Ireland to marry Irish men. These women often became Irish citizens through marriage.

(iv) Post-1997. Migration during the Celtic Tiger boom years, which Grabowska (2005: 32) describes as having a 'dual character'. Some migrants were outsourced by their multinational or Irish company bosses but most came to Ireland through the process of chain migration. This is a process whereby personal contacts and developed networks of migrants in the destination country lead to an induction process: 'One migrant inducts another. Whole networks and neighbourhoods leave to work abroad, bringing back stories, money, know-how and contacts' (Hochschild, 2006: 214).[5] Factors influencing an individual's decision to migrate are complex (Grabowska, 2005: 31) but the post-1997 migration flow is characterised as primarily economically-motivated in nature (ibid.: 32). This was facilitated by the fact that Ireland (along with the UK and Sweden) did not require Polish citizens to hold a work permit in order to gain employment after Poland's accession to the EU in 2004.

There has been much debate about the actual number of Polish nationals living in Ireland but with no definitive conclusions. According to the 2006 Census (www.cso.ie/statistics/nationalityagegroup.htm), the number of non-Irish nationals living in Ireland rose to almost 420,000, accounting for c. 10% of the total population of the country. This is a substantial increase amounting to a doubling of the estimated 5% of migrants who lived in Ireland before the mid 1990s (OECD, 2009: 15). Within this figure of 420,000 the great majority came from European Union countries (almost 276,000), with 63,276 from Poland, meaning that Poles represented, on paper at least, 15% of the total non-Irish population. Of the 63,276 Poles in the 2006 Census, 5,900 of these were aged 0–19 (Ní Laoire et al., 2009: 20).

However, since Census 2006, reports in the media (cf. MacCormaic, 2007) suggest that the number of Poles in Ireland actually hovers somewhere close to 200,000. A figure which might appear helpful in determining how many Polish nationals have moved to Ireland since EU accession is the number of Personal Public Service Numbers (PPSNs). From 2004–2009, a total of 321,976 PPSNs were issued to Polish nationals (www.welfare.ie/EN/Topics/PPSN/Pages/ppsn_all_years.aspx). Unfortunately, this figure cannot be treated as an accurate indicator of the Polish population in Ireland as not every migrant registers nor does a person have to deregister if he/she decides to leave Ireland. In conclusion, there are no accurate statistics on how many Poles have actually migrated to Ireland nor, more currently, on how many have chosen to remain.

METHODOLOGY

There was a total of 103 young people aged 9–19 involved in the wider study (Nestor) – 61 males and 42 females. Each participant had moved to Ireland since

EU accession in 2004. There were two research sites, one urban and one rural, and the research was conducted in the young people's schools for the most part. On the rare occasion that this was not possible, the researcher gathered data in the young person's home. Seventy-five of the young people were living in a rural area and 28 lived in an urban area. The difference in sample sizes was due to the nature of access in both research sites. The researcher was given permission to conduct research in more schools in the rural area. Of the total number of participants, 77 (45 males and 32 females) agreed to take part in the interview process. The interviews lasted between 35 minutes and 2 hours. In general, where possible, the researcher spoke to the young person for an hour or longer. Sometimes the age of the young person indicated that one hour might be too long and tiring; on other occasions, the natural dynamics of school life meant that the interview lasted for less than one hour.

Speakers were recorded in semi-directed interviews (cf. Tagliamonte, 2006); however, for the most part, the interviews were largely guided by the young people's own interests. In the broader research project, the interview data will be analysed quantitatively and qualitatively for the production of particular linguistic variables (see endnote 2). For the purposes of this chapter, the authors have chosen to draw on one case study in particular in order to elucidate the link between language and identity. The first author speaks Polish fluently after a significant amount of time spent in Poland. She translated any Polish used during the interviews or in the ethnographic questionnaire[6]. Her Polish language proficiency also gave her the status of 'insider' during the field study period.

THE YOUNG POLISH PEOPLE IN THIS STUDY

As mentioned previously, Census 2006 returned a figure of 5,900 for Poles aged 0–19 years old. It can be assumed that a relatively significant number of these children and teenagers are in fulltime education (however, no accurate data exist on this). The young people in this study have all migrated to Ireland from Poland since 2004. The decision to migrate was always taken by one or both parents, sometimes with but sometimes without the agreement of the young people. The young people generally live with both parents, and, in some cases, other members of the extended family live in the same house or close by. In other cases, the family remains frag-mented due to migration (one parent in Poland and one in Ireland), or has fragmented since arrival.

Since leaving Poland, these young people have experienced the various ups and downs of the migration process. They have felt excitement at the prospect of living in a new country, making new friends, attending a new school, and having new experiences. They have also felt homesickness and loneliness, the anxiety brought on by the separation from family and friends, the insecurities associated with 'fitting in', and the often tricky dynamics of friendship-forming while maintaining a consistent commitment to old friends in Poland.[7] Because these young people are sometimes more proficient in the language of the receiving country, they often become the mouthpieces of their parents in various situations (cf. Suárez-Orozco & Suárez-Orozco, 2002). Since the beginning of Ireland's economic downturn (2008), many of these young people have shared the anxieties of financial and job insecurity borne by their parents. Not least, these young people have had to carry the often overwhelming burden of coping with the demands of a new curriculum through a second language in a very different school system.

ETHNOGRAPHIC QUESTIONNAIRE

The ethnographic questionnaire was designed to elicit biographical, linguistic, socio-psychological and linguistic-educational data. There were two versions of the questionnaire (one for younger children and one for teenagers), and the participants (N=103; 61 males and 42 females) could complete the questionnaire in Polish or English. The mean age of the participants was 13 years and two months. The mean length of residence in Ireland was one year and five months. The majority of the participants (86%) returned to Poland between one and three times per year, and throughout the interviews, this return to Poland was an important area of discussion.

The participants generally displayed confidence in their own language abilities (Table 1, i). When considering home language usage (Table 1, ii), it is no surprise that Polish is dominant but the results for English-language usage with family members are interesting. One reason for this could be that some of the young people's close relatives have non-Polish-speaking partners and therefore English has become one of the languages of communication at home. Equally as unsurprising is the result for English-language usage at school (Table 1, iii) but Polish is also used frequently, indicating involvement in Polish-speaking networks. This result is further supported by the balance of daily language use (Table 1, iv). The participants regard their multilingual language abilities very positively (Table 1, v).

When asked about national identification (Table 2), the majority of the participants chose 'Polish', but 20% chose to identify as 'Irish-Polish'. Two of the participants identified as 'Other'. One chose a regional identification, while the other (pseudonym: Ola) identified as something 'between' Polish and Irish. Because of the uniqueness of Ola's answer to this question, the authors have chosen to focus on her case in this chapter.

Table 1. Language

First contact with English (mean age)	8 yrs 9 mths
Receiving formal language instruction?	65% attending English classes (for the most part English as an Additional Language (EAL) at school)
Self-reported language proficiency[i] How well do you speak English? (like a native/very well/well/quite well/a little/not at all)	28% quite well 37% well 17.5% very well 6% like a native

Table 1. (Continued)

Language use in the family[ii]	
How often do you use Polish with your family? (always/often/sometimes/rarely/never)	96% always or often
How often do you use English with your family? (always/often/sometimes/rarely/never)	26.2% often or sometimes
Language use at school[iii]	
How often do you use English at school? (always/often/sometimes/rarely/never)	84.5% always or often
How often do you use Polish at school? (always/often/sometimes/rarely/never)	54% often or sometimes
Language use and bilingualism[iv]	
Balance of Polish and English in your daily life?	40% a balanced use of both languages 54% use more Polish
How happy are you about the fact that you can speak both Polish and English?[v] (very happy/happy/neutral/unhappy/very unhappy)	95% very happy or happy with their bilingualism

Table 2. Identity

How do you identify? (Polish, Irish-Polish, Other)	78% Polish 20% Irish-Polish 2% Other

THE CASE STUDY

A case study method is appropriate when 'a researcher wants to better understand a particular case' and is undertaken because of the unique set of features that characterise the case: 'it is because of its uniqueness or ordinariness that a case becomes interesting (Creswell, 1998; Stake, 1994, 2000)' (Berg, 2007: 291). Case studies can provide 'extremely rich, detailed, and in-depth information' (ibid.: 283) and they open the door to, as Weick (1995, cited in Berg, 2007: 285) described it, 'the "sensemaking" processes' employed by individuals and others. This 'sensemaking' is 'the manner by which people, groups, and organizations make sense of stimuli with which they are confronted, how they frame what they see and hear, how they perceive and interpret this information, and how they interpret their own actions and go about solving problems and interacting with others' (ibid.: 285). The authors are fully aware that by focussing on one participant the benefits of comparability and generalisability are lost. However, we feel that this loss is mitigated by the many gains which come from this approach. In our chapter, we have highlighted the fact that the Intercultural Education Strategy places an emphasis (among other emphases) on the language-identity nexus. But what does this mean? How should educators and other stakeholders understand the link between language and identity, and, in addition, how should they understand this link for those who are learning a new language in a new living situation? Against this background, we have tried to problematise the language-identity link to demonstrate that the issue is by no means a straightforward one. As we shall see, in a small group such as Ola and her peers, there were multiple competing identities with multiple competing benefits on offer. The reality of life at school and outside of school for Ola was 'kaleidoscopic, complex and complicated, often a patchwork of overlapping activities' (Blommaert & Dong, 2010: 11). In this respect, the ethnographic approach of the case study method is critical as it serves to illuminate the complexity of this reality while other research methods have as their aim the 'simplification and reduction of complexity' (ibid.). Through Ola, we are able to view the contested space of identity. She describes herself as neither Polish nor Irish but as something in between, and in this way, invokes Block's third place identity (Block, 2007). While her experiences cannot be generalised across the cohort of Polish young people in the wider study, we feel that Ola's case is important to discuss precisely because it is different.

The School and the Participant

Íascairí Mara School (pseudonym) is a non-denominational post-primary school in a rural area. The School has been designated as disadvantaged by the Department of Education and Skills on the basis of levels of social and economic disadvantage in the student cohort. At the time of the interview, Ola had been living in Ireland and attending Íascairí Mara for two and a half years. She was almost seventeen and about to sit her Leaving Certificate. Her ambition after Leaving Certificate was to work in the medical field, and she had already taken up a part-time job in her chosen field which she had found as part of her school work experience the previous year.

Language as an Investment in the Future

Ola's family had had some experience of migration before moving to Ireland. Her father had been working in Germany (and previously in the Netherlands) when the family decided that they no longer wanted to live separately, and, as there were no employment opportunities for her father in their home town in Poland, the whole family (Ola, her parents, and her older brother) moved to Ireland. Through the prism of investment in the future, Ola saw this as an opportunity to improve her language skills. Over time, she embraced the change determinedly and pragmatically and viewed the move very positively.

> I think it's very good because I learn, like, English a lot and I think that will help me in the future.

The parents interviewed in the doctoral study (Nestor) unanimously agreed that moving to Ireland was a long-term investment in their children's futures and Ola accommodated to this discourse. She was clearly invested in the long-term benefits of acquiring English and was an active agent in her own learning. She sought out opportunities to use the language, thus providing favourable learning opportunities (Spolsky, 1989, cited in Norton Peirce, 1995).

Language and the Identity of 'the Fretful, Frustrated Parent'

Ola's positivity about the move to Ireland was in sharp contrast with her mother's sadness during the first few months in Ireland. Ola's proficient language skills contrasted sharply with her mother's difficulty with learning the language (evidenced by the fact that Ola and her brother translated constantly for their mother) and Ola, ever the pragmatist, self-assuredly believed that low language proficiency was the root cause of her mother's depression and desire to return to Poland.

> I think she would prefer to live in Poland because she was very – what will I say – depressed for the first couple of months in here cos all the friends and everyone. Especially the English is so hard for her.

In speaking about her mother, Ola constructed the identity of 'the fretful, frustrated parent'. Language and language proficiency were central to the construction of this identity. Ola's concern about her mother's lack of proficiency in English led to a reversal in the traditional parent-child roles: in this context of the perceived lack of success in a form of learning, Ola became the concerned parent and her mother became the dependent child.

In Norton Peirce's terms, Ola viewed her mother's lack of investment in the language as having led to a low return: general unhappiness with life in Ireland, an inability to put down roots (hence the desire to return), and an unsatisfying job. Interestingly, it was Ola who felt dissatisfied with her mother's (perceived) low occupational status which she pinpointed as being due to her mother's low language proficiency ('she works in fish factory because she doesn't speak English at all'); she never commented on whether her mother actually *felt* dissatisfied. In fact, the large Polish community in the area, which provided Ola's mother with opportunities to speak Polish and socialise with other Poles, seemed to have helped mitigate her mother's feelings of isolation and dissatisfaction, and Ola acknowledged this in the interview: 'There's like huge Polish community in here so she works with Polish people and meeting Polish friends'. It seems that, in line with the identity of 'the fretful, frustrated parent', Ola's wishes for her mother may not have tied in with her mother's own wishes. Ola's comment, 'she doesn't speak English at all', while perhaps not necessarily possessing truth value, indicates that Ola saw her mother's lack of proficiency as having rendered her invisible when and where Ola felt it mattered, i.e., on the job market and in creating new social networks (understood perhaps as English-speaking networks, given Ola's later comments about learning to speak English well because she chose to make friends with Irish girls in school). In line with the family's primarily economic reasons for migrating and her identity as 'the fretful, frustrated parent', Ola expressed her disappointment at what she perceived to be her mother's lack of agency and urgency about her language skills and, consequently, concomitant static occupational mobility and closed social networks.

Ola expressed frustration at her mother's over-reliance on her children for linguistic support and struggled to understand her mother's lack of agency, but concluded that this had to be due to sheer intransigence on her mother's part.

> I think she *thinks* she doesn't have to [learn English] because she can always ask me for something, my brother as well.

Ola laughed as she made the above statement but her frustration was evident. She found it difficult to understand why her mother would continue to reject (as Ola perceived it) the idea of learning English, particularly given the fact that Ola and her brother would not always be available to translate for her. Ola believed that her mother must have deliberately chosen not to learn English because she could always rely on her children.

> But you know, the thing is, inside her head there's little block saying that, "It's ok. You don't have to study English. Every time, like, you have to translate something, you've Ola and [brother]", you know.

Again, the identity of the 'fretful, frustrated parent' was evident here. Ola could not understand her mother's refusal to learn English despite all of the opportunities available to her and the obvious benefits (as Ola saw it) that this would bring. Ola perceived her mother as taking advantage of the linguistic safety net that her two children provided and she could not understand her mother's refusal to accept the inevitable: that one day she would be out on her own with no more safety nets on offer.

> She has to learn because like I'm leaving. I'm going to college or I might go to Poland or something with my brother. And what she'll do then?

Ola impatiently desired to 'cut the linguistic apron strings' and felt that her mother, just like she and her brother had done, would have to face up to the challenge of learning English and overcome her insecurities.

> It wasn't easy either to go into school like with no English and all the people were like, "Where are you from? What's your name?" la la la. "I'm from like uh", like all the questions and I didn't know how to answer anything, and I was like, "Oh". I had the dictionary, the, the whatyoucallit, the em the electronic one so that was quicker than book so, but still, it wasn't good at all.

In conclusion, the above discussion illustrates the central role that language played in the resetting of the parameters of a mother-daughter relationship against the backdrop of the migration experience (for similar discussions, see e.g., Hagan, MacMillan & Wheaton, 1996; Kwak, 2003; Lutz, 1998; and Suárez-Orozco and Suárez-Orozco, 2002, chapter 3). While it is impossible to generalise from one individual's migration story, what we have attempted to demonstrate here is that, although Ola's mother may have overcome her initial feelings of depression, Ola continued to see an acceptable knowledge of English as key to a happier life. Indeed, many second language speakers see language proficiency as central to the success of their migration experience. This was something which Ola embraced wholeheartedly for herself and which she found the rejection or refusal of difficult to accept in others.

Language and the Identity of 'the New Kid on the Block'

Despite her identity as 'the fretful, frustrated parent', Ola was not completely un-sympathetic to her mother's feelings of despair. She had also felt depressed on leaving Poland and had found the challenge of starting school in Ireland both lonely and daunting, primarily due to the language barrier. With hindsight, however, she felt that her novel status in the school helped to remedy this.

> I had to leave all my friends and I was so depressed and I didn't want to go to school because, you know how it's like, few days you don't know anyone, my English wasn't so good and that was awful. I was lucky that I came in as a first Polish em person in the school. Together with my brother so but em everyone was really nice and wondering em asking questions and (sic).

Ola became known (and is still remembered) as the 'first' Pole in the school. Indeed, she saw her identity as 'the new kid on the block' as central to her successful language learning. As she was novel and new, she became the centre of attention and made friends easily which, she said, was the reason she learned English so easily. She continued to prefer to socialise with her Irish peers throughout her time at school. In this regard, she compared herself to the other Polish students who arrived later than her. She suggested that they did not learn English as well as she had because they had chosen to socialise with each other and speak Polish, rather than focusing on making Irish friends and improving their English.

Ola was also 'new' in other ways: she arrived in a town and a region with a long history of emigration and thus embodied the bucking of this long-debilitating trend. In the school, she also bucked other trends: unlike some members of the broader student body, she was courteous at all times, she was dedicated to learning, she was very hardworking, and on numerous occasions, despite the language barrier, she outshone her Irish peers by scoring higher than them in various school and State exams. She thus embodied the identity of 'model student'. In conversations with the staff at the school, it was clear that Ola was well-liked and her academic success granted her somewhat of a 'Wunderkind' status among both the Irish and other minority students. The authors suggest that Ola was positioned in a model-minority discourse at work in the school and that through her identity as 'model student', she accommodated to this discourse.

Language, Resistance and Ruptured Identities

Language was an important element in each of the social identities constructed by Ola. She had invested heavily in her own process of language learning and had, as Norton Peirce would assert, also invested in her various social identities in equal measure. These identities clearly became a site of struggle when a number of other young Polish people enrolled in the school a year after Ola had arrived. During the fieldwork, Ola reported that she no longer identified as Polish but that she also did not identify as Irish. Rather, she identified as something 'between' (her own description).

This rupture in her identity was brought about by what she perceived as anti-social behaviour on the parts of some of the 'new' Poles in the school. The type of Poland she felt she represented through her identity as the 'model student' and her accommodation to the model-minority discourse was not the type of Poland represented by some of the new Poles. In a clear case of 'distinction' which 'depends on the suppression of similarities that might undermine the construction of differentiation' (Bucholtz & Hall, 2010: 24), Ola railed against the behaviour of some of these new Polish students and re-positioned herself as both linguistically and socially separate from them.

> I don't feel Polish anymore because I'm not, like, living in Poland and actually em actually I adopted more to Ireland but and I don't like the- what's happening in Poland now. If the Polish people coming in and putting me in shame and giving me bad reputation, I don't like to be Polish anymore, like. But em I don't feel Irish either because I'm Polish (laughs).

In McKay and Wong's study (1996), the strategy of resistance was actively adopted by one student in their study, Michael Lee. As a Chinese ESL (English as a Second Language) student, he used various resources to 'put together his own counter-discourse in order to exercise agency' (ibid.: 594) and resisted his positioning as only-academically-oriented in the model-minority discourse which was at work in the school. McKay and Wong (ibid.) argue that, through this counterdiscourse, Michael worked against himself academically. They suggest, however, that the agency he gained from his various social identities (as athlete and friend) were sufficiently satisfying so as to subvert the need for academic success. The arrival of the large group of new Polish students in Ola's school resulted in a severe rupture in her repertoire of social identities. Language became a tool by which many of these new students were othered (by the linguistic majority) and which the new students used to resist this othering. Through sheer numbers, the opportunities to speak Polish in school increased and naturally the students availed of these opportunities. While this lessened the opportunity to practise and learn English, what became clear was that the return on the investment the new students would have to make in learning English did not appear to provide the right type of gains for these students at this particular time. Just like Michael Lee in McKay and Wong's study, these students gained agency through the construction of a counterdiscourse. Both Willis (1977) and Giroux (1983a), though primarily in a discussion about social class, outline how the notions of agency and resistance play out in the site of the school. Students can 'refuse, reject and dismiss the central messages of the school' (Giroux, 1983b: 260) by engaging in oppositional behaviour (i.e., a counterdiscourse), even though, ultimately, this behaviour may lead to 'class subordination and political defeat' (ibid.). In a demonstration of resistance through 'distinction' (see above; Bucholtz & Hall, 2010: 24), some of the new Polish students resisted their positioning in the model-minority discourse and instead engaged in a counterdiscourse which enabled them to construct alternative identities such as 'the Polish speaker', 'the lazy student', and so on. This resistance undercut Ola's own sense of self. She felt othered by her own in-group and, through the new students' resistance, her identity became a site of struggle. Block (2007) notes that an individual's sense of identity becomes unstable when he or she moves across 'geographical and psychological borders, immersing themselves in new sociocultural environments' (ibid.: 864) but cautions against assuming that the new identity which may emerge from this period of destabilisation will simply be a combination of the old-plus-new or a half-and-half mixture, whereby 'the individual becomes half of what he or she was and half of what he or she has been exposed to' (ibid.). Rather, what emerges is 'a third place' (ibid., citing Bhabha, 1994 and Hall, 1996) where there is a 'negotiation of difference' (ibid., citing Papastergiadis, 2000) during which 'the past and the present "encounter and transform each other" in the "presence of fissures, gaps and contradictions"' (ibid., citing Papastergiadis, 2000: 170). In order to challenge the counterdiscourse of her peers, Ola re-negotiated her own identities, remaining a 'model student' and a 'hard-working person' but rejecting a national identification as Polish. She renegotiated her national identification away from both dominant identifications in the school – Polish or Irish – to position herself in a third, undefined space in between.

The consequences of the emergence of the new students' counterdiscourse had wide-ranging and long-term effects across the student body. Over the course of the research, the researcher noted a heightening of tension between some of the linguistic majority and some of the linguistic minority students in the school. Ola blamed her Polish peers for this, claiming that they did not make an effort to be friendly towards the Irish students. Through a process of distinction (i.e., they are not 'novel', they are not polite, they do not use the language of the majority), Ola sharpened the boundaries of her own social identity. In interactions between the linguistic majority and the linguistic minority, language – and the Polish language in particular – became a powerful tool of resistance, inclusion and exclusion.

> Now, I must say, all the other Polish people that came in are not really em (laughs) in centre- in centre of attention or anything. They're just kind of ignored. I think the Polish people just really bad for the Irish people in school cos they call them names and talk in Polish to the Irish people so (laughs) that's annoying.

The new Polish students drew on their bilingual abilities in the creation of the counterdiscourse and the use of bad language in Polish became a common tool in this process. Ola disapproved strongly of this and distanced herself from this behaviour.

> I was here a year on my own like, the only Polish person in the school like together with my brother. They [the linguistic majority students] never know what's "fuck" or "fuck off" or stuff like that. And the minute the Polish- the other Polish people came in, there's like "suka" [*bitch*], "kurwa" [*whore/fuck*] and you know.

Interestingly, the linguistic majority, whose dominant position in the language stakes had been undermined by name-calling in Polish, appropriated the language of the linguistic minority in a powerful counter-move. When the linguistic minority used Polish expletives in interactions with the linguistic majority, members of the linguistic majority countered with the same.

This struggle also manifested itself in an ethno-territorial division of space in the common area, a large area inside the school where students gathered during break times. The Irish non-Traveller and Traveller students congregated around the edges of the common, the Poles sat together at tables in the centre of the area, and the small number of Pakistani students in the school retreated to the very fringes of this area. During this time, stories in the media served to heighten tensions further. Dell announced that it was moving its operations to Poland (Scally, 2009) and reports appeared in local, regional and national newspapers about Polish firms refusing to recruit Irish workers in Poland (the infamous 'No Irish Need Apply' story (McDonald, 2009)). At the conclusion of the fieldwork period, the students maintained these in-group social networks.

CONCLUSION

While Ola's story is unique to one person in one place at one time, it is informative in that it illustrates the struggle to achieve self-representation in the linguistic majority language and reminds us that identity is not static or fixed but that it is multiple, fluid, and changing across time and space (Weedon, 1987). Ola invested heavily in her own language learning on the basis that she expected a long-term sustained return. The arrival of the new Poles in the school challenged her sense of self and her accommodation to the model-minority discourse. Educators may position linguistic minority students in particular discourses without taking into account the individual's agency. Often, the agency gained from competing social identities is sufficiently satisfactory and the individual does not feel the need to accommodate to positionings desired for him/her by the relevant authorities (teachers, parents, policymakers, and so on). Just like Michael Lee in McKay and Wong's (1996) study and the new Polish students in this study, a rejection of the dominant school and wider societal discourses led to a situation whereby the students challenged these (undesirable) positionings through the creation of a counterdiscourse and the construction of alternative identities.

These insights are useful for policy makers and teachers in a number of important key respects. While the importance of the influence of Polish parents' desire for their children to achieve self-expression in the majority language (and, thus, future academic and career success) is indubitable, it cannot be taken for granted that each young person will work to fulfil this desire. Policymakers should, therefore, not lose sight of the individuals for whom policy is designed. Polish young people in Ireland demonstrate that they have a multitude of subjectivities and diverse circumstances which they must negotiate in a variety of situations. Despite the best intentions of parents, educators, and policymakers, the struggles and ruptures that these young people face are not accounted for in policy.

The authors suggest that it is in this respect that the school becomes crucial. We see as one of the significant challenges facing the implementation of the IES in Ireland the willingness of educators, with particular reference to those in school management and other important stakeholders (Parents' Council, Board of Management, the wider community), to approach the implementation of the policy across the whole school. The implementation of the policy cannot become the sole remit of EAL teachers. In order to support these young people on their path to academic achievement and personal fulfilment and to ensure the participation and integration of all young people in the wider society, all those carrying the different and varying responsibilities in a school should be made aware of and encouraged to play their role in the implementation of the IES for his/her school. On-going training, both at the pre-service and in-service stages, is vital in this respect.

The publication of the IES at this stage is both timely and welcome. Over the following years, as this Strategy begins to come into effect, it will be crucial to monitor its impact on the ground, with mechanisms in place to encourage and facilitate feedback from all interested stakeholders, and to ensure that adjustments are made in a timely and a structured way in response to changing circumstances and contexts, both at national and local levels.

NOTES

[1] This research has been made possible through the support of the Irish Research Council for the Humanities and Social Sciences. The authors would like to thank Breda Naughton and Sarah Miley at the Integration Unit of the Department of Education and Skills for their generous assistance. The authors would also like to thank the anonymous reviewers for their constructive comments. Needless to say, any errors are our own.

[2] This list is by no means exhaustive. See Mac Éinrí and White (2008) for a more comprehensive review of research available on migrant children in the Irish context.

[3] Variationist sociolinguists are interested in language change. People can say the same thing in different ways, and this language variability is seen as a 'necessary condition for change' (Johnstone, 2006: 46). Variationist sociolinguists explore the social meaning of linguistic variables (e.g., Eckert, 2000) in order to understand broader questions of language change (Johnstone, 2006). A good example of a variable which is currently receiving increased attention in the literature is quotative *like* (e.g., *I was like, "Who does she think she is?"*). In this case, the speaker could alternatively use one of the more 'traditional quotatives', *say, go, think* (among others) (Tagliamonte and Hudson, 1999: 147), which act as competing variables.

[4] See also Wei & Wu (2009) for a description of how bilingual Chinese-English pupils use language to resist positioning in particular discourses and to construct identities in complementary schools in Britain.

[5] The authors would like to thank Diane Sabenacio Nititham for her valuable help with this section.

[6] The ethnographic questionnaire is designed to elicit important background information about the participant, particularly the kind of information which variationist sociolinguists believe may have an impact on the way the person speaks, e.g., sex, age, length of residence in the host country, previous contact with English, use of Polish, and so on.

[7] For a discussion on emotions and human mobility, see the 2008 Special Issue of the *Journal of Intercultural Studies*, 29(3) entitled 'Transnational Families: Emotions and Belonging'. Also, Suárez-Orozco and Suárez-Orozco (2002) devote a chapter to the psychosocial impact of immigration.

REFERENCES

Berg, B. L. (2007). *Qualitative research methods for the social sciences* (6th ed.). Boston: Pearson Education Inc.

Bhabha, H. (1994). *The location of culture*. London: Routledge.

Block, D. (2007). The rise of identity in SLA research, post Firth and Wagner (1997). *The Modern Language Journal, 91*(5), 863–876. Retrieved August 10, 2010, from http://onlinelibrary.wiley.com/doi /10.1111/j.1540-4781.2007.00674.x/pdf

Blommaert, J., & Dong, J. (2010). *Ethnographic fieldwork. A beginner's guide*. Bristol, UK: Multilingual Matters.

Bucholtz, M., & Hall, K. (2010). Locating identity in language. In. C. Llamas & D. Watt (Eds.), *Language and identities* (pp. 18–28). Edinburgh: Edinburgh University Press.

Central Statistics Office, Ireland. Retrieved March 20, 2010, from http://www.cso.ie/statistics/nationalityage group.htm

Creswell, J. W. (1998). *Qualitative inquiry and research design: Choosing among five traditions*. Thousand oaks, CA: Sage.

Department of Education and Skills and the Office of the Minister for Integration. (2010). *Intercultural education strategy, 2010–2015*. Retrieved September 16, 2010, from http://www.education.ie/servlet/blobservlet/mig_intercultural_education_strategy.pdf

Department of Social Protection, Ireland. Retrieved August 9, 2010, from http://www.welfare.ie/EN/Topics/PPSN/Pages/ppsn_all_years.aspx

Devine, D. (2005). 'Welcome to the Celtic Tiger?' – Teacher responses to immigration and increasing ethnic diversity in Irish schools. *International Studies in Sociology of Education, 15*(1), 49–71.

Devine, D. (2009). Mobilising capitals? Migrant children's negotiation of their everyday lives in school. *British Journal of Sociology of Education, 30*(5), 521–535.

Devine, D., & Kelly, M. (2006). 'I just don't want to get picked on by anybody': Dynamics of inclusion and exclusion in a newly multi-ethnic Irish primary school. *Children & Society, 20*(2), 128–139.

Devine, D., Kenny, M., & McNeela, E. (2008). Naming the 'other' – Children's construction and experience of racisms in Irish primary schools. *Race, Ethnicity and Education, 11*(4), 369–385.

Eckert, P. (2000). *Linguistic variation as social practice*. Malden, MA: Blackwell Publishers.

Eckert, P., & McConnell-Ginet, S. (1992). Think practically and look locally: Language and gender as community-based practice. *Annual Review of Anthropology, 21*, 461–90.

Ellis, R. (1994). *The study of second language acquisition*. Oxford: Oxford University Press.

Giroux, H. (1983a). *Theory and resistance in education*. South Hadley, MA: Bergin and Garvey.

Giroux, H. (1983b). Theories of reproduction and resistance in the new sociology of education: A critical analysis. *Harvard Educational Review, 53*(3), 257–293.

Grabowska, I. (2005). Changes in the international mobility of labour: Job migration of Polish nationals to Ireland. *Irish Journal of Sociology, 14*, 27–44.

Hagan, J., MacMillan, R., & Wheaton, B. (1996). New kid in town: Social capital and the life course effects of family migration on children. *American Sociological Review, 61*(3), 368–385.

Hall, S. (1996). Introduction: Who needs 'identity'? In S. Hall & P. du Gay (Eds.), *Questions of cultural identity* (pp. 1–17). London: Sage.

Hochschild, A. R. (2006). Love and gold. In D. M. Newman & J. A. O'Brien (Eds.), *Sociology. Exploring the architecture of everyday life. Readings* (6th ed., pp. 212–220). Thousand Oaks, CA: Pine Forge Press.

Johnstone, B. (2006). A new role for narrative in variationist sociolinguistics. *Narrative Inquiry, 16*(1), 46–55.

Keogh, A., & Whyte, J. (2003). *Getting on? The experiences and aspirations of immigrant students in second level schools linked to the Trinity Access Programmes*. Dublin: The Children's Research Centre, Trinity College.

Kirwan, D. (2009). *English language support for newcomer learners in Irish primary schools*. Unpublished PhD thesis, Trinity College, Dublin.

Kwak, K. (2003). Adolescents and their parents: A review of intergenerational family relations for immigrant and non-immigrant families. *Human Development, 46*, 115–136.

Labov, W. (1963). The social motivation for a sound change. *Word, 19*, 273–309.

Labov, W. (1966). *The social stratification of English in New York City*. Washington, DC: Center for Applied Linguistics.

Labov, W. (1972a). *Language in the inner city*. Philadelphia: University of Pennsylvania Press.

Labov, W. (1972b). *Sociolinguistic patterns*. Philadelphia: University of Pennsylvania Press.

Leki, I. (1995). Coping strategies of ESL students in writing tasks across the curriculum. *TESOL Quarterly, 29*, 235–260.

Lutz, H. (1998). The legacy of migration: Immigrant mothers and daughters and the process of inter-generational transmission. In M. Chamberlain (Ed.), *Caribbean migration. Globalised identities* (pp. 96–110). London and New York: Routledge.

MacCormaic, R. (2007, September 17). Level of immigration 'underestimated'. *The Irish Times*, p. 4. Retrieved January 9, 2010, from ProQuest Newspapers. Document ID: 1336733291.

MacÉinrí, P., & White, A. (2008). Immigration into the Republic of Ireland: A bibliography of recent research. *Irish Geography, 41*(2), 151–179.

McDaid, R. (2009). *Tears, teachers, tension and transformation? Minority language children reflect on the recognition of their first languages in Irish primary schools*. Unpublished PhD thesis, St. Patrick's College, Drumcondra, Dublin.

McDonald, B. (2009, January 2). 'No Irish need apply' – Polish builders get their own back. *The Irish Independent*. Retrieved January 4, 2009, from http://www.independent.ie/national-news/no-irish-need-apply--polish-builders-get-their-own-back-1589265.html

McKay, S. L., & Wong, S. C. (1996). Multiple discourses, multiple identities: Investment and agency in second-language learning among Chinese adolescent immigrant students. *Harvard Educational Review, 66*(3), 577–608.

Miller, J. (1999). Becoming audible: Social identity and second language use. *Journal of Intercultural Studies, 20*(2), 149–165.

Ní Laoire, C., Bushin, N., Carpena-Méndez, F., & White, A. (2009). *Tell me about yourself. Migrant children's experiences of moving to and living in Ireland*. Retrieved February 12, 2010, from http://migration.ucc.ie/children/finalreport.html

Norton, B. (2000). *Identity and language learning: Gender, ethnicity and educational change*. Harlow, UK: Pearson Education.

Norton Peirce, B. (1995). Social identity, investment, and language learning. *TESOL Quarterly, 29*(1), 9–31.

Nowlan, E. (2008). Underneath the band-aid: Supporting bilingual students in Irish schools. *Irish Educational Studies, 27*(3), 253–266.

OECD. (2009). *OECD reviews of migrant education: Ireland*. Paris: OECD. Retrieved March 21, 2010, from http://www.oecd.org/dataoecd/1/50/44344245.pdf

Ogbu, J. (1978). *Minority education and caste: The American system in cross-cultural perspective*. New York: Academic Press.

Papastergiadis, N. (2000). *The turbulence of migration*. Cambridge, UK: Polity.

Pavlenko, A., & Blackledge, A. (Eds.). (2004). *Negotiation of identities in multilingual contexts*. Clevedon, New York, Ontario and Church Point: Multilingual Matters.

Rampton, B. (1995). *Crossing: Language and ethnicity among adolescents*. London: Longman.

Regan, V., & Nestor, N. (2010). French Poles, language and identity: An intergenerational snapshot. In V. Regan & C. Ní Chasaide (Eds.), *Language practices and identity construction by multilingual speakers of French L2. The acquisition of sociostylistic variation*. Modern French Identities (Vol. 80, pp. 145–158). New York: Peter Lang.

Scally, D. (2009, January 9). Firm invites existing 500 Polish staff to seek jobs in Łódź. *The Irish Times*, p. 11. Retrieved March 11, 2009, from ProQuest Newspapers. Document ID: 1623698801.

Schumann, J. (1978). *The pidginization process: A model for second language acquisition*. Rowley, MA: Newbury House.

Smyth, E., Darmody, M., McGinnity, F., & Byrne, D. (2009). Adapting to diversity: Irish schools and newcomer students. Dublin: The Economic and Social Research Institute. Retrieved March 28, 2010, from http://www.esri.ie/publications/latest_publications/view/index.xml?id=2783

Spolsky, B. (1989). *Conditions for second language learning. Introduction to a general theory*. Oxford: Oxford University Press.

Stake R. E. (1994). Case studies. In N. K. Denzin & Y. S. Lincoln (Eds.), *Handbook of qualitative research* (pp. 236–247). Thousand Oaks, CA: Sage.

Stake, R. E. (2000). Case studies. In N. K. Denzin & Y. S. Lincoln (Eds.), *Handbook of qualitative research* (2nd ed., pp. 435–454). Thousand Oaks, CA: Sage.

Suárez-Orozco, C., & Suárez-Orozco, M. M. (2002). *Children of immigration.* Cambridge, MA: Harvard University Press.

Tagliamonte, S. (2006). *Analyzing sociolinguistic variation.* Cambridge: Cambridge University Press.

Tagliamonte, S., & Hudson, R. (1999). *Be like* et al. beyond America: The quotative system in British and Canadian youth. *Journal of Sociolinguistics, 3*(2), 147–172.

Ward, T. (2004). *Education and language needs of separated children.* Dublin: City of Dublin, VEC, County Dublin VEC, Dun Laoghaire VEC.

Weedon, C. (1987). *Feminist practice and poststructuralist theory.* London: Basil Blackwell.

Wei, L., & Wu, C.-J. (2009). Polite Chinese children revisited: Creativity and the use of codeswitching in the Chinese complementary school classroom. *International Journal of Bilingual Education and Bilingualism, 12*(2), 193–211.

Weick, K. E. (1995). *Sensemaking in organizations.* Thousand Oaks, CA: Sage.

Willis, P. (1977). *Learning to labour. How working class kids get working class jobs.* Farnborough: Saxon House.

Niamh Nestor and Vera Regan
School of Languages and Literatures
University College Dublin, Ireland

ANGELA VEALE AND EMILY KENNEDY

4. INDIAN YOUNG PEOPLE NEGOTIATING TRANSNATIONAL IDENTITIES

INTRODUCTION

The aim of this chapter is to explore how migrant Indian young people living in Ireland negotiate the normative task of adolescent identity development in the 'here and now' while undergoing acculturative change as a result of migration. Simultaneously, youth are engaged in thinking about the future and they are developing imagined 'future selves'. Migrant adolescents are now growing up in an era whereby migration to a host country may not be a fixed 'end point' but rather a point-in-time process of multiple returns and migrations. Certainly, global communication technology and better access to transatlantic travel means there is less disconnect with one's country of origin (Bhatia and Ram, 2004). In an increasingly globalised world, there is an important question to be asked as to how adolescents see themselves negotiating their lives now and into the future. This chapter focuses on the psychological implications of how participation in processes of migration may affect Indian migrant adolescents' identity or sense of self. It takes a socio-cultural psychological view of the development of "present" and "desired future" identities as embedded in cultural, political and economic processes. It also considers the participants' shifting positions of power/agency or powerlessness as they negotiate identity formation as transnational actors.

THEORETICAL UNDERPINNINGS

Prominent in psychological research in youth and migration is Berry's acculturation strategies model (Berry, 1980). This model refers to four distinct strategies that immigrants may use in a new cultural context. Integration is said to happen when an individual seeks to maintain contact with both native and host culture. Assimilation describes individuals who adapt to the dominant group whilst not maintaining their own cultural identity. Separation relates to those who preserve their cultural identity without seeking to make contact with the host group. Marginalisation relates to those who appear to be confused and lose ties with home culture but do not develop a clear orientation towards the host culture. In a study of immigrant young people in 13 countries, Berry et al. (2006) found that a third of youth demonstrated an integration profile, which predicts consistently more positive outcomes than alternative strategies, and the remainder were more or less equally divided among the other profiles. In another study, South Asian adolescents aged 13–18 years in Britain

Darmody, Tyrrell, Song (eds.), The Changing Faces of Ireland: Exploring the Lives of Immigrant and Ethnic Minority Children, 53–69.
© *2011 Sense Publishers. All rights reserved.*

found that the majority of Indian youth adopted integration strategies whereas Pakistani Muslim youth fitted an ethnic or separation profile (Robinson, 2009).

Recently, Berry's acculturation framework has come under sustained critical reflection. His model promotes an illusion of stable psychological identifications among migrants and fails to capture how macro-level processes such as changing economic and political circumstances in the lives of migrants who are experiencing change, may be inextricably intertwined in immigrant identity (Lichtsinn and Veale, 2007; Hermans, 2001a). Bhatia (2008) has argued that the model fails to address the psychological impact of migration for identity as it does not account for the dynamic, 'culturally distinct and politically entrenched experiences' of transnational migrants (p. 225). It also does not capture the impact for migrant adolescents of growing up outside their homeland as part of transnational diasporas.

'Transnational diasporas' are communities that 'forge and sustain simultaneous multi-stranded social relations that link together their societies of origin and settlement' (Glick-Schiller et al., 1995, p. 48). Kleist (2008) argues that in academic writing, a 'diaspora' is often characterised as a marginalized community which experiences social and cultural problems in adapting to life in Western countries. On the other hand, in political contexts, the term may denote 'agency, solidarity and resources' (p. 1139). There has been little exploration in the literature of adolescent's identities as participants in diasporic communities. Political leaders in India and Ireland have recognised the potential for members of the respective diaspora to act as transnational political actors in the reconstruction and political development of their countries.[1] How do migrant adolescents position themselves in this political domain? Importantly, a sense of agency and solidarity with homeland may relate to how migrants negotiate identities within transnational diasporic communities. More interestingly, perhaps we can ask how do adolescents themselves negotiate this acculturation journey?

Research to date suggests that this acculturation journey places special demands on the developing identities of young migrants. Naidoo (2007) notes that among the Indian diaspora in Australia, parents' greatest fear is that their children will become too "Australianised" and begin to relinquish the core cultural values and practices of their family. Indian parents also tend to establish strict rules for their children's behaviour in order to exert some control in the face of cultural change and foreign influence. Naidoo (2007) also argues that religion and religious affiliations in the host country are used by parents in order to instil core cultural and religious values in the second generation.

Similarly, Das Gupta (1998) notes that during the process of negotiation, Indian migrants to the USA make a considerable effort to maintain their Indian identity in their host countries and to resist cultural change. They familiarise the next generation with their Indian heritage and traditions through their participation in cultural celebrations and communal festivals in the host country. Physical links with the homeland are maintained through frequent trips to India, while psychological ties are fostered through a process of reinventing "Indian culture" in the host country (Bhattacharjee, 1992). In global, diasporic societies, Bhatia and Ram (2009) ask 'Who carries the burden of transmitting 'culture and traditions' across generations and taking on the responsibility of acculturating their children in the new world' (p. 143).

These studies suggest that parents are invested in the developing identities of young Indian migrants and expect their children to resist cultural change and retain important aspects of their ethnic identity.

Talbani and Hasanali (2000) conducted a study exploring the social and cultural experiences of 22 adolescent girls of Indian, Pakistani and Bangladeshi origin in Canada. The participants (15–17 years) were second-generation immigrants who had been educated in Canada. A key concern identified in their study related to parental control of socialisation, going out, parties and dating. Many of the participants discussed the restrictions they faced with respect to socialising, especially with members of the opposite sex. The researchers noted signs of change in the traditional power or family structure as participants discussed their changing dress codes, less frequent participation in community activities and increasing levels of dissent. Talbani and Hasanali (2000) note that their participants expressed dissent with parental control in different ways. Some rebelled openly against their parents, others went 'behind their parents back', while some suppressed their feelings of frustration and accepted the expectations of their parents.

Naidoo (2007) argues that many Indian families migrate because they are motivated by the prospect of being able to provide their children with better educational opportunities abroad. Educational and economic success is highly valued by the Indian community and regarded as an honour to the family (Naidoo, 2007). Desai and Subramanian (2000) note that 'many parents are willing to experience downward mobility in their careers and social status as they see it as a sacrifice they are making to ensure a better future for their children' (p. 60). Naidoo (2007) argues that children of the Indian diaspora are thus, often under a great deal of pressure to perform well academically and take on professional careers that are highly valued in the community. As such, the migrant families tend to resist cultural changes in this regard and strive to maintain their high standards of education regardless of the surrounding academic standards.

Yet, acculturation theory is limited in its ability to provide insight into the complex identity processes of adolescents journeying as transnational migrants. For adolescents in our study, identity and a sense of a future self are being formed in a context where culture, macrolevel political and social 'markers' are also changing. One theoretical lens recognised to be potentially useful for this study is the theory of the dialogical self, proposed by Hermans and Kempen (1998). Hermans and Kempen argue that in an era of increasing globalisation and transmigration, it is useful to conceptualise the self as a dynamic, multivoiced and dialogical entity. This notion challenges the existence of both a core essential self and a core essential culture (Hermans, 2001b). While the rational self is believed to be 'context-free' and separate to society, culture and history, the dialogical self is defined with respect to its historical and cultural context (Fogel, 1993, as cited in Hermans (2001b)).

In this model, the self is conceptualised, not as one coherent voice but instead as a multiplicity of different voices in different and relatively autonomous I-positions expressing their own ideas and accompanying and opposing each other in a dialogical relation. Hermans (2001a) argues that when an individual migrates to another country, a number of new 'I' positions may enter the subjective horizon of the self. He notes that these new positions may find themselves in conflict or may coexist relatively independent of each other. It is also a possibility that they may fuse so that hybrid combinations emerge in the form of multiple identities (e.g. African American). The self is not therefore necessarily unified, continuous or organised but may be pulled in many different directions by internally inconsistent or externally driven forces. In response to this process, an ongoing negotiation of identity takes place. According to Hermans (2001b), the asymmetry of dialogic relations is critical to our understanding of the dialogic self. He challenges such notions as the 'integration strategy' which assumes that the migrant individual can freely choose between two or more cultural positions. He argues that conceptions such as this, fail to acknowledge the tensions and power relations which may exist between different I-positions localised in time and space.

Bhatia and Ram (2009) argue that psychology as a discipline has only recently begun to recognise the advancements which have been made in postcolonial and diaspora studies, in developing an understanding of the migrant's experience of acculturation. They argue that researchers need to explore the larger historical, sociocultural and political structures that are inevitably implicated in both acculturation dynamics and the formation of immigrant identity (Bhatia and Ram, 2009,) In dialogic terms, Bhatia (2008) argues that we need to think of acculturation as process rooted in history, culture and politics which involves an 'ongoing, contested negotiation of voices from here and there, past and present, homeland and hostland, self and other' (p. 37). Embedded in this may be asymmetrical power relations between the majority and minority world, particularly in a globalised world. Hermans (2008) notes, 'In particular, the uncertainty and instability of a globalizing world increases the desire for stability, safety, and survival as universal biological needs' (p. 32), and draws attention to what he refers to as the 'shadow side of globalization': neoliberal international market-driven approaches to economic and social policies, the removal of job certainty in the middle and lower classes, and terrorism. Transnational migrant adolescents have to face the challenge of adapting not only to their (situated) local culture but also to global society. Hermans (2008) argues it is likely transnational adolescents develop a bicultural identity but this is an underresearched area and needs further understanding.

The Asian population in Ireland accounts for 1% of the population, just 46,952 individuals in a population of just over 4 million people (CSO, 2006). However, while important studies have examined the experiences of African, Latin American and returned Irish migrant children and youth in Ireland (Ní Laoire et al., 2009; Bushin and White, 2009), Asian youth have been largely invisible. Bearing the above literature in mind, this chapter seeks to explore how Indian migrant adolescents' living in Ireland negotiate their transnational identities.

DATA AND METHODOLOGY

Six participants (4 boys and 2 girls) of Indian nationality participated in the study. Inclusion criteria were adolescents (13–18 inclusively), shared nationality among participants, recent migration to Ireland (within past 3 years); and ability to speak and understand English fluently. Four focus group discussions were conducted with all participants and each discussion lasted 60 minutes approximately. This allowed for topics that emerged in focus groups to be reflected upon by the researcher and brought back to the group for further discussion and analysis. Following this, the six participants also participated in paired interviews each lasting approximately 50–60 minutes. Pseudonyms are utilised in the analysis. Participants were as follows: Avani, (female aged 15 years), Rahul (male, aged 14 years), Nikhil (male, aged 14 years), Pranav (male, aged 15 years), Jyoti (female, aged 13 years), and Anand (male, aged 16 years).

A constructivist approach to grounded theory is employed in this study (Charmaz, 2006). Through the method of "constant comparison", the analysis engaged in a process of simultaneously identifying similarities and differences between the meanings and experiences of participants. Respondent validation (Pigeon, 1996) was incorporated into interviews and discussions. For example, if participants emphasised certain words or terms in their narratives, they were asked to explain what the terms meant for them. Memos were used to develop conceptual ideas. In the course of this analysis, it became evident that a dialogical perspective was required that brought attention to the different voices and counter voices in the transcripts and also their emotional character (e.g. anxiety, uncertainty, confidence), and the ways in which adolescents positioned themselves with respect to forces of globalisation (e.g. a future transnational job market). The transcripts were read utilising dialectical principles (Hermans, 2008) addressing the tensions evident in the data. Using dialectical principles in a grounded-theoretical analysis has precedent in socio-cultural research (Rawlings, 1998).

AGENCY AND POWER (LESSNESS) IN TRANSNATIONAL MIGRATION

In making the decision to move to Ireland, the participants reported that their parents wanted to avail of transnational opportunities and enhance the future prospects of their children. Rahul explained that his father had always aspired to live abroad and notes that his parents anticipated "a better education...and a better life like" for their son in Ireland. Avani and Anand both suggest that their parents were motivated to migrate by the prospect of making and investing money in a world of global currency opportunities.

> Avani: But the thing is if you look at euros and rupees, they were bigger, ya like one euro is like almost sixty rupees so like yeah that's a big thing...so if we work here, when we go back we will be probably very rich.(laughs)...yeah so that's why she came here..

Most interestingly, four of the six participants had lived in other countries as well as having lived in India before their move to Ireland. Avani had previously lived with both parents in the Middle East when one parent got a job in Ireland and she decided to move with her mother to Ireland. When asked how she felt about moving to Ireland, she responded:

> Avani: I...first of all I disagreed, that I won't come because...I dunno, I just you know...just don't want to make up new friends...I had so many friends

there and then you come to this new country and...like everyone knew me in that school like and then when you come here, you are...I know the feeling of changing schools....

With an emphasis on *knowing* the feeling of changing schools, Avani. is letting us know that she is an experienced migrant, she knows what is involved, and this made it a difficult decision. She conveys agency and choice in noting that she disagreed with moving and that she would not come, but then "*I dunno, I just you know...*" possibly also indicates a lack of power in this being truly her decision. As an adolescent caught between dependence on parents and emerging self-responsibility, this dialectic tension is conveyed in this sentence. When asked about this, she noted:

Avani: Back then I just said, yeah because I missed my mum so much so ok if she's staying there (Ireland), ok let's go...Yeah I had been living with my Dad for more than a year so...yeah so that time I missed my mum really because I didn't talk much to her and it would take a lot of money and so I just went and to tell the truth, I didn't know there was a place known as Ireland (laughs)...seriously yeah (laughs) because when I looked at the map I was like...ok she is telling Ireland...where is that?

Rahul: ...Yeah, Ireland was like low in nurses and stuff.

The external, authoritative voice of her mother is conveyed by "OK, she is telling Ireland." and her own confusion "Where is that?" Avani is a member of a growing number of transnational families separated because of parents work. Rahul chimed in to explain the workplace demand in Ireland for nurses "and stuff" as explanatory, conveying simultaneous understanding and confusion.

Rahul also exhibits this dialectical tension of agency-powerlessness in the familial decision to migrate:

Rahul: I didn't want to come over here like, but first time I said, I'm not coming. I'll stay here with my grandparents or something...but then I just came and I liked it here.

Nikhil was the only participant who felt that it was fully his choice to move. He explained that his parents gave him the choice of remaining in India in boarding school, and he feels is was his own decision to move to Ireland. As will emerge in the analysis, all participants experienced their migration to Ireland as one destination country in a possible open-ended migration trajectory.

"They don't want us to Change but we are Changing"

In early focus group discussions, the group were very interested to talk about how they felt they had changed as individuals since moving to Ireland. The group highlighted an identity position- the "good" Indian boy or girl- as one they struggled with. They explained, for example, that their parents expected them to be "good" Indian boys and girls and avoid changing "too much" in response to Irish culture.

Identification as a "good" Indian boy or girl was found to be loaded with cultural and gender specific meanings for the participants. For boys, it appeared to evoke mainly moral connotations. A "good" Indian boy is identifiable as a boy who refrains from drinking and smoking, respects his elders, goes to church, catechism and confession and does not have a girlfriend until he is over the age of 18. A "good" Indian girl, on the other hand, evokes both moral and cultural connotations. According to Avani, a "good" Indian girl is identifiable due to her devotion to God, kindness to others, appropriate dress, ability to cook, to take care of the house, and ability to be shy, that is, to be demure while still capable of asserting her rights.

Avani notes that her parents have adapted their expectations somewhat, with regard to how Avani can identify herself as a "good" Indian girl in Ireland. Avani also asserted that she feels a "little bit" more free to express herself in Ireland and gives and an example that she tends to think less before shouting at her mother during an argument. It appears that some identity positions can be incorporated more easily than others and that this may depend on the participant's level of flexibility regarding older identity positions. For example, Anand continues to hold a firm belief that "You should have some respect for your elders"; and when he sees Irish peers being disrespectful, he wants to "get at them and hit them", and it makes him very angry. He exercises personal agency in maintaining his core value. On the other hand, as a member of a minority group in Ireland, he is forced to accept the behavioural norms of the majority group around him which he experiences as a position of powerlessness.

Rahul is also negotiating the dilemma of incorporating conflicting positions of identification in his developing identity. Rahul, however, finds himself in opposition to his parents as he begins to identify with the freedom of Irish teenagers.

Rahul: Irish people, they are allowed to go out anytime they want…but like, our parents will be mad if we're going out with girls and stuff…They just want us to be…

Pranav: "Good boys"

As part of forging his own autonomous identity, Rahul has adopted different values which stand in conflict to the values of his parents. For example, Rahul's parents do not approve of their son dating a girl in Ireland and that they think "it's wrong", and "if you do that you are going to go to hell or something". Rahul's beliefs in this regard are reinforced by his understanding of cultural "norms" in Ireland and in this way we can see that migration to Ireland has affected his sense of values and identity.

Rahul: Like I don't see anything wrong with it like…it's normal to like someone.

In negotiating his own personal autonomy in this situation, Rahul explains that he is seeing a girl in Ireland but he has not told his parents. Similar to Anand, Rahul appears to feel a certain degree of frustration as he engages in the process of negotiating between two conflicting identity positions and notes "sometimes you feel like you have to be like a saint or something". When asked to reflect on how they feel they have changed since moving to Ireland, the group all concurred that there was a shift in the part of self relating to parents and through that relationship, to Indian traditions and culture:

Pranav: Our behaviour to our parents. (laughs)

Rahul: If I was in India I would be more obedient but here I'm not as much as in India, at home or in school like India is changing to like it is in Ireland, it's changing to European style.

Researcher: And how do you think your parents feel about that?

Pranav: They want us to keep up the traditions like... they don't want us to really change too much to the culture.

Avani: Our culture has been attacked for some years, like you pass it down to your children and like.

Rahul: They don't want us to change but we are changing.

There is recognition that it is their parents' responsibility to pass on their cultural heritage which has "been attacked" but also an agentive push that although "they" (their parents) do not want them to change, the participants themselves note "we are changing". These findings point to the way in which participants can be forced to negotiate between conflicting and asymmetrical identity positions as they participate in migration.

Facing a Transnational Threat to Identity.

A significant part of the change participants notice in themselves is an emerging critical voice with respect to their homeland. Their dialogue shows evidence of a developing politicised voice that is becoming more socially aware but is also working out their own 'situatedness' in respect to the different socioeconomic and social welfare models of Ireland and India. Most interestingly, these different structural models are very 'live' for them as they grapple to understand that the choices they make now as adolescents in their work ethic and education will impact their future adult identities. As they talked this out, one of the negotiations they are engaged in as participants in transnational migration is to manage identity tensions in the 'here and now' that may impact on positions they may occupy in the future in different socioeconomic and political systems. This is sparked by an emerging political consciousness. Rahul begins this discussion:

Rahul: Because since I came to Ireland I don't really like India now because if I compare Ireland to India, it's a way dirtier and... and like people don't really care about other people in India and...there's no peace...there's robbery and crime and everything.

Avani: Yeah, like just last summer I went to India and I saw India in a way I usually didn't see...Like just before I went, a few months back, we did this recycling project. But then I went to India and I was travelling a lot, I did notice at that time that there was a lot of rubbish and something had to be done…I usually didn't notice that because I was used to it. I didn't know why the government wouldn't do anything about that. Then I asked my eldest cousin why they don't do something here and she said that it had to do with the economics and everything.…

In the positions adopted in discourse, there is a distancing from identification with India that begins in observations in daily life and develops into a critical political position that has to do with "economics and everything". In the discussion, Avani emphasised the inefficiency of the government in India. Rahul noted the greed of the politicians and their apparent neglect of the poor. Avani blamed politicians for sustaining religious division, while Nikhil stressed the occurrence of violent political strikes and "dirty politics". Rahul's growing sense of identification with a "happier", more "peaceful" life in Ireland, is clearly shaped by his personal experiences of political unrest in India. Two of the participants in this study (Anand and Nikhil) lived in the suburbs and felt that they were not "affected" by politics. They appeared to desire, and identify with, the freedom of Ireland to a lesser extent than the other participants but also felt that life was easier here. Nikhil relates this to an observation that "like, Irish people get more support from the government like". The researcher asked Nikhil to explain what he meant:

Nikhil: Well, if you are unemployed, like they will get money...or monthly payments or something and social welfare and that kind of stuff...and they can keep up their family when they are elder like...but like in our country, we don't get...the government won't support us...so if we don't study and if we don't get good marks and no job, it will be hard for our future. The government helps people out here.

Avani: Yes, in India job that is best to get in India is a government job because it is secure, a job that you know you will have like. Sometimes you can get a pension from that in your old age like but I don't want to work in my country...believe me I don't want to get in that stress...in that hot place (laughs) so I am going to work abroad and maybe only settle in India when I'm old like.

An observation that some Irish people get support from the Government quickly moves from an observation about external social conditions to an introjected identity threat about what it means for self to live in a system without social protections. Security emerges as a very central concept in their discussion, the dialectic opposite of insecurity. "Working abroad" offers security but in India, education is your security to order to be competitive in a challenging job market, which would get you *in that stress* (emphasis in original). Stress is not desirable. This brings an inner conflict. A 'good' Indian boy/girl identity is closely tied to school and good grades. There is a threat/danger if you do not do well at school. As good education is so closely tied to parental and cultural values of success, they struggle to negotiate their personal positions, resisting the stress associated with the need to succeed within the Indian community in Ireland but also to be suspicious or even derogatory of the perceived more relaxed attitudes of their Irish peers. This indicates that the values and beliefs of the participants are fluid in nature as they shift between different positions of identification and negotiate between the contrasting Indian and Irish value systems and systems of education. For example, they enjoy feeling less pressure at school to a certain extent:

> Rahul: ...if I was in India, I would get a better education but like there would be more pressure on me.

Similarly Avani noted, "If you study in India you will probably be way smarter but it's quite a tough life...".

On the other hand, they identify strongly with the persona of the "unchallenged" student.

> Anand: We don't have much competition here...you know if you want to be the best you have to compete against the best.

> Avani: That's the thing about Ireland, we are the only competitors...they don't want to compete (referring to Irish people)...they agree that we are smart but they don't want to like fight with us and I get bored like...In India that's what happens...when you study, you have to study more so that you become number one...no matter what. ...if you go back, you are going to be dumb, we are going to be dumb actually (laughs).

Behind this is the threat of what it means as members of a transnational community should they fall behind real or imagined peers in India.

The participants shared the view that they would have poor job prospects in India as a result of their studies abroad, as Anand notes, "You can study in India and come out, but you can't study out and go back in for a job. You can go in but...". For the participants, their sense of self is distilled with a sense that they have the potential to be successful and the desire to actualise their potential in this regard. Yet their involvement in migratory processes, and their perception that they are availing of a lower education level in Ireland, has led to them fearing that their desired identity in this regard may come under threat upon return to India, particularly if they were to try and get a job there as their friends would me "*much more intelligent*". Avani, Anand and Rahul all expressed anxiety that their identity as strong performers to date, would come under threat in India:

> Rahul: If I go back to India, I will probably fail everything.

> Avani: That's why I'm scared because my mum is considering that we will go back...in India, maths is one of the toughest subjects...It's a little bit harder to go back then and do really hard stuff and that's why it scares me because when I go back I will be totally blind, I wouldn't know what they're doing at all. I might be even two classes behind which means I will be maybe two years elder than I should be.

This dialogical tension between security-insecurity is a source of anxiety for all participants, and in particular, causes Nikhil to feel a significant sense of regret. Speaking from an agentive, choosing, 'I' position, he takes ownership of his decision to migrate but this has emotional consequences as he rejects a possible position of dependency on parental decision-making and locates responsibility for any consequences of that decision within himself.

Nikhil: I think I am more secure in India.

Researcher: Ok…can you tell me why Nikhil?

Nikhil: I don't know…I think always that if I stay in India that my future would be more secure, I will get a good job or something like that…I don't think I'm secure here because the education level of here compared to over there is much different… I'm thinking like that I made a bad decision to come over here (leans forward and lowers head almost to his knees).

Researcher: Ok…but was that your decision Nikhil?

Nikhil: Yeah, it was mine (sits upright again)....my family came over here first, but they asked me if I wanted to come over here or stay studying there in boarding school.

A sense of psychological 'safety' for participants depended on the extent to which they were able to perform well on key culturally-expected tasks for adolescents, such as doing well in school. This also gave them confidence in their developing present and future identities. While peripheral values could be adapted more easily as seen in the last section (dress, eating, habits, etc.), the participants' comments show that a threat to a core identity position ("to be the best") can cause considerable anxiety and insecurity. This is particularly the case as they perceive they are likely to experience future migrations and this is as yet unknown. There is a developmental tension also, most evident in Nikhil's account, of being caught between positions of dependency and autonomy. In claiming personal responsibility for the decision to move, Nikhil even begins to feel a considerable degree of regret. While exercising his own personal agency in "choosing" to come to Ireland, he now grapples with what he perceives as the negative consequences of his decision.

Future Selves: Multiple Possibilities

This section explores was adolescents' negotiation of identity in an environment of significant uncertainty as members of transnational families whose parents are willing to move with the ebb and flow of global opportunities. In their dialogue, the participants talked of their imagined future possible selves. Markus and Nurius (1986) defined possible selves as "self knowledge (that) pertains to how individuals think about their potential and their future"; that is, "selves that we would very much like to become," "selves we could become," and "selves we are afraid of becoming" (p. 954). For participants in this study, foremost in the factors that impinged on thinking about "selves they would very much like to become' or 'selves we are afraid of becoming" was uncertainty about future return or migrations. Settling, thinking about settling, not having a chance to settle, suddenly moving was part of Avani's experience and in the following utterance, there is a sense that she is trying to take control of this in thinking about her own future. She initially positions herself within the social group of all Indians, of whom "no one tries to settle abroad" to formulating her own plan which will involve leaving Ireland.

> Avani: But no one tries to settle abroad because, I don't know, it's like, every time you think about settling, you don't want to. Now my mum and dad never thought they were going to come here. Everyone thought we were going to go back but suddenly we just moved and we couldn't settle in India again because we came here. It was like, *fast*...I didn't know, I thought we were all going to go back, you know, everything was going to be normal but then we just came here and everything changed. So every time we think about settling, something happens that we don't have a chance to settle... I will maybe stay in Ireland until my studies (laughs) but after that I will go.

Avani's view of the future, that of future migrations, is shared by all members of the group. One of the group points out that Rahul will be moving to Australia and he clarifies that this will take place after his Junior Certificate (a State examination in secondary school) as his mum is getting a job there. Pranav announces, "I might be going to Australia too...and Nikhil too...". Anand comments that there is a kind of rumour that most of the Indian community are going to Australia as jobs are being lost in Ireland, and there will be less money to be had and says, "Yeah, like many of the Indians lost their job here...like in the hospitals in Dublin and stuff". The researcher asks about whether the migration route itself is important:

> Researcher: So they are thinking it makes more sense to go to Australia from Ireland rather than from India to Australia.

> Pranav: It's because you get PR (Permanent Residency) there if you go there.

> Anand: But what do you think? Would it be better to go from a third class country or from a first class country...I mean like would they take you as seriously going to Australia from India as from Ireland?

Interestingly, in the above analysis, the young people include macro-level political factors such as migration laws (being able to achieve a status of Permanent Residency) and the development status of different nation states as factors in possible migrations. This is integrally tied to their identity and the desire to be a person that is taken seriously. The sense of "self" that Anand, for example, might be afraid of becoming is someone who is not taken seriously and someone who is perceived to be from a "third class country". The dialectical tensions of opportunity/threat and security/insecurity identified in the previous section in particular crystallises for young people around their future selves. For Nikhil, the struggle to negotiate the threat to his core value of education and the perceived threat to his desired "future self" was confounded by the political consequences of migration. In returning to India, he would also have to deal with the difficulties associated with a new political status.

> Nikhil: …If I go back I will be a "Non Resident Indian"…so if I want to join the army or something like that, it could be difficult for me.

The participants' comments suggest that in order to understand present identity challenges, it is important to understand the core values of the participants in the context of their desired "future self". It seems that the participants will experience less psychological stress if they can find a way to reduce any threat to their core identities and thus preserve their future 'desired self'.

Identifying as a Transnational Agent of Political Change

During the course of the research, both Avani and Anand evidenced a strong sense of political and patriotic loyalty to their own country. Both recognised negative aspects of life in India but identified themselves, as members of a "future generation" with political responsibility to their country of origin. It is in this context that a strong identification of I-as-Indian self is evident. This is provoked by reflection on the external threats to India posed by terrorism, which in turn mobilises a strong national identity and identification with the collective 'people' of India. An agentive and powerful I-as-diaspora self also emerges for some of the young people who articulate an ongoing sense of connection and responsibility. On the contrary, others in the group recognise internal and external threats to their home country, but they dissociate themselves from responsibility to solve the problems and do not feel any power as part of the Indian diaspora.

> Rahul: That's why I don't really like India that much…because of that…Like the people are like destroying the whole India, like you know the thing that happened in Mumbai.

> Nikhil: That's Pakistan (Pranav agrees).

> Avani: …The thing is…even though India is dirty, you know polluted and has like the dirtiest politics I have ever seen, I still like it because, you can't just say you hate your country and be away from it. You have to be, that's patriotism, you can't just say you love your country and do nothing. You have to go there, experience it and try to solve because you are the people, you have to do something.

> Rahul: You can't do anything.

> Pranav: That's democracy- for the people, by the people…you know.

> Avani: That's what democracy means and our country is one of the number one democracies, still now, although the government is made by the people,

the government...they make false promises that the people just don't get. Now only they realise that so we have to fight back. We are, what do you say?

Pranav: The future generation.

Avani: The future generation who are going to handle that country like.

Anand is considering returning to India and therefore can exercise his political responsibility upon his return. However, Avani is intending to remain abroad to pursue other personal ambitions. Two aspects of Avani's identities are therefore in conflict: her ambition to succeed abroad and her simultaneous identification as one of "people" of India who has a political responsibility to her country. We suggest that Avani negotiates this dilemma by identifying herself as a transnational agent of political change. Her comments reveal that she sees herself as one of the many "educated" Indian citizens abroad, who can return at election time in order to bring about political change in India.

Researcher: But Avani, did you tell me earlier that you weren't going to go back to India?

Avani: Yeah (laughs).

Researcher: So where will the future generation be who are going to make this difference?

(Pranav: points at Anand and all laugh).

Avani: No like I will go and study abroad, I will work a little bit abroad but I will come back and vote and everything...if educated people from abroad come back to India... they might pick a good Prime Minister who might actually know what is happening in this country like. Avani's identification with this group is strengthened by her assumption that educated Indian citizens abroad, the Indian diaspora share her belief that political change is needed and that they can have influence in the future of India. In identifying as a trans-national agent of political change, Avani appears to negotiate the challenge of incorporating new identity positions within the self while simultaneously preserving her core values and her "desired future" identity.

CONCLUSION

As a result of their active participation in the process of migration, the participants in this study are engaged in a process of negotiating their developing transnational identities. While living in Ireland, the participants are expected to maintain and foster certain aspects of their ethnic identity including cultural values, traditions and religious practices. These findings clearly support the findings of Naidoo (2007) and Das Gupta (1998) who noted the resistance of Indian parents to cultural change and their commitment to instilling core cultural and religious values in the second generation.

Participants have also begun to identify with other aspects of life in Ireland. These positions of identification were unavailable to the participants prior to their migration to Ireland, but they now draw on these identifications as they engage in critical reflection of life in India as they become politicised. Identity processes are clearly embedded in dynamics of globalisation and the pull from the majority (poorer) world to the opportunities in the minority (wealthier) world. However, global recession beings uncertainty and the migration trajectory is open-ended in the imagination and lives of these young people. Dialectics of adventure and un-certainty sit beside those of security and insecurity. While adolescents live their lives in the 'here and now', they are struggling to keep open a future that has many possible 'future selves' in Ireland, a move to another country, or a return to India. This presents challenges both to the fixed categories of Berry's acculturation theory and Hermans' (2008) contention that it is likely that only transnational adolescents develop a bicultural identity.

Participants experience threats to a future successful identity. The value they place on education and their determined drive to succeed appear to be compromised by their perception of a lack of challenge and lower education system in Ireland. The participants are clearly negotiating their developing transnational identities as they find themselves simultaneously identifying with the lack of pressure in Irish schools but they also identify strongly with the persona of the "unchallenged" student. The findings of this study lend further support to the Dialogical Model of Self as the participants' comments suggested the fluid nature of their identifications as they shifted between different positions of identification and navigated between the contrasting Indian and Irish value systems and systems of education at different times and in different contexts.

It appears that due to their experiences of a threatened identity in Ireland, the participants and their parents have engaged in a process of changing their future migration plans. In light of the perceived lower standards of education in Ireland, they are also considering a move to other, more competitive locations and young people show a readiness to avail of transnational opportunities once again in order to enhance their future prospects.

Due to her participation in the process of migration, Avani is forced to negotiate her own personal drive to succeed with her strong sense of patriotic and political responsibility as an Indian citizen. While she feels that her own personal prospects are better supported abroad, Avani identifies as a member of the "future generation" and thus feels a strong sense of patriotic and political responsibility to her country. She appears to negotiate this dilemma by identifying as a transnational agent of political change within a diaspora community who can bring about political change in India from the outside. In this way, she manages to actualise her personal drive to succeed abroad, while simultaneously upholding her political responsibility as an India citizen. In dialogical terms, it might be argued that by engaging in this process of negotiation, the two relatively autonomous 'I' positions have fused to form a hybrid combination in a developing transnational identity.

For all participants, there is a sense of trying to keep a number of different balls in the air as they imagine future identities in their country or origin, Ireland or a third country. They convey their openness to multiple journeys of return and migration in a globalised world of opportunities across different geographic locations. This is also fuelling insecurities in their lives in the current moment as they try to prepare for a future that may make many different demands of them within different socioeconomic and political contexts.

NOTES

[1] In 2006, during the fourth annual Pravasi Bharatiya Divas (celebration of the homecoming of global Indians), the Indian Prime Minister recognised the potential for members of the Indian diaspora to act as transnational political actors in the reconstruction and political development of India. A similar point was made by the Irish President, Mary McAleese with respect to harnessing the power of the Irish Diaspora. President Mary McAleece, Address to the Global Irish Economic Forum, Farmleigh, Dublin, 18–20 September, 2009. http://www.europeanirish.com/news_details.php?news_id=1091

REFERENCES

Berry, J. W., Phinney, J. S., Sam, D. L., & Vedder, P. (2006). Immigrant youth: Acculturation, identity, and adaptation. *Applied Psychology: An International Review, 55*(3), 303–332.

Bhatia, S., & Ram, A. (2009). Theorizing identity in transnational and Diaspora cultures: A critical approach to acculturation. *International Journal of Intercultural Relations.* doi: 10.1016/j.ijintrel. 2008.12.009

Bhatia, S., & Ram, A. (2004). Culture, hybridity, and the dialogical self: Cases from the South Asian Diaspora. *Mind, Culture, and Activity, 11*(3), 224–240.

Bhatia, S. (2008). 9/11 and the Indian Diaspora: Narratives of race, place and immigrant identity. *Journal of Intercultural Studies, 29*(1), 21–39.

Bhattacharya, G. (2008). The Indian Diaspora in transnational context: Social relations and cultural identities of immigrants to New York City. *Journal of Intercultural Studies, 29,* 65–80.

Bhattacharjee, A. (1992). The habit of ex-nomination: Nation, woman, and the Indian immigrant bourgeoisie. *Public Culture, 5,* 19–44.

Bosma, H. A., & Kunnen, E. S. (2008). Identity-in-context is not yet identity development in context. *Journal of Adolescence, 31,* 281–289.

Bushin, N., & White, A. (2009). Migration policies in Ireland: Exploring the impacts on young people's geographies. *Area, 42,* 170–180.

Central Statistics Office, Ireland. (2006). Census data. http://www.cso.ie/statistics/popnclassbyreligion andnationality2006.htm

Charmaz, K. (2006). *Constructing grounded theory.* London: Sage Publications.

Dasgupta, S. D. (1998). Gender roles and cultural continuity in the Asian Indian immigrant community in the U.S. *Sex Roles, 38,* 953–973.

Desai, S., & Subramanian, S. (2000). Colour, culture, and dual consciousness: Issues identified by South Asian immigrant youth in the greater Toronto area. In P. Anisef & K. M. Kilbride (Eds.), *Managing two worlds: The experiences and concerns of immigrant youth in Ontario* (pp. 1–82). Toronto: Canadian Scholar's Press.

Eastmond, M. (2007). Stories as lived experience: Narratives in forced migration research. *Journal of Refugee Studies, 20*(2), 249–263.

Glick-Schiller, N., Basch, L., & Blanc, C. S. (1995). From immigrant to transmigrant: Theorizing transnational migration. *Anthropological Quarterly, 68,* 48–63.

Hermans, H. J. M. (2001a). The dialogical self: Toward a theory of personal and cultural positioning. *Culture and Psychology, 7*(3), 243–281.

Hermans, H. J. M. (2001b). Mixing and moving cultures require a dialogical self. *Human Development, 44,* 24–28.

Hermans, H. J. M., & Kempen, H. J. G. (1998). Moving cultures: The perilous problems of cultural dichotomies in a globalising society. *American Pscyhologist*, *53*, 1111–1120.

Hondagneu-Sotelo, P., & Ernestine, A. (1997). "I'm here, but I'm there": The meanings of Latina transnational motherhood. *Gender and Society*, *11*, 548–557.

Kleist, N. (2008). In the name of Diaspora: Between struggles for recognition and political aspirations. *Journal of Ethnic and Migration Studies*, *34*(7), 1127–1143.

Lichtsinn, I., & Veale, A. (2007) Between 'here' and 'there': Nigerian lone mothers in Ireland. In B. Fanning (Ed.), *Immigration and social change in the Republic of Ireland*. Manchester: Manchester University Press.

Mahler, M. (1977). *Separation-Individuation: Selected papers of Margaret S. Mahler*. New York: Aronson.

Markus, H., & Nurius, P. (1986). Possible selves. *American Psychologist*, *41*, 954–969. http://www.flipkart.com/book/separation-individuation-margaret-mahler-selected/1568212240/margaret-s-mahler/5

Naidoo, L. (2007). Renegotiating identity and reconciling cultural ambiguity in the Indian immigrant community in Sydney Australia. *Anthropological Special Issue*, *2*, 53–66.

Ní Laoire, C., Bushin, N., Carpena-Mendez, F., & White, A. (2009). *Tell me about yourself: Migrant children's experiences of moving to and living in Ireland*. Cork: University College Cork, Ireland.

Orellana, M. F., Thorne, B., Chee, A., & Lam, W. S. E. (2001). Transnational childhoods: The participation of children in processes of family migration. *Social Problems*, *48*(4), 572–591.

Pigeon, N. (1996). Grounded theory: Theoretical background. In John T. E. Richardson (Ed.), *Handbook of qualitative research for psychology and the social sciences* (pp. 79–85). Oxford: Wiley Blackwell.

Rawlings, W. (1998). Writing about friendship matters: A case study in dialectical and dialogical inquiry. In B. Montgomery & L. Baxter (Eds.), *Dialectical approaches to studying personal relationships*. London: Psychology Press.

Robinson, L. (2009). Cultural identity and acculturation preferences among South Asian adolescents in Britain: An exploratory study. *Children & Society*, *23*, 442–454.

Sabatier, C. (2008). Ethnic and national identity among second-generation immigrant adolescents in France: The role of social context and family. *Journal of Adolescence*, *31*, 185–205.

Talbani, A., & Hasanali, P. (2000). Adolescent females between tradition and modernity: Gender role socialization in South Asian immigrant culture. *Journal of Adolescence*, *23*, 615–627.

Angela Veale and Emily Kennedy
Department of Applied Psychology
University College Cork

PART 2: IMMIGRATION, EDUCATION AND SCHOOLING

DYMPNA DEVINE

5. SECURING MIGRANT CHILDREN'S EDUCATIONAL WELL-BEING

Perspectives on Policy and Practice in Irish Schools

INTRODUCTION

Internationally increasing attention is being given to children's well-being as nation states recognise the value of investment in children for long term sustainability and economic development (Unicef, 2009). The renewed focus on children's well-being is also underpinned by a recognition of children's rights as outlined in the United Nations Convention on the Rights of the Child (1989), not only to a safe, healthy and fulfilling childhood, but also one in which their views and perspectives on matters which directly affect them are taken into account. Education continually emerges as a key factor influencing children's well-being and comparative research across countries globally (e.g. PISA studies OECD, 2006) highlights substantial differences in children's education outcomes. Migrant children emerge consistently as one group around which there is cause for concern, yet basic accounts of 'outcomes' on a narrow range of indicators (typically maths, science and literacy) fail to capture the complexity of children's responses to their learning, nor to the factors and processes which give rise to different experiences of educational well-being, broadly defined. Furthermore, in spite of the increasing recognition being given to children to be involved in decisions about their lives, education systems appear slow to embrace the idea of real and meaningful engagement with children about their educational experiences (Devine, 2003). This is then another key element of their educational 'well-being' and has very explicit consequences for children, such as those from an immigrant background, who may differ from the cultural and social norms which predominate in schools. This chapter highlights not only migrant children's perspectives but also how they actively construct and contribute to processes of integration, accommodation (and indeed assimilation) through their work in schools. It argues that securing migrant children's educational well-being involves not only focusing on skills acquisition in the areas of English language, but fundamentally on providing such children with an experience of education which recognises the totality of their personal, social and cultural background. It also involves recognising and being sensitive to the complex processes of positioning, negotiation and identity formation which migrant children undergo in adjusting to their lives both inside and outside of school. Two central themes are developed, related to the experience of learning and how this is influenced not only by issues

Darmody, Tyrrell, Song (eds.), The Changing Faces of Ireland: Exploring the Lives of Immigrant and Ethnic Minority Children, 73–87.

related to class, gender and age, but also the desire to manage their ethnic identities. This latter is developed further with respect to social and racial dynamics in schools.

CHILDREN, MIGRATION AND SCHOOLING

Children's educational well-being is influenced by a range of factors, including the actions of adult stakeholders (parents, teachers, principals) who shape the trajectory of their lives (Devine, forthcoming). Such shaping is of course itself dependent on broader structural dynamics in society, most especially related to class, race and gender – creating different dynamics and modes of reaction/interaction locally in schools and communities. Children's well-being is also influenced by how they themselves interpret and experience what happens to them. Gaining insights into children's own perspectives provides a clear indicator of the impact of policy and practices in schools, as well as the skills and complex negotiations migrant children must draw upon in order to cope with school. Consistently what emerges in the emerging research in this area is the absence of deep and meaningful engagement with the perspectives and values of minority ethnic children and youth, that is reflected in an a-critical approach to multi-cultural education (Banks, 2009; Modood, 2007). While there is some research on minority ethnic pupils' perspectives on the curriculum and learning (e.g. Archer and Francis, 2007; Chan, 2007), studies of first generation immigrant children's voices in relation to schooling are rare, with the exception of research on the area of refugee children (e.g. Rutter, 2006) and recent work here in Ireland such as that of Ní Laoire et al. (2009) and other work reflected in this volume.

THEORISING MIGRANT CHILDREN'S PERSPECTIVES:
AGENCY, IDENTITIES AND BELONGING

For the newly arrived migrant child, learning to adjust to the school situation, become familiar with new subjects and languages, as well as try to negotiate relations with peers provides a difficult set of challenges which they must overcome. Such challenges are coupled with those which may also prevail in the wider community as the immigrant family seeks accommodation and work, often in the context of split families and differentiated access to financial, cultural and social supports (Devine, forthcoming). In considering how migrant children perceive and experience their education, my analysis is informed by constructs of children as competent and agentic, framing their identities in hybrid and multiple ways (Butler, 1993). It is also informed by an assumption that learning is not simply a cognitive event – it is also a social process that is embedded in the relationships we form with one another (Vygotsky, 1978). It involves a complex set of dispositions that draw not only on some predefined 'ability' or readiness to learn, but also on sensitivity to the responses we get from others – teachers, parents and peers, in relation to our learning. This is especially so with children.

The concept of social and cultural capital (Bourdieu, 1986) is especially pertinent in discussions about schooling and the experiences of migrant children (Devine, 2009). Yet within adult-centred perspectives and analyses, children are typically portrayed as receptors of adult capitals (Morrow, 1999; Holland et al., 2007). Migrant children are constructed as the carriers of their parent's hopes and expectations for achievement and success in the receiving society. Simultaneously they represent the mechanism used by the State, through the work of teachers, in assimilating into the norms of the host society. In this sense children are also constructed as the targets for adult intervention, both at home and at school. An inter-generational perspective however highlights the social competency of children and of how through their participation in school children mobilise the social and cultural capital of the family, facilitating processes of economic and social development (Devine, 2009; Morrow, 1999). This is not a simple process however. Migrant children 'have' to go to school and 'integrate' in a way in which their migrant parents do not. Their sense of themselves and their place in school is influenced by the broader society which 'shapes' them according to certain norms. As active managers of their social identities, children negotiate and perform their identities in a manner which is certainly mediated by their gender, class and ethnicity, but also by the specific context or locale in which the interaction takes place (Devine, 2007). Children are not cultural 'dupes' to be moulded unquestioningly into the 'adult' (be it parent or teacher) way of doing things. For many a tension exists as they straddle diverse worlds, seeking approval and recognition from teachers and parents, while simultaneously retaining status and recognition from peers. Participation in child and youth cultures brings with it relief and autonomy from the constraints and obligations of formal schooling, but challenges vulnerabilities in relation to the assertion of 'self', 'otherness', 'belongingness' and recognition in relations with peers. In this scenario the situation for migrant children is especially challenging.

The remainder of this chapter presents some findings from research I have been involved with in a range of primary and secondary schools over the past ten years. It does so with respect to two main themes. The first relates to the strategic mobilization of capitals through children's learning while the second details children's perspectives on social and racial dynamics in schools.

MOBILIZING CAPITALS THROUGH CHILDREN'S LEARNING

A number of key themes consistently emerged from interviews with migrant children in relation to how they positioned themselves with respect to the learning environment in school. These related to the significance of language to the learning process, adjusting and accommodating to the curriculum in Irish schools, and the resources and support they would like in order to do well in school. Reflecting both a strategic and pragmatic approach to schooling, students consistently spoke about their desire to achieve and make the most of the opportunities to do well in school. For some this was linked to specific ambitions expressed by their parents, for others it was about having skills they could use if they returned to their 'home' countries:

Interviewer: Is it good for children to come to a different country?

Andrew: Yes. When they go back to their own country, they'll be different… they'll be smarter (Lithuanian boy, Riverview primary)

I won't say we have a great life, we don't. But for those who want to try…we believe we can make more, study, have an education (Rwandan boy, Bellview secondary)

The desire to do well was, in many (but not all) cases influenced by the children's own classed positioning. Martha, a Muslim girl whose Syrian parents were both professionals, displayed a strong sense of entitlement and confidence in relation to her integration into Irish society. She was ambitious to enter politics and achieve the highest political standing as a woman, keen to assert her place in Irish history!

First I wanted to be the President but then Mr Murphy [teacher] told me that I should be the first female Taoiseach [prime minister] so I am planning to be the first female Taoiseach and then the President… my parents are supporting me in wanting to be the President (Oakleaf primary)

This sense of expectation and valuing of education consistently emerged across all interviews and while it can be attributed to high education levels among the children's parents (Devine 2011), this was not always the case. The children's families were clearly differentiated in terms of both the social, economic and cultural resources they could draw upon, evident for example from the children's own different experiences of access to extra-curricular activities and participation in cultural and social events at weekends. It has been difficult to make generalisations about the class positioning of different immigrant groups in the study schools, given the diversity of occupations within groups themselves.[1] As Anthias (2010) notes, traditional classed, gendered and ethnic binaries do not map easily to transnational mobilities in modern global economies. Nonetheless, the very decision to migrate, as well as capacity to do so, is indicative of 'goal directed' activity that is centred on working actively toward improving familial life chances, which will in itself be reflected in positive orientations and work effort in school.

Gender dynamics were also significant to the children's positioning as learners. For boys especially, a tension had to be managed between competing constructs of masculinity, compounded in working class schools where hegemonic masculinities (centred on sporting prowess rather than academic success) prevailed. This tension is reflected in the comments of Mahmoud (see below), as he struggles not to appear 'too good' contrary to the constructs of masculinity operating among his (working class indigenous Irish) friends, while simultaneously not doing 'too bad' given his parents' expectations that he do well in school. What is also of significance is how he draws on his construction as a migrant as a basis for potential teasing:

I used to do maths really fast but now I do it sort of slow… like not the first to finish cos some children they say you are trying to show off just because you are from a different country. [Other children agree]: 'just because we are trying to do our best' (Mixed gender group, Oakleaf primary)

For girls, the tension around how they positioned themselves related to contrasting constructs of femininity in terms of appropriate 'rules' for dress, freedom to roam (especially after school) and romance relations with boys.

With respect to language, the acquisition of fluency was something that was mentioned by students whose first language was not English and its relevance to engaging with the curriculum to a level and standard they sought. All of the children received some form of EAL [English as an additional language] support, but this seemed to be relatively ad-hoc in second level, more structured in the primary school:

> The grammar is so hard. We're always making mistakes. We do have extra English, but we don't find the TEFL teacher good (Vietnamese junior girl, Parkway college)

For children whose mother tongue was not English, the additional work they had to do in order to achieve well in school was evident from the language or 'code' switching (Cummins, 2001) they engaged in as they sought to master the material they were learning across a range of subjects. An additional challenge for students was learning the Irish language,[2] which most seemed to talk about in a positive way. While Irish was perceived as an additive extra rather than core to the children's success in the Irish system, it did have cultural and symbolic value. Their proficiency in speaking and learning Irish was reflective of a willingness to adapt to the 'rules' of schooling in Ireland, as well as to take on board distinctly 'Irish' traditions:

> I don't have to do it but it is my choice cos I like it (Salma, Saudi Arabia, Oakleaf primary)

For older students in second level schools, a more circumspect view was evident, that tied in with more specific constructs of their own national/ethnic identity as 'non-Irish':

> The Irish students seem to think it's not fair that we don't learn Irish…I think it's fair enough because we already have our own language 'cos we come from our own country with our own life but I know we live in Ireland culture and we to have learn their rules and laws (5th year Kosovo, Spireview girls Secondary)

In taking account of these challenges the students placed considerable priority on their relationships with their teachers, as they were perceived as the primary sources of support and information for learning. Listening to the older secondary school students, it was clear that their positive behaviour was rooted in patterns of inter-generational relations in their home country centred on respect for adult authority, most often mentioned by girls, as well as an appreciation of their opportunity to learn in Irish schools:

> I think the manners and the education is a bit different here…they really don't respect the teachers…they don't appreciate that they are being taught like…they take it for granted…too much freedom (Malaysian girl, 5th year, Spireview secondary)

However this could be a double-edged sword, as their relative silent demeanour in the classroom ensured that they could feel overlooked by their teachers and less likely to get the support they needed. Our own subsequent observation of teacher practices in schools has confirmed a tendency for less engaged teaching with such children in mainstream classrooms, especially where there are a higher number of immigrant students present (Devine et al., 2010). A related issue concerned the view that migrant students felt they were not pressed upon to do better in school, a factor which could be reinforced by being placed in a lower stream in second level, the absence of provision of instruction during 'free' periods when other students were learning 'Irish' or a class below their age level in primary school:

> Sometimes you don't have something to do in Irish class. I don't know maybe reading, or we don't know much about computers, or typing... (Mark, Nigerian, Bellview boys secondary)

> It's not easy, we also need to be taught... but sometimes we need more help (Peter, Polish, Riverview primary)

With respect to the curriculum, secondary school students critiqued the absence of a broader focus in subjects such as history and geography. Inevitably their experiences were rooted in what they had learned in their home country, but also concerns over level of preparedness for State examinations in Ireland:

> Our geography teacher writes notes basically on Europe and America, Ireland and England. In history we've done Ireland, England, Europe and America (Leaving Cert, Rwanda, Bellview boys)

> We have dreams but it's kind of hard to achieve them...and in the leaving certificate exams...they don't know the paper, its not from an ordinary Irish person...that makes it hard (Ukrainian, 5th year student, Spireview girls secondary)

Students at this level also voiced concerns about the impact of this Eurocentric focus on indigenous Irish students in terms of their awareness of cultures other than their own. Their comments link not only to the diasporic identities of many of these migrant students, but also their positive attitudes toward globalisation and multicultural identities:

> Andreus: They [Irish students] say: where are you from? And I say 'Moldova' and they say where is that? And I ask where do you think it is and they say 'Africa'! (Junior Cert boy, Ashleaf college)

> Interviewer: Is it good there are lots of people from different countries?

> Natasha: Yes. You get to know about other countries and other religions...it's kind of like fruits. If you only had banana, you wouldn't know what kiwis and oranges tasted like (Iraq, Oakleaf primary)

WHO IS' (SE) NORMAL, WHO '(SE) CULTURE?

However there is a tension in this issue of cultural recognition that is underpinned by processes of inclusion, exclusion and belonging for these students. We see this more clearly in the following excerpt from an interview with one group of immigrant students in Spireview girls' secondary school, although similar issues arose in a number of other schools. In an attempt to embrace cultural diversity, the school had initiated a 'cultural celebration' day in which all 'foreign national' students were invited to come up on the school stage, in front of the entire school, dressed in their national dress to speak about their culture. Reflecting the unintended consequences of the exercise of power at capillary level (Foucault, 1979), the initiative highlighted the 'otherness' of many of these students, mirroring the concept of the 'tourist curriculum' approach to cultural diversity that is often employed by schools (May, 2009). While the intention behind such initiatives may be positive, they also increase the tendency of highlighting the difference and 'otherness' of minority students, especially when the majority culture is not similarly put on 'display'. The contrasting perception of these events by the majority 'we' and minority 'them' is succinctly reflected in the voices of the young people themselves below:

> Student 1: Well last term we had the culture day...people from different countries would dress up in their own costume and say where they were from and...it was good

> Dympna: Did you get up and say where you came from?

> Student 1: No it wasn't us...it was the girls from the foreign countries...there was actually loads wasn't there [emphasis added]

> Dympna: Would you have liked to get up on the stage and talk about where you come from?

> Student 2: No it was only for the cultureds...everybody knows me. (Majority ethnic, seniors, Spireview girls Secondary)

Viewed from the perspective of the migrant students, this event highlighted the tension they feel between visibility and invisibility in school. While they were not overtly critical of such events, recognising the effort the school was making to be 'inclusive', queries were raised as to the effectiveness in improving cultural tolerance in the absence of direct instruction about tolerance of difference:

> They [indigenous Irish] don't really learn like...we had a mixed show and you say where you are from and I got up and I said I was from Trinidad and then I got off the stage and someone said; 'so what part of Jamaica are you from' and: 'say something funny' (Group interview, Spireview girls secondary)

In essence their perspectives query the rhetoric of inclusion, when it is not supplemented by real and meaningful engagement with the substantive exclusionary processes and practices which can permeate school life (Bryan, 2010; Kitching, 2010). Further, a number of students in other schools signalled that while they saw value in indigenous Irish students learning about their cultures, they wanted to be treated the same as their majority peers:

> Dympna: Do you think other students should be made aware of your cultures, if the school drew attention to your culture, like some schools have a cultural day?

> Student 1: What I'd prefer that if they teach them projects on how to accept them... we just want to be treated the same

Student 1: The thing is the school can teach but education really comes from your own family. There should be a course for parents as well. (Vietnamese, male, senior class, Parkway College)

Younger children also displayed a certain ambiguity around whether or not specifics of their culture and background should be highlighted in school. Cultural validation appeared to be a strong component in the support that was provided to these children in their activities with the language support teachers. Taking place away from the 'mainstream' classroom, this may have been a 'safer' place for the children to engage with their culture and background. Nonetheless, it is this very 'separation' which reinforces the notion that diversity education is about and for the minority 'them' rather than also about and for the majority 'us'. The children's perspectives were also influenced by their ethnic background, as well as personal experiences (related to trauma and separation) and the extent to which they differed from the Irish norm. Children from Africa and Asia were most circumspect:

I would not like her to talk about my language and country because I have to think back every time. I don't like answering questions. (Francis, 5th class boy, Sierra Leone, Riverview Primary)

I would tell them songs and the way we dance, but we dance funny dances and they might laugh at me. They might think it's something disgusting. (Georgia, Nigerian girl, Sea view primary)

Implicit in the children's perspectives was the 'use' and 'exchange value' (Bourdieu, 1986) of cultural recognition for all children, as part of the general process of cultural/capital accumulation in the class, rather than as an extra for celebration and display. Where the children saw authentic engagement with their cultures and identities and the teacher was clearly comfortable with it, then they also felt at ease. In one of the field trips, for example to Oakleaf primary, this was reflected when a missionary nun came to visit the school and spoke effortlessly to some of the children in Arabic:

Dympna: So what's that like when someone comes in and speaks like that [in your own language]?

Sarah: Cool! [Laughs] and she is Irish!.. it makes you feel very comfortable. (Group interview, Oakleaf primary).

Undercutting the children's experiences were not only dynamics related to gender and social class but also patterns of belonging and separateness that derived from their ethnic/cultural identities and desired levels of visibility/invisibility in school. This was also a key issue in the negotiation of peer relations in school.

SOCIAL AND RACIAL DYNAMICS IN CHILDREN'S PEER RELATIONS: MOBILIZING SOCIAL CAPITAL

There is considerable research which highlights the complex dynamics that underpin children and young people's relations with one another, patterns which become strongly embedded in relationships in the adolescent years (Troyna and Hatcher, 1992; Gaganakis, 2006). Across my own research in primary schools, it was clear that a varied pattern existed, with a blend of core ethnic groupings in some classes (consisting for example of a pairing or threesome of one ethnic group) combined with an inter-mingling of minority/majority ethnic children in other friendship groups. Of note however were Roma children, clustered in Riverside Primary school[3] who were consistently observed in the school yard as playing together, or standing on their own by the school wall. Further, Muslim children in Oakleaf Primary, especially a number of girls, also tended to cluster together in paired groupings. In secondary schools, evidence of inter-ethnic friendships was more sparse, with a clearer demarcation of student friendships along ethnic lines, that was especially evident in the clustering of students during break times. For their part, a mixed response was evident among the second-level sample of students in relation to their levels of interaction and integration with indigenous Irish peers. While some spoke of having made friends in school, others identified difficulties in making 'deep friendships':

> I think, it's not that you can't make deep friends out of them, but it takes a long time for them to get used to you and it takes a long time for us to get used to them. (Tanzanian, female, Ashleaf College)

Where some of these students mentioned their difficulty in making friends with their indigenous Irish peers, their feeling of relative isolation, especially after school was notable:

> I've been here for one year now, and I can say everybody here is having an Irish friend, but it's in the school… we have friends here, we have friends in our class but I wouldn't know what they think sometimes…They don't know anything about black, anything about me, they don't feel comfortable inviting me to their house. (Rwandan senior student, Bellview Boys Secondary)

The experience of racism and exclusion in peer relationships is influenced by constructs of difference/sameness that operate in children's social and cultural worlds (Devine et al., 2006; 2008). It is the perception and experience of difference/sameness which leads to stronger bonding between children of the same ethnic/migrant background, while simultaneously making it difficult to 'bridge' with students from other ethnic groups. Children of all ages spoke of this experience of 'otherness' and sense of being different which proved challenging for them:

> Student: Some students see us as some kind of freaks or something.

> Interviewer: How do they show that?

> Student: Wink in the first place, more psychological. I can see it in their faces. (Mixed interview group, Bellview boys secondary)

What is important to bear in mind is that inclusion/exclusion and sameness/difference operates along a graduated continuum giving rise to some fluidity of movement across groups that signals caution in overly simplistic analyses of children's friendship patterns. Children's social world is embedded in identity work, as they position and reposition themselves, drawing on discourses related to gender, sexuality, dis/ability, social class and ethnicity in their relations with one another. For example, intensive case study analysis of friendship patterns in Oakleaf primary indicated intra-ethnic tensions between three Muslim girls and the subsequent positioning of Karina as more like her indigenous Irish peers in terms of dress, taste, and modes of self presentation (Devine and Kelly, 2006). In contrast, Salma positions herself more clearly with her Muslim/Arabic peers:

> I'm a Muslim but my Mum was brought up not wearing scarves and all the Muslims jeer me because I'm not like them … Sometimes I wear scarves when I go to the Mosque. Since me and Karla use to be friends because we are both Muslims and everyone used to think we had loads of things in common. (Karina, Syria, Oakleaf primary)

> First I didn't know where I belong…now I only like to be friends with Arabs cos I tried to be friends with Irish but it just didn't work…they have really different stuff they do that we don't do [especially for girls]. (Salma, Palestine, Oakleaf primary)

For boys, affiliation to sport proved important in friendship patterns irrespective of ethnic/immigrant status, although the latter could be used as a basis for racist name calling on the sports field:

> Please people who are listening to this, pick up some sport or you get slagged. You have to be good at sport. (Marcus, Libya, Oakleaf primary)

> Racism mainly takes place in sport…sometimes white people are picked first or if a coloured person hacked you or side tackled you then you could give them a punch. (Tony, majority ethnic boy, Oakleaf primary)

All of the children had a practical/grounded understanding of racism (both cultural and colour based) that was not so evident in the more incomplete and disconnected (Peck et al., 2008) narratives of their indigenous Irish peers. This racial tension was most explicitly felt by children who came from Asia or Africa, evident in the narrative of this mother (from Pakistan) who spoke of having to remove her son from his previous primary school because of the racial abuse he was subjected to by one child. In referring to this colour based racism, what is significant is how she links her son's feelings to 'ownership' (they don't feel they own the place) and feeling 'out of place' because of his 'difference':

> My son had a problem with a boy who always called him 'black' and stuff like that and mentally he tortured him so much. So usually he would come to me to ask me, "Am I very black?" It's very obvious that he is not from Ireland. So, they feel that they are not comfortable with their environment, and they don't feel they own the place (Parkistani mother)

At secondary level, aspects of youth culture (dress, going out, relative freedom – especially for girls), coupled with the high level of 'slagging' that is typical of adolescent groups, especially among boys, created difficulties for some students to integrate socially. Issues of both ethnic identity as well as social class influenced these experiences. In Spireview girls secondary for example, 'the attitude' of Martha from Zimbabwe, was interpreted by her as a reason for racism directed against her and which she responded to in a defiant manner, that included fighting back:

> Sonia: I think it's not fair that they come to you and shout at you… because if you are a nice person it doesn't matter what colour you are...and I was passing by the lockers and Martha was walking along and a first year kicked her and I was 'what? What are you doing?'
>
> Interviewer: And why was Martha being kicked?
>
> Tara: Because she has attitude
>
> Dympna: Martha has attitude?
>
> Martha: No, but when I am talking to my friends I have a different attitude than when I am talking to them (Irish girls)….if they talk to me in that way I won't allow it cos they call me a mean nigger….and they can't just call me that for fun…I don't take it that way…and if you don't stand up to them they just see you as a fool. (Mixed African, females, junior class, Spireview Girls Secondary)

Class dynamics were also at play here, Martha's 'attitude' undoubtedly linked to her own positioning from a diplomatic family background that perhaps gave her the confidence to stand up for herself when racially abused. Her experience of racism however underlies the additional 'work' that is required because she is black in order to retain her class position, especially in a context where she is attending a mixed social class school. A similar situation was identified in a primary school with respect to Ava, a Nigerian girl who also was teased because of her overt confidence and 'being good' at Irish (Devine et al., 2008). Minority ethnic, especially non-white children, are at continual risk of racial abuse and it was something that all were aware of and sensitive to. This is not to suggest it was a pervasive aspect of their lives in school, yet it was clear that racialised dynamics most especially came into play when minority children became 'more visible', unsettling existing status hierarchies in the classroom. Confident, assertive minority ethnic children were especially at risk of racial abuse because in their 'attitude' they have queried (and resisted) their minoritized positioning. In this sense they have crossed over normative boundaries to remain relatively invisible, in spite of/or because of their 'visible' difference. Standing up for oneself, putting oneself 'out there' can be a threat to 'our own' and derives from insider/outsider status that is a challenge for migrant children to negotiate.

Similar experiences emerged for young people from the Vietnamese community in Parkway College, a number of whom had been born in Ireland, or who had attended primary school in Ireland, yet still remained 'on the outside'. The disjuncture between their family and school lives is evident in Lee's comment below:

> You can't talk about yourself or your culture, you have to hide it. It's like living another life. (Vietnamese, Senior level, Parkway college)

Some of these students spoke of their frustration with the stereotypes they faced in relation to being 'foreign' that ranged from 'not having a sense of humour' to being seen to be abusers of the 'system'. This was more evident in interviews with secondary school students, whose reaction to such stereotyping was often a desire to position themselves academically in school:

> I want to do well in school...get a good job and more money. We're being slagged now but that would make us happy, proud if we did well in our exams. (Vietnamese, male, senior class, Parkway College)

> One day I was sitting somewhere and the cleaner came downstairs and... knocked my glasses from the desk and they got broken. All she said was: 'Oh the social will replace them'. She is invariably telling me now that whatever I am today, is the 'social'...which is not proper, as a matter of fact. What it does seem as a statement is what impression she has of me. (Rhwandan, senior class, Bellview Boys Secondary)

Perceptions must also be understood in the context of broader community class dynamics. Students spoke of the tensions they experienced, most especially in marginalised urban communities where competition for resources is scarce and lack of trust, that is essential for building strong social capital, is evident:

> There are too many immigrants [in this area]. They [Irish] think the government is going to feel sorry for them all [immigrants]. They'll lose out and they are afraid of immigrants taking over. (Polish boy, Bellview boys secondary)

Neither should it be assumed that the experience of racism occurs only between majority/minority ethnic groups, or indeed that 'whiteness' conveys automatic privilege, which in relation to for example Traveller children is clearly not the case (Devine et al., 2008). Notwithstanding these challenges, there was also evidence of strong friendship bonds between migrant children and their indigenous Irish peers and this led to forms of social capital which enabled them to cope better with life in school. In secondary schools, it was opportunities often outside of the formal curriculum – participation in team sporting and social events which facilitated more authentic social engagement. In Ashleaf college for example, the work of the student council in putting together a fashion show allowed a blending of diverse traditions (a form of cultural hybridity) signalling what could happen when the students themselves worked on creating hybrid forms of being and doing:

> Student: We have fashion shows. Not only to involve European fashion shows but we could also involve African things like...but we can use even modern things, we can also even use entertaining things, to mix the Irish and the African styles

> Interviewer: Not just to mix the traditions but also to mix the modern African and the modern Irish.

> Pupils (all): Yeah! Yeah! (Mixed ethnic group, females, Ashleaf College)

CONCLUDING DISCUSSION

This chapter has documented issues which were to the forefront of the children's experience in school: the impact on their friendships, the opportunities created for wider learning (about themselves and others) as well as broader questions related to the dynamics of power and control in their relations with others that was influenced by perceptions of and attitudes toward cultural and ethnic difference. The strong motivation the migrant children and youth displayed toward learning and achieving well in school can be understood in terms not only of their immigrant status, but also the influence of family social background and expectations on the part of their parents that they do well in school[4]. However in most instances, the children's struggle to integrate into their schools was their own – they did so often in the absence of parent's knowledge of the Irish school system as well as lack of fluency in English. Through their school activities the children were acquiring new forms of knowledge (cultural capitals) with the intention of improving their own life-chances, as well as that of their entire family. The general ambitiousness to do well was evident in their desire for continual focused instruction and correction from their teachers, as well as a willingness to learn and adapt to 'Irish' ways of doing things. The children were, for the most part, reluctant to be critical of their experiences of teaching and learning, appreciative of the efforts being made by schools. This is indicative perhaps not only of their minoritized position as migrant 'others' (and the power imbalances this implies) but also of culturally embedded inter-generational patterns which foreclosed criticism of what teachers, as adults, were doing.

What is evident also is that there are as many differences between immigrant children as there are similarities, suggesting that a one size fits all approach to diversity in schools is not sufficient. Neither is 'diversity' about and for immigrant children, rather it is embedded in all children's lifeworld in school and should be taken as normative in itself. A range of identity signifiers related to, for example age, gender, social class, ethnicity, dis/ability and sexuality intersect as children position and reposition themselves in their relations with teachers, peers and parents. Recognition is key however to the children's educational well-being – in terms of visibility as persons with a voice to be heard and expressed, as well as in being validated and meaningfully supported in their efforts at work and play in school.

NOTES

[1] If we consider the Nigerian group for example, some worked within the IT sector, while others worked as Taxi drivers, others had come through the asylum process and were still waiting for their applications to be processed.

[2] Irish is compulsory in schools, but students over the age of 12 years who have not been resident in Ireland up to that point are entitled to a dispensation.

[3] More in-depth analysis of these patterns is provided in Devine and Kelly 2006.

[4] These are interlinked in complex ways. Ability to migrate to a country in itself demonstrates social and cultural capital on the parts of parents to access knowledge in relation the host country and finds the means and resources to travel there.

REFERENCES

Anthias, F. (2010). *Intersections and translocations: New paradigms for thinking about identities and inequalities*. European Conference of Educational Research, University of Helsinki.

Archer, L., & Francis, B. (2007). *Understanding minority ethnic achievement*. London: RoutledgeFalmer Press.

Banks, J. (Ed.). (2009). *The Routledge international companion to multicultural education*. New York: Routledge.

Bourdieu, P. (1986). The forms of capital. In J. G. Richardson (Ed.). *Handbook of theory and research for the sociology of education* (pp. 46–58). New York: Greenwood Press.

Bryan, A. (2010). Corporate multiculturalism, diversity management, and positive interculturalism in Irish schools and society. *Irish Educational Studies, 29*(3), 253–269.

Butler, J. (1993). *Bodies that matter: on the discursive limits of 'sex'*. London: Routledge.

Chan, E. (2007). Student experiences of a culturally sensitive curriculum: Ethnic identity development amid conflicting stories to live by. *Journal of Curriculum Studies, 39*(2), 177–194.

Connolly, P. (1998). *Racism, gender identities and young children*. London: Routledge.

Crul, M., & Holdaway, J. (2009). Children of immigrants in schools in New York and Amsterdam: The factors shaping attainment. *Teachers College Record, 111*(6), 1476–1507.

Cummins, J. (2001). Empowering minority students – A framework for intervention. *Harvard Educational Review, 71*(4), 656–676.

Devine, D. (2003). *Children, power and schooling*. Stoke-On-Trent, Trentham Books.

Devine, D. (2007). Immigration and the enlargement of children's social space in school. In H. Zeiher, Devine, D. Kjorholt, A. Strandell, & H. Odense (Eds.), *Flexible Childhood? Exploring children's welfare in time and space*. University Press of Southern Denmark.

Devine, D. (2009). Mobilising capitals? Migrant children's negotiation of their everyday lives in schools. *British Journal of Sociology of Education, 30*(5), 521–535.

Devine, D. (forthcoming, 2011). *Immigration and schooling in Ireland – Making a difference?* Manchester: Manchester University Press.

Devine, D., & Kelly, M. (2006). I just don't want to get picked on by anybody: Dynamics of inclusion and exclusion in a newly multi-ethnic Irish primary school. *Children & Society, 20*(2), 128–139.

Devine, D., & Kenny, M., et al. (2008). Naming the 'other': Children's construction and experience of racisms in Irish primary schools. *Race, Ethnicity & Education, 11*(4), 369–385.

Devine, D., Fahie, D., MacGillicuddy, D., MacRuairc, G., & Harford, J. (2010). *Report on the use of ISTOF (International System for Teacher Observation and Feedback) - Challenges, issues and teacher effect*. Dublin: School of Education, UCD.

Evergeti, V., & Zontini, E. (2006). Introduction: Some critical reflections on social capital, migration and transnational families. *Ethnic and Racial Studies, 29*(6), 1025–1039.

Foucault, M. (1979). *Discipline and punish: the birth of the prison*. New York, Vintage Books.

Gaganakis, M. (2006). Identity construction in adolescent girls: The context dependency of racial and gendered perceptions. *Gender and Education, 18*(4), 361–379.

Holland, J., Reynolds, T., & Weller, S. (2007). Transitions, networks and communities: The significance of social capital in the lives of children and young people. *Journal of Youth Studies, 10*(1), 97–116.

James, A., & James, A. (2004). *Constructing childhood: Theory policy and social practice*. New York: Palgrave.

Kitching, K. (2010). An excavation of the racialised politics of viability underpinning education policy in Ireland. *Irish Educational Studies, 29*(3), 213–229.

May, S. (2009). Critical multiculturalism and education. In J. Banks (Ed.), *The Routledge international readers in multicultural education*. New York: Routledge.

Modood, T. (2007). *Multiculturalism: A civic idea*. Cambridge: Polity Press.

Morrow, G. (1999). Conceptualising social capital in relation to the well-being of children and young people: A critical review. *Sociological Review, 4*(4), 744–765.

Ni Laoire, C., Bushin, N., Carpena-Mendez, F., & White, A. (2009). *Tell me about yourself - Migrant children's experiences of moving to and living in Ireland*. Cork: University College.

OECD. (2006). *Where immigrants succeed - A comparative review of performance and engagement in PISA 2003*. Paris: Author.

Peck, C. S. A., & Donaldson, S (2008). Unreached and unreasonable: Curriculum standards and children's understanding of ethnic diversity in Canada. *Journal of Curriculum Inquiry, 38*(1), 63–92.

Rutter, J. (2006). *Refugee children in the UK*. Maidenhead: Open University Press.

Troyna, B. A., & Hatcher, R. (1992). *Racism in children's lives – A study of mainly-white primary schools.* London: Routledge.

UNICEF. (2009). *The state of the world's children.* New York: United Nations.

Vygotsky, L. (1978). *Mind in society – The development of higher psychological processes.* London: Harvard University Press.

Dr Dympna Devine
University College Dublin
Ireland

KARL KITCHING

6. THE MOBILITY OF RACISM IN EDUCATION

Contested Discourses and New Migrant Subjectivities in Irish Schooling

INTRODUCTION

Racism is an ideology which is continually changing, being challenged, interrupted and reconstructed, and which often appears in contradictory forms. As such, its reproduction in schools, and elsewhere, can be expected to be complex, multifaceted and historically specific (Rizvi, 1993, p. 15).

The purpose of this chapter is to discuss and analyse the interplay of potentially racist, common sense, and anti-racist understandings around and between 'new migrant' and 'indigenous' students and teachers in one Irish post-primary school. Taking inspiration from Rizvi (1993), this focus serves as a means of being vigilant to the mobility and multi-faceted nature of both overtly racist ideas and well-intentioned actions that may have racist effects. The first section of the chapter discusses national and international research on institutional racism, focusing on schools in particular. It notes how, despite decades of research evidence of institutional racism, official 'intercultural' and 'anti-racist' stances in institutions can constantly become diluted to racist effect, both as a result of wider state measures and shifting, exclusionary meaning making. School marginalisation is often rendered through 'common sense' understandings about immigration, citizenship and educational participation in schools. It is repeatedly crystallized through the rendering of students in racialised achievement hierarchies internationally.

Given such a complex climate, the second section argues that the unexpectedly exclusionary effects of previous attempts to tackle racist outcomes through research might lead us to adopt more nuanced, open-ended approach to 'knowledge production'. An analysis of the multiple potential meanings and desirable/undesirable subjective locations taken up, newly created, and strategically resisted in one Dublin post-primary school is then pursued, using post-structural discourse analysis. Drawing upon several brief school moments, I demonstrate the mobility of meaning-making processes, and show how minority and majority ethnic school subjects (i.e., students and their teachers) constantly work to include and exclude learners and peers on terms that may be maintained or may change. In light of this analysis, it is argued that space must be created within the Irish school system to critically interrogate the interplay of old and new meanings of 'race' and racism, with and through already recognised forms of inequality. Such a space should allow for schools, teachers and students to deconstruct how desirable and undesirable subjectivities are rendered in continuous ways, by examining everyday, context-bound practices of identity.

Darmody, Tyrrell, Song (eds.), The Changing Faces of Ireland: Exploring the Lives of Immigrant and Ethnic Minority Children, 89–104.

ONGOING PROBLEMS WITH THE RECOGNITION OF INSTITUTIONAL RACISM

Research has demonstrated several ways in which barriers are enacted at structural-institutional level for new migrant and minority ethnic groups in Ireland, and how failures to support these groups repeatedly occur. The recent accounts include barriers in accessing higher education and training (Linehan and Hogan, 2008), marked failures for asylum-seeking children (Fanning, Veale and O'Connor, 2001), difficult relationships for Travellers, Nigerians and Muslims with the Gardaí (Ionann, 2004), problems within the criminal justice system (Culleton, 2007), and ongoing failure by local authorities to provide adequate accommodation for Travellers (Watt and Charles, 2009).

Mainstream policy discourses in Ireland have a limited history of recognising institutionally racist processes in schools. Moreover, such discourses persistently fail to define the exclusion of Travellers from educational participation and achievement as a form of systematic racism (Kenny, 1997). In curricular texts, anti-Traveller biases are often referred to in terms of 'discrimination' or 'prejudice' rather than racism (Bryan, 2007). But while Irish educational research has made scant direct reference to 'race' historically, important critical perspectives have recently emerged in the work of Devine (2005, 2009) and Bryan (2007, 2009, 2010) in particular. An extensive history of exposing racialised exclusions is readily available from the sociology of education in the UK. This work demonstrates the constant salience of skin colour and cultural and religious background to experiences of schooling and achievement. Gillborn (1990) suggests ethnocentrism is a key way in which often well-meaning teachers may act to racist effect within school boundaries. The constitution of youth styles of blackness as a threat to school authority, and the assumption of Asian students as 'model' minorities have been suggested as common ways in which teachers render 'Other' students in terms of learning and behaviour (Archer and Francis, 2007; Gillborn, 1990; Mac an Ghaill, 1988; Youdell, 2003). Furthermore, schools marginalise across generations in Ireland and elsewhere through overt streaming and tracking processes, which can contribute to determinist, fixed constructions of minority ethnic and working class student's ability and educational potential amongst teachers (Gillborn and Youdell, 2000; Lynch and Lodge, 2002).

Ongoing Racisms and the Politics of Definition in Anti-racist Institutions

Significant anti-racist policy advances have been triggered by black and minority ethnic struggles internationally, and masses of research on institutional racism has accumulated since the concept was coined in the US in the 1960s. However, in spite of – or perhaps even because of – its narrow official recognition in state legislation and institutional policy, failure to tackle institutional racism may have intensified. Liberal states can adopt contradictory stances with respect to 'recognising' institutional racism, while failing to combat it at the level of the judiciary, economic or immigration policy. The politics of state policy formation can also lead to a failure to encourage agents to look beyond good intentions, towards the non-neutral outcomes of institutional procedures. These politics were quite strongly in evidence in Macpherson Inquiry's ultimate separation of 'overt individual' racism from the structural inequalities engendered through institutional processes (see Murji, 2007). Lentin and McVeigh (2006) contend that the notion of institutional racism was instantly diluted within the Irish criminal justice system when it adopted the Macpherson definition. They argue for the concept of *constitutional* racism, in order to foreground the manner in which the Irish state re-defines, racialises and excludes 'non-nationals' via immigration, legislation and citizenship control.

From this perspective, the singular 'anti-racist' policies that the State espouses for schools (e.g. National Council for Curriculum and Assessment [NCCA], 2005) can be understood as predicated on, or working in tandem with the wider exercise of control around Ireland's borders. This exercise of control expressly turned to racialise citizenship in a 2004 referendum (Lentin and McVeigh, 2006), and to hierarchise migrants along lines of economic desirability: a form of 'corporate multi-culturalism' (Bryan, 2010; Kitching, 2010a). Unsurprisingly, migrant status has been shown to have a major impact on the lives of minority ethnic youth in Ireland (Ní Laoire et al., 2009), while perceptions of 'asylum seeker vs. economic migrant' students have been suggested as a conduit for Irish teachers to construct racialised understandings of their students (Devine, 2005).

In response to the frustrations of anti-racist struggle and the contradictory stances adopted in state policies, researchers informed by post-structural ideas have provided more nuanced accounts of the ways in which the state, individual subjects and popular and political discourses are implicated in these contradictions. These ideas, which examine the continuous construction of *acceptable and unacceptable citizen and student subjectivities in the public sphere*, are taken up here (Titley, in press; Youdell, 2006a). A particular point of concern for this form of anti-racist thinking is the reflexive uptake of mainstream research knowledge about various forms of excluded identity in popular and political discourse (e.g., by institutional actors such as teachers). Youdell (2006a) shows how the identity politics of social movements are now no longer entirely controlled by the groups that may construct and use them, as they can 'circulate in mainstream and hegemonic discourses and in so doing, may well act against the interests of the individual and groups so named' (p. 28). Examples from the UK include 'Black and African interchanged with West Indian, Negro… Men substituted by girls' (Youdell, 2006a, p. 28). Mindful that there are several tensions in arming ourselves with 'anti-racist' intent when we attempt to research racisms in institutions, this approach explicitly confronts how contentious the effects of research knowledge can be. I turn next to the complexity (while not forgetting the necessity) of producing contemporary knowledge about racism in liberal societies, with a view to adopting a particular methodological stance with the data that is analysed in the third section.

ANTI-RACIST TENSIONS AND RACIST CONTINUITIES: THE SUBJECTIVE
UPTAKE OF KNOWLEDGE OF EXCLUSION

Lentin (2004) suggests that the identities of those who consider themselves to use 'anti-racist' thinking are heterogenous, differently located and often contested. They range from those who see the State and its institutions as protecting against racism, to those who view the state as complicit in racism. Different stances on the drive to name 'objective' inequality while (subjectively) attempting to recognise what is 'racist', 'not racist' and 'anti-racist' are often tacitly adopted amongst researchers, and none of these positions are dilemma-free.

Problems with recognising and tackling the persistence of inequality on the basis of ethnic, religious or other differences are ultimately part of the tension of creating normative and/or interpretive research knowledge. For example, the names that are offered in well-intentioned statistical reports offer a constant problem in terms of how they might reify and normalise constructions of the 'racial Other' (Goldberg, 2000). As alluded to in the previous section, 'objective truths' espoused by statistics which monitor achievement by ethnicity can also be taken up by teachers to inform determinist, racialised understandings of fixed student potentials (Gillborn and Youdell 2000; Mirza 1998). A recent report from the Economic and Social Research Institute (ESRI) on racism in employment in Ireland usefully highlights a vast degree of racism in the Irish labour market (O'Connell and McGinnity, 2008). However, using Census 2006 categories, the report refers to 'black' and 'Asian' peoples as *national/ethnic* groups, despite that people in Ireland who identify using the often largely political term 'black' may have hugely diverse ethnic and national origins, not to mention differing experiences of material advantage/disadvantage (e.g. from doctors to asylum seekers). While the aforementioned report follows decades of a move beyond the pseudo-science of biological racial difference, the potential for *ethnicity and nationality* to be taken up as the cultural placeholders of racial meaning have been strongly problematised in educational research and elsewhere (Mirza, 1998). As Hall (2000) argues:

> The more 'ethnicity' matters, the more its characteristics are represented as relatively fixed, inherent within a group, transmitted from generation to generation, not just by culture and education, but by biological inheritance, stabilized above all by kinship and endogamous marriage rules that ensure that the ethnic group remains genetically, and therefore culturally 'pure'. (p. 223 in Gunarantam, 2003, p. 4).

The fixing of statistical measures of identity such as those critiqued in the Irish ethnic census question may not be extricated from racialising processes (Cadogan 2009). However, the subjective 'truths' of more radical qualitative anti-racist research also are prone to the danger of simular essentialist singularities, e.g. by equating 'being white' with dominance and 'being black' with victimhood. Such representations which risk oversimplifying the feelings, experiences and identities of those constituted as dominant or powerful. The murder of 13 year-old Bangladeshi student Ahmed Ullah in Burnage High School (Manchester, England in 1986) is a tragic example of perhaps an oversimplified approach to anti-racism, which failed to account for the resentment of white working class students who may be marginalised in other ways.

Locating the School and its Subjects? Open-ended Discourse Analysis

Conscious of these difficulties, I made the contested and equivocal ways in which subjects take up knowledges about themselves, others and school and social issues a central part of recursive processes of ethnographic data generation, analysis *and writing* in this particular project. The forthcoming analyses are underpinned by post-structural readings: namely, how desirable, undesirable and recognizable subjectivities are constantly, almost endlessly made by, while also 'making' school settings (following Youdell, 2006a, 2006b). Teachers and students, as subjects,[1] construct their understandings of racism, desirable/undesirable students, and inclusive and exclusionary practices according to available discursive resources. 'Discourse' may refer to

> Ways of constituting knowledge, together with the social practices, forms of subjectivity and power relations which inhere in such knowledges and relations between them. They constitute the 'nature' of the body, conscious and un-conscious mind and emotional life of the subjects they seek to govern (Weedon, 1987, p. 108).

The mobile, context-dependent and multi-faceted ways in which knowledge around racism and 'the Other' are created and taken up was more than a momentary concern in this study. I wished to explore potential moments where claims and perspectives around racism, school achievement and student and classmate desirability are end-lessly centred and decentred at local and official policy levels. Analyses of the maintained and shifting notions of what is acceptable or unacceptable in schools (e.g. policies, subjective stances, etc.) are particularly helpful in demonstrating the continuity, mobility and contestation of racism.

The data below was generated in a Dublin Community School, during the 2007–2008 school year. 'Dromray', the pseudonym for the school, is situated in a region of county Dublin fictitiously named 'Termonfort'. Termonfort has experienced some of the highest levels of change in population in Ireland in the past decade. Twenty-two percent of Termonfort's inhabitants are immigrants of first generation and early second-generation, and this group is largely of minority ethnic heritage. Nigerian and Polish migrants, followed closely by British and Lithuanian groups represent the largest new minorities in Termonfort. Usually one or two days were spent per week in the school during the year, particularly with Junior Certificate (3rd year, usually 15 year-old) students. Time was spent observing performance of identity in lessons, chatting with staff and students in the staffroom, on the corridor, on the yard and while going for lunch. Recorded interviews were also conducted with students and staff. Key themes discussed below are subjects' constructions and performances of *racism, ability and individual effort*. Knowledges and silences around these themes largely reflect the embeddedness of 'monoculturalism' and internally classed and gendered norms around desirable and undesirable classmates and learners that tacitly underpin Irish school sites (Lynch and Lodge, 2002; Kitching, 2010b).

Discourse analysis was drawn upon as a means of understanding how certain ways of knowing the world and living everyday life become used, assumed, avoided and/or contested in ordinary school moments and in subjects' constructions of events and others. In the analyses that follow, I am not attempting to present a sealed narrative of teachers' and students' understandings and identity performances. I do not view their understandings, or performances of self as fixed truths that are closed to being rethought. Nor is my analysis free from the equivocal, contested nature of interpretation: Dromray is not either a simply either a good or bad school, as it does not stand apart from the politics of society, economy and self. Following Youdell (2006b), it is not that I am seeking to offer a collection of 'real' or 'actual' discourses. Researchers are wholly constrained by their own discursive repertoires and capacity to build and name discourses: 'I am, then, absolutely entangled in the data I generate and the representations I produce' (ibid, p. 513). Instead, I focus on *potentially* guiding discourses that frame meaning in various moments of data generation in an open-ended manner. Certainly such a stance cannot, in the short term, transcend the constant binds of racialised subjectivity and authorial authenticity. However, it refuses foreclosure on subjective understandings of Same/Other relations, as a pro-active, critical and ethical stance against the embeddedness of school inequality in 'tolerant' societies (Kitching, 2010b).

SUBJECTIVITIES AND CONTESTED DISCOURSES: RACISMS, ABILITY AND DESIRABILITY IN SCHOOL

During the study, moments of racist and anti-racist knowledge production, and per-formances of acceptable/unacceptable learner, classmate or friend identity played out along multiple lines such as sporting ability, youth subculture, and various 'pro-school' and 'anti-school' practices. As previous research in Ireland, the UK and Australia indicate, the terms of subjectivity that make these practices of identity possible are underpinned by racialised, classed and gendered norms circumscribing the school site (Devine and Kelly 2006; Ní Laoire et al., 2009; Youdell, 2006a). A range of meanings were taken up and avoided in the classroom setting by student and teacher subjects in order to construct, approximate or avoid un/desirable selfhood. In the fieldnotes below, for example, discourses of the feminine Other are worked to negatively position a 'rocker' kid who is knowable within school discourses as an acceptable, or even good learner. During a five minute break in their A-Band (upper tier) Spanish class, I tried to get to know to some 3rd year students. Rainey, Aoife and Sarah[2] – three girls who regularly demonstrate ambivalence and subtle resistance towards school expectations – reiterate their position in our conversation. They introduce me to Jack – a 'quiet' white-Irish boy who has long black hair and sallow skin – as "Pocahontas".

Fieldnotes, December 2007

A number of students get up out of their seats and gather around my seat towards the back of the classroom. I ask how many people in the class are Irish. Rainey comes down beside us and sits on the boys' table at the back. Rainey points to two white boys who are sitting alone: Tomas from Moldova, and Jack from Ireland, saying "he's not Irish, he's not Irish". Then they point over to Cian, who they say *was* from Canada. Aoife and Sarah point back then to Jack, and tell me that he is from Pocahontas-land. They shout "Pocahontas! Pocahontas!" at Jack, expecting him to respond. All Jack does is look over and look away again. I feel extremely uneasy. The girls then recite a common catchphrase of theirs, "good one!", and laugh in a high-pitched giggle.

As in the example above, racialising meanings might not necessarily be overtly directed towards minority or new migrant students: they can be deployed to draw certain boundaries between white-Irish students. It is also interesting that it is unlikely that the term 'Pocahontas' would have been available to be mobilised by the girls before the popular Disney film about the colonisation of Native Americans. However, exclusionary meanings could also be deployed in subtle, tacit and un-expected ways around or towards new migrant, black and minority ethnic students. Below, a girl answers a question about Asia in Geography class: following this, her (white-Irish) classmate Louise turns around and recites a pop song that draws upon racialised notions of sexual desirability. This 'rap' is immediately and uncomfortably juxtaposed with Louise's rendering of Carlos, who has come from the Philippines in recent years:

Fieldnotes, May 2008

"They're all in Asia", answers the girl beside Louise to the teacher's question. At mid-volume, Louise spontaneously quotes Janet Jackson's recent hit *Feedback*. At more than a whisper, she mock-raps "light skin, dark skin my Asian persuasion, I got them all that's why these girls out here hatin' cause I'm sexy". Louise then swings around to Carlos and casually says "where's your bumchum"? Carlos mumbles something inaudible. Louise chirpily repeats her question, and Carlos does not reply.

In this brief instance, Carlos may appear passive to how Louise positions him. But while not denying "racist comments" or actions were directed at them, it was possible for new migrant and minority ethnic students to draw upon a range of discourses to avoid/deny victimhood. They could dismiss or contest their significance and meaning, depending on their subjective location. Christian, who describes himself as Belgian but of Congolese origin, cites available 'equal opportunities' logics when it comes to racism below: we can *all* be racist.

KK:	Are there many racist comments (heard in the school)?
Christian:	Yeah, there is like, for the laugh. But there's no serious one 'cause they know they'd just get beat again.
Tank:	(laughs)
KK:	Who em, can say it (racist remarks) as a laugh?
Christian:	(elusively) Everyone, anyone can say it.
KK:	Like what?
Christian:	Like what? What kind of racist comments? ... I'm not comfort-able, like, if we're outside school I say all of them
Tank:	(laughs)

KK:	And what about inside school?
Christian:	It's like a hou(se) – like a church. You wouldn't say it in a church. 'Cause you're not used to saying it in a church. You're not used to saying it in a school.

Certainly, Christian's equalization of racist comments may not necessarily produce positive effects, at the very least because it re-deploys racist thinking, and is inadvertently fatalistic about challenging racism. While Christian could not be faulted in his suggestion that racist comments are equally available for use by all, his position is underpinned by the uptake of a subculturally desirable, transnationally popularised black masculine subjectivity, discussed elsewhere (Kitching, in press-a). Christian's identity was, in this school, largely irreconcilable with successful learner subjectivity and often required him to, in his words, "keep it low", and be strategic about how he contested school norms in Dromray. However, other minority ethnic students were differently positioned as learners to Christian, and were thus capable of questioning/ showing resistance to the 'beneficence' of official school rules in ways that did put them somewhat at risk of being as strongly considered as 'undesirable learners'. Steve, a white-Irish working class 3rd year student, and his friend, Jonathan, a working class black-Nigerian boy, were classmates in the lower (B) Band. They exhibited frustration at being 'good learners' who were often subtly rendered as undesirable through negative teacher interpretations of their fun-loving behaviour in class. Below, they discuss an experiment they conducted which contested implementation of school uniform rules.

KK:	Do you think the school is heavy on people?
Steve:	Depends on the teacher really.
Jonathan:	I'd say half of the school is racist.
KK:	Would you?
Jonathan:	Yeah.
KK:	Why?
Jonathan:	Alright. Em, yesterday, we had an experiment, right? I have this green jacket, right. If I wear it to school, every teacher that sees me complains about it. So I told – he wanted to wear it to see, right? So he wore it yesterday and nobody gave out to him.
Steve:	Nobody said *anything* to me
Jonathan:	To the last minute they stopped school, nobody complained to him but when I wore it all the teachers would be all angry and stuff.
KK:	Do you think that happens to other people Jonathan or?
Jonathan:	I'd say, I'd say they're just racist. I don't think it's only me.

Instead of assuming that the school's prohibition of racism effectively dealt with its presence, their experiences led them to construct an understanding that institutional practices themselves were not neutral. However, the boys did not take the risk of exposing this to their teachers, even though they liked a number of them, and recognised that many teachers wanted to help them. Such a risk might/might not challenge prevailing understandings of racism amongst their teachers, many of whom associated racism *less with institutional practices* and *more with inter-student conflict*. I often reached awkward places with well-intentioned teachers when we probed the meanings of skin colour, ethnicity and culture in the school. In the instance where a potential meaning about "colour" was broached below, Ms. Regan, remains open to learning, but contingently reverts to ambiguous, positive rhetoric about '(non) nationals' and 'integration':

KK: Is there talk about, amongst the students and amongst the staff themselves about colour, since you mentioned it?

Ms. Regan: Talk as in?

KK: Is it talked about, am I creating an issue for example by saying "is it an issue?" or is it something that...

Ms. Regan: I don't think it's an issue in the classroom, or it's not an issue in the staffroom, that there's nations – I actually welcome, multicultural... (sic) in the school. I think it's good, it's an education in itself. But as I say, I would prefer socially if they were better, if they were integrated more and I think we –maybe should be thinking about doing something about that in the school. You know?

Many teachers were reluctant to characterise students as learners in terms of their ethnicity. This may could speak to the newness of mass immigration to Ireland, the lack of discourses available on student ethnicity and achievement in a 'previously monocultural' setting, or a positive unwillingness not to pigeonhole or stereotype new communities. However, some who constructed understandings of ethnicity – as it related to school participation and achievement – overtly assessed students in terms of their 'cultural fit' to (Irish, Dromray) school life. Migrant students could become constructed in relation to, or through teachers' already existing, determinist, classed and gendered conceptions of Irish students' ability, motivation and behaviour as *fixed*. Given the systemic constraints operating on teachers in Dromray, it is some-what understandable that culturalist discourses could become used to construct understandings of individual students' and groups' achievement and behaviour, sometimes with clearly racist underpinnings.

Ms. Mahony: My (first year) maths class are quite, in terms of ability they're quite mixed. I have kids that can't add without a calculator and kids that are very well able to do it. I would say there's a good 5 or 6 in that class that would be capable of doing higher level.

KK: Do you have many kids of minority ethnic background?

Ms. Mahony: There is (sic) a few... and in general

KK: I know that class, I know James and Stefan and Michael and Lukasz (Nigerian, Polish, Nigerian, Polish students respectively)

Ms. Mahony: And Mahmood and Joseph as well (Pakistani, Indian).

KK: How would those kids be faring?

Ms. Mahony: In general I find the kids from Asian backgrounds are very hard-working and work really hard to get what they want to do and em, in the older classes I find the Eastern European kids would be hard working as well, in Junior Cert not so much. Just in terms of the kids I'm dealing with, not necessarily all of them. And, the kids from African backgrounds, em, are, somewhere in the middle really, they can go either way depending on the child themselves I suppose.

Teachers' understandings could both elide *and* enforce racial meaning by reflexively and inconsistently referring to 'Other' students and their families in terms of gender, geographical origin, class, etc. As discussed in the first two sections of this chapter, such understandings could return conversations to determinist, 'trait' notions that 'explain' the difficulty with certain students. The following discussion of Christian's friend Tank, a 'disruptive' black South African boy, draws on discourses of problematic (black, Other) masculinities within non-nuclear family structures, while at the same time 'relating' to Tank's mother through gender:

Ms. Thornton: I think you've got certain students who are very motivated and I think you always find, I mean I don't know how this sounds, you always find that students from Asian countries are very motivated, whereas the students where you have problems with, are the African countries are probably not very motivated. And I think it's an awful lot to do with women sometimes. Like I know that I spoke to Tank's mother and she said to me "I know, I'm a woman" and the way she said it, "I'm a woman too, I know what's"... it was like she knew that he wasn't going to pay me any attention because I was a woman. You know, and Tank's kind of, I had to struggle very much with Tank last year because it was very much like he didn't want to be told anything by a woman. Obviously he and I have gotten used to each other and have a bit of an arrangement now at this stage.

By helping students with their subject, with exam preparation, or with the English language, the well-intentioned, caring aspects of teacher identities could be made apparent. There were important ways in which the school manipulated (pre-recession) general resource allocations to further develop the academic proficiency of their students, by taking time beyond the two-year provision.

Mr. Hanrahan: I usually concentrate the ESL on helping them with their spell – with their vocabulary and with their grammar. Because I feel if they can get a handle on these two, the rest will come. Also try to help them develop more unique ways of going about doing, we'll say the Leaving Cert, the Junior Cert exam. For example we've recently been doing a few classes on developing ideas for essays. And, it's just very basic, coming up with points, developing these points into paragraphs and then a paragraph into an essay. That sort of process. And for the majority of the students they actually very much enjoy it.

The practice of ensuring as many students as possible would participate in 'honours' classes and Junior Cert examinations had been part of school policy for some years, despite its A/B Band tier system. Omolara and Adeola, who both came from Nigeria in their later primary years and settled in Termonfort after 2–3 moves around Ireland, demonstrated strong aspirations in terms of engagement in education. Below, we discussed being/not being motivated to do well in exams.

Omolara: If I start dossing and don't do any work, that's gonna be my fault, there's nobody else to blame when my Leaving or Junior comes and I fail, God forbid! Like it's gonna be my fault and it's gonna be my fault I don't get to do what I want to do after I leave school.

Adeola: You're gonna be like working in the shopping centre or something

Omolara: (laughs) McDonalds!

KK: That's not the kind of thing you want

Adeola: No. I want to be a lawyer.

Omolara: I want to be a paediatrician.

KK: Right, em, can you tell me about the other kids in the class and people who don't have the same view about school and about studying. Who are they? In the class

Adeola: Like. Some people, I don't know why they don't study. Like, they're not gonna get a good job, like their parents probably do have good jobs and it's like – think money grows on trees?

Omolara: Some people just aren't bothered. Like, it's like "oh yeah, whatever, I study on the last week". Do you get me? Which is like, I think impossible to do

Adeola: It is

Omolara: But that's the way some people are. But it's not really the girls, it's mostly the guys. And they're just like, "oh yeah, whatever, I'll study in the last couple of nights".

It is significant and important that these girls consistently adopted highly positive stances towards school; indeed, their experiences of school immediately troubles fatalistic readings of black and minority ethnic experiences in schooling. However, earlier research warns of the risks attached to downplaying the significance of cultural capital and social structure to educational success, as students' aspirations can often be taken up to 'colour blind' effect. For example, Mirza's *Young Female and Black* (1992) demonstrated how the positive efforts of black female students in UK were thwarted by unequal education structures. While Adeola and Omolara were recognised as significantly pro-school by their class tutor, this was in the context of their B Band positioning: their chances of achieving such goals through school participation were suggested by their tutor as slim. It is also significant that the girls mobilise the prevailing discourse that achievement is premised on 'good (girl, migrant)' and 'bad (boy, working class)' student groups being dichotomous in terms of their motivation: "it's not really the girls, it's mostly the guys". This logic has already been worked to tacitly opposition 'independent, motivated' migrant and 'dependent, unmotivated' working class learners in Irish political discourses on immigration and education (Kitching, in press-a, b).

In the fragment below, Ms. Greaney views language support as inclusive practice, along with the 'tweaking' of A and B Band placement by manoeuvres in certain subject areas. However, these somewhat minor moves still capitulate to the constraints placed on the school by the slow march towards the major issue: competitive examinations.

> Ms. Greaney: My suspicion is that a lot of the reason that non-Irish kids get into the B Band is because of their English and that is going to bring them down if you like. But in the maths department at the end of first year, we take thirty of the top kids from the B Band and give them a chance to do higher level. And that is when those kids who are very good mathematically but not particularly good through English will get a chance to do honours maths… that's a difficult group to teach because they've been because they've been going at a much slower pace and have less work covered in first year and then you're taking them into second year and third year to try and bridge the gap… they've less class time because they're scheduled for less classes in a week, and you can't break them out of that group… unless they're very good mathematically, they're not going to be getting As or Bs but they are getting the chance to do honours Maths for the Junior Cert. Which is a huge advantage to them for Leaving Cert maths.

It is possible that routine constraints on teachers and the school can aid a determinist reinforcement of achievement hierarchies, rather than rethinking of culturalist understandings of students' motivations and abilities (Gillborn and Youdell, 2000; Kitching 2010c). However, as I suggest in the concluding paragraphs, it is critical to one's understandings about meaning-making, subjective location and discourse that teacher and learner subjectivities are constantly open to being mobilised differently. As the interpretive approach and the above examples demonstrate, there are constant points of intervention in school discourses and subjective constructions where alternative meanings and critical lines of analysis can be transformatively explored.

UNRAVELLING SCHOOL AND SELF: RUPTURING RACISMS IN CONTEXT

As the first section outlined, the problem of institutional racism has not been seriously combated in Ireland or elsewhere; in fact, the UK case suggests that policy attempts to 'deal with' the problem of embedded, racialised inequality has been at best mild, and at worst counterproductive. Irish social and education policy has adopted under-standings of institutional racism in a way that disarms critical engagement with the state's implication in exclusion (Lentin and McVeigh, 2006). The adoption of an uncritical understanding of institutional racism in Irish school guidelines (e.g. NCCA, 2005) is perhaps sadly predictable, given the legacy of Traveller exclusion from education and social participation that preceded recent mass immigration. But our relationships to school, and the way we construct understandings of Others are always preceded by our *subjection* to a range of social conditions such as these. Seemingly personal conditions and individual understandings are always already social, and our influenced by, for example, the history of our educational experiences our social position(s) in and out of school.

One way of challenging institutional racism is to critically analyse how privileged and marginalised students and families are made subject to an array of conditions (or, as this paper has termed them, discourses), that circumscribe their affiliation to the institution, their relationships to others and, of course, their identities. Discourses are inherently imbued with power relations and politics, but, to quote an adage, politics is the art of the possible. While students and teachers are made subject to certain conditions (e.g. prevailing monoculturalism and a weak understanding of anti-racism), they are at the same time 'speaking', and 'acting' subjects who might intentionally or inadvertently rupture and contest the terms of their positioning in school and society (Kitching-in press, a; Youdell, 2006a). A direct example of an inventive rupture could be Jonathan and Steven's experiment to prove that teacher enforcement of the uniform rule was racially biased. However, politics is a tricky art. Other challenges to exclusionary practices may replay rather than challenge current conditions: Christian's strategy of countering racism *with* racism could not be seen to be effective for him individually, in a location that exerts a higher level of surveillance over black boys. The intentional and unintentional contestation and acquiescence of these students had everything to do with *context*: their racialised, classed, gendered and indigenous/migrant school biographies, and the particular 'pro-school' or subcultural investments that shaped their identities.

Unfortunately, inventiveness and context is also the means by which racism is sustained by subjects in practice. An example of how terms of identity (from research and political struggle) are used in 'everyday', mobile and injurious ways included the deployment of the term 'Pocahontas', a term which sustained racial meaning and directed it at an unpopular (white) Irish classmate. Teacher interviews also showed ways in which teachers create understandings of migrant students by drawing on long-embedded discourses of meritocracy (i.e. educational success is about individual, hard work and has nothing to do with social ascription), and aligning them with notions that learning potential is fixed (i.e., uninfluenced by banding, biased testing, everyday forms of exclusion from participation such as an ethnocentric and abstract curriculum, etc.) As subjects who operate under maintained and shifting school and social contexts, teacher understandings can deploy a limitless repertoire of ideas, such as gendered conceptions of good and bad learners, constructions of helpful and unhelpful family structures (e.g. nuclear versus one-parent), and fatalism around social class.

There is much work that can be done to unpack the politics of meaning around immigration, racialisation and Othering, both by and for students and teachers. Calls to action should first critically focus on how one is constantly positioned across a matrix of privileged and marginalised experiences. A critical pedagogy that examines inclusion-exclusion implications *with students and teachers in their own school and community settings* could form a key part of a curriculum process that is committed to situated *anti-racisms*. Topics might include the effect of constant 'trait' inscriptions about majority and minority ethnic students that imbued with racialised ability discourses, and also the manner in which racial and other meanings are reflexively used by peers to construct desirable and undesirable classmate identities. As in the case of Ms. Regan, difficult meanings around students and 'colour' can become further broached/opened up to support and extend inclusive intentions. 'School' and 'self' need to be constantly critically examined (Kitching, 2010b): teachers and students must be aided by a more radical, context-based approach to anti-*racisms*, which encourages them to gain critical literacy around subjective contradictions and contested discourses constituting Ireland's shifting educational and social terrain.

NOTES

[1] Suggesting that subjectivity is only possible through iterated reliance on available discourses, Judith Butler argues that there is no 'doer' behind the deed – the doer is "variably constructed in and through the deed" (Butler, 1990, p. 142). Contesting the notion of an apparently self-contained, autonomous identity, this notion of *decentred subjectivity* views identity as fragmented, non-unitary and unstable, because it both becomes recognisable only in discourse, and in turn can only then work within/with/against to shape discourses.

[2] Staff and student names cited above are pseudonyms.

REFERENCES

Archer, L., & Francis, B. (2007). *Understanding minority ethnic achievement: Race, gender, class and 'success'*. London: Routledge.

Bryan, A. (2010). Corporate multiculturalism, diversity management, and positive interculturalism: A vertical case study of the racialised dynamics of inclusion and exclusion in Irish schools and society. *Irish Educational Studies, 29*(3), Pages unavailable at present.

Bryan, A. (2009). The intersectionality of nationalism and multiculturalism in the Irish curriculum: teaching against racism? *Race, Ethnicity and Education, 12*(3), 297–317.

Bryan, A. (2007). The (mis)representation of travellers in the civic, social and political education curriculum. In P. Downes, & A. L. Gilligan (Eds.), *Beyond educational disadvantage* (pp. 247–258). Dublin: IPA.

Butler, J. (1990). *Gender trouble: Feminism and the subversion of identity*. New York: Routledge.

Cadogan, M. (2009). Fixity and whiteness in the ethnic census question. *Translocations, 3*(1), 50–68.

Culleton, J. (2007). Institutional racism in Ireland: Ethnic religious minorities in criminal justice and social care provision systems. *European Journal of Social Education, 12/13*, 51–62.

Devine, D. (2005). Welcome to the Celtic Tiger? Teacher responses to immigration and increasing ethnic diversity in Irish schools. *International Studies in Sociology of Education, 15*(1), 49–70.

Devine, D. (2009). Mobilising capitals? Migrant children's negotiation of their everyday lives in school. *British Journal of Sociology of Education, 30*(5), 521–535.

Devine, D., & Kelly, M. (2006). "I just don't want to get picked on by anybody": Dynamics of inclusion and exclusion in a newly multi-ethnic Irish primary school. *Children and Society, 20*(2), 128–139.

Fanning, B., Veale, A., & O'Connor, D. (2001). *Beyond the pale: Asylum-seeking children and social exclusion in Ireland*. Dublin: Irish Refugee Council and the Combat Poverty Agency.

Gillborn, D. (1990). *'Race', ethnicity and education: Teaching and learning in multi-ethnic schools*. London: Unwin Hyman.

Gillborn, D., & Youdell, D. (2000). *Rationing education: Policy, practice, reform and equity*. Buckingham: Open University Press.

Goldberg, D. T. (2000). Racial knowledge. In L. Back & J. Solomos (Eds.), *Theories of race and racism: A reader* (pp. 154–180). London: Routledge.

Gunaratnam, Y. (2003). *Researching race and ethnicity: Methods, knowledge and power*. London: Sage.

Ionann Management Consultants. (2004). *An Garda Síochana human rights audit*. Available at http://www.garda.ie/Documents/User/Garda%20Human%20Rights%20Audit.pdf

Kenny, M. (1997). *The routes of resistance: Travellers and second level schooling*. Aldershot: Ashgate Publishing.

Kitching, K. (2010a). An excavation of the racialised politics of viability underpinning education policy in Ireland. *Irish Educational Studies, 29*(3), 213–229.

Kitching, K. (2010b). *Justifying school... and self: An ethnography on race, recognition and viability in education in Ireland*. Unpublished PhD thesis, Institute of Education, University of London.

Kitching, K. (2010c). *The politics of "doing English": Three critical lenses on being a subject of English language support policy in a new migrant context*. Paper presented at the Educational Studies Association of Ireland annual conference, Dundalk. 25th–27th March 2010.

Kitching, K. (in press-a). Interrogating the changing inequalities constituting school/subculture in Ireland: New migrant student recognition, resistance and recuperation. *Race Ethnicity and Education*.

Kitching, K. (in press-b). Understanding class anxiety and race certainty: moments of in/coherent home, school, body and emotion configuration in 'new migrant' Dublin. In K. Bhopal, & J. J. Preston (Eds.), *Intersectionality and race in education*. London: Routledge.

Lentin, A. (2004). *Racism and anti-racism in Europe*. London: Pluto Press.

Lentin, R., & McVeigh, R. (2006). *After optimism? Ireland, racism and globalisation*. Dublin: Metro Éireann Publications.

Linehan, M., & Hogan, E. (2008). *Migrants and higher education in Ireland*. Cork: CIT Press.

Lynch, K., & Lodge, A. (2002). *Equality and power in schools: Redistribution, recognition and representation*. London: Routledge/Falmer.

Mac an Ghaill, M. (1988). *Young, gifted and black*, Milton Keynes: Open University Press.

Mirza, H. S. (1992). *Young, female and black*. London: Routledge.

Mirza, H. S. (1998). Race, gender and IQ: The social consequence of pseudo-scientific discourse. *Race, Ethnicity and Education, 1*(1), 109–126.

Murji, K. (2007). Sociological engagements: Institutional racism and beyond. *Sociology, 41*, 843–855.

National Council for Curriculum and Assessment. (2005). *Guidelines for intercultural education in the post-primary school*. Dublin: Government Stationery Office.

Ní Laoire, C., Bushin, N., Carpena-Méndez, F., & White, A. (2009). *Tell me about yourself: Migrant children's experiences of moving to Ireland.* University College Cork. Available at http://migration. ucc.ie/children/Tell%20Me%20About%20Yourself%20Full%20Report.pdf

O'Connell, P. J., & McGinnity, F. (2008). *Immigrants at work: Nationality and ethnicity in the Irish labour market.* Dublin: Equality Authority/ESRI.

Rizvi, F. (1993). Critical introduction: Researching racism and education. In B. Troyna (Ed.), *Racism and education* (pp. 1–17). Buckingham: Open University Press.

Titley, G. (In press). Mediated minarets, intolerable subjects: The crisis of "multiculturalism" in Europe. *European Journal of Cultural Studies.*

Watt, P., & Charles, K. (2009). *Housing conditions of Roma and travellers.* Available at http://fra.europa. eu/fraWebsite/attachments/RAXEN-Roma%20Housing-Ireland_en.pdf

Weedon, C. (1987). *Feminist practice and post-structuralist theory.* London: Blackwell.

Willis, P. (1977). *Learning to labour: How working-class kids get working-class jobs.* Westmead, England: Saxon House Press.

Youdell, D. (2003). Identity traps, or how black students fail: The interactions between biographical, sub-cultural and learner identities. *British Journal of Sociology of Education, 24*(1), 3–20.

Youdell, D. (2006a). *Impossible bodies, impossible selves: Exclusions and student subjectivities.* Dordrecht: Springer.

Youdell, D. (2006b). Subjectivation and performative politics – Butler thinking Althusser and Foucault: Intelligibility, agency, and the raced-nationed-religioned subjects of education. *British Journal of Sociology of Education, 27*(4), 511–528.

Karl Kitching
School of Education
University College Cork
Republic of Ireland

AUDREY BRYAN AND MELÍOSA BRACKEN

7. 'THEY THINK THE BOOK IS RIGHT AND I AM WRONG'

Intercultural Education and the Positioning of Ethnic Minority Students in the Formal and Informal Curriculum[1]

INTRODUCTION

The trend of immigration that accompanied the Celtic Tiger economy resulted in a newfound emphasis on issues related to cultural diversity, interculturalism and 'integration' in an Irish context, as well as rising levels of public concern about, and negative sentiment towards, migrants in Ireland (Devereux & Breen, 2004; Garner, 2004; Hughes, McGinnity, O' Connell & Quinn, 2007). Against a backdrop of increased immigration and growing evidence of hostility towards minorities, the education system, and intercultural education in particular, has come to be viewed as 'one of the key responses to the changing shape of Irish society and to the existence of racism and discriminatory attitudes in Ireland' (NCCA, 2005, p. 17). Intercultural educational guidelines produced by the National Council for Curriculum and Assessment (NCCA) - a statutory body with responsibility for advising the Minister for Education and Skills on curriculum and assessment issues—define intercultural education as a 'synthesis of the learning from multicultural and anti-racist education approaches...used internationally in the 1960s to the 1990s' (NCCA, 2005, p. 6).

This chapter seeks to advance our understanding of how intercultural education is practised on the ground in schools, based on findings from a twelve month critical ethnographic case study of one school's efforts to promote a policy of 'positive interculturalism'. Combining ethnographic and discourse analytic techniques, it offers a critical exploration of how ethnic minority cultural identities are represented in the formal and informal curriculum. In so doing, it subjects the philosophy and practices of interculturalism to critical scrutiny. It explores ethnic minority students' perceptions of formal curricular knowledge about their ethnic identities (along religious, cultural and nationality lines), and their experiences of engaging with, and negotiating, this knowledge in the classroom. Collectively, the chapter seeks to advance our understanding of the problems associated with 'add diversity and-stir' approaches to curricular and school reform which seek to accommodate the presence of ethnic minorities without altering the existing curriculum or school policies and practices to any significant extent (Bryan, 2008a). In other words, it seeks to demonstrate the limitations of existing educational responses to cultural diversity in an Irish context and stresses the need for radical curricular and educational reform as

Darmody, Tyrrell, Song (eds.), The Changing Faces of Ireland: Exploring the Lives of Immigrant and Ethnic Minority Children, 105–123.

it relates to inclusion, equity, and curricular justice for ethnic minority students (Connell, 1993).

The chapter is organised as follows: The first section presents an overview of the conceptual and methodological frameworks underpinning the study. The next section offers an account of how interculturalism is practised at 'Blossom Hill College' (BHC), a community college based in the greater Dublin area which has been identified as a model of best practice where issues of interculturalism, inclusivity and equality are concerned.[2] Drawing on participant observation and in-depth and small group interviews with ethnic minority students who attended BHC, we seek to demonstrate the ways in which some intercultural interventions have the ironic effect of reinforcing an ethnically homogenous Irish (white, Christian) centre, against which the Otherness of ethnic minority students is highlighted or exposed to ridicule. We also seek to demonstrate the ways in which instructional materials can reinforce overly-negative and inaccurate portrayals of ethnic minority cultures while simultaneously endorsing restrictive, ethnic nationalist understandings of Irishness. The concluding section discusses the need for radical curricular and educational reform as it relates to inclusion, equity, and curricular justice for ethnic minority students.

CONCEPTUAL FRAMEWORK: INTERCULTURAL EDUCATION AS SYMBOLIC VIOLENCE

Within recent years, intercultural education has become the preferred educational policy response to cultural diversity and the existence of racism in Irish schools and society. In 2010, an Intercultural Education Strategy was published, with the aim of ensuring that 'all students experience an education that "respects the diversity of values, beliefs, languages and traditions in Irish society and is conducted in a spirit of partnership"' and that 'all education providers are assisted with ensuring that inclusion and integration within an intercultural learning environment become the norm.' (Department of Education and Skills and the Office of the Minister for Integration, 2010, p. 1). Some years earlier, in 2005 and 2006, intercultural education guidelines for primary and post-primary schools were produced by the NCCA and were subsequently distributed to schools throughout the country. The guidelines define intercultural education as 'education that respects, celebrates, and recognises the normality of diversity in all aspects of human life, promotes equality and human rights, challenges unfair discrimination, and provides the values upon which equality is built' (NCCA, 2005, p. 169).

The intercultural educational guidelines include recommendations for how diversity can be embraced in schools, such as 'organising a special event or awareness day to celebrate diversity in the school' (NCCA, 2005, p. 64), while active-learning methods such as role play are promoted as an effective means of enabling students to develop empathy with those who are discriminated against. In recent years, celebratory events and activities of this nature have become commonplace in schools throughout Ireland as a means of embracing and enacting intercultural principles (Bryan, 2009a), despite evidence to suggest that these kinds of interventions are tokenistic and risk confirming the 'other' status of migrant students in the eyes of the majority Irish student population (Devine, 2009). A wealth of scholarly criticism of these practices in other geographical contexts highlights their failure to recognise the persistent (discursive) constitution of race/ethnicity as markers of difference and stratification, or to acknowledge historical and contemporary exploitation, and of failing to acknowledge, let alone challenge, the ongoing dominance of the majority race/ethnicity (Youdall, 2006).

Existing research on how intercultural education has been conceived and enacted in an Irish context suggests that it is unlikely to alleviate racism because it constitutes an additive approach (Bryan, 2008a). In other words, the focus of intercultural education is on adding to, adapting and mediating the existing curriculum, as opposed to altering it significantly. Contrary to the emphasis within interculturalism on underscoring the normality of diversity in all aspects of human life, existing instructional materials problematically, if unwittingly, abnormalise diversity in Irish society and actually reinscribe narrow and restrictive, ethnically-nationalist versions of Irishness (ibid.). Furthermore, the very discourse of 'respecting,' 'celebrating,' 'valuing,' and 'appreciating' diversity is problematic because it has the effect of denying the possibility of a national 'we,' which is itself diverse (see Ang, 1996; Bryan, 2009b; Hage, 1998). Rather than promoting equality, models of inclusion based on celebrating diversity reinforce the privileged status of culturally dominant groups within society by positioning them as the 'embracer' or 'tolerator' of difference, who get to decree the acceptability (or otherwise) of the ethnic Other.

Theorising intercultural education as a form of symbolic violence (Bourdieu, 2001; Bryan, 2009c; Hage, 1998), we suggest that the current implementation of intercultural education in schools fulfils a political function of providing an educational palliative to minorities. This approach effectively mutes any consideration of alternative policy responses that would yield genuine egalitarian outcomes and effects for ethnic minorities in Ireland. In what follows, we offer an in-depth critical exploration of how interculturalism is practised on the ground in one school where the discourse and practice of celebratory interculturalism has become institutionalised through a policy of 'positive interculturalism'. In so doing, we seek to highlight the exclusionary effects and negative impact of tokenistic or 'add and stir' intercultural educational curricular content and practices for ethnic minority students in schools, and seek to demonstrate ways in which positive, celebratory versions of interculturalism position ethnic minorities as Other while subtly reinforcing the normative, hegemonic status of culturally dominant groupings in Irish society.

METHODOLOGY

Methodologically, the larger study on which this chapter is based combined critical discourse analysis (CDA) of policy documents and curriculum materials, as well as observational analysis of, and in-depth interviews with, students about daily life and interculturalism at BHC which were carried out between September 2004 and December of 2005. This chapter draws exclusively on those interviews conducted with ethnic minority students attending BHC to provide insights into their perceptions of how their cultural identities are represented in the curriculum, as well as their attempts to negotiate more accurate and legitimate representations of their cultural identities within the school. Additionally, we utilise CDA techniques to critically examine representations of ethnic minority students' cultures (along religious, cultural and nationality lines) within instructional materials currently used to teach subjects such as Geography, Civic, Social and Political Education (CSPE) and Religious Education (RE) to show how these materials re-inscribe narrow and restrictive understandings of Irishness while misrepresenting and homogenising aspects of ethnic minority students cultural identities.

Cherishing the Students of All Nations Equally?

BHC is a large, co-educational, ethnically diverse community college located in a middle-class suburb of Dublin. At the time of field work, approximately 10% of the student body was characterised as 'international', a term which reflected a policy decision taken by the school administration to emphasise the extent to which 'international students are seen as a positive part of Blossom Hill' (BHC Yearbook, 2004), as opposed to the term 'non-national' commonly used in media, political and public discourse. In actuality, the terms 'non-national' and 'international' were used interchangeably by staff and students at BHC to refer to ethnic minority students, irrespective of whether they had Irish nationality or were Irish born.

BHC proudly proclaims its culturally diverse student body and maintains that it 'cherish[es] the students of all nations equally' (BHC yearbook, 2004). Because BHC has been identified as a model of best practice where interculturalism is concerned, it offers a useful case study from which to examine the philosophy and practices of intercultural education in schools. In this section, we seek to provide an ethnographic illustration of some of the subtle mechanisms through which the cultural (in this instance, religious) values of dominant cultural groupings in Irish society are banally reinforced as cultural and institutional norms at BHC, under the guise of positive interculturalism.

Community colleges (also known as vocational schools) comprise about a third of all post-primary schools in the Republic of Ireland, and cater for a similar proportion of post-primary students. They are administered by local Vocational Educational Committees (VECs), which are statutory bodies with responsibility for providing a broad range of educational and training programmes, including the management and operation of post-primary and further education colleges. Secondary schools, which comprise just over half of all of post-primary schools in the Republic, are, by contrast, privately owned and managed, in most cases by religious communities (predominantly Catholic), and can give preference in enrolment to students whose religious identification supports the ethos of the school.[3] Community colleges are formally non-denominational, in the sense that they neither admit nor refuse to enrol students on the basis of their religion; in practice, however, the underlying ethos or spirit of many such schools often remains overtly or subtly Christian, and a commitment that RE would be taught in these schools was provided when they were established. Some community colleges are named after Christian saints and/or have Christian emblems or symbols as the basis of their school crest. At times, competing claims to promoting pluralism and Christianity co-exist as part of the school's mission statement, with one midlands-based community college, for example, describing itself as 'a multi-denominational school which aims to provide an education that is truly Christian.'[4]

While neither religious terminology nor iconography are explicit features of BHC's identity, special events to mark important occasions within the school initially took the form of a Catholic mass. As the student body became more culturally diverse during the Celtic Tiger era, the school was forced to re-think its approach to religious services and events at the school. As the school Chaplin (a Catholic nun) explained: 'In the beginning it was a Catholic service, then it was ecumenical and then it moved to interfaith, arguing that 'when it was just one or two <students of non-Christian faiths> it didn't matter.' (field notes, January, 2005). Despite some initial resistance to the idea of replacing a Catholic mass with an interfaith service from some members of the school's board of management (which comprises religious representatives from the Protestant and Catholic traditions, but not of other faiths), the interfaith celebrations and ceremonies have come to represent some one of the main mechanisms through which the school's positive intercultural policy is promoted. The annual first year 'multi-faith celebration', for example, is characterised as the 'spiritual highlight of the first term,' (School Yearbook) while other special occasions, such as the school's anniversary celebration was also marked by an interfaith service. Tolerance, respect, and the celebration of cultural (and in particular religious) diversity were the main themes of these services, with official publications making explicit that it is the school's 'policy and privilege to support all faiths' and expressing its pride in 'cherish[ing] the culture and each faith tradition' within the school (School Anniversary Celebration Booklet).

As one of hallmarks of BHC's positive intercultural policy, the school's interfaith or multi-faith events were generally viewed by students and staff alike in a positive light. Siddhi, a Hindu student who has lived in Ireland for most of her life and who identifies as both Indian and Irish, describes the inclusive nature of these events as follows:

> *Siddhi*: And in our interfaith services…when we are reading out prayers and stuff, they don't just ask all the Irish people to read them out, they try and get all of us involved in their services as much as possible.
> (15 years, Hindu, India, female).[5]

Despite being positively received by members of the BHC community, these formal attempts to be inclusive of multiple 'cultures and faith traditions' sometimes had the ironic effect of undermining the perspectives of those who subscribe to non-monotheistic or non-theistic belief systems. At the interfaith service for incoming First Year students, which took place in October of 2004, the local parish priest encouraged those present to be tolerant and respectful of religious diversity by emphasising that human beings are all 'made in the image of God' and underscoring the importance of having a religious value system in one's life.

> No matter who your God is, whether Christian or Muslim, you must have respect for your own religion and for other people's religion. Ethnic origin is not a Christian value, or a Muslim value, but a human value. It doesn't matter whether your God is Christian, Muslim, Buddhist or Jewish. What is important

is to have a religious value system in your life. We are all human beings made in the image of God (field notes, October 2004).

Furthermore, although non-Christian, ethnic minority students may indeed be 'involved' in these interfaith events, Christianity remains the dominant, yet unmarked reference point. Against this Christian benchmark, non-Christian students are marked as Other, thus resulting in qualitatively different modalities of belonging to these events for religious minority and majority students (as in 'this is my event' or 'I belong here') (Bryan, 2009b; Hage, 1998). Furthermore, to the extent that religious figures from only Catholic and Protestant Churches attended these events, efforts to 'involve' and include students of non-Christian faiths by having them represent, or speak on behalf of, their religion can be seen as tokenistic at best.

A core component of the interfaith service held to mark the school's anniversary celebrations, which took place in October of 2005, comprised recitals of various 'interfaith prayers for peace' by students of different religious backgrounds (fieldnotes, October 2005). The prayers were identified—in both the booklet accompanying the service, as well as the introductions to the prayers during the service—as follows: an 'Opening prayer,' a 'Hindu prayer for peace,' a 'Buddhist prayer,' 'An Islamic prayer,' 'a Jewish prayer,' 'a Christian prayer,' the 'Peace Prayer of St. Francis,' and 'Concluding Prayer.' Despite the professed 'inter-denominational' and 'multi-denominational' nature of BHC's interfaith celebrations, we argue that this event actually had the effect of reinforcing Christianity's normative status within the school. Although the Hindu, Buddhist, Islamic and Jewish prayers were all explicitly named as such, neither the opening and concluding prayers, nor the *Peace Prayer of St. Francis*, were identified as being associated with a specific faith tradition. Yet the opening prayer, which arguably set the tone for the entire service, was overtly Christian in tone. It began with the statement: 'Lord, may your spirit hover over the chaos of your broken world so that divided people will do the work of justice and bring about peace, and ended with the 'we ask this through Christ our Lord.' Moreover, the peace *Prayer of Saint Francis* is a Christian prayer widely attributed to the 13th-century saint Francis of Assisi, the Catholic Church's patron saint of animals and the environment.

The failure to mark the opening, closing or *Peace Prayer of St. Francis* as 'Christian' prayers effectively secures Christianity as the unmarked reference point against which the difference of 'other' religious traditions is highlighted. Moreover, the disproportionate emphasis devoted to Christianity during the service implies that Christianity represents more than simply one faith among many to be celebrated and respected at BHC. The normative status of Christianity is thus secured through its unacknowledged presence as the invisible centre against which the 'otherness' of different belief systems is named and marked (Giroux, 1992; Leonardo, 2004). Further evidence of the hegemonic status of Christianity at BHC is presented below in a section concerning the teaching of RE.

Despite BHC's best efforts to 'support all faiths' and 'cherish the culture and each faith tradition', tokenistic attempts to embrace different faith traditions can have the ironic effect of making certain ethnic minority students feel marginalised, forgotten, or excluded within the school's policy of positive interculturalism, as the following discussion of the school's 'meditation room' and journal reveals.

Siddhi: The meditation room is supposed to be a place where all faiths are recognised and stuff, because they have the Bible and they have the book of Judaism and they have the Koran and the mat and the hat and everything, but they didn't have anything for Hinduism. Nothing! Like I went in there in First Year and my religion the teacher said, 'oh no, we are getting it.' Second Year there was still nothing there. Third Year there was still nothing there. And this year, there still is nothing there. (15 years, Hindu, India, female)

[....]⁶

Asmitha: <Interrupting> Yeah like even in the journals they have all of these religions you know and there are festivals, and they have them written down on the days, but there's absolutely none from Hinduism whatsoever. (15 years, Hindu, India, female)

Another of BHC's intercultural gestures which was designed to sensitise members of the school community to the cultural or religious practices of ethnic minority students was the placing of signs asking students to be 'mindful' that Muslim students were fasting during the month of Ramadan. However, instead of promoting greater awareness, or understanding of the Islamic faith, this call for 'mindfulness' resulted in taunting and teasing of some fasting students by their non-Muslim peers, as the following vignette reveals.

Kiran: Some children what they do is they start making fun of you and stuff. Like the Ramadan posters, when they went up, people were just making fun of them and stuff and then they used to come up to you and asking you are you fasting and stuff like that. Even when they know stuff about it….. (13 years, Muslim, Pakistan, female).

Zoran: <interrupting> And they eat in front of you like…. (15 years, Muslim, Bosnia, male).

Kiran: Even when they know stuff about it, they just keep kind of asking you and stuff, again and again and it is really annoying.

Shoma: Like they would say they are really hungry and stuff in front of you and stuff and take out something and start eating it in front of you. And they know very well that you are fasting and probably you are hungry as well. ….. (13 years, Muslim, Pakistan, female).

Clearly, BHC's efforts to recognise and celebrate diversity, and to sensitise students to aspects of ethnic minority students' cultures, were well-intentioned. Nevertheless, as the foregoing scenarios reveal, tokenistic gestures can have a range of unfortunate and unintended consequences, including reinforcing ethnic minority students' pre-existing sense of otherness, making them feel that their cultural identities are unimportant, or exposing their cultural practices to ridicule by majority ethnic students.

'The Irish are Still Catholic'

This section seeks to highlight the ways in which the formal curriculum, which purportedly embraces culturally diverse perspectives, has the effect of securing the hegemonic positioning of dominant cultural groups within society. We initially present evidence to suggest that the teaching of RE had a range of marginalising, Othering and delegitimising effects for non-Christian students. In so doing, we seek to draw attention to some of the problems posed by a curriculum which professes to be 'multicultural' and inclusive of all faiths but which continues to position Christianity as the central referent point against which other religious traditions are compared, evaluated, and/or marginalized.

Some ethnic minority students described how they were initially excluded from taking part in RE lessons at BHC, presumably because the programme was deemed unable to 'accommodate' non-Christian students. For others, the strongly disproportionate emphasis devoted to Christianity within the syllabus resulted in them choosing to opt out of Religious Education:

> *Siddhi*: Well, we had to actually ask them, they didn't actually give us a choice. We had to ask them could we be examined for religion… (15 years, Hindu, India, female)

> *Amel*: Yeah there is…last year they told us it's a mixture of religions of the world, like the world religions, but last year it was mostly Christianity. So that is why this year I am not doing it (13 years, Muslim, Pakistan, female).

Ethnic minority students who did not participate in RE were typically permitted to do their homework in the class while RE was being taught, or were withdrawn from class during this period to take 'extra English' lessons. That these practices can reinforce students' pre-existing perceptions of being, and made to feel like the 'Other,' by drawing attention to their 'difference' in front of teachers and peers has been well documented in the literature (e.g., Bryan, 2009c; Devine, 2005; Nolan, 2008).

The privileging of Christianity in both RE textbooks and classroom instruction is reflected, to some degree, in the Junior and Leaving Certificate syllabi which aim to 'expose' students to 'a broad range of religious traditions and to the non-religious interpretation of life' (NCCA, 2000, p. 8), while 'offering opportunities to develop an informed and critical understanding of the Christian tradition in its historical origins and its cultural and social expressions' (NCCA, 2003, p. 7).[7] While the aims of both the Junior and Senior Certificate syllabi emphasise RE over religious instruction, the prominent positioning of Christianity ensures that the exploration of different faiths is usually initiated from a 'host' position and through a Christian lens. From this perspective, Christianity maintains its hegemonic status while 'other' faiths are relegated to peripheral positions – 'them' but not 'us'.

The failure to acknowledge religious diversity as a feature of Irish society is evident in a number of RE textbooks designed for use at Junior cycle level. *Exploring Faith* quotes an excerpt from an analysis of the status of Roman Catholic faith and practice in Ireland at the start of the third millennium by Dr Andrew Greely, which includes the statement: 'If the proper measures of Catholicism are faith and devotion, then the Irish are still Catholic' (cited in Goan & Ryan, 2004, p. 245). Homogenising 'the Irish' as 'still Catholic' is problematic for two reasons – first it is indicative of a casual disregard for the fact that faith and devotion can also be expressed by Irish people belonging to 'other' faiths and secondly, it conflates Irishness with Catholicism (Bryan, 2008a). Similarly, in *All About Faith* (Boyle & Boyle, 2005) examines 'communities of faith in Ireland today' with chapters on Catholicism, Protestantism and Ecumenism, but makes no reference to the multitude of non-Christian faiths which are also practiced in Ireland,

At Senior cycle level, one of the most notable examples of the failure to acknowledge religious diversity as an historical feature of Irish society is contained in *Religion: The Irish Experience* (Gunning & De Barra, 2006). Ignoring the fact that Ireland has, in fact, a long history of multiculturalism and religious diversity, it provides an almost exclusively Christian narrative, acknowledging only briefly that 'other major world religions are *now* gaining a foothold in Ireland' (Gunning & De Barra, 2006, p. 18; emphasis added). Saturated in Christian, mostly Catholic, imagery, it succeeds in setting out a selectively theocentric view of Irish history, with only tokenistic references to 'other' religious faiths. Only two pages, in the very last chapter, discuss, in limited detail, the notion of pluralism, and this is done solely from a Christian 'host' perspective. The text emphasizes tolerance and respect for various religious traditions 'irrespective of their size or influence' while denying the dominant position of Catholicism and Christianity in Ireland:

> The situation in Ireland, where no constitutional honour or privilege is now given to any religious faith, means that no religion can become dominant in society and instead each has a voice that needs to be heard (Gunning & De Barra, 2006, p. 93).

The section continues with a selecting out of 'elements' of non-Catholic faiths that can 'enlighten Catholics' and which have been 'embraced' by many Catholics, for example 'meditation', the 'simplicity of these faiths' and 'their lack of dependence on material possessions' (ibid, p. 94). That 'other' religions are reduced to a set of practices that can be viewed favourably by Catholics further legitimizes the hegemonic status of Catholicism in the text. While the text may endorse 'respect' and 'dialogue' between 'us' (read: Christian) and 'them' (read: Baha'i, Buddhist, Hindu, Jewish, Muslim, Sikh), its rigid identification of Irishness with Christianity actively works against the notion that 'they' are, in fact 'us'.

This failure to acknowledge that the national 'we' is itself already diverse is one of the fundamental weaknesses of the philosophical underpinnings of dominant celebratory models of interculturalism. Speaking about multiculturalism in the Australian context, Hage (1998) argues:

> The 'we appreciate' diversity, 'we value' ethnic contributions, etc. attitudes which abound in the dominant political discourse in Australia create a gulf between the 'we' and that which is appreciated and valued. In so doing, they work to mystify the real possibility, grounded in the very composition of Australian society, of a national 'we' which is itself diverse. (Hage 1998, p. 139)

'We are Just Going to Stick with the Book'

Ethnic minority students' legitimate concerns about the disproportionate emphasis devoted to Christianity within the RE curriculum were often compounded by inaccurate or false claims about their faiths contained in school texts and class discussions.

> *Siddhi*: It is not that we didn't want to do it [RE] because it was mostly Christianity, it was more that we looked through the syllabus, and we saw what was in it and we thought this was unfair, we can't really do this. If you are saying that it is multicultural syllabus we can't agree with it because there is five chapters based on the whole world religions and they are not even true, so how can we partake in something that we know is not true? (15 years, Hindu, India, female)

> *Karim*: Yeah I remember last year. We were talking about religion about like how it works. The facts they had were very, very wrong. But I didn't want to argue because like I couldn't be bothered like. It's not my business, it's the book's. I couldn't say anything because there are so many people in that class who are not Muslim like. (16 years, Muslim, Saudi Arabia, male)

Karim further explained his reluctance to 'argue' or contest this inaccurate knowledge in terms of the perception among teachers that textbooks were *the* legitimate source of knowledge, where the relaying of information about minority religious practices and customs was concerned.

> *Karim*: So like if you argue with them, they think the book is right and I am wrong.

Karim's belief that teachers would not accept his competing knowledge claims was corroborated by a number of other students who actually did take steps to highlight inaccuracies, or to provide alternative understandings or representations to those presented in the textbooks. Having been asked to write a report on Hinduism by her RE teacher, Siddhi maintained that her teacher subsequently decided not to use any of the material in class and failed to acknowledge her concerns about the prescribed textbook's portrayal of Hinduism.

> *Siddhi*: Sometimes what they portray isn't accurate....Because my teacher in First Year, she got me to do a really long report on Hinduism and I put my heart and soul into it and I got my Dad to help me and I typed it up and everything. And I handed it up to her and not once in that whole time she was teaching us did she open it and use it. I don't think she read it at all. And I felt really bad because I spent my time doing that and she is not even trying to teach the class what it said, because in that report I was correcting some of the things that it said in the book, and I don't think she wanted to accept that, and she was like 'You know what? We are just going to stick with the book.' And I didn't really feel that that was nice. (15 years, Hindu, India, female)

Shoma and Muhammad explained how teachers' reliance on textbooks as the definitive source of knowledge about specific religions impacted negatively on the results they were awarded in their 'Christmas exams'. In Shoma's case, the discrepancy between her *own* understanding of her faith (Islam) and how it was represented in RE textbooks resulted in her receiving a lower grade in an exam than she would have otherwise received, had she simply based her answer on what was in the book, despite her best efforts to demonstrate that the book had 'gotten it all wrong.'

> *Muhammad*: And in the textbook, like if you have an exam, it gives the wrong information, but if you already know about your religion and you write down the right information, you will get it wrong. (12 years, Muslim, Pakistan, male)

> *Shoma*: Yeah like last year in my Christmas exams I wrote down in religion… I wrote down the right information and the teacher deducted marks for it because that is not what it said in the book. And I went 'Miss, that is the right information.' And I had to go home and prove it and go on the internet and print out about ten pages and proved it and brought it back in, but she said 'it is on my record and in my book so I can't give you any marks.' (13 years, Muslim, Pakistan, female)

> *Muhammad*: It's like you have to pay attention to the book.

> *AB*: So your grade wasn't changed?

> *Shoma*: My grade wasn't changed even though I did all that.

While teachers can play a significant role in altering misperceptions about the ethnic minority students' cultures, these scenarios suggest that they can also play a detrimental role in devaluing the primacy of students' personal knowledge and experiences, and hence invalidating what they already know and bring to the classroom. Asmitha recounted an incident whereby her RE teacher dismissed her knowledge of Indian culture as invalid by privileging her own personal experience of having travelled to India.

> *Asmitha*: We were actually doing something about the Hindu religion last year in class and there, she [the teacher] was just talking about cremation and everything and she was saying something about cremation I told her that it wasn't true and we don't do that and she was like…she wouldn't believe me. She said 'no I went to India and I saw it actually happen.'…The whole class thought it was totally sick and everything what she told us, and I was like it's not true. But she was like it is and the students would be more likely to believe her than me because she's the teacher… (15 years, Hindu, India, female)

In privileging her own personal experience ('no I went to India and I saw it actually happen'), the teacher simultaneously dismissed Asmitha's understandings about her own cultural practices and traditions as irrelevant or inaccurate, while promoting the ideas that feed racism ('The whole class thought it was totally sick'). In other words, she legitimates her own view by linking the subject matter to her own experience while delegitimizing Asmitha's personal understandings and experiences of her own culture.

'They Only Show the Bad, they Never Show the Good'

Geography was another subject area which proved problematic where representations of the countries of origin of ethnic minority students were concerned. Asmitha critiqued the tendency within Geography texts to present a one-dimensional and overly negative portrayal of India, where she was born, which did not conform to her own personal experiences or -perceptions.

> *Asmitha*: … We are actually from the South of India, and the cities we are from are so like urbanized. They are very urban cities. They only show the bad, they never show the good. Like in that textbook <referring to a Geography text>, it talked about it [India] being a Third World country, it being poor and the people being illiterate all the time. And they never once showed the prosperity of the country, they never showed the real riches, they never showed, just how people are in India, how intent they are on education, on getting somewhere, on getting sort of a mark on the world. They never said anything about that. Nothing about the economy or anything about that. Just that it is a Third World country (15 years, Hindu, India, female)

An analysis of the imagery and accompanying narrative used in both Geography and CSPE textbooks supports the view that the complexity and diversity of so-called 'Third World' countries is often overlooked in favour of homogenized assumptions of desperate poverty, helplessness and/or ignorance. Understandings about the 'developing world' presented in these texts are informed by Eurocentric perspectives which reconstruct 'other' cultures as alien or problematic or in terms of what they lack in comparison to those in the 'developed' world, as the following examples taken from two senior cycle Geography textbooks illustrate:

> [Caption beneath two photographs]: 'The domestic possessions of the Yadev family in India [showing a family with few possessions] and the Calvin family in the USA [showing a family surrounded by large stacks of possessions]. Study the photographs and use the images to explain the meaning of economic development and quality of life (O' Dwyer, Brunt & Hayes, 2007, p. 130).

> The peoples of North America and Western Europe (the North) generally earn high incomes, live in comfortable homes, eat well, consume most of the world's fuel and have a long life expectancy. In contrast, the peoples of Africa, Asia, and Central and South America (the South) are generally poor and lack a balanced diet. In addition, basic services such as clean drinking water, medical care and transport are in short supply (Quinn, 2007, p. 319).

Harris (1987) has critiqued the 'gross distortion' of such simple dichotomies, arguing that 'even the so-called poorest countries has its clutch of millionaires…. [while] each so-called rich country has, trapped in the interstices of its economy, thousands of hungry and poor' (pp. 200–201). These narratives highlight a lack of appreciation for the complexities of community, culture and continent and for the heterogeneity of social, cultural and political histories (Bryan, 2008b; Escobar, 1995; Slater, 2008). Similarly, within the CSPE curriculum, the continent of Africa and the sub-continent of India are at times presented as undifferentiated and homogenous land masses. One CSPE text, for example, describes 'two examples of development' wherein development workers visited 'a community in India' and 'local people in a community in Africa' (Harrison & Wilson, 2007, p. 119), as if all or at least most communities in Africa and India are indistinguishable.

Underpinning this 'discursive homogenisation' (Escobar, 1995) in textbook representations of 'developing' countries, are numerous photographs of bedraggled children, decrepit shanty towns, overcrowded classrooms and polluted environments, which represent and objectify entire countries or continents. For example, in one Junior cycle Geography textbook, *New Complete Geography*, the 'problems' of Kolkata in India are illustrated with several, vivid photographs. One such photograph shows several semi-clad children outside their dwelling, a 'temporary shack' while a second depicts a Kolkata street with an open sewer and piled high with garbage (Hayes, 2009, p. 206). In a later chapter, the Patel's home – a bustee squat – is depicted, which according to the text is 'the size of an average Irish kitchen' (ibid, p. 273). On the following page a series of images are used to illustrate Kolkata's 'urban problems' – women queuing to fill plastic containers from a street tap; cramped children in a 'poorly built, badly equipped' bustee school and finally, the ubiquitous sight of men, women and children, crowded onto the of an old, rickety bus (ibid, p. 274). Short passages of text do nothing to contextualize the images shown, giving only a brief description of the 'problem' without any examination of its underlying structural or historical causes (Bryan & Bracken, forthcoming). Nor is there any attempt to balance the bleak depictions of poverty and deprivation as another Geography textbook – *New Geo* – manages to do, offsetting negative portrayals of poverty in Kolkata with references to its status as 'a great manufacturing city and a major port' with many amenities such as a famous university, modern hospitals, excellent underground rail transport and widely available internet access (Ashe & McCarthy, 2009, p. 230). However, even this textbook's more balanced representation is let down somewhat by its photographic illustrations – one image of a ramshackle shanty town and another of a crowded and polluted city street. While the text does seek to provide a balanced view of Kolkata, the vivid photographs illustrating the text emphasise only the negative and, arguably, leave a more lasting impression.

Over-generalized comparisons of the so-called 'developed' and 'developing' world strip entire continents of nuance and context and close off consideration of the underlying structures of global inequality. In doing so, crude us-them dichotomies are reinforced, which afford 'us' a way of knowing and defining 'ourselves' as 'developed' 'modern' 'wealthy', 'lucky' and 'concerned' and 'compassionate' about less fortunate 'others', 'corrupt governments' and geographical contexts that exist 'over there' (Heron, 2007). One of the CSPE texts we examined seeks to instill in the national consciousness the notion of Ireland as a developed country—one of *the* most developed countries in the world in fact—as distinct from those who are developing at a 'very slow pace'.

In a country such as Ireland, we are now seen as one of the most developed societies in the world. We have enormous wealth and so are regarded as a developed country. However, many countries throughout the world are not as lucky and often are developing at a very slow pace. These countries experience many problems which slows down their rate of development (Murphy & Ryan, 2006, p. 6.18).

CSPE texts, while ostensibly informing students about geo-political contexts and situations outside of Ireland, are undergirded by narratives about Ireland's role as a fearless campaigner for the cause of human rights globally and as a generous and compassionate provider to the less fortunate in the world (Bryan, 2008b). Meanwhile, countries and people 'over there' are constructed as objects of NGO and western salvation; steeped in an ideology of modernization, the developing world is constructed as lagging behind a Western world which it seeks to emulate (ibid.).

Equally problematic is the way in which the themes of human and children's rights in CSPE texts promote an understanding of the Western experience of childhood as somehow superior to that of 'developing' countries, and the construction of 'Third World' countries as lacking a fully developed conception of childhood (Nieuwenhuys, 2009). For example, a unit on Human Rights in CSPE text *One World* (Murphy & Ryan, 2006, p. 110) presents a human interest story of a young child labourer from Kolkata called Sanjay who describes the poverty and poor living conditions which his family endures. Students are asked to 'make a list of the rights that Sanjay and his family are being denied', to 'Compare Sanjay's life to yours' and to 'List some rights that you have under the UDHR which Sanjay does not have'. Similarly, *Taking Action Now* (Quinn & O' Flynn, 2009, p. 54) provides a case study of '14 child labourers [who] were rescued from New Delhi by the Save the Childhood Movement and the police', which depicts children between the ages of 8–14 in a four storey building with 'rooms crammed with children and adults' working on the embroidery tables. Readers are further informed that 'the air was pungent with the stench of the open toilets and overflowing with filth'. Meanwhile, the same text offers diary extracts from a young Ugandan child, Jean Marie, who was 'forced into combat when she was just ten years of age' (ibid, p. 53). Representations of this nature have the effect of affirming the North's (and Ireland's) putatively superior record where children's rights are concerned, while defining children in the developing world in terms of what they 'lack', relative to some Western norm (Roberts, 1998; cited in Aitken, 2001). In other words, they leave little room for alternative views other than one which portrays children in the developing world as being robbed of the proper experiences and categories of childhood (ibid.).

DISCUSSION

The foregoing analysis has attempted to demonstrate the ineffectiveness of models of interculturalism premised upon an 'add diversity and stir' logic. It is argued that when intercultural educational content and classroom practices are merely 'tacked on' to existing frameworks, practices and curricula they reinscribe ethnically nationalist understandings of identity, misrepresent minority culture and offend and delegitimise ethnic minority students. The analysis comprises part of a larger effort to analyse the implications and effects of dominant discourses and understandings about 'race', ethnicity and cultural diversity 'in those institutions that play so large a part in defining what counts as official knowledge and in helping to form identities around these definitions' (Apple, 1993, p. vii).

As this case study of an ethnically diverse, 'best practice' model of interculturalism suggests, even within so-called non-denominational community colleges, Christian activities and philosophies continue to permeate school events, reflecting 'a "ghostly rhythm" that gives expression to a religious worldview...almost unselfconsciously' (Williams, 2006, p. 129). Observational analysis of intercultural events at BHC reveals how Christianity is reproduced as the normative and invisible centre against which 'Otherness' is produced and highlighted. Within such contexts, dominant cultural identities are at once re-affirmed and rendered invisible through the very intercultural activities and discourses that seek to assure minorities that they *too* belong.

The underlying logic of these practices is that Other students can be part of *our* Irish family *too*, i.e., that 'we' accept and tolerate 'them' *even though* they are outsiders and *even though* they are different to *us* (Ang, 1996). Meanwhile, the very possibility of a national 'we' which is already diverse is denied, and a gulf between 'us' and the 'them' whom 'we' celebrate and accept through the very discourse and practice of interculturalism is created (Hage, 1998). Interculturalism thus constitutes a form of symbolic violence—a subtle, invisible violence—which is difficult to contest, precisely because it assures minorities that they are to be welcomed, tolerated, accepted, even celebrated. Yet it is precisely this logic, the very *raison d'être* of interculturalism in fact, which subtly reinforces the privileged status of culturally dominant groups within society by positioning them as the 'embracer' or 'tolerator' of difference. Accordingly, it is the dominant groups who get to decree the acceptability (or otherwise) of the ethnic Other, thereby negating the possibility of true equality ever being achieved. In other words, power imbalances are constructed and reinforced through the very discourses and practices which claim to be promote equality and human rights (Hage, 1998).

In the absence of major changes to existing curricular context, restrictive under-standings of what it means to be Irish will continue to be promoted, wittingly or unwittingly. Accordingly, ethnic minority students are likely to continue feeling invalidated by overly-simplistic, one-dimensional and inaccurate portrayals and depictions of their cultural identities in instructional materials. While textbooks do not solely determine what is taught and learned in and through schools (Kuzmic, 2000), their dominance in classroom practice endows them with what Rizvi (1993) terms an effective *steering capacity* which *steers* readers *towards* certain inter-pretations, while *steering* them *away* from others. The need to interrogate dominant textual representations and understandings of cultural diversity is all the more urgent therefore, when we consider that teachers tend to rely on textbooks to teach those subjects which lend themselves to a consideration of issues of diversity and interculturalism (Gleeson, King, O'Driscoll & Tormey, 2007). The reliance on text-books as the authoritative and definitive sources of knowledge means that when these inaccuracies are contested by students, their own beliefs and experiences are de-legitimised. The fact that the NCCA is engaged in ongoing work where curriculum review and planning are concerned offers potential for more inclusionary and accurate curricular representations of ethnic minority identities within the formal curriculum. However, to the extent that the NCCA currently has no role in determining or 'vetting' the content of textbooks, this potential may be limited.

Recent studies suggest teachers often feel-ill prepared to address issues of 'race' and racism in their classrooms which reflects gaps in anti-racism pedagogy in teacher education programmes and indicates an urgent need for greater opportunities for pre and in-service teachers to engage critically with issues of 'race' and racism (Bryan, 2009; 2010b; Bryan & Bracken, forthcoming; Devine, 2005; O'Brien, 2009; Smyth, Darmody, McGinnity & Byrne, 2009). The purpose of the foregoing critique is not to 'blame' individual teachers or schools for limited or tokenistic responses to cultural diversity, which are often rooted in good intentions. Existing research demonstrates how macro processes and discourses operating at the level of Irish state policy intersect with, and constrain, local level school responses (Bryan, 2010b; Devine, 2005). Relatedly, teachers' engagement with diversity and with ethnic minority students is often constrained by a lack of adequate statutory support and resources to schools (See e.g., Lyons, 2010).

It is also important to acknowledge that schools are not the only place where young people develop their understandings of cultural diversity. Indeed, while schools can play an important role in promoting positive attitudes towards diversity, and teaching against racism, schooling occurs within specific social and political-economic contexts that may mitigate – or even reverse – its progressive effects (Vavrus, 2003). This implies a need for radical alternative pedagogical anti-racist strategies in tandem with broader political-economic reforms (Bryan, 2009c; 2010b).

The foregoing attempt to render curricular representations problematic, should not be read as a naïve call for additive approaches to the curriculum, which offer 'fuller' representations of ethnic minority cultures, 'one that gets things right' (Talburt, Rofes & Rasmussen, 2004, p. 8). Rather, it seeks to argue that there is an urgent need for a radical redefinition of school knowledge from the multiple perspectives and identities of ethnic minority groups that goes beyond the discourse of 'inclusion' and 'celebrating diversity,' to address issues of representation and the unequal distribution of material resources and power within society (McCarthy, 1993). An integral part of this radical redefinition is curricular justice (Connell, 1993), that is, the reconstitution of curricular knowledge from the point of view of those who are marginalized within society, and the displacement of normative versions of identity, along, *inter alia*, class, racial, ethnic, gender, and sexuality lines.

NOTES

[1] The findings presented in this chapter draw on a larger qualitative vertical case study (Vavrus & Bartlett, 2009) concerned with both school and national-level policy responses to cultural diversity and racism in Ireland during the so-called 'Celtic Tiger' era. We would like to acknowledge the support of a Dean's Grant for Student Research in Diversity and a President's Grant for Student Research from Teachers College, Columbia University, a Conflict Resolution Network Interdisciplinary Ph.D. Award from Columbia University, and a Spencer Foundation Research Training Grant in enabling this research to be carried out. We would also like to thank Andy Storey, two anonymous reviewers and the editors of this volume for their helpful feedback on an earlier version of this chapter.

[2]   All names in this chapter are pseudonyms. The source of this quotation is deliberately omitted to protect the anonymity of the school.

[3]   There is a strong tradition of Church involvement in, and control over, social institutions in an Irish context. Church and state entered into a "marriage of convenience" in post-independence Ireland, enabling the Catholic Church to wield considerable ideological control and institutional power over such institutions as education, health and social welfare (Tovey & Share, 2000, p. 322). Although this unusual position is increasingly challenged, the Catholic Church continues to play a dominant role in the management and provision of education, particularly at primary level. Secondary schools, although privately owned institutions under the management of religious communities, boards of governors or individuals, are formally recognised, funded and regulated by the Department of Education and Skills (Tovey & Share, 2000). Historically, these schools have provided an 'academic' curriculum and have been oriented towards students from middle class backgrounds. A small percentage of secondary schools charge fees and are highly socially selective. A majority of secondary schools are denominational (mostly Roman Catholic) and a small majority are single-sex. Community colleges (formally known as vocational schools), are administered by and funded through the Vocational Education Commiteers (VECs) of local government, are non-denominational and are entirely funded by public monies. These schools, which were established in the 1930s, were originally designed to provide a vocational rather than academic curriculum, and catered to children from working-class, small-farming and lower middle class backgrounds and today cater for approximately 34 percent of all post-primary students. The remainder of students attend community and comprehensive schools, which are administered jointly by the VEC and a designated religious body and are effectively denominational. They cater to a wide cross-section of students along social class lines.

[4]   See the website of Banagher College, Co. Offaly. http://www.bccns.ie/

[5]   Participants are identified by their age, religion (if they identified with a particular faith), their country of origin, and their gender,

[6]   Denotes that some of the conversation has been omitted.

[7]   The committee responsible for drawing up guidelines for both of the national syllabuses in RE included members from Catholic and Protestant denominations but not from other faiths (NCCA, 2000, p. 52).

REFERENCES

Aitken, S. C. (2001). Global crises of childhood: Rights, justice and the unchildlike child. *Area, 33*(2), 119–127.

Ang, I. (1996). The curse of the smile: Ambivalence and the 'Asian' woman in Australian multiculturalism. *Feminist Review, 52*, 36–49.

Apple, M. W. (1993). Series editor's introduction. In C. McCarthy & W. Crichlow (Eds.), *Race, identity and representation in education* (pp. vii–ix). New York & London: Routledge.

Ashe, L., & McCarthy, K. (2009). *New Geo: Junior certificate Geography.* Dublin: EDCO.

Billig, M. (1995). *Banal nationalism.* London; Thousand Oaks, CA: Sage.

Bourdieu, P. (2001). *Masculine domination.* Cambridge, England: Polity Press.

Boyle, A., & Boyle, N. (2005). *All about faith: Complete junior certificate religion.* Dublin: Gill & MacMillan.

Bryan, A. (2008a). The co-articulation of national identity and interculturalism in the Irish curriculum: Educating for democratic citizenship? *London Review of Education, 6*(1), 47–58.

Bryan, A. (2008b). Researching and searching for international development in the formal curriculum: Towards a post-colonial conceptual framework. *Policy and Practice: A Development Education Review, 7*(1), 68–79.

Bryan, A. (2009a). Pedagogies of privilege: Re-thinking interculturalism and anti-racism in education. In S. Drudy (Ed.), *Education in Ireland: Challenge and change,* (pp. 226–240). Dublin: Gill and Macmillan.

Bryan, A. (2009b). The intersectionality of nationalism and multiculturalism in the Irish curriculum: Teaching against racism? *Race, Ethnicity and Education, 12*(5), 297–317.

Bryan, A. (2009c). "Migration nation": Intercultural education and anti-racism as symbolic violence in Celtic Tiger Ireland. In F. Vavrus & L. Bartlett (Eds.), *Critical approaches to comparative education: Vertical case studies from Africa, Europe, the Middle East and the Americas* (pp. 129–146). New York: Palgrave Macmillan.

Bryan, A. (2010a). 'Common-sense citizenship', 'citizenship tourism' and citizenship education in an era of globalisation: The case of Ireland during the Celtic Tiger era. In A. Reid, J. Gill & A. Sears (Eds.), *Globalisation, the nation-state and the citizen: Dilemmas and directions for civics and citizenship education* (pp. 143–157). Routledge: New York.

Bryan, A. (2010b). Corporate multiculturalism, diversity management and positive interculturalism in Irish schools and society. *Irish Educational Studies, 29*(3), 253–269.

Bryan, A., & Bracken, M. (forthcoming). *Learning to read the world?: Teaching and learning about global citizenship and international development in post-primary schools.* Irish Aid.

Connell, R. W. (1993). *Schools and social justice.* Philadelphia: Temple University Press.

Department of Education and Skills and the Offie of the Minister for Integration. (2010). Intercultural Education Strategy 2010–2015. Dublin: DES.

Devereux, E., & Breen, M. (2004). No racists here: Public opinion and media treatment of asylum seekers and refugees. In N. Collins & T. Cradden (Eds.), *Political issues in Ireland today* (pp. 168–187). Manchester: Manchester University Press.

Devine, D. (2005). Welcome to the Celtic Tiger? Teacher responses to immigration and ethnic diversity in Irish schools. *International Studies in the Sociology of Education, 15*(1), 49–70.

Devine, D. (2009). Mobilising capitals? Migrant children's negotiation of their everyday lives in schools. *British Journal of Sociology of Education, 30*(5), 521–535.

Escobar, E. (1995). *Encountering development: The making and unmaking of the third world.* Princeton, NJ: University Press.

Garner, S. (2004). *Racism in the Irish experience.* London: Pluto.

Giroux, H. A. (1992). *Border crossings: Cultural workers and the politics of education.* New York; London: Routledge.

Gleeson, J., King, P., O'Driscoll, S., & Tormey, R. (2007). *Development education in Irish post-primary schools: Knowledge, attitudes and activism.* Shannon Curriculum Development Centre, University of Limerick and Irish Aid.

Goan, S., & Ryan, T. (2004). *Exploring faith: Junior certificate religious education.* Dublin: The Celtic Press.

Gunning, T., & de Barra, M. (Ed.) (2006). *Religion: The Irish experience.* Dublin: Veritas.

Hage, G. (1998). *White nation: Fantasies of white supremacy in a multicultural society.* Annandale, NSW; West Wickham, Kent, UK: Pluto Press.

Harris, N. (1987). *The end of the third world: The newly industrialising countries and the decline of an ideology.* London: Penguin.

Harrison, C., & Wilson, M. (2007). *Make a difference! Junior certificate civic, social and political education.* Dublin: Folens.

Hayes, C. (2009). *New complete Geography* (4th ed.). Dublin: Gill & McMillan.

Heron, B. (2007). *Desire for development: Whiteness, gender and the helping imperative.* Ontario, CA: Wilfred Laurier University Press.

Hughes, G., McGinnity, F., O'Connell, P., & Quinn, E. (2007). The impact of immigration. In T. Fahey, H. Russell, & C. Whelan (Eds.), *Best of times? The social impact of the celtic tiger* (pp. 217–244). Dublin: Institute of Public Administration, Economic and Social Research Institute.

Kuzmic, J. (2000). Textbooks, knowledge, and masculinity: Examining patriarchy from within in N. Lesko (Ed.). *Masculinities at school.* (pp. 105-126). Thousand Oaks, CA: Sage.

Leonardo, Z. (2004). The colour of supremacy: Beyond the discourse of "White privilege". *Educational Philosophy and Theory, 36*(2), 137–152.

Lyons, Z. (2010). Articulating a deficit perspective: A survey of the attitudes of post-primary English language support teachers and coordinators. *Irish Educational Studies, 29*(3), 289–303.

McCarthy, C. (1993). After the canon: Knowledge and ideological representation in the multicultural discourse on curriculum reform. In C. McCarthy & W. Crichlow (Eds.), *Race, identity and representation in education* (pp. 289–305). New York & London: Routledge.

Murphy, D., & Ryan, J. (2006). One world: Studies in civic, social, political education for junior certificate. Dublin: EDCO.

National Centre for Curriculum and Assessment. (2000). *Junior certificate religious education syllabus (ordinary and higher level)*. Dublin: The Stationery Office.

National Centre for Curriculum and Assessment. (2003). *Leaving certificate religious education syllabus (ordinary and higher level)*. Dublin: The Stationery Office.

National Centre for Curriculum and Assessment. (2005). *Intercultural education in post-primary school: Guidelines for schools*. Dublin: NCCA.

Nieuwenhuys,O. (2009). Is there an Indian childhood? *Childhood, 16*(2), 147–153.

Nolan, E. (2008). Underneath the bandaid: Supporting bilingual students in Irish schools. *Irish Educational Studies, 27*(3), 253–266.

O'Brien, J. (2009). Institutional racism and anti-racism in teacher education: Perspectives of teacher educators. *Irish Educational Studies, 28*(2)193–207.

O'Dwyer, P., Brunt, B., & Hayes, C. (2007). *Dynamic economic Geography: Syllabus core and economic activities*. Dublin: Gill & McMillan.

Quinn, R. (2007). *Eco* (2nd ed.). Dublin: Folens.

Quinn, R., & O'Flynn, O. (2009). *Taking action now: civic, social and political education*. Dublin: C.J. Fallon.

Rizvi, F. (1993). Children and the grammar of popular racism. In C. McCarthy & W. Crichlow (Eds.), *Race, identity, and representation in education* (pp. 126–139). New York: Routledge.

Slater, M. (2008). *Geopolitics and the post-colonial: Rethinking north-south relations*. Oxford: Blackwell.

Smyth, E., Darmody, M., McGinnity, F., & Byrne, D. (2009). *Adapting to diversity: Irish schools and newcomer students*. Dublin: ESRI.

Talburt, S., Rofes, E., & Rasmussen, M. L. (2004). Transforming discourses of queer youth and educational practices surrounding gender, sexuality and youth. In M. L. Rasmussen, E. Rofes, & S. Talburt Youth (Eds.), *Sexualities: Pleasure, subversion, and insubordination in and out of schools* (pp. 17–39). New York: Palgrave.

Tovey, H., & Share, P. (2000). *A sociology of Ireland*. Dublin: Gill & Macmillan.

Vavrus, F. (2003). *Desire and decline: Schooling amid crisis in Tanzania*. New York: Peter Lang.

Vavrus, F., & Bartlett, L. (2009). *Critical approaches to comparative education: Vertical case studies from Africa, Europe, the Middle East, and the Americas*. New York: Palgrave Macmillan.

Williams, K. (2006). Religion and the civic space. *Studies: An Irish Quarterly Review, 378*(95). Retrieved March 23, 2010, http://www.studiesirishreview.ie/j/page129

Youdell, D. (2006). Subjectivation and performative politics–Butler thinking Althusser and Foucault: Intelligibility, agency and the raced nationed-religioned subject of education. *British Journal of Sociology of Education, 27*(3), 511–528.

Audrey Bryan
Department of Human Development
St. Patrick's College, Drumcondra, Dublin 9

Meliosa Bracken
School of Education
University College Dublin

EMER SMYTH AND MERIKE DARMODY

8. RELIGIOUS DIVERSITY AND SCHOOLING IN IRELAND[1]

INTRODUCTION

During recent decades, many European societies have become increasingly culturally diverse. Local neighbourhoods now include people from different ethnic, linguistic and religious backgrounds. The extent to which different communities integrate has implications for social cohesion in the receiving countries. In addition, schools across Europe face growing pressures to respond to immigration and adopt more inclusive practices (Faas, 2010). It is generally accepted that schools play an important role in the integration of ethnic minority[2] students and in promoting their feeling of inclusion through involvement in the academic and social spheres (Darmody et al., forthcoming). The importance of integration is evident in the rhetoric on multi-cultural and intercultural education in various policy documents across Europe (see, for example, European Commission, 2008). Some sources have referred to various barriers to integration at school (Caulfield et al., 2005; Devine and Kelly, 2006). One of the areas where potential tensions may arise is in relation to the provision of religious education and to the broader religious ethos of the school.[3]

During the 'Celtic Tiger' period of economic boom, labour shortages in the Republic of Ireland allied with the expansion of the European Union resulted in rapid large-scale immigration and significant change in the student composition of Irish schools (Byrne et al., 2010). In their recent study, Smyth et al. (2009) estimated that in 2007 ethnic minority students made up approximately 10 per cent of the primary school-going population and 6 per cent of the secondary population. The distribution of these students across schools in the two sectors was found to differ. The vast majority of secondary[4] schools had at least one ethnic minority student but the overall proportion of these students in this sector was relatively modest. The situation was very different in primary schools: while there were no ethnic minority students in a significant number of primary schools, in others (mainly located in cities), these students made up more than a fifth of the total cohort. Importantly, these ethnic minority children represent a wide variety of cultures, linguistic groups and faith systems.

Increasing cultural diversity in Ireland has had implications for the religious profile of the population, though nationality and religious affiliation intersect in complex ways. Data from the 2006 Census of Population indicate that 92 per cent of Irish 4–12 year olds are reported as Catholic compared with 57 per cent of children with non-Irish nationality (CSO, Special Tabulation). Looked at another way,

Darmody, Tyrrell, Song (eds.), The Changing Faces of Ireland: Exploring the Lives of Immigrant and Ethnic Minority Children, 125–144.

children with non-Irish nationality make up 5 per cent of Catholics, 32 per cent of non-Catholics and 26 per cent of those with secular beliefs. Immigration has therefore increased religious diversity in the context of the long-standing presence of religious minorities and a growth in the number without formal religious affiliation in the Irish population.

Not surprisingly, religious diversity is a challenge for the Irish school system which, particularly at primary level, is largely denominational in nature. Increasing debate is taking place regarding the issue of school governance and the potential of the educational system to encompass children and young people of different beliefs and none. A good deal of the focus of research on immigration into Ireland has been on linguistic and cultural issues, with relatively little attention paid to the implications of religious diversity. This chapter draws on a pioneering large-scale mixed methods study on ethnic minority children in Irish primary and secondary schools to address this gap in research. The chapter focuses on the provision of religious education in Irish primary and secondary schools in the general context of intercultural education. In particular, the chapter explores to what extent schools in Ireland accommodate religious diversity among the student population and how ethnic minority students feel about religious education. The chapter is organised into five main sections. Section one explores previous research on the provision of religious education in multicultural settings. Section two gives a brief description of the Irish educational system and the position of religious education in it. The chapter then moves on to introduce the methodology and data used in the study. Section four presents the research results while the concluding section discusses the implications of these findings.

PREVIOUS RESEARCH ON THE PROVISION OF RELIGIOUS EDUCATION IN MULTICULTURAL EDUCATION SETTINGS

Growing plurality and globalisation in contemporary societies has brought the issue of provision of religious education in formal educational settings increasingly to the fore in many countries, including Ireland. Most European countries offer religious education as a school subject. However, its mode of delivery and content tend to vary significantly across countries (see Dommel and Mitchell, 2008) and a number of different models of religious education have been identified (see Jackson et al., 2007). The main distinction is between education into religion and learning about religion (see Schreiner, 2005). Education *into* religion focuses on faith formation, teaching specific religious doctrine and preparing children for religious rites of passage. Learning *about* religion involves exploring different major religious and moral issues but without seeking to transmit particular belief systems. It is important to note, however, that different types of religious education are not always mutually exclusive. As well as differing in the nature of religious education, European countries also differ in the relative role of the State and/or religious communities in managing schools and providing religious education. Furthermore, religion and religious education have recently come into focus as an important component of supporting intercultural education and citizenship education in schools (Jackson, 2004; Jackson et al., 2007). Increasingly, classrooms now contain students from a number of religious belief systems and none, presenting schools with considerable challenges in catering for the needs of this diverse student population.

Religious education in multicultural societies is a contentious subject. Bates, Durka and Schweitzer (2006) talk about 'tensions between multiculturalism and intercultural learning, between learning about religion and learning from religion, between pedagogy and theology, context and tradition, initiation and critical thinking, universal human rights and particular religious convictions' (see also Mercer and Roebben, 2007). Several studies have pointed towards potential discord between what is taught in school and what is transmitted at home, which is likely to have an impact on minority faith or secular students' integration at school (Caulfield et al., 2005). Mercer and Roebben (2007) argue that the religious diversity of local communities should be reflected in what is being taught at school. Nevertheless, despite the rhetoric of intercultural or multicultural education, schools often adopt an assimilationary approach, expecting those of different beliefs to 'fit in' with the majority culture (Faas, 2010).

While research on the integration of ethnic minority students in Ireland is steadily growing, there is a general paucity of empirical research on the provision of religious education in Irish schools and the implications for minority students. A study by Lodge (1999), which focused on minority belief parents whose children attended Catholic schools, indicated that the emphasis on sacramental preparation in these schools was a problematic issue for parents and students, with some children reporting being teased or bullied as a result of not participating and feeling that the schools undervalued diversity. In her study, Devine (2005) found that minority belief children in primary schools had to remain in class for religious education or withdraw from class, thus highlighting their 'difference'. This issue was seen as less problematic within secondary schools where some schools provided additional English language support during religious education classes (Devine, 2005). These studies indicate that the way in which schools address religious diversity is clearly an important issue for ethnic minority parents and students.

The treatment of diversity relates to much broader concepts of multicultural and intercultural education. Faas (2010) notes that multiculturalism is a contested concept. While interculturalism promotes communication, integration and dialogue, multiculturalism describes reciprocity, dialogue and civic integration (ibid.: 13). The two concepts have been defined by UNESCO:

> Multicultural education uses learning about other cultures in order to produce acceptance, or at least tolerance, of these cultures. Intercultural education aims to go beyond passive co-existence, to achieve a developing and sustainable way of living together in multicultural societies through the creation of understanding of, respect for and dialogue between the different cultural groups (UNESCO, 2006: 18).

The way in which education systems across Europe address cultural diversity varies from country to country. Whether the policy focus is on multicultural or intercultural education often reflects the historical background of migration and resulting diversity as well as broader notions of the nature of the State. In general, policy documents in Ireland have tended to adopt the term 'intercultural education'. The National Council for Curriculum and Assessment (NCCA) has published *Intercultural Guidelines* for primary and secondary schools (NCCA, 2005, 2006); the Irish National Teachers' Organisation has also published intercultural guidelines for schools (INTO, 2005). According to the NCCA, '[i]ntercultural education is a synthesis of the learning from multicultural education approaches and anti-racist education approaches which were commonly used internationally from the 1960s to the 1990s' (2006: i). The *Intercultural Guidelines* for secondary schools note that religious diversity has become a feature of Irish society and that the numbers of individuals belonging to minority or no religion groups have increased over the years. It clearly states that '[i]ntercultural education promotes an engagement with a diversity of cultures for students of all ethnic groups and religions' (ibid, p. 27). However, while stating that the school should 'celebrate special events in the calendars of a diversity of cultures' and that 'all students irrespective of their colour, ethnic group, religion or ability can feel at home and represented within the school', it does not make specific recommendations on how the provision of religious education should be treated.[5] In the remainder of this chapter, we explore the extent to which the desired 'intercultural education' approach is influenced by the way in which religious education is provided in Irish schools and by broader school ethos, that is, day-to-day practices and interactions within the school.

THE IRISH EDUCATIONAL SYSTEM AND THE PROVISION
OF RELIGIOUS EDUCATION

This section outlines the structure of the educational system in the Republic of Ireland and the provision of religious education in primary and secondary schools. Education is compulsory for children from the ages of six to 16, with the transition from primary to secondary education occurring at around 12–13 years of age.

A distinctive feature of the Irish primary school system is the predominance of faith, mainly Catholic, schools. The denominational nature of the system can be traced back to the early nineteenth century and the Churches' response to the establishment of a national school system intended to be multidenominational in character (Coolahan, 1981). The vast majority (92%) of primary schools are currently owned and managed by the Catholic Church. One in twenty schools are owned and managed by the Church of Ireland with a small number of Presbyterian schools and one Methodist school. There are two Muslim faith schools and one Jewish school, all located in Dublin city. There is a growing number of multidenominational schools under the patronage of Educate Together; these schools emphasise the development of a culturally inclusive and democratic ethos. There are also seven multidenominational schools under the auspices of An Foras Patrúnachta, the body which owns and manages Irish language medium schools. The latter body also runs 14 interdenominational schools, which are explicitly designed as interfaith (Catholic-Protestant) schools. A new model of school patronage has emerged in recent years, the community primary school run by Vocational Educational Committees (VECS); two such schools were created in response to the needs of growing religious diversity among the student body. The issue of school governance has been the subject of on-going debate in policy and media circles, with discussions under way regarding the potential 'transfer' of some Catholic schools to State control.

In general, parents in Ireland are free to choose a primary school for their children. However, in practice, their choice may be limited as some of the schools can be oversubscribed and/or employ specific selection criteria which may include the religious background of the family (see Smyth et al., 2009 for further discussion). Furthermore, the provision of minority faith and Educate Together schools is geographically variable. As a result, the majority of principals of Catholic schools (75%) report that they have at least a few students of minority (or no) belief (see Smyth et al., 2009).

Irish primary schools follow the new Primary School Curriculum (introduced in 1999), devised by the National Council for Curriculum and Assessment. It is an integrated curriculum which aims to promote active learning and comprises seven curriculum areas, including religious education. However, the formulation of the religious curriculum has been the responsibility of religious authorities and patron bodies. In Educate Together and other multidenominational schools, a specific ethical curriculum, *Learn Together*, has been developed which combines a focus on ethics and values with a comparative view of world religions. This approach is similar to what Schreiner (2005) describes as 'learning *about* religion'. In Catholic schools[6], a common religious education programme, *Alive-O*, is taught to children, and children receive preparation for sacraments, including Communion and Confirmation, within the school day. In Catholic primary schools, religion often permeates the school day with prayers and observation of religious festivals important features of school life, making schools a central mechanism in religious socialisation (Inglis, 1987). Thus, religious education in primary Catholic and other faith schools in Ireland focuses on 'education *into* religion', that is, faith formation.

The Education Act (1998) does not 'require any student to attend instruction in any subjects which is contrary to the conscience of the parent of the student or in the case of the student who has reached 18 years, the student' (p. 30). Therefore, parents whose children attend faith schools may opt out of religious education. Some secular groups (such as the Humanists) have strongly criticised this approach, arguing for the crucial differentiation between religious education ('learning *about* religion') and religious instruction ('education *into* religion'). The NCCA notes that 'it is the responsibility of the school to provide a religious education that is consonant with its ethos and at the same time to be flexible in making alternative arrangements for those who do not wish to avail of the particular religious education it offers' (NCCA, 2006: 86). The operation of this practice at the school level, and the implications for ethnic minority students, will be explored in the following sections of the chapter.

School structure and curriculum at secondary level in the Republic of Ireland is quite distinct from that at primary level. Secondary schools fall into four broad sectors: voluntary secondary schools, vocational schools (including community colleges), community schools and comprehensive schools. Voluntary secondary schools are owned and managed by religious communities (increasingly in the form of trusteeship rather than direct involvement), boards of governors or individuals; they make up just over half (53%) of all secondary schools. The vast majority (94%) of voluntary secondary schools are Catholic. Vocational schools, which make up 34 per cent of all secondary schools, are owned and managed by local VECs. They are formally termed 'interdenominational' in character but, at their inception, a commitment was given that religious education would be provided in vocational schools. In addition, religious trustees are represented on the board of management of community colleges, which fall under the VEC remit. Community schools are managed by boards of management, which contain three nominees of religious authorities. The Deed of Trust for community schools explicitly states that religious education must be taught for a minimum of two hours (or three class periods) per week and principals of comprehensive schools are required to facilitate religious worship. If a community school has a significant number of students of a minority religious persuasion, the board of management has an obligation to provide appropriate religious instruction. Nine of the 14 comprehensive schools fall under the trusteeship of the local Catholic bishop while the remaining five fall under the trusteeship of the Church of Ireland Board of Education. In sum, while secondary school structures are much more heterogeneous than at primary level, religious bodies continue to play a role in the management of many schools.

Until the 1998 Education Act, the State had been precluded from setting examinations in religious education. Prior to this period, religious education was provided as a non-exam subject in secondary schools, with the emphasis being on faith formation ('education into religion') and the religious education syllabus designed by the relevant faith bodies. As at primary level, students could opt out of the subject. Religious education as an exam subject at junior cycle (lower secondary level) was introduced in 2000, with the curriculum designed by the National Council for Curriculum and Assessment, and first examined in 2003. In 2008, religious education was taken as an exam subject by 46 per cent of Junior Certificate (lower secondary examination) candidates. The NCCA-designed senior cycle (upper secondary) religious education syllabus was introduced in 2003 and first examined in 2005. Religious education as an exam subject was taken by only two per cent of Leaving Certificate (upper secondary) exam candidates in 2009. In addition to guidelines for the exam subject, the NCCA has introduced guidelines, which are optional for teachers, for the teaching of religious education as a non-exam subject.

The religious education exam syllabus appears to focus on a 'learning about religions' approach, stating that 'Religious Education should ensure that students are exposed to a broad range of religious traditions and to the non-religious interpretation of life' (NCCA, 2000: 4). Williams (2005) suggests that the religious education examination syllabus at secondary level focuses on the theoretical aspects of religion and risks not communicating to young people 'the lived richness of a religious tradition' (p. 83). However, the Irish Catholic Bishops' Conference (2003) suggests the development of a school policy on the religious education of Catholic students to ensure the meshing of 'content' and faith formation aspects of religious education. Subject inspections of religious education would appear to imply that religious education is being interpreted in the context of existing school ethos.

However, there is no available research on the implementation of the religious education curriculum and its relative focus on learning about and into religion.

METHODOLOGY

This chapter draws on data collected for the *Adapting to Diversity* study, the first national study on provision for the needs of ethnic minority students in Irish primary and secondary schools. This study built upon previous small-scale research in the Irish context to combine national survey data with in-depth case-studies from primary and secondary school sectors. While the focus of the study was on provision for ethnic minority students in general, it yielded original and interesting information on how schools handle religious diversity, an issue which has been relatively neglected in existing research.

The study involved a postal survey of all (733) second-level principals and a sample of 1,200 primary principals selected to be representative of all primary schools in size, location and disadvantaged (DEIS) status.[7] The survey focused on the views of principals as it was felt that they would be in the best position to give an overview of available resources and support structures within the school. The topics included in the survey were based on international research and on prior consultations with key stakeholders in the Irish educational system.

The questionnaire collected detailed information on a number of aspects of school policy and practice regarding ethnic minority students, including:
- The number and profile of ethnic minority students in the school;
- Admissions policies in the school;
- General support structures and specific supports for ethnic minority students;
- Language support provision: practice and perceptions;
- Perceived academic outcomes of ethnic minority students (including achievement, motivation and aspirations);
- Perceived social integration of ethnic minority students.

To supplement survey data, 14 case-study schools were chosen to further explore school provision for ethnic minority students and challenges that schools face catering for growing ethnic and religious diversity. To provide a contrast, two schools without any ethnic minority students were also chosen as case-studies within each sector. The profile of the case-study schools is presented in Table 1. As indicated, all of the case-study primary schools were Catholic schools. The other secondary schools without ethnic minority students were both Catholic voluntary secondary schools. Among the secondary schools with ethnic minority students, two were community schools, one was a vocational school and three were Catholic voluntary secondary schools. Across the schools, a total of 82 in-depth interviews were conducted with school principals, language support teachers, and designated personnel dealing with ethnic minority students. Focus group interviews were conducted with 43 separate groups of Irish and ethnic minority students to explore students' own experiences. In this chapter, we focus on presenting the perceptions of religious education among ethnic minority students, given the focus of the book.

Table 1. Profile of the case-study schools

School	Sector	Size	Rural/ urban	Disadvantaged (DEIS) status	Proportion of ethnic minority students
Primary schools					
Adams Street	Catholic	Small (<100)	Rural	Disadvantaged	High (>20%)
Dobbins Road	Catholic	Large (>300)	Urban	Not disadvantaged	None
Durango Street	Catholic	Large (>300)	Urban	Not disadvantaged	High (>20%)
Glendale Avenue	Catholic	Small (<100)	Rural	Not disadvantaged	None
Greenway Road	Catholic	Large (>300)	Urban	Not disadvantaged	Low/medium (<10%)
Jefferson Street	Catholic	Small (<100)	Urban	Not disadvantaged	Low/medium (<10%)
Thomas Road	Catholic	Small (<100)	Urban	Disadvantaged	High (>20%)
Van Buren Street	Catholic	Large (>300)	Rural	Disadvantaged	Low/medium (<10%)
Secondary schools					
Adwick Street	Catholic voluntary secondary	Large (600+)	Urban	Not disadvantaged	None
Ashville Lane	Catholic voluntary secondary	Small (<400)	Urban	Disadvantaged	High (>10%)
Bentham Street	Community school	Medium (400–599)	Rural	Not disadvantaged	Low/medium (<10%)
Brayton Square	Community school	Medium (400–599)	Rural	Disadvantaged	High (>10%)
Grange Park	Catholic voluntary secondary	Small (<400)	Urban	Disadvantaged	None
Huntington Road	Catholic voluntary secondary	Medium (400–599)	Urban	Not disadvantaged	Low/medium (<10%)
Lowfield Street	Catholic voluntary secondary	Medium (400–599)	Urban	Not disadvantaged	Low/medium (<10%)
Wulford Park	Vocational school	Small (<400)	Rural	Not disadvantaged	High (>10%)

Note: Pseudonyms are used to protect the anonymity of schools.

RESEARCH RESULTS

This chapter has outlined the way in which the issue of religious diversity has been relatively neglected in existing research on ethnic minority children and young people in Ireland. In this section, we draw on case-studies of primary and secondary schools to explore the implications of the nature of school provision for the experiences of students. The discussion focuses on two issues: how schools handle religious education in the context of religious diversity and how young people themselves view religious education at school.

School Provision and Religious Diversity

Section two outlined the pertinence of religious affiliation to school ownership and the provision of religious education in Irish schools. Where schools are oversubscribed, religious affiliation may be one of the criteria used for allocating school places. Thus, a survey of school principals indicated that in oversubscribed primary schools, 31 per cent selected students on the basis of religious affiliation (Smyth et al., 2009).[8] In Greenway Road primary school, for example, parents put their child's name down for entry to the school as soon as they are born or as soon as they arrive in the area; both 'religion' and 'having a sibling in the school' are taken into account in allocating places. The principal referred to the school as a 'Catholic school for Catholic children':

> We get two applicants for each place ... so the prioritisation in our enrolment policy is brothers and sisters of children already enrolled... and because it is a Catholic school, Catholic children of this parish. So usually we fill our places from those cohorts, so that can sometimes make it difficult for a child from another country who does not have a brother or sister with us or who is not a Catholic. (Principal, Greenway Road primary school)

Similarly, in Dobbins Road school, the principal indicates the role played by religious affiliation in determining school admissions:

> Because we are a Catholic school, we accept all Catholic children in the parish ... first right and then ... siblings of children coming to this school and to the boys' school.... Then it's all other children. So definitely Catholic children have priority ... but we have quite a number of children of other denominations and no faith at all. (Principal, Dobbins Road primary school)

However, in the case of other schools, their Catholic nature was explicitly seen as requiring that they adopted an inclusive approach to admissions:

> The Catholic ethos is something that the school espouses and we don't turn away regardless of colour or creed. (Principal, Adams Street primary school)

> We're a Catholic school, a Catholic parish and a Catholic bishop is the patron but we accept children of all nationalities and all religions and no religion. And it's actually under our enrolment criteria, religion is not under the criteria,

so we've never refused anybody on grounds of religion. (Principal, Van Buren Street primary school)

In general, specifying religion as an admission criterion is likely to disproportionately impact on ethnic minority families but so too are other criteria, such as length of time on a waiting list.

Secondary schools were much less likely to mention religion as an admissions criterion than primary schools; only 7 per cent of secondary principals in oversubscribed schools did so. One principal even indicated that the school does not collect information on religious affiliation:

Interviewer: What is the religious background of foreign students in your school?
There would be a mixture, the Polish on the whole would be Catholic, although in fairness, on an application form I don't ask this question. (Principal, Huntington Road secondary school)

As in the primary sector, criteria such as giving preference to those with siblings in the school and to those on the waiting list may indirectly affect access to oversubscribed secondary schools for ethnic minority families. One principal highlighted sectoral differences, emphasising the inclusive nature of community schools:

A community school has to be inclusive … And the tradition of religion is one that we don't just provide for one religion. (Principal, Brayton Square secondary school)

All of the case-study schools indicated having at least a few students of minority faith or secular beliefs. Understandably, the provision of religious education raised questions for these families, most of whom were from ethnic minority backgrounds. The main approach taken in Catholic primary schools was for students to opt out of religious education class. In one school, Muslim students carried on with their school work in another classroom during the religious education (RE) class:

We have a few Muslims here as well and we observe their religion, they take part in all the classes and when religion is going on they're involved in another activity, usually in the room or an adjacent room. (Principal, Van Buren primary school)

In practice, however, there were often logistical difficulties in supervising children in another setting so many students remained in class doing other schoolwork or homework during RE class. Alternatively, some schools attempted to timetable language support classes so that students would be withdrawn from religion class.

Well if we have to take anybody out, they will go out at religion time, now just say they need individual work or anything, that is the time that is allocated to them. (Principal, Jefferson Street primary school)

While this approach can be seen as avoiding highlighting difference, it may in fact reinforce the equation of 'Irish' with 'Catholic' rather than allowing for the existence of religious diversity among both Irish and ethnic minority students.

It is important to note that the religious nature of Catholic primary schools is a significant part of the whole school day, with prayers and attending religious services an important feature. While, in general, minority faith children attended (even if they did not participate in) religion classes, they were not obliged to go to Mass with the other students and generally stayed with another class while carrying on with their school-work.

> Some religions perhaps wouldn't want their children to be involved in liturgies or in sacramental preparation. That's fine, we accommodate them, they can do work in another class if we're going to the Church or whatever. (Principal, Van Buren primary school)

> In religion classes, the children remain in their classroom and they do another activity at that time. In Church celebrations, if the parent wishes their child to go and be present in the Church and be present for the celebration or to join in … they go. If their parents wish for them to remain in the school, we timetable it in such a way that they can remain supervised in the school. (Principal, Greenway Road primary school)

In one primary school, major difficulties around religion were reported with a Muslim family that was concerned that the children would be indoctrinated into the Catholic faith:

> They had a huge difficulty around religion, because it is a Catholic school and they were Muslim themselves, but they had a fear, somewhere along the line they had a fear that we would try to change their children to Catholics and we didn't have Kurdish and they didn't have English to explain, every child is welcome. … If we say a prayer they don't say their prayer, they get quiet time and things like that, you know. (Teacher, Jefferson Street primary school)

While participation in religious education class or attending Mass meant that children were sometimes separated along faith lines, some schools in our study attempted to include and engage the minority ethnic students by acknowledging their beliefs and engaging them in different activities, such as singing in a choir:

> But like that we would welcome the children to bring it [school-work related to Koran] in, like they go to classes after school and they would be doing the Koran etc., but we praise them when they bring us in their copies on the Koran, wouldn't have a clue what is in it, but we would tell them that it is beautiful and that they are working so hard and their mums must be so proud of them and dad, to value that as well. … We are a Catholic school but we welcome all religions. (Principal, Jefferson Street primary school)

> Even in the first Holy Communion celebrations, some children of different faiths and of different nationalities participate in the choir or participate in the celebration afterwards with the photographs. (Principal, Greenway Road primary school)

The situation regarding religious education was somewhat different in secondary schools due, in part, to the nature of the subject. Not surprisingly, participation in religious education class among ethnic minority children ran along faith lines:

A lot of them will participate in religion class, the Polish will very much participate in religion class or whatever but we would have some Muslims who would not ... be part of it. (Chaplain, Huntington Road secondary school)

As at primary level, some minority faith students opted out of RE class but remained within the class doing homework or other schoolwork. One principal indicated that the lack of extra space and resources in the school meant that the school could not supervise students in another setting during RE class:

I don't have anywhere else for them to go during religion class and I would have to say to parents, look the building is reasonably small, we don't have any supervision or classroom, so I couldn't have them not in the class ... not from a religion point of view but because I simply have nobody to look after them.... So you might need to rethink whether you send your child here, if you don't want them in religion class, because I have nowhere else to put them, you know so. (Principal, Huntington Road secondary school)

The lack of provision for minority faith students was seen as a matter of concern by some teachers:

And yet now with 50 kids in the school, 40 of them [who may be]... different religions, they still have to sit in religion class. Unless I can withdraw them for English, they sit down the back and study. Because where else can they go? (Principal, Brayton Square secondary school)

In the same vein, the principal of Adwick Street school noted that should parents request the provision of alternative faith education, it was likely to be left up to the parents themselves to organise:

Well I suppose, being honest it hasn't arisen so far, ... if there were a request, I suppose more realistically I mean I would imagine we would kind of facilitate it but I would suspect we would be leaving it to kind of the parents perhaps unless we had someone to organise it. (Principal, Adwick Street secondary school)

However, another principal indicated their desire to be able to provide religious education to other faith groups in the school:

If we are to provide, then let us have the backup and resources, let us have, let us employ a religion teacher from, what's an Islamic, mullah, is it? I don't know what they are called, but let me, let me source a local guy and say now I'm going to pay you to come up at this time, this time, and take these for their religious classes. It's not going to happen. (Principal, Brayton Square secondary school)

In other schools, however, all students were timetabled to take RE and opting out of religion class was very rare.

Everyone is required to be in the classroom. Now if a parent requests that a child, or a student, be left out of the religion class, they're legally entitled to do so. ... In my experience, in the last seven years, I think I've received two notes from parents, in general, like you don't, it doesn't really happen. (Teacher, Ashville Lane secondary school)

Religion class, they just go with the class that's here. I haven't found any of them asking to stay out of religion, not that I'm aware of. (Teacher, Wulford Park secondary school)

Many secondary school teachers thought that religion classes should be suitable for everybody as the curriculum took a broad approach to teaching the subject, focusing mostly on comparative religion allied with ethics and morals.

There's at least four, if not six, Muslims in the class, and none of them except [exempt] themselves from class. .... They actively participate in class, you know. ... The role within the class is not evangelical, we're not trying to convert people, I see my job as giving people information, and allowing them ... to make a decision on their own, whether they make that decision this year, next year, or in ten years' time, is up to them, because everyone will come to their own understanding and maturity at a different time. (Teacher, Ashville Lane secondary school)

One principal felt strongly that all students should attend the class:

As a community school we are inter-denominational so ... religion class is part of our curriculum and students are obliged to attend. (Principal, Bentham Street secondary school)

However, students at this school indicated that attendance at religious education was not, in fact, 'compulsory' (see below). Ethnic minority students themselves were also reported as taking part in religious education class in order not to be singled out as different.

Actually I would say a 100 per cent of them want to be there ... some of them will go to religion class but won't necessarily say at home that they are going but they want to be there and they want to be part of what is happening. That is an interesting one. (Teacher, Huntington Road, secondary school)

As at primary level, a clear distinction was drawn between attending religious education class and acknowledging students' right not to attend religious services:

They don't have to take part in the Mass and all that kind of stuff. They do have to sit in the religion class because that's where they are timetabled for. (Principal, Bentham Street, secondary school)

Ethnic diversity in the classroom was considered to be an asset by some of the teachers who felt that sharing different viewpoints was valuable and enriching:

They actually form a very important part of the class, because they do, they spice things up at times. (Teacher, Ashville Lane secondary school)

The larger study upon which this chapter draws pointed to a number of support structures put in place in secondary schools to cater for ethnic minority students (Smyth et al., 2009). Some of the case-study schools attempted to acknowledge and celebrate cultural and religious diversity. Feeling that some recognition should be made of ethnic minority students, one school chaplain had tried to provide some other forms of involvement for these students:

> I suppose being the school chaplain I have involved them in our carol service at Christmas. … We have a girl in Leaving Cert [upper secondary exam year] from Pakistan, so she dressed up in her Pakistani dress and she spoke about Christmas in her country. The Polish, one Polish girl spoke about Christmas in her country, the Trinidad girl spoke about Christmas in her country and she brought in the Christmas cake, a rum cake, and we passed it around and you know people sampled it and tasted it and then we got the girls to carry up the flags of their different countries as well, during the carol service. So people really appreciated that because they felt it was, you know, I suppose an integration exercise, and the kids were delighted, they were absolutely thrilled to be part of it, very, very, willing to be part of it. (Chaplain, Huntington Road secondary school)

According to teachers, some ethnic minority (minority faith) students engaged in religious festivals outside school that the Irish school tried to accommodate. For example, the principal in Grange Park secondary school noted that a Muslim student was given a day off for that purpose. However, the principal admitted that celebrating minority religious festivals was something that 'did not come into school':

> I think her mother is Irish and her father is Muslim. And she's being reared a Muslim. But … it doesn't come into the school as such. Now again that's something that's maybe lacking, that's not discussed. Or it's not brought in, I don't know if our religion teacher has actually gone down that road. But I know she observes the Muslim tradition so I presume she must get instruction outside school but I never actually asked her. (Principal, Grange Park secondary school)

It is interesting to note that the principal appears to conflate 'Irishness' with 'Catholicism' in discussing this particular student's situation, reinforcing the view of Islam as 'other'. The principal in Ashville Lane also noted that minority faith students engage with their religion outside school:

> Well, I know a lot of the Muslim lads go over to [the mosque] … and when things like Ramadan tend to impact on the school here, they have their fasting period. A lot of them are quite ill at that time because they are fasting and it's difficult for them to come in and from dawn to dusk not to eat food and you can see that they are wilting. But they would practise, a lot of them would practise outside the school their own religions. (Principal, Ashville Lane secondary school)

The latter principal noted that they have developed a policy in the school 'which will cater for, and be open to, all other religions'. The school had provided a prayer room for all students:

> We did have an oratory which was just primarily a Catholic Church, if you like, part of it, that is now being developed into what we would call a prayer room, but we won't lose our own identity within that, but we would certainly be open to, and cater, for all others. (Principal, Ashville Lane secondary school)

Brayton Square school also made an oratory available for students of different faiths:

> We totally refurbished the oratory recently and we've all the symbols of different religions outside it... that's an issue, religion is a massive issue. (Principal, Brayton Square secondary school)

In general, interviews with staff in primary and secondary schools showed that both sectors try to address the needs of minority ethnic/faith parents and students where possible. This was done by either withdrawing students from religious education class or, if students attended the class due to lack of alternative resources, they were not obliged to participate. Only in one school were minority ethnic students encouraged to bring in religious work they had done outside the school. Two of the schools also provided a quiet space for all students who needed it. In general, whether the school had more options in place for ethnic minority students did not relate to the proportion of ethnic minority students in the school. Rather, it seemed to depend on the ethos of the school or, in particular, the motivation of specific teachers.

Students' Perspectives on Religious Education

During focus group interviews with primary and secondary school students, children and young people were asked about their experiences in school, including attending and participating in religious education classes. The focus groups comprised of students from a wide range of countries (including Latvia, Lithuania, Somalia, Moldova, South Africa, the Czech Republic, Poland, etc.), and most did not have English as their first language.

In Durango Street primary school, ethnic minority students seemed to think that religious education was for Christians and not part of their curriculum:

> Interviewer: [There are] no religion classes?
> Well for Christians.
> Yeah they have it but it's not part of our curriculum. (4th class ethnic minority students, Durango primary school)

As already indicated by the principals, ethnic minority students with different faiths were either withdrawn from religion class, or stayed in the class but did not participate. Students themselves reported engaging in a different task or doing their homework during RE classes.

> [We] do a job for the teacher or you can sit down and draw.
> Read a book.

> Or finish something that you haven't done. (4th class ethnic minority students, Durango Street primary school)

Perhaps not surprisingly some students found this approach boring:

> You do work in your class.
> It's boring in class.
> Interviewer: Why?
> Because always do homework. (3rd to 6th class ethnic minority students, Jefferson Street primary school)

Students also indicated that they did not participate in religious services alongside the rest of their classmates:

> Sometimes we have to stay, when they go to the Catholic Church sometimes because we don't go. (3rd/4th class ethnic minority students, Thomas Road primary school)

Other students reported that there were 'much more' religion classes than in their home country (Adams Street primary school). Overall, interviews with primary school children did not indicate their reluctance to be in the classroom when the other students studied religion. However, it could also be that they found it difficult to talk about the issue.

A few additional issues were highlighted by the ethnic minority students attending secondary school. Schools appeared to differ as to whether minority faith students were required to attend religious education class. In some schools, all students were required to attend class:

> We have no choice, we have to go to every class. (Junior cycle ethnic minority students, Huntington Road secondary school)

In other schools, students were allowed to opt out of RE class. In Brayton Square secondary school, for example, students came from a range of countries, including Nepal, Lithuania, Romania, and Nigeria. These students noted that it is generally left up to the student whether she/he wants to participate in religion classes or not and that students from a Christian background tended to participate:

> Interviewer: And does everyone have to go to religion?
> Yeah.
> I do religion, I always do religion … I'm Christian anyway.
> Interviewer: And if someone isn't a Catholic, do they still have to do religion?
> No, they don't have to if they don't want to.
> If they don't want to they can, if they don't want to. In first year I did not do it because I was going to the [language support] classes.
> You can ask if you don't want to do it or not. (Junior cycle ethnic minority students, Brayton Square secondary school)

However, some students were reluctant to single themselves out as 'different' by opting out of RE class. Thus, students in Bentham Street, a vocational school, indicated that religion is not compulsory and it is up to the students if they attend or not:

> But yeah you can go, it's not compulsory, you can go do something else but everybody usually goes because you wouldn't want to be an outsider. (Junior and senior cycle ethnic minority students, Bentham Street secondary school)

Students who participated in religious education reported that classes often focused on learning about world religions and/or discussing general social issues, reflecting the different focus of the RE secondary curriculum compared with primary level.

> We just talk about topics, different topics like today we were talking about drugs and once we talked about euthanasia and stuff like that. (Senior cycle ethnic minority students, Huntington Road secondary school)

Senior cycle students in Ashville Lane school came from Cambodia, Armenia, Somalia and Poland, and noted that religion classes were not really about religion but 'talk and conversation'.

> Well we don't actually do it [religion] in class, we talk about drugs or something.
> Yeah, it's like CSPE [Civic, Social and Political Education], religion and that type of thing together. (Senior cycle ethnic minority students, Ashville Lane secondary school)

Many students were positive about religious education class:

> Just that one day, that one 35 minutes you can relax, it's nice. (Senior cycle ethnic minority students, Ashville Lane secondary school)

> Well the teacher tells us about like you know the believing and everything like to the god in heaven and hell and the devil and things like that. But he doesn't tell about hell but (laughing) yeah I like it. (Junior cycle ethnic minority students, Wulford Park secondary school)

However, other criticisms centred on the lack of discussion of a sufficient variety of religious perspectives and the potential differences between them:

> We only get to taught about five religions, that's about it and they don't even go into real detail.
> They tell you just the basics and that's it, they move on, the same with religion, religion has so much conflict between [viewpoints], they don't explain that to you, they don't do anything on it. (Junior cycle ethnic minority students, Huntington Road secondary school)

The previous subsection indicated that some schools actively attempted to acknowledge the different cultures and beliefs of minority students. However, some students were uncomfortable with being highlighted in this way and felt reluctant to talk about their culture(s) during an open forum in front of other students:

> Like during Christmas the teachers, our religion teacher got us to write out a thing about our cultures and stuff like that and we had to go into the cathedral

and talk about it. We didn't want to do it but she made us do it and I don't see the point. Why would we do these things so that other people would know about us? If they wanted to know they'd go and find out by themselves. (Junior cycle ethnic minority students, Huntington Road secondary school)

This perspective indicates the difficulty for schools in balancing recognition of diversity with the danger of singling out ethnic minority students as 'other'.

CONCLUSIONS

Recent large-scale immigration to Ireland has contributed to growing religious diversity in the population. However, religious diversity has been given much less attention in policy and research terms than linguistic or cultural diversity. This chapter set out to explore the implications of religious diversity for primary and secondary schools in Ireland, drawing on the accounts of teachers and students themselves.

Educational policy in Ireland has aimed at bringing about intercultural education, which recognises and celebrates diversity and promotes equality and human rights (NCCA, 2006). The NCCA Guidelines for Primary Schools (2006) can be seen as promoting a 'learning about religion' approach, suggesting that:

The religious education class provides a significant opportunity to promote tolerance and understanding between faiths and those with no expressed religious belief system. (p. 86)

However, the potential use of religious education in this way must be seen in the context of the existing structure of primary schooling, and the content of the religious education syllabus, in Ireland. The vast majority of primary schools are Catholic in ownership and management. As a result, most Catholic primary schools have several students of minority or no faith. Within these schools, religious education tends to assume the 'education into religion' model, that is, one of faith transmission. Minority faith students may 'opt out' of religious education classes, but are in the position of accommodating to the majority religion and culture, and opting out may in effect reinforce the notion of difference. Many Catholic principals and teachers in the case-study schools report the tension between trying to maintain the school's religious ethos and promoting inclusive practice. A number of the case-study schools had tried to recognise and celebrate religious and cultural diversity. However, the cathechical nature of religious education in primary schools would appear, at least potentially, to limit the capacity to use the subject to actively promote intercultural education.

The situation at secondary school level is somewhat different from that at primary level. There is a diversity of school ownership and management structures. Furthermore, 'the syllabus for Religious Education, at both junior and senior cycle, places great emphasis on the value of religious diversity and on mutual respect for people of all beliefs' (NCCA, 2005: 74). The way in which the subject is taught in secondary schools appears to combine strands of 'learning about (world) religions' and the exploration of ethical and moral issues. However, the relative emphasis on faith formation in religious education as a secondary exam and non-exam subject is little understood, and a number of minority faith students in secondary schools opt out of religious education class while others participate in order not to be seen as 'different'. Some secondary students report a positive view of religious education as a space to discuss and reflect. It is crucial that this experience is built upon to promote a genuinely intercultural education.

NOTES

[1] The original study was funded by the Department of Education and Skills. We would like to acknowledge Dr Fran McGinnity and Dr Delma Byrne who were co-authors of the original report 'Adapting to Diversity', the data from which have been re-analysed for this chapter.

[2] Our definition of 'ethnic minority students' refers to students from families where both parents were from outside Ireland, whether or not the student's first language was English/Irish. This excludes children born abroad with Irish parents (return migrants), and those with one Irish and one immigrant parent.

[3] For the purposes of this chapter we define religious education as a subject area at primary and secondary level that deals with religion, morals and values. Our definition excludes instruction in families and in organisations run by faith communities.

[4] In the Irish context, the term 'second-level' is generally used to relate to schools catering for 12 to 18 year olds as the term 'secondary' is sometimes taken to refer to a particular school sector (voluntary secondary schools). However, throughout this chapter, the term 'secondary' is used to refer to all second-level schools, in keeping with the practice in other European countries.

[5] The Guidelines do recommend that teachers find out 'what is the student's religion, how is it practised, and has this any implications for classroom planning?' (NCCA, 2006: 32).

[6] The Church of Ireland schools use the 'Follow Me' series that is broadly modelled on the *Alive-O* programme.

[7] The DEIS (Delivering Equality of Opportunity in Schools) programme provides targeted funding to schools on the basis of the representation of children and young people from disadvantaged communities in their student body.

[8] It is important to note, however, that schools generally consider a number of factors in allocating places.

REFERENCES

Bates, D., Durka, G., & Schweitzer, F. (Eds.). (2006). *Education, religion and society: Essays in honour of John M. Hull.* London: Routledge.

Byrne, D., McGinnity, F., Smyth, E., & Darmody, M. (2010). Immigration and school composition in Ireland. *Irish Educational Studies, 29*(3), 271–288.

Caulfield, C., Hill, M., & Shelton, A. (2005). *The transition to secondary school: The experiences of black and minority ethnic young people.* Glasgow: Glasgow Anti Racist Alliance.

Coolahan, J. (1981). *Irish education: Its history and structure.* Dublin: IPA.

Darmody, M., Smyth, E., Byrne, D., & McGinnity, F. (2010, forthcoming). New school, new system: The experiences of immigrant students in Irish schools. In Z. Bekerman & T. Geisen (Eds.), *International handbook of migration, minorities, and education – understanding cultural and social differences in processes of learning.* Amsterdam: Springer.

Devine, D. (2005). Welcome to the Celtic Tiger? Teacher responses to immigration and increasing ethnic diversity in Irish schools. *International Studies in Sociology of Education, 15*(1), 49–70.

Devine, D., & Kelly, M. (2006). "I just don't want to get picked on by anybody": Dynamics of inclusion and exclusion in a newly multi-ethnic Irish primary school. *Children and Society, 20,* 128–139.

Dommel, C., & Mitchell, G. (Eds.). (2008). *Religion education on the boundaries between study of religions, education and theologies: Jürgen Lott and the Bremen approach in international perspective.* Atglen, Penn.: Schiffer Publishing.

European Commission. (2008). *Migration and mobility: Challenges and opportunities for EU educational systems*. Brussels: EC.

Faas, D. (2010). *Negotiating political identities: multiethnic schools and youth in Europe*. Farnham: Ashgate.

Inglis, T. (1987). *Moral monopoly: The Catholic Church in modern Irish society*. Dublin: Gill and Macmillan.

Irish Bishops' Conference. (2003). *Towards policy on religious education in post-primary schools*. Available online at www.dioceseofkerry.ie/.../towards_a_policy_in%20_religious_education.pdf

Irish National Teachers' Organisation [INTO]. (2005). *Intercultural education in the primary school*. Dublin: INTO.

Jackson, R. (2004). Intercultural education and recent European pedagogies of religious education. *Intercultural Education*, *15*(1), 3–14.

Jackson, R., Miedema, S., Weisse, W., & Willaime, J.-P. (Eds.). (2007). *Religion and education in Europe: Developments, contexts and debates*. Münster: Waxmann Verlag GmbH.

Lodge, A. (1999). First communion in Carnduffy: A religious and secular rite of passage. *Irish Educational Studies*, *18*, 210–222.

Mercer, J. A., & Roebben, B. (2007). Europe: Just do it! Recent developments in European religious education research. *Religious Education*, *102*(4), 438–450.

NCCA. (2005). *Intercultural education in the primary school: Guidelines for schools*. Available online at www.ncca.ie/uploadedfiles/publications/intercultural.pdf

NCCA. (2006). *Intercultural education in the post-primary school: Guidelines for schools*. Available online at www.ncca.ie/uploadedfiles/publications/interc%20guide_eng.pdf

Schreiner, P. (2005). *Religious education in Europe*. Germany: ICCS Comenius-Institut.

Smyth, E., Darmody, M., McGinnity, F., Byrne, D. (2009). *Adapting to diversity*. Dublin: ESRI.

UNESCO. (2006). *Guidelines on intercultural education*. Paris: UNESCO.

Williams, K. (2005). *Faith and the nation: religion, culture and schooling in Ireland*. Dublin: Dominican Publications.

Emer Smyth and Merike Darmody
The Economic and Social Research Institute
Dublin, Ireland

MERIKE DARMODY AND SELINA McCOY

9. BARRIERS TO SCHOOL INVOLVEMENT

Immigrant Parents in Ireland[1]

INTRODUCTION

As is evident from the contributions throughout this book, Ireland's social fabric has changed significantly in recent decades. While there has always been some degree of ethnic diversity in Ireland, since 2004 Irish immigration reform legislation opened the doors to many more ethnic minority families whose cultures, mother tongues and beliefs were vastly different from the majority culture. The immigrant and ethnic minority population arriving in Ireland has been diverse, with large groups arriving from the UK, Africa, Eastern Europe and elsewhere, resulting in over hundred different languages being spoken in the country. The economic situation of the new arrivals has also been the subject of a number of studies – while previous research has shown that many immigrants have high levels of education, there is now considerable evidence of immigrants not working in jobs commensurate with their skills in Ireland. It is also important to note here that there are no well-established ethnic communities or ethnic 'enclaves' in Ireland, hence the majority of the new arrivals have needed to adjust to the new society, largely without the help of established social networks.

Many new arrivals have been accompanied by school-aged children, which has necessitated establishing links with local schools that their children attend. Most of these children are not second-generation but true 'immigrants'[2] so issues concerning knowledge of the school system, language proficiency and integration have been particularly pertinent. International research indicates that establishing family-school links may be complicated by different kinds of social and cultural capital the new arrivals possess. We feel that investigating immigrant parental involvement in schools also contributes to a greater understanding of the experiences of ethnic minority children in Ireland as it highlights the potential barriers that both families and schools need to overcome to ensure the educational success of these children. With this in mind, in this chapter we explore the topic of immigrant parents' involvement in their child's school-based education drawing on Bourdieu's framework of capitals – particularly cultural and social capitals. By focussing on this relationship between home and school, we can identify the potential barriers to school involvement for ethnic minority parents and the potential implications these may have for the experiences and successes of their children in schools in Ireland.

Focusing on ethnic minority populations in the Irish context is important since the number of new arrivals in Ireland has increased significantly over the past decade,

Darmody, Tyrrell, Song (eds.), The Changing Faces of Ireland: Exploring the Lives of Immigrant and Ethnic Minority Children, 145–163.

and earlier studies have demonstrated that both immigrant parents and children are facing a number of challenges trying to navigate their way in a new country with an unfamiliar educational system (Devine, 2005; Smyth et al., 2009). Dealing with ethnic minority families also poses considerable challenges to schools that are not sufficiently equipped to address the needs of an ethnically and culturally diverse student body and their parents. Further challenges have been posed by the recent economic downturn that saw many educational resources previously available to ethnic minority groups severely cut (Smyth et al., 2009).

This chapter draws on the data gathered for a large-scale research project funded by the Department of Education and Skills in Ireland which explored how primary and secondary schools cope with the growing heterogeneity of the student population (see Smyth, et al., 2009 for a more detailed discussion). This chapter specifically focuses on secondary school teachers' perspectives on the school-based involvement of ethnic minority parents. We focussed on second level education in particular, because of the significance of this stage of schooling with regard to the further educational pathways of students and their longer-term social and occupational outcomes. The objective of this chapter is to illuminate the challenges schools face when interacting with ethnic minority parents and identify major barriers to their school-based engagement. In line with Perez et al. (2005), we argue in this chapter that parents' engagement in their child's education needs to be understood through the extent to which these parents are able to participate in this process. Recent work in Ireland by Bleach (2010) highlights the need to keep parents informed of their own children's learning, as well as ensuring their involvement in decision-making at all levels within the school and education system. However, immigrant parents still remain on the margins of the home-school interface in this regard.

In this chapter we begin by introducing a theoretical framework which considers possibilities for analysing immigrant experience in relation to social and cultural capital. We then consider the work that has focussed on parental involvement, paying particular attention to those authors who have applied the concepts of cultural and social capital to the study of ethnic groups. This is followed by research findings based on extensive in-depth interviews with secondary school teachers. In conclusion, we raise some possibilities for interpreting the engagement of ethnic minority parents through the lens of social and cultural capital and offer some recommendations on how best to support immigrant parents.

THEORETICAL UNDERPINNINGS

We approach our understanding of interactions between immigrant parents and schools in a receiving country from a socio-cultural theoretical framework. This framework highlights the interdependence of social and individual processes in the construction of knowledge drawing on Vygotsky's theoretical contributions to the development of curricula and teaching strategies (Vygotsky, 1978). According to Vygotsky, social experience shapes ways of thinking about and interpreting the world. Current conceptualizations of socio-cultural theory draw heavily on the work of Vygotsky (1986). Tharp and Gallimore (1988) argue that this perspective has strong implications for understanding schooling and education processes. Learning conceptualised as being embedded within social events and the environment is useful in developing our understanding about parental school-based involvement. Parents can be seen as agents of culture (Trevarthen, 1988) – carriers of specific cultural knowledge. In this chapter, we argue that socio-cultural theory helps to elucidate factors relevant in dealing with cultural diversity within rapidly changing culturally diverse local and global conditions. In line with Lim and Renshaw (2004), we argue that this theory is especially relevant for developing approaches that value difference in inclusive environments.

In addition, in this chapter we also make use of the conceptual tools developed by Bourdieu. In particular, we utilise his concepts of social and cultural capital in exploring the school-based involvement of ethnic minority parents in Ireland. Bourdieu (1998) has advanced a theory of cultural capital that encompasses styles of interaction as well as the knowledge and skills that are products of an individual's position in a social space that is always relational to others. Bourdieu (1986) differentiates between objectified, incorporated and institutionalised cultural capital. Cultural capital is objectified in cultural articles, while incorporated cultural capital constitutes the sum and the quality of acquired knowledge and skills as well as values and dispositions which are manifested in the habitus of a person. The incorporation takes place over time and its content is dependent on the cultural capital of the family. In addition, cultural capital is to a large extent created through early childhood. Cultural capital can also be institutionalised in institutions and is expressed in terms of certificates, diplomas and examinations (Bourdieu and Passeron, 1977; Bourdieu, 1977). Bourdieu (1998) points out that cultural capital, especially with reference to schooling, is initially passed down by the family and that the sorting function of schooling further differentiates people with respect to capital, by giving more to those who have more capital and less to those with less. Cultural capital refers to the possession of knowledge and experiences that result in behaviours and practices aligned to the values of those who are in a position to legitimize them. Parents who understand the knowledge and behaviours rewarded in schools may pass these on to their children and may enhance their opportunities for the future. Different forms of cultural capital (e.g. language, culture-specific knowledge and skills) are dependent on the context and society in which they have been acquired and may be devalued in the immigration context. Some authors argue that immigrant families have little knowledge of the majority culture educational system and may not have extensive knowledge of the educational systems of their countries of origin (Portes, 1998; Valdes, 1996). However, others note that despite the high value many immigrant families place on education it rarely translates into success for their children (Goldenberg and Gallimore, 1995). While the desire to succeed academically is often prominent among these families, these aspirations are not often matched by knowledge of how to achieve academic success. Transferring knowledge and skills may be difficult since the type of institutionalised cultural capital they possess is often not recognised in the receiving country. In the context of majority culture schools, where teachers enforce the rules, monitor and reward practices aligned with the majority culture, the cultural and social capital of immigrant groups may lose their worth. Bourdieu (1986) argues that cultural capital becomes recognised and activated only in its alignment to the preferences of those in power. Those parents who have the 'feel of the game' and understand what is rewarded in schools may experience fewer difficulties in the home-school interface. Lareau and Horvat (1999) argue that 'to be of value in a given field, social and cultural capital must be activated. The ability to activate social and cultural capital and the way in which it is activated influence its value in a field of interaction' (ibid.: 39). Hence it is important to recognise each individual's skill and ability in activating capital. The success of doing so depends on familiarity with school standards.

Another relevant concept for discussing immigrant experience is social capital. Bourdieu is generally considered to be among the first to explore social capital theory, being particularly interested in how the dominant class reproduces itself. However, Bourdieu's work suggests that families lacking in economic capital may be able to use other capitals to achieve their educational aims and goals (see Bourdieu, 1986). Social capital has two components: it is a resource (e.g. information) that is connected with group membership and social networks. Bourdieu, (1986: 249) argues that 'the volume of social capital possessed by a given agent ... depends on the size of the network of connections that he can effectively mobilise'. The membership can be used in efforts to improve the social position of the actors in different fields. Social capital is also based on mutual cognition and recognition and is, through this process, transformed into symbolic capital (see Bourdieu, 1986). Bourdieu (1985: 204) notes that 'symbolic capital...is nothing other than capital, in whatever form, when perceived by an agent endowed with categories of perception arising from the internalisation (embodiment) of the structure of its distribution, i.e. when it is known and recognised as self-evident'. Symbolic capital defines what forms and uses of capital are recognised as legitimate in any given society. With regard to immigration, social capital tends to consist mostly of relations within the ethnic group that has migrated, thus the network is limited. Heckmann (2008) argues that 'one central aspect of lack of social capital that is relevant for succeeding in the education system of the immigration country is the generally weak or non-existent relations between educational institutions, teachers and the parents of migrant children'.

We argue in this chapter that it is possible to see ethnic minority background as operating as a set of shared norms and values, as a form of social or cultural capital that is likely to have an impact on children's' outcomes.

PREVIOUS STUDIES ON PARENTAL INVOLVEMENT IN EDUCATION

There is an extensive international research literature on parental involvement in children's education, mostly originating from the United Kingdom and America (see Domina, 2005; St. Clair and Jackson, 2006; Grolnick and Slowiaczek 1994). Some research is also available in the Irish context (see Conaty, 2003; Cregan, 2008). Various authors have put forward definitions of parental involvement that include interactions with schools and with their children to promote academic success both at school and at home (see Hill and Tyson, 2009; Comer, 1995; Grolnick and Slowiaczek, 1994). There seems to be a consensus among the researchers that home-school interaction is relevant as active parental involvement contributes to the socialisation of children into recognising the importance of education (Domina, 2005) as well as for children's academic and behavioural outcomes (Becker and Epstein, 1982). In the Irish context, previous studies (see Smyth et al., 2004) have discussed parental involvement in their child's education with reference to checking homework, discussing the child's progress in school and discussing school choice. International research evidence seems to suggest that active parental involvement in school and education related issues improves the academic outcomes of children (Fan and Chen, 2001; Jeynes, 2003; 2010). Other types of parental school-based involvement include participating in parent-teacher meetings and functions, and receiving and responding to written communications from the teacher (Becker and Epstein, 1982), which are beneficial also with regard to the information flow between schools and parents.

It is important to note that the relationship between parents and the formal institutions of education is complex and may be different for different groups of parents (Cregan, 2008). Research by Hanafin and Lynch (2002) on the views of working-class parents on home-school links in Ireland shows that parental involvement in school is limited to the giving and receiving of information, restricted consultation and engagement in some supplemental responsibilities. The authors note that although parents participating in the study were interested, informed and concerned regarding their children's education, they also felt excluded from participation in decision-making processes at the school level, about issues that had personal and/or financial implications to them, and about their children's progress at school. To date, research into the first-hand experiences of immigrant parents in Ireland is lacking, although international experience indicates that these parents may experience a number of barriers in dealing with the formal institutions of education.

According to some studies, particular issues emerge when examining the involvement of ethnic minority parents in their child's schooling (see Li, 2006). In this context, specific barriers can be identified. Among these parents, the amount of time spent in the receiving country and majority language proficiency have been found to be positively associated with school based involvement (Turney and Kao, 2009). The authors argue that barriers to involvement serve as another source of disadvantage for ethnic minority parents and their children. In some cases the social and cultural capital the newly arrived ethnic minority families bring into the receiving country and its educational system is considered to be in the 'wrong' currency and therefore requires 'conversion'. In fact, the new arrivals are often viewed through a 'deficit' lens, i.e. lacking certain cultural attributes that are valued by the majority culture (Dwyer et al., 2006). It follows that in so doing, the majority school culture (largely mediating white middle class values), replicates existing inequalities and operates to disadvantage newly arrived ethnic minority families. While all individuals have social and cultural capital to activate or convert in various fields, the capital possessed by some groups may be considered less valuable. This social reproduction perspective is particularly useful in understanding how race and class influence the transmission of educational inequality (Lareau and Horvat, 1999).

Previous studies also point to the impact of the socio-economic status, culture and educational attainment of parents (Lareau, 1989; Moles, 1993) on participation in their children's schooling. Moles' (1993) study on ethnic minority parents indicated that the latter often felt ill at ease when visiting their children's school due to their limited knowledge of English. In addition, they were unfamiliar with the technical language used by teachers when talking about the curriculum and school processes. These parents tended to be unsure about the school's expectations of them in terms of their role in the school process. This is in line with work by Reay (2004) in the British context. The parent-school interface may be further exasperated by the limited time some teachers spend with ethnic minority parents (Bernhard and Freire, 1999) or by teachers holding low expectations for their children due to their ethnic origin (Villenas and Deyhle, 1999; Stevens, 2006). It is generally acknowledged that teacher-student and teacher-parent relationships are central for student achievement in any educational system (Heckmann, 2008). Schofield (2006: 94) observes that 'students who are not very verbal or who fail to initiate much interaction with their teachers are more likely than others to generate low teacher expectations irrespective of their potential, which has important implications for their achievement gap since immigrant students may be especially likely to evidence such behaviours due to being less familiar with the language of instruction than their non-immigrant peers'. It is possible that the teacher-immigrant parent relationship in Ireland may have similar characteristics to the above.

It is important to fully understand the factors influencing parental involvement, as minimal participation at school may refer to existing barriers to involvement rather than parental lack of interest in their child's schooling. Importantly, Cummins (2000: 8) argued that 'if ability to speak English and the knowledge of North American cultural conventions are made prerequisites for parental involvement, then many of those parents will be defined as apathetic and incompetent and will play out their pre-ordained role of non-involvement'. It is important to acknowledge that many ethnic minority parents can be quite involved with their children in their home environment. This is demonstrated in several studies: by Melzi, Paratore and Krol-Sinclair (2000) on ethnic minority (Latino) mothers' storybook reading with their children at home; Xu's (1999) study on Chinese and English literacy practices; and Li's (2003) study on home-based support for education among a Chinese-Canadian family. However, the latter study revealed that the enthusiasm at home for educational success did not necessarily translate into positive results in terms of their children's 'success' at school.

In the American context, Turney and Kao (2009) examined immigrant status differences in the barriers to parental involvement at school. Compared to native-born parents, ethnic minority parents perceived greater barriers to school-based participation. Among those parents, time spent in the United States and English language proficiency were positively associated with school-based involvement. The authors argue that barriers to involvement serve as another source of disadvantage for immigrant parents and their children. Also in America, Annette Lareau (2002) explored childrearing practices among Black and White families, arguing that the mechanisms through which parents transmit advantage to their children are imperfectly understood, and pointed to the need to recognise social class position as an important variable. She noted that 10-year old White and Black children both showed the effects of social class on interactions inside the home. While middle-class parents engaged in concerted cultivation by attempting to foster children's talents through organized leisure activities and extensive reasoning, working-class and poor parents engaged in the accomplishment of natural growth, providing the conditions under which children could grow but leaving leisure activities to children themselves. Overall, Lareau (2002) found that race had much less impact than social class. Writing in the American context, Li (2006) argues that immigrant children whose families had been successful in the educational system of the receiving country had the necessary social capital to gain the cultural capital to succeed in school. Their skills and practices were in alignment with the expectations of teachers. In addition, their families had knowledge of how to structure their children's education, what were the characteristics of good schools and what to expect and demand of schools on behalf of their children. Many ethnic minority children (particularly those from lower socio-economic backgrounds, speakers of languages other than English, etc.) are at a significant disadvantage with respect to culture and social capital given that their parents have little knowledge of how majority culture schools function, of the practices and behaviours rewarded by teachers and schools, and even of their rights with respect to educational issues. Although children can learn the social norms valued in schools, this will likely take years of participation (see Bourdieu, 1986; Vygotsky, 1979).

BACKGROUND, DATA AND METHODOLOGY

This chapter focuses on secondary school teachers' perspectives. The data used in this chapter derives from the study *Adapting to Diversity* which is the first national study on provision for the needs of ethnic minority students in Irish primary and secondary schools. The aim of the original study was to explore the types of schools which have ethnic minority students relative to those who have none, how different kinds of schools address the language needs of, and provide support to, these students, and to consider the perceived adequacy of the curriculum and teaching methods used in schools in catering for a diverse student population. The study was a mixed method study, incorporating a postal survey of primary and secondary school principals and qualitative case study research.

This chapter draws on the perspectives of teachers, from eight case study secondary schools. The profile of these case-study schools is presented in Table 1. The schools, which have been assigned pseudonyms, reflect a mix of school sizes and urban/rural locations. Importantly, they include both schools targeted for additional funding, through disadvantaged schools status, and non-disadvantaged schools, and schools with different numbers of immigrant students. The authors of this chapter acknowledge the limitations of the analysis provided here as it draws on the perspectives of teachers, rather than providing the 'voices' of immigrant parents themselves (the study did not collect information from parents). While possibly providing us with only part of the story, we feel that considering the lack of published empirical research in this area on the first-hand experiences of immigrant parents, at the time of writing, drawing on the views of teachers allows us to go some distance in

Table 1. Profile of the case-study schools

School	Size	Rural/ urban	Disadvantaged (DEIS) status	Proportion of newcomers
Adwick Street	Large (600+)	Urban	Not disadvantaged	None
Ashville Lane	Small (<400)	Urban	Disadvantaged	High (>10%)
Bentham Street	Medium (400–599)	Rural	Not disadvantaged	Low/medium (<10%)
Brayton Square	Medium (400–599)	Rural	Disadvantaged	High (>10%)
Grange Park	Small (<400)	Urban	Disadvantaged	None
Huntington Road	Medium (400–599)	Urban	Not disadvantaged	Low/medium (<10%)
Lowfield Street	Medium (400–599)	Urban	Not disadvantaged	Low/medium (<10%)
Wulford Park	Small (<400)	Rural	Not disadvantaged	High (>10%)

Note: Pseudonyms are used to protect the anonymity of schools.

understanding the possible barriers to parental school-based involvement. Furthermore, similar international studies have drawn on teachers' perspectives (see Karlsen Baeck, 2010).

RESEARCH FINDINGS

Barriers to Parental Involvement

To date, research on ethnic minority parents in the Irish context is sparse, with occasional glimpses provided by studies exploring the school experiences of migrant children (see Devine 2005; Ní Laoire, 2009; Smyth, *et al.*, 2009). The original study *Adapting to Diversity*, commissioned by the Department of Education and Skills, that drew on teacher and student perspectives, identified language proficiency and cultural distance as factors that acted as potential barriers to parent's participation in their child's education and schooling. International studies have shown that the gap between the language of the home and school remains the greatest barrier to successful communication partnerships (Peterson and Ladky 2008). In line with Peterson and Ladky (2008) we found that proficiency in the English language was a significant factor in immigrant parents' involvement at school and a poor proficiency in English can act as a barrier to meaningful participation in the school and in the child's educational activities. It is important to remember, that immigrants in Ireland are a very heterogenous group, representing various nationalities and languages and this is likely to pose a considerable challenge for schools.

The study collected information from a number of teachers in the case study schools including Principals, Guidance Counsellors, Resource and Language support teachers and others who had involvement with ethnic minority students and parents. Among other issues, they were asked to identify potential issues they felt arose when dealing with immigrant parents. The majority of teachers interviewed observed that low language proficiency acted as a significant barrier to parents' involvement in school. It was also evident that schools had put some thought into how these parents could be included as is evident from the following extract:

> Interviewer: And can you think of any ways they [immigrant parents] might become more involved in the school?

> Teacher: I think if we can overcome the language barrier first of all. And then that will give them a level of confidence that would facilitate participation. And then again like all parents, and in particular the newcomer parents, you have to find the areas that they would have the most interest in, it may not necessarily be an educational interest initially but the idea is to physically get them into the school first and become comfortable with the school environment so I would look to see what courses, classes, what talks might be of interest to them. And work from there. [Bentham Street]

This issue of limited proficiency in English became particularly pertinent when accessing resources and supports for their children, both of an educational nature and more generally:

> Interviewer: What are the main issues that arise [with immigrant parents]?

> Teacher: ... a lack of ability to access the resources that they need. For example at the moment we would have a family whose student has special needs, they are having emotional difficulties. And alongside that there's the language barrier, so they need access to social services but they also need access, language access within those social services. So it's quite difficult to try and make all the connections for them from that point of view. [Bentham Street]

However, the implications of communication difficulties and language barriers were complex and had consequences across a number of aspects of the home-school relationship. Firstly, teachers and other school personnel were concerned about being able to communicate effectively with parents. Several teachers felt frustrated when trying to communicate with parents who had no English or whose English language proficiency was very poor, and as a result often relied on the student to translate the relevant information for their parent(s):

> Interviewer: And are there any issues around language proficiency when you deal with parents?

> Teacher: .... I had to contact the parents on the phone [in relation to an event] and I didn't, I just couldn't communicate with them, I had to get the child to say in her own language what I wanted so it was virtually impossible through the phone anyway to communicate with them. And sometimes the would have to bring in an interpreter when they come, some of the parents, you know [student name] parents now they have no English, so if they come to the school they have to have somebody with them, like [student name] herself at this stage has much more English than her parents. [Huntington Road]

Interviewer: What about the level of English that the parents have?

Teacher: Very little, they would have much, much less than the children, much less, much less. [Huntington Road]

Consequently, the need for interpretation services was an important issue in a number of schools and an area where school personnel felt greater support was required. As well as relying on the students to translate for their parents, school personnel were often relying on neighbours or friends of the family to assist with ensuring the parents could understand the relevant information.

Teacher: Its difficult at times, because very often many of them haven't, have very little English, so you'd be looking for students to help out with interprettation, sometimes ... It can be difficult, like we've one family now, one lad, he's from Iraq, and he's in third year, and he's the youngest, and his parents are very, very old, and they have no English, and its extremely difficult. ... So [name of home-school liaison teacher] has to look for somebody who has, there is some neighbour, or some friend of theirs, who negotiates with them, so [name of teacher] has to look for that person to negotiate with, and talk about, or even when you go down, you do sign language. [Brayton Square]

The teachers were asked if they felt that ethnic minority parents were actively involved in their children's education and if they got involved in school life more generally. To some extent responses reflected a level of diversity among migrant parents, not dissimilar to the diversity found among other parents – some were involved and participated in school events and others did not. However, many responses came back to the language barriers faced by these parents and the difficulties this posed for their day-to-day involvement with the school and hence acted as a barrier to activating their social and cultural capital.

Interviewer: And how involved are foreign parents in this school?

Teacher: I suppose the question is how involved are parents generally, I mean we have a parents' committee, there isn't a foreign parent on that parents' committee, for whatever reason, I don't know, maybe my numbers are quite small at the moment, also from a language point of view, once again I know I keep coming back, the children would have better English than the parents, so that would stop them you know but they would come to, like if we had say a parent-teacher meeting, they would always come. [Huntington Road]

Having limited knowledge of the English language also presents immigrant parents with many practical challenges and difficulties that schools variously attempt to overcome. In some cases it meant that they had difficulty understanding the organisation and polices of the school, such as homework requirements or the uniform code.

Teacher: .... for example a very simple thing, at senior level they have one type of uniform, at junior cert level they have a different type of uniform so that's even important on the day, that they don't end up with the wrong uniform ... just little things like that. ... at the very beginning [of the school year] it's getting books and support and all that type of thing. [Ashville Lane]

Teacher: ... there's issues around their understanding of how the school works and the procedures of the school, things like parent teacher meetings, even though a letter has gone out and announcements have been made. You know sometimes, its difficult for them. [Lowfield Street]

In another case, the school provided practical assistance in the form of helping immigrant parents to apply for a bus ticket for their son/daughter, assisting with the relevant paperwork and the application process. While this may seem a simple form of support, being able to access school transport was clearly of great importance for the school attendance of that student.

Now the biggest problem is that the parents can't read, they can't read in English, so this slip comes back from CIÉ [to apply for a bus ticket] and they actually have it in the house but they can't read it, because the slip comes back and it's telling them to send forward the forty-five euro or fifty euro but they think that's the ticket and they can't understand. So I had the problem and I had to negotiate all of these since September now to try and actually get them the bus tickets so they would actually bring in their paperwork to me and I would have to liaise and get a copy of their medical card (from them). [Wulford Park]

A third issue that was prominent in discussions with teachers was that of attendance at parent-teacher meetings – concerns over levels of attendance emerged and the implications this had for parents' awareness of their child's progress and the home-school relationship more generally.

Above and beyond parent-teacher meetings, attendance at other school events and initiatives specifically targeting parents also were discussed. The home-school-community liaison officer, a position not available in all schools, played an important role in attempting to promote the involvement of parents, and particularly newcomer parents, in the school. However, a number of them noted that access to parents was not always straightforward – a parent working long hours was often cited as a reason for the home-school-community liaison officer finding it difficult to meet parents. In addition, cultural differences emerged and parents were not often aware of the identity of the home-school-community liaison officer and were suspicious of knocks on the door. The legal status of some parents further hindered their participation and involvement in the school and impinged on the opportunity for parents to engage in the home-school relationship.

... I don't meet the parents as much as I should. For a number of reasons, one I don't get out as often as I should get out. Two, when I go they don't have the language. Like even in here I'm using the fellows in fifth and sixth year to translate stuff for me. And three, if I do go out they are working, they are working, they are working long hours in poorly paid jobs ... So when you put all those factors together I don't meet them that much. [Ashville Lane]

Well I'll tell you what the biggest issue in relation to my interaction with them is, the difficulty of actually interacting, of making contact with them in the home. ... they may be out working, or they may be at the shops, but I mean

I would have certainly been quite convinced, you know, on occasions, that somebody would be at home, but wouldn't answer the door, I think there is a certain kind of reticence in there … they don't know who it is that is calling … Whether their status is, you know, in question, or whatever, and they think maybe I'm from the, well I suppose, what, the Authorities, in one guise or another, you know. [Brayton Square]

Again, the difficulties home-school liaison officers face in addressing language barriers were prominent and their efforts to overcome serious communication difficulties were noted. In particular, the comments suggested a need for some form of foreign language support to be introduced.

...the language barrier there again is an issue … now maybe there's home-school liaison as well but what use is the home school liaison teacher who doesn't speak French or Arabic? No point in calling to the house unless you can speak it. There is obviously a need for some kind of home school liaison or visiting teacher who has a few of these languages. Communication is a problem. [Ashville Lane]

However, some schools did speak about the impact of courses and social events as an effective means of bringing parents (and other family members such as siblings) into the school. Where courses were well-established and had developed a reputation in the community, they were seen as a way of promoting both interaction among parents and boosting the home-school relationship more generally.

… we used to have an occasional sort of social evening, social night, you know, for parents, and that was a success in its time … so we were talking about actually actively thinking about reviving that, you know, even if its just in terms of, you know, establishing a kind of a rapport, getting more parents to sort of come in … I know certainly in the last concert we had, we had a number of them, a number of the students, I think they were African students actually mainly, and they were a great hit altogether, they were terrific, and their parents and siblings would have been there. [Brayton Square]

...at the moment we are running night classes, one of the night classes is for English for non-nationals and … I'm promoting courses for parents, have made a point of actually making contact with particular parents to take part in that course. Now not with all of them, not with all the newcomer parents because a lot of them are working. … So you are dealing with the, you know, the fact that some of them would do night shifts, you are trying to find something that would I suppose facilitate them. But there are some parents who have indicated that that's what they want and we've worked with them to try and provide that. … we have international days and we have kind of dress days and that kind of thing. And different schools have, they celebrate different festivals, food festivals and dance festivals and all that type of thing. We have done a certain amount of that here but, and I suppose in a sense we could be doing an awful lot more of it. [Ashville Lane]

The implications of language barriers were apparent across many of the interviews and across virtually all schools with ethnic minority students that participated in the research. The day-to-day difficulties posed by language barriers in terms of allowing parents to understand the organisation and policies of the school, to engage in parent-teacher meetings and other forms of home-school interaction were widely noted by the secondary school teachers, but perhaps more importantly, the implications of such language barriers for broader processes of social integration were perhaps best captured by one home-school-community liaison officer:

> And a lot of people talk about inter-culturalism and integration, I'm more convinced now than ever before that if you can't give the people a language you can't have integration. Because if the person doesn't have it they are isolated, they are frustrated, they are left out, they feel they are being talked about, they are looked at differently. The people that don't understand them and look at them suspiciously, so to me I suppose I would see the school has 'gone for the jugular' in the sense that they are trying to give them the language and if, if you give them the language children can make their views known to me or whatever else and you can put things in place. [Ashville Lane]

It was clear that overcoming language barriers and developing the ability to communicate effectively allowed parents to unlock their own social and cultural capital and in the process acquire the social and academic capital valued in Ireland.

> Language is the main issue, if they have the language I think they can overcome a lot of the other sort of issues but if they don't have the language it's extremely difficult. [Lowfield Street]

This section has demonstrated that immigrant parents faced a number of issues with regard to effectively communicating with the school of their child. As we can see, the main obstacle is proficiency in English, followed by limited information about the way schools function in Ireland. The cultural and social capital that they possess that had currency in their country of origin, proved to have limited value in the new country. Language proficiency proved to be one of the main difficulties in activating their capitals. The analysis provided here builds upon existing literature in the area of the home-school interface between schools and ethnic minority parents in that it details the variety of areas where low proficiency of English and cultural distance can be a problem. These include accessing information from school, not being able to get involved in their child's education, having to rely on their child when communicating with teachers, not being able to access relevant resources for their children, and difficulties accessing outside agencies. It can be argued that this may have an impact on the educational outcomes of their children in the receiving country and beyond.

DISCUSSION AND CONCLUSIONS

Recent policy documents have pointed to the need to strengthen the contacts with immigrant parents and migrant communities in order to enhance the success of immigrant children in the receiving countries (see European Commission, 2009; Niessen and Huddleston, 2009; Heckmann, 2008). It has been found that parents with a lower socio-economic status, including immigrants, tend to have lower levels of school involvement (Niessen and Huddleston, 2009). With this in mind, this chapter focused on Irish secondary school teachers' experiences in dealing with ethnic minority parents. Increased ethnic diversity in Irish schools due to rapid and large-scale immigration has resulted in a situation whereby the majority of Irish schools now have at least some ethnic minority students. Establishing a link with the homes of these families that would enable greater parental involvement has proven to be a challenge, in some cases due to language and cultural barriers (Smyth et al., 2009). Schofield (2006) argues that 'in fact it is common for immigrant, minority and low-income parents to feel alienated, powerless, and culturally estranged from their children's school and to avoid involvement in them. ... In addition, immigrant parents may have quite different ideas regarding the proper role of schools and parents than do their children's teachers or feel different or embarrassed interacting with teachers, especially if they lack fluency in the language of the host country or have little education themselves' (ibid.: 101).

It is important to note that the immigrant population in Ireland is highly diverse with families arriving from a wide range of countries. Furthermore, over a hundred and fifty languages are currently spoken by the new arrivals. This is likely to present a challenge for the home-school interface and parental involvement. Ireland is an interesting case particularly with regard to the heterogeneity of immigrants: on the one hand there are parents from the UK who may not have language-related difficulties (part of cultural capital) when dealing with the school, but who, on the other hand may have limited social capital (social networks) to draw on. Many families from African countries, for example, may experience difficulties in both areas. Eastern European parents, usually perceived to be expressing a positive disposition towards academic achievement and motivation by teachers, may also experience difficulties in both areas. All these parents may experience some challenges in the home-school interface process, but these challenges may be different for different (groups) of parents. For most parents, parts of the capital that they possess become devalued in the migration process – language and location-specific knowledge of the education system and the labour market being some of the examples. This is likely to effect the education of their children in a variety of ways: language barriers and cultural distance may influence school choice, home-school interaction, ensuring the necessary resources for their children in contacting external agencies, as we have seen in this chapter. In turn, this may have an impact on the immigrant child's later life-chances.

Schools in Ireland are largely denominational, representing White, middle class Christian values. A meeting of the 'two worlds' that both possess different cultural and social capitals can be a challenge for the school and home as well as an opportunity. International research has indicated that parental school-based involvement is crucial for students' socialisation as well as their academic success. While this chapter specifically focuses on immigrant parents, it is worth noting that there is considerable variation in levels of home-school contact among Irish parents, both between schools and also within schools (see Cregan, 2008). Cregan's study of Irish parents' school involvement suggests that while parents largely valued education, social class differences could be identified in terms of the levels and types of school involvement.

Immigrant parental involvement can be limited due to a number of factors acting as barriers: proficiency in the language of the receiving country, limited knowledge of the educational system and school processes, and differences arising from their cultural backgrounds. In addition, barriers to participation also include limited financial resources, feelings of being unwelcome in the new school environment and different cultural expectations in terms of parents' role in the educational process (Niessen and Huddleston, 2009).

In this chapter we argue that all people have social and cultural capital that has developed in a specific socio-cultural context. Arriving to a receiving country, while possibly having limited economic capital at their disposal, ethnic minority families possess different cultural and social capital that may or may not be 'aligned' with what is valued in the culture of the receiving country. In order to be successful in the new environment, immigrant parents need to activate their capital to build upon the resources they already have. They can only do this through acquiring the language of the receiving country. With proficiency in this language, it is easier to get access to information about the new education system and understand what is valued in this system – in other words, 'what has currency' in the new country. Being proficient in the language of the receiving country, parents can become more actively involved and greater involvement may translate into increased academic success for their children, in line with international research. Schools, on the other hand, are also developed in specific socio-cultural contexts. Overall, they carry the culture of the middle classes and uphold middle class values – particular standards count, specific behaviour is rewarded and certain types of social conventions are accepted. In order to create more meaningful home-school links, it is necessary to acknowledge the background of new immigrants and see what they have to offer rather than adopting a 'deficit' model. It is important to 'allow parents' life experiences and cultural capital to inform schools' cultural worlds' (Carreon, et al., 2005: 494).

In this paper we explored teachers' perceptions of the involvement of immigrant parents in their child's formal education. In so doing, we have drawn on a socio-cultural perspective in order to position the cultural and social capital and argue that, contrary to the deficit perspective utilised in a number of studies, all ethnic groups have cultural and social capital in specific socio-cultural contexts that have developed over time. In order to function successfully in a new country, the new arrivals need to 'activate' their existing capital. Ireland is an interesting case as its immigrant population differs from many other countries in terms of its profile. Previous studies have shown that the majority of new arrivals to Ireland are highly educated; their knowledge and skills could easily be utilised in the new society. Their children often have been perceived by teachers in Ireland as highly motivated and ambitious (Smyth et al., 2009). It is likely that the social and cultural capital they possess reflects the social norms in Ireland, yet they are likely to experience similar barriers to many other immigrants. In this study we found that the major barrier to activating the cultural and social capital of ethnic minority parents is a lack/low proficiency in English and unfamiliarity with the new educational system. This prevented many parents from actively engaging with their child's school. In particular, the secondary school teachers noted that language barriers made it difficult to explain the school processes to the parents and to engage them in parent-teacher meetings. Occasionally children, who often had better English than their parents, had to act as interpreters between teachers and schools. Limited language proficiency among these parents is likely to influence children's academic achievement as the parents may not be able to seek additional assistance from school or monitor their homework. In addition, at secondary school level children in Ireland need to make subject choices that are likely to affect their future options. If they are not able to fully participate in school life, ethnic minority parents with very different social and cultural capital will be further disadvantaged.

We feel that it is important to recognize the importance of the home-school interface and to assist ethnic minority parents in activating their social and cultural capital and not adopt a deficiency perspective. Portes and Rumbaut (2006) feel that schools should be proactive in establishing a link with ethnic minority parents. We also feel that in this process every single school matters. In her study, Creagan (2008) found that the institution of the school varies in relation to how it interacts with these families.

To assist parents, it is necessary to devise culturally sensitive programmes that would provide ethnic minority parents with the necessary know-how about the educational system of the receiving country and encourage their meaningful participation in school life. This participation should recognize the importance of the cultural background of ethnic minority families and use it as a resource rather than simply attempting to assimilate the newcomers into the majority culture. The process of involving ethnic minority parents in the school that their child attends should include a critical dialogue between the home and the school, and culturally sensitive parental education initiatives that should recognize the cultural background, values and beliefs of ethnic minority families (Gorman and Balter, 1997). The Home-School-Community Liaison Scheme in Ireland has proved effective in establishing contact with parents; unfortunately this scheme is in place in only a limited number of schools and the officers are likely to encounter language barriers when dealing with some immigrant parents. Perhaps one way forward would be to include officers from immigrant communities that would liaise between immigrant families and schools. A European Commission (2009) report also suggests that the lack of accessible information on the education system of the country of residence can pose considerable obstacles for immigrant parents. The recommendations include information programmes targeting these parents, the involvement of community mediators, translation/interpretation services and the provision of guidance in the language of origin. In addition, addressing the learning needs of both parents and children has been highlighted (Niessen and Huddleston, 2009). At present, in order to support immigrant parents, information on the school system is available from the Department of Education and Skills in the main immigrant languages; in addition, the

Reception and Integration Agency has produced an information booklet in the main languages of the immigrant population. At the time of writing, several initiatives to empower immigrant parents to get more involved in their child's education are being devised.

Lave and Wenger (1991) argue that in order to fully benefit from the education system of the receiving country, ethnic minority families need full participation to legitimise and validate their cultural and social capitals that have socio-culturally developed in the context of the country of origin. For this approach to be successful, we conclude that teacher training programmes in the receiving country should adopt equality and intercultural education perspectives, encouraging all parents as partners in process of educating children. Finally, we would like to stress that by being responsive to the needs of parents, schools have an important opportunity to help immigrant parents to integrate into the society of the receiving country.

NOTES

[1] The authors would like to acknowledge Prof. Emer Smyth, Dr Fran McGinnity and Dr Delma Byrne who were the authors of the original Diversity Study that provided data that was re-analysed for this chapter. The original study was funded by the Department of Education and Skills. The views expressed in this chapter are those of the authors. The authors would like to thank two external reviewers and editors for useful comments on an earlier version of this chapter.

[2] Rather than transmitting (ethnic) disadvantage across generations.

REFERENCES

Bankston, C. I., & Zhou, M. (2002). Social capital and immigrant children's achievement. In B. Fuller & E. Hannum (Ed.), *Schooling and social capital* (pp. 13–39). Amsterdam: Jai Press.

Becker, H. J., & Epstein, J. L. (1982). Parent involvement: A survey of teacher practices. *Elementary School Journal, 83*(2), 85–102.

Bleach, M. J. (2010). *Parental involvement in primary education in Ireland*. Dublin: The Liffey Press.

Bourdieu, P. (1977). *Outline of a theory and practice*. New York: Cambridge University press.

Bourdieu, P., & Passeron, J.-C. (1977). *Reproduction in education, society and culture*. London: Sage.

Bourdieu, P. (1985). The social space and the genesis of groups. *Social Science Information, 24*(2), 195–220.

Bourdieu, P. (1986). The forms of capital. In J. G. Richardson (Ed.), *Handbook of theory and research for the sociology of education*. New York: Greenwood Press.

Bourdieu, P. (1998). *Practical reason*. Stanford, CA: Stanford University Press.

Byrne, D., & Smyth, E. (forthcoming). *Parental involvement in post-primary education*. Dublin: The Liffey Press/ESRI.

Carreon, G. P., Drake, C., & Barton, A. C. (2005). The importance of presence: Immigrant parents' school engagement experiences. *American Educational Research Journal, 42*(3), 465–498.

Comer, J. P. (1995). Racism and African American adolescent development. In C. V. Willie, P. P. Rieker, B. M. Kramer & B. S. Brown (Eds.), *Mental health, racism, ...* Pittsburgh, PA: University of Pittsburgh Press.

Conaty, C. (2002). *Including all: Home, school and community united in education*. Dublin: Veritas.

Central Statistics Office [CSO]. (2007). *Census 2006* (Vol. 4). Dublin: Stationery Office.

Cregan, A. (2008). *Sociolinguistic perspectives on the context of schooling in Ireland*. Working Paper. Dublin: Combat Poverty Agency.

Cummins, J. (2000). *Language, power, and pedagogy. Bilingual children in the crossfire*. Clevedon, England: Multilingual Matters.

Devine, D. (2005). Welcome to the Celtic Tiger? Teacher responses to immigration and increasing ethnic diversity in Irish schools. *International Studies in Sociology of Education, 15*(1), 49–70.

Domina, T. (2005). Leveling the home advantage: Assessing the effectiveness of parental involvement in elementary school. *Sociology of Education, 78*(3), 233–249.

Dwyer, C., Modood, T., Sanghera, G., Shah, B., & Thapar-Bjokert, S. (2006, March 16–17). *Ethnicity as social capital? Explaining the differential educational achievements of young British Pakistani men and women*. Conference paper presented at the Leverhulme Programme conference on Ethnicity, Mobility and Society at University of Bristol. Retrieved from http://www.bristol.ac.uk/sociology/leverhulme/conference/conferencepapers/dwyer.pdf

European Commission. (2009). *Commission staff working document. Results of the consultation in the education of children from a migrant background*. Brussels: Author.

Fan, X. T., & Chen, M. (2001). Parental involvement and students' academic achievement: A meta-analysis. *Educational Psychology Review, 13*, 1–22.

Goulbourne, H., & Solomos, J. (2003). Families, ethnicity and social capital. *Social Policy and Society, 2*(4), 329–338.

Goldenberg, C. N., & Gallimore, R. (1995). Immigrant Latino parents' values and beliefs about their children's education: Continuities and discontinuities across cultures and generations. In P. Pintrich & M. Maehr (Eds.), *Advances in motivation and achievement* (Vol. 9, pp. 183–227). Greenwich, CT: JAI Press.

Gorman, J. C., & Balter, L. (1997). Culturally sensitive parent education: A critical review of quantitative research. *Review of Educational Research, 67*(3), 339–369.

Grolnick, W. S., & Slowiaczek, M. L. (1994). Parents' involvement in children's schooling: A multidimensional conceptualisation and motivational model. *Child Development, 65*, 237–252.

Hanafin, J., & Lynch, A. (2002). Peripheral voices: Parental involvement, social class, and educational disadvantage. *British Journal of Sociology of Education, 3*(1), 35–49.

Hill, N. E., & Tyson, D. F. (2009). Parental involvement in middle school: A meta-analytic assessment of the strategies that promote achievement. *Development Psychology, 45*(3), 740–763.

Jaramillo, J. A. Vygotsky's sociocultural theory and contributions to the development of constructivist curricula. *Education*. Find Articles.com. Retrieved March 30, 2010, from http://findarticles.com/p/articles/mi_qa3673/is_n1_v117/ai_n28677164/

Jeynes, W. (2003). A meta-analysis: The effects of parental involvement on minority children's academic achievement. *Education & Urban Society, 35*(2), 202–218.

Jeynes, W. (Ed.). (2010). *Family factors & the academic success of children*. Thousand Oaks, CA: Sage.

Karlsen Baeck, U.-D. (2010). We are the professionals': A study of teachers' views on parental involvement in school. *British Journal of Sociology of Education, 31*(3), 323–335.

Lareau, A., & Horvat, E. M. (1999). Moments of social inclusion and exclusion: Race, class, and cultural capital in family–school relationships. *Sociology of Education, 72*, 37–53.

Lareau, A. (1989). *Home advantage: Social class and parental intervention in elementary education*. London: Falmer Press.

Lareau, A. (2002, October). Invisible inequality: Social class and childrearing in black families and white families. *American Sociological Review, 67*(5), 747–776.

Lave, J., & Wenger, E. (1991). *Situated learning: Legitimate peripheral participation*. Cambridge, UK: Cambridge University Press.

Li, G. (2006). What do parents think? Middle class Chinese immigrant parents' perspectives on literacy learning, homework, and school-home communication. *School Community Journal, 16*(2), 27–46.

Lim, L., & Renshaw, P. (2004). The relevance of socio-cultural theory to culturally diverse partnerships and communities. *Journal of Child and Family Studies, 10*(1), 9–21.

Niessen, J., & Huddleston, T. (2009). *Handbook on integration for policy-makers and practitioners*. Brussels: European Commission.

Moles, O. (1993). Collaboration between schools and disadvantaged parents: Obstacles and openings. In N. Chavkin (Ed.), *Families and school in a pluralistic society* (pp. 21–49). Albany, NY: State University of New York Press.

Perez, G., Drake, C., & Barton, A. (2005). The importance of presence: Immigrant parents' school engagement experiences. *American Educational Research Journal, 42*(3), 465–498.

Portes, A., & Landolt, P. (1999). The downside of social capital. *The American Prospect, 26*, 1–5. Retrieved from http://tap.epn.org/prospect.html/archives/26/26-toc.html

Portes, A., & Rumbault, G. (2006). *Immigrant America. A portrait* (3rd ed.). Berkely, CA; Los Angeles; London: Univeristy of California Press.

Reay, D. (2004). Exclusivity, exclusion, and social class in urban education markets in the United Kingdom. *Urban Education, 39*(5), 537–560.

Schofield, J. W. (2006). Migration background, minority – Group membership and academic achievement. Research evidence from social, educational and developmental psychology. *AKI Research Review, 5*.

Smyth, E., Darmody, M., McGinnity, F., & Byrne, D. (2004). *Adapting to diversity*. Dublin: ESRI.

Smyth, E., McCoy, S., & Darmody, M. (2004). *Moving up: The experiences of first year students in post-primary education*. Dublin: The Liffey Press.

St. Clair, L., & Jackson, B. (2006). Effect of family involvement training on the language skills of young elementary children from migrant families. *School Community Journal, 6*(1), 31–41.

Stevens, P. (2007). Researching race/ethnicity and educational inequality in English secondary schools: A critical review of the research literature between 1980 and 2005. *Review of Educational Research, 77*(2), 147–185.

Sy, S. R., & Schulenberg, J. E. (2005). Parent beliefs and children's achievement trajectories during the transition to school in Asian American and European American families. *International Journal of Behavioral Development, 29*(6), 505–515.

Turney, K., & Kao, G. (2009). *Barriers to school involvement: Are immigrant parents disadvantaged? (Report)*.

Villenas, S., & Deyhle, D. (1999). Critical race theory and ethnographies challenging the stereotypes: Latino families, schooling, resilience and resistance. *Curriculum Inquiry, 29*(4), 413–445.

Valdes, F., McCristal Culp, J., & Harris, A. (2002). *Crossroads, directions and a new critical race theory* (pp. 243–250). Philadelphia: Temple University Press.

Vygotsky, L. S. ([1933] 1978). *Vygotsky and education: Instructional implications and applications of sociohistorical psychology* (L. C. Moll, Ed.). New York: Cambridge University Press.

Wertsch, J. V. (1991). *Voices of the mind: A sociocultural approach to mediated action*. Cambridge, MA: Harvard University Press.

Xu, J. (1999, April). *Reaching out to families from diverse backgrounds: A case study*. Paper presented at the annual meeting of the American Educational Research Association, Montreal, Quebec, Canada.

Zhou, M. (1997). Growing up American: The challenge confronting immigrant children and children of immigrants. *Annual Review of Sociology, 23*, 63–95.

Zhou, M., & Bankston, C. L. (1998). *Growing up American: How Vietnamese children adapt to life in the United States*. New York.

Dr Merike Darmody and Dr Selina McCoy
The Economic and Social Research Institute
Ireland

PART 3: IMMIGRATION, WELL-BEING AND RISK

BRYAN FANNING, TRUTZ HAASE AND NEIL O'BOYLE

10. IMMIGRANT CHILD WELL-BEING AND CULTURAL CAPITAL

INTRODUCTION

This chapter draws on extensive survey data on child, family and neighbourhood well-being in the Republic of Ireland (hereafter Ireland) to examine the nature and extent of immigrant social exclusion. Social inclusion, hitherto defined in terms of income and employment, increasingly is defined in terms of well-being and social capital and as such, constitutes an essential ingredient of immigrant integration. Our aim in this chapter is to use a narrow focus on immigrant child well-being (understood in terms of social and behavioural outcomes) as a means of contributing to broader academic debates about the integration of recent immigrants from a social policy perspective. More specifically, the wider debates to which this chapter contributes concern the empirical relationships between social inclusion, well-being and social capital on one hand, and normative understandings of the relationship between social inclusion and integration on the other.

This chapter is divided into four parts. In the first part we investigate increasing convergences and commonalities in debates about integration and social inclusion, especially where these include concerns about child well-being. The Irish experience of recent globalisation-led immigration is fairly typical of a wider international pattern in which new migrants generally possess high levels of human capital relative to the host population (OECD, 2007). Analyses of small area data from the 2006 Irish census found that in all areas of Dublin immigrants lifted overall educational levels (Fahey and Fanning, 2010). As might be expected, the relative educational advantages of immigrants compared to Irish citizens were most pronounced in deprived areas (O'Boyle and Fanning, 2009).

In the second part of the chapter we present detailed findings from a combined analysis of five studies into the well-being of children, families and neighbourhoods in Ireland (hereafter WBCFN studies), focusing in particular on the results for an area known as 'the Liberties' in Dublin (in which immigrants are overly-represented). Here we specifically compare child well-being scores of immigrant and Irish families and consider how and to what extent parental immigrant human, social and cultural capital explain these findings. Our study examined the impact of immigration within a sample of hitherto mono-cultural deprived communities using indicators of socio-economic well-being and deprivation, psychological well-being, cultural capital and social capital. Whilst the employment status of many migrant respondents was not found to reflect their skills and education, many were found to have lower

Darmody, Tyrrell, Song (eds.), The Changing Faces of Ireland: Exploring the Lives of Immigrant and Ethnic Minority Children, 167–182.

levels of socio-economic deprivation than their Irish neighbours; in essence, many had middle-class characteristics yet lived in comparatively deprived localities. Adult migrants were found to experience poorer well-being than their (socially-excluded) Irish neighbours yet there were indications that migrant children experienced considerably better psychological well-being than Irish children within such communities. There were also indications that such children performed better at school. In the third part of the chapter we place these findings in a wider context by relating them to the findings of other studies that have examined the experiences of immigrant children within the Irish educational system. For example, we discuss growing evidence that African children encounter distinct barriers within Irish schools, which cannot be understood without taking into account racism and discrimination encountered by black people in Irish society. Finally, in the fourth part of the chapter, we consider the challenges of researching this topic and make some suggestions regarding future studies.

SOCIAL INCLUSION AND INTEGRATION

Social inclusion debates turn on understandings of the interdependent factors that enable people to participate meaningfully in the economic and social life of society and have widened to include holistic conceptions of welfare (UNICEF, 2007). As such, psychological well-being and social capital are increasingly understood to be interdependent (Helliwell, 2005). Social capital, which is generally measured in terms of trust and reciprocity, is understood as a mediating variable between inequality and health outcomes (Kawachi et al., 1997) and has been repeatedly found to be affected by education. Relatively high education, in turn, is claimed to positively contribute to well-being (Helliwell, 2005). However, educational achievement is also strongly influenced by socio-economic status and by what Pierre Bourdieu (1985) depicted as a hidden curriculum of cultural capital manifested in the skills and dispositions that confirm social advantage upon individuals. Our approach is informed by Bourdieu's emphasis on social resources (or capital) used by agents to navigate social fields and which in turn are transmitted to the next generation. Cultural capital affects the life chances of individuals even as it reproduces a specific social order; it confers status-enhancing forms of knowledge, norms and habits.

Just as education, health and well-being scores are indicators of social inclusion, so too are these potential indicators of integration (Berry, 1997). Nevertheless, social inclusion and integration differ in some respects. In particular, the literature on acculturation and integration holds that the maintenance of ethnic identities is conducive to immigrant well-being where such retention occurs alongside adaptation to the host society. When such identities are suppressed or marginalised, the well-being of immigrants has been found to deteriorate (Phinney et al., 2001). Cultural identities are generally not emphasised within social inclusion debates, nor is *kultur* much emphasised in current normative debates on integration. In a context where multiculturalism has lost political ground, integration debates tend to implicitly emphasise human capital, social capital and cultural capital, the latter referring to skills and dispositions that confirm social advantage upon individuals in specific social contexts rather than upon members of minority or majority ethnicities (Directorate-General for Justice, Freedom and Security, 2007).

A shared key concern of both social inclusion and integration debates are the risks of inter-generational exclusion. Again, overlaps between both are to be found in concerns about child well-being and the nature, extent and distribution of child poverty (UNICEF, 2009). For example, research in the United States, where children experience comparatively high risks of poverty by OECD standards, finds that immigrant youth tend to be protected from poverty-associated risks including infant mortality, low birth weight, acute and chronic health problems, early sexual activity, delinquency and substance abuse, but that this advantage tends to decline with their length of time in the United States and from one generation to the next. For example, first generation immigrant adolescents are less likely to report that they engage in risky behaviour, such as sexual intercourse at an early age, delinquent or violent behaviour, the use of cigarettes and substance abuse. However, immigrant children whose parents have little formal education and who live in linguistically-isolated households are found to face considerable risks of poverty (Kamerman et al., 2003; Hernandez and Charney, 1998). The Irish case study here examines a quite different scenario. It compares findings for immigrant and indigenous children in a series of studies of families living in deprived areas. These indicate that immigrant children in such areas possess considerable educational cultural capital advantage over indigenous children. The methodology and findings of this research are outlined in the following section. The findings are then considered alongside those of various studies of immigrant children in Irish schools.

WELL-BEING OF CHILDREN, FAMILIES AND NEIGHBOURHOODS
CASE STUDY

The 2006 Irish Census of Population (CSO, 2006) found the heaviest concentration of immigrants to be in inner-city Dublin and the north-west suburbs of the city (an area where urban population growth has rapidly expanded). Analysis of census findings indicates a strong correlation between the availability of private rented accommodation and immigrant settlement patterns at an electoral area level. In effect, immigrants in Ireland are concentrated where private rented accommodation is most available. This chapter draws particular attention to an area known as "the Liberties" in inner city Dublin, which is a deprived area where residents face multiple forms of disadvantage. This area also has a disproportionately large immigrant population by overall Irish levels. Immigrants in the Liberties mostly reside in newly-built apartments rather than in the older social housing stock that is characteristic of this area.

The composite data used in this chapter were obtained from a combined analysis of five studies into the well-being of children, families and neighbourhoods undertaken in Ireland during 2007 and 2008. Each focused on a sample population within a relatively deprived neighbourhood or client group using identical instruments to measure aspects of well-being, social exclusion and social capital. The component studies were undertaken by a single research consultancy on behalf of five client agencies working with socially-excluded families and children: Barnardos, the Respond! Housing Association, the Bray and Wicklow Partnerships and the Liberties Regeneration Area. The combined WBCFN dataset comprised 1,633 households distributed across 117 sample clusters. The analysis presented here of immigrants living in socially-excluded communities draws on a re-examination of this composite data. With 28 per cent of its respondents consisting of non-Irish citizens, the Liberties was over twice as diverse as Ireland as a whole. Some 14 per cent of the population were from EU countries other than the UK (predominantly Poland and Lithuania); some eight per cent were Asian and six per cent were from other countries. As such, the Liberties area (Figure 1) offers an appropriate site in which to examine immigrant social exclusion.

Inevitably, understandings of well-being are not the preserve of any one discipline. Notably, the various contributory literatures reflect different paradigms. For example, efforts to develop indicators of child well-being have conceptualised well-being in terms of both sociological understandings of material deprivation and psychological welfare (Bradshaw, 2007: 146). In the case of the former, claims about the role of cultural capital in reproducing educational disadvantage tend to emphasise educational outcomes. Examples of the latter include Strengths and Difficulties Questionnaires (SDQ) used to assess the psychological well-being of children, based on the perceptions of parents. However, to some extent SDQ scores offer a proxy for cultural capital; children with serious behavioural difficulties patently lack many of the dispositions and attributes that confer educational advantage upon individuals,

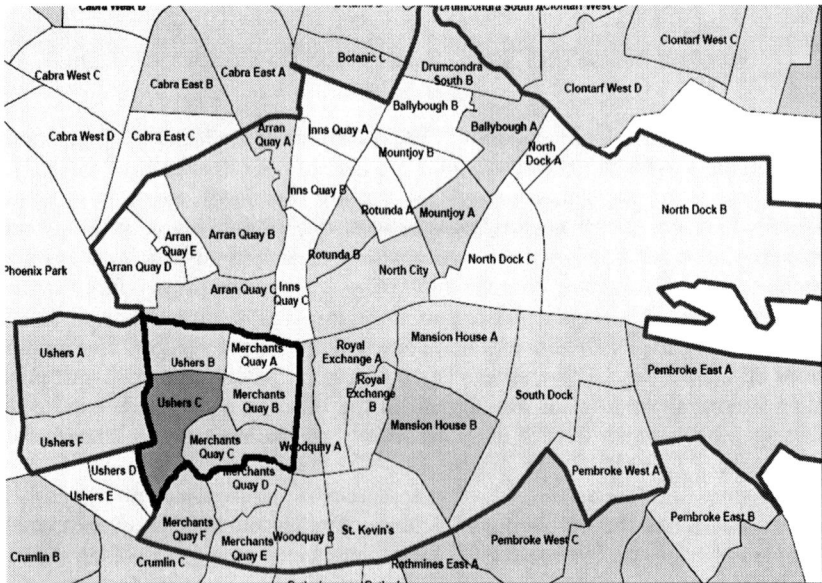

Figure 1. The liberties (Five EDs encircled in thick black line).

what Bourdieu (1985) depicts as a hidden curriculum. In one Irish study teachers working in deprived areas were found to idealise migrant pupils as "extremely well-behaved, courteous, polite and dedicated", as possessing "values regarding respect for authority" and as potential role models for Irish-born pupils in disadvantaged areas (Devine, 2005: 54). Immigrant pupils ostensibly possessed forms of cultural capital that were lacking in Irish-born pupils in deprived areas.

Our reading of Bourdieu's cultural capital perspective suggests a hypothesis that both familial (parental human, social and cultural capital) and environmental factors (levels of deprivation) influence child 'habitus' and well-being. Longitudinal research finds that children who experience material disadvantage perform more poorly on cognitive tests. Poverty impedes the capacity of parents to nurture their children but also contributes to the social exclusion of children in distinct ways (Kamerman et al., 2003). Across OECD countries, child well-being outcomes are understood to result from the interplay between resource and risk factors. These can be seen to change as a child develops, with, for example, the highest risks to child development due to poverty incurred when children are very young (Bradshaw et al., 2007). Such findings variously suggest that immigrants or their children may (or may not) possess social and cultural capital advantages that contribute to (or ameliorate) risks of social exclusion within specific spatial settings.

From a psychological perspective, SDQ indicators measure individual behavioural characteristics; however, theorised from a sociological perspective, following Bourdieu, they may indicate aspects of cultural capital. Bourdieu, who emphasises structural inequalities in social relations, might resist ranking individual-level attributes and characteristics but would emphasise that some such attributes (detectable, for example, by indicators of child well-being) confer advantage or disadvantage. In the WBCFN studies, child (psychological) well-being was assessed using a 25-item SDQ questionnaire, based on the perceptions of parents (Figure 2). The 25 items comprised five sub-scales measuring: (i) conduct problems, (ii) emotional symptoms, (iii) hyperactivity, (iv) peer problems and (v) anti-social/pro-social behaviour. Within each of these, child well-being (as revealed in parental perceptions) was assessed according to whether the child had 'no difficulties', 'some difficulties', or 'serious

Parent-Child Relationship	Parent-Child Relationship Inventory (PCRI)* comprising 20 items and four sub-scales: (i) satisfaction with parenting, (ii) involvement with child, (iii) communication with child, (iv) limit-setting.
Parent-Child Conflict	Parent-Child Conflict Tactics Scale (CTS-PC)** comprising 18 items and four sub-scales: (i) non-violent discipline, (ii) psychological aggression, (iii) minor physical assault, (iv) severe physical assault.
Strengths and Difficulties	Strengths and Difficulties Questionnaire (SDQ)^ comprising 25 items. Five sub-scales: (i) conduct problems, (ii) emotional symptoms, (iii) hyperactivity, (iv) peer problems, (v) anti/pro-social behaviour.
*Adapted from Gerard (1994) **Straus et al. (1995) ^Available at: http://www.sdqinfo.com/	

Figure 2. Child well-being indicators.

difficulties'. The SDQ has been used in more than 50 countries to assess behaviour disorders of children and adolescents and is available in over 40 languages. Assessments of the risks of cultural bias support European evidence of "good psychometric properties and clinical utility" of this questionnaire (Woerner et al., 2004: 1147). In other words, what are measured are characteristics and capacities widely understood to affect well-being outcomes.

In the WBCFN studies, the overall percentage of Irish children found to experience serious difficulties (10%) is consistent with findings from the United Kingdom, which used similar SDQ indicators of child well-being (Lindsay et al., 2008). The UK study (based on a representative sample of 10,000 children) found that 10 per cent of children had a clinically-defined mental disorder, mainly of a conduct or emotional nature, with higher rates among boys than girls, and higher rates among older children compared to younger children. Similarly, in the WBCFN studies a strong positive correlation between percentages of children experiencing serious difficulty and poor socio-economic status was found when children of medical card holders (18%) and those not entitled to a means tested medical card (6%) were compared. Unsurprisingly, the greatest relative concentrations were found amongst children within vulnerable families (43%). Serious difficulties scores were more than twice as high for lone parents (17%) as for those in two-parent families (8%). By housing type, the scores for local authority, housing association and private rented were around twice as high as for owner occupied accommodation. The finding for private rented sector (16%) is particularly relevant insofar as immigrant children were predominately located in this sector (see Table 1).

The serious difficulties scores for immigrant children shown in Table 1 are striking. One hundred per cent of EU migrant child respondents were found to be experiencing *no difficulties* at all. Again, no (0%) children of respondents in the 'Other EU' and 'Other' categories were found to be experiencing serious difficulties, whilst 12 per cent of EU migrants reported some difficulties. Of non-EU migrants, 88 per cent were found to be experiencing no difficulties. The differences in SDQ scores between Irish respondents (many with high levels of social exclusion) and immigrants (many with comparatively higher socio-economic status and educational advantage) may also owe something to the distinct human capital attributes of such self-selecting migrant families. Overall these findings suggest that (non-UK) immigrant children living in the five WBCFN areas/communities exhibit considerably higher levels of well-being than indigenous children. This contrast becomes even more dramatic in the Liberties, where the strongest correlation between spatial deprivation and children with severe behavioural problems was found and where most of the immigrants in the WBCFN samples resided.

Somewhat similar findings emerged with respect to levels of parental conflict with children, as measured using the Parent Child Relationship Inventory (PCRI) and Conflict Tactics Scale (CTS-PC) (see Figure 2). The PCRI includes 78 items covering seven distinct scales: parental support, satisfaction with parenting, involvement, communication, limit setting, autonomy, and role orientation. Parental responses to questions range from 'strongly agree' to 'strongly disagree'. The CTS-PC examines behaviours rather than attitudes. Items are categorised as either mild or severe and

Table 1. Children's difficulties by key categories

Category	Total Difficulties	Percentage of Children having Difficulties		
	Mean	None %	Some %	Serious %
Family Type				
Two parents	8	84	8	8
One parent	10.1	74	9	17
Housing Tenure				
Owner occupied	8	84	8	8
Rented from LA	9.4	76	9	16
Rented from VB	9.4	77	9	14
Private rented	10	76	9	16
Nationality				
Irish	8.6	82	8	11
UK	9.2	76	14	10
Other EU	6.9	100	0	0
Other	8.3	88	12	0
Other Categories				
Medical card	10	74	8	18
No medical card	7.7	86	8	6
Vulnerable families	14.6	50	7	43
Travellers	10.5	67	8	25
Homeless	n/a	n/a	n/a	n/a
Gender (Child)				
Boy	8.7	81	10	9
Girl	8.4	83	6	11
Ireland (est.) *	**8.5**	**82**	**8**	**10**

*Estimate based on the combined data of the 5 surveys, re-weighted to match the national population characteristics according to family type, housing tenure and nationality.

the frequency of each item is rated on an eight point scale: 'never', 'once', 'twice', '3–5 times', '6–10 times', '11–20 times', 'more than 20 times', and 'not in the past year but did happen before'. Conflict scores for the Liberties and 5 study areas are shown in Table 2 (with higher scores indicating higher levels of conflict). Compared to the WBCFN baseline of 11.3, the score for the Liberties was 30.7; in other words far higher parental conflict scores than found in any of the other study areas. Within the Liberties, Merchants Quay A had the highest conflict score (44.9) followed by Ushers C (30.7), Ushers B (29.2), Merchants Quay B (22.5) and Merchants Quay C (18.2). By comparison, the children of EU migrants had much lower parental conflict scores of 12.3, with a markedly higher score of 24.3 for non-EU immigrant children.

These findings are in keeping with research in other countries, which has examined the relationship between socio-economic status and child well-being. Study after study has found that poverty and insecurity take their toll on parental mental health and detrimentally affect relationships between parents and their children (Duncan, 2005; UNICEF, 2007). In the Irish case, amongst the most vulnerable WBCFN groups, a strong correlation between poverty and poor psychological well-being was clearly identified. Poverty experienced in early childhood has been found to be

*Table 2. Parent-child relationship and parental expectations
of child educational achievement*

Liberties EDs	Conflicts with children	Parent's expectation that child will attend college (%)
Merchants Quay A	44.9	30
Merchants Quay B	22.5	90
Merchants Quay C	18.2	39
Ushers B	29.2	66
Ushers C	30.7	42
5 Study Areas*	**11.3**	**59**

*Estimate based on the combined data of the 5 surveys, re-weighted to match the known characteristics of the respective study areas

a strong predictor of children's ability and achievement (Shonkoff and Phillips, 2000). However, this literature also emphasises that depression and other forms of psychological distress affect the ways parents interact with their children (ibid.). In the WBCFN studies, adult migrant respondents with comparatively low social exclusion scores were found to have comparatively poor well-being scores. However, their children were found to have comparatively high well-being scores. These findings suggest a need to tease out the different factors which respectively contribute towards higher and lower child well-being. One hypothesis might be that an absence of relative poverty amongst immigrants (which in this sample did not include asylum seekers) contributed to child well-being as did the comparatively high educational capital possessed by their parents. Comparative OECD data show that only two other developed countries (Canada and Australia) have higher proportions of foreign-born with third-level educational qualifications. Except in a handful of Western countries (including the United States, Finland, Belgium, France and Germany) immigrants are now more likely to possess tertiary education than the native born population (though educational levels may differ between immigrant communities). Here again, however, Ireland is in a somewhat extreme position in that immigrant educational advantage over the native population is quite large. This holds in Dublin, even in areas that are not disadvantaged. According to the 2006 census (CSO 2006), over half (52.5%) of non-Irish/non-UK-born persons living in Dublin had third level qualifications (compared with 34.6 per cent of natives); of these, less than 15 per cent had low education (primary or lower secondary level only) compared with 37 per cent of natives.

Migrants have a distinctively youthful age-profile – a large majority is aged between 20–39 years, an age-group in which education levels amongst natives are also quite high. When the comparison is restricted to this age-group, the educational advantage of the non-Irish/UK-born reduces a great deal: 55.6 per cent have third level qualifications compared with 50.6 per cent for native Dubliners. Yet, it is significant that even when age effects are taken into account immigrants still retain an educational advantage. In the case of deprived areas, where immigrants living in Dublin have been found to settle disproportionately, these are found to have considerably higher educational levels than indigenous residents (Fahey and Fanning, 2010). Unsurprisingly then, in the case of immigrant children identified in the WBCFN data, many of their parents had middle class educational capital, even if this had not translated into employment status. Likewise, immigrant children were considerably less likely to be in one-parent households than WBCFN respondents as a whole.

However, the findings of this study suggest that a pronounced generation gap exists in respect of the well-being of immigrant adults and children in the Irish case. Something of an inverse relationship between low social exclusion and well-being emerged when well-being was defined as including social capital indicators as well as psychological ones. In essence, the main barriers to adult well-being were social capital deficits. Immigrant adults were also under-employed given their education levels. The well-being of children was measured in considerably greater detail than that of adults. Well-being scores for immigrant children were extremely high compared with the children of their Irish neighbours; the zero percent SDQ 'serious problem' scores of both EU and non-EU immigrant children are striking. The 25 point SDQ questionnaire utilised has been found to be robust in a large variety of cultural settings. These results strongly suggest that immigrant children have cultural capital resources not possessed by the children of their Irish neighbours in deprived communities. These findings are to some extent corroborated by qualitative research on the responses of Irish schools to immigrant children where teacher interviewees were found to idealise immigrant pupils (Devine, 2005). This suggests that low levels of child well-being (defined by factors such as conduct problems, emotional symptoms, hyperactivity, peer problems and anti-social behaviour) amongst Irish-born pupils were in effect interpreted as a deficit in cultural capital.

Of particular note is that adult immigrant respondents in the WBCFN studies were also markedly more optimistic about the educational prospects of their children than were Irish respondents. These differences were most dramatic when scores for migrants were compared to those for the Liberties overall. Considerably lower educational expectations were found in the Merchants Quay A electoral district of the Liberties, where just 30 per cent expected that their children would access third level education. Low scores were also found for Merchants Quay C (39%) and Ushers Quay C (42%). Yet 90 per cent of respondents in Merchants Quay B (the Liberties electoral division with the lowest percentage of Irish citizens at 55%) expected that their children would access third level education (Table 2). Whilst hardly definitive, this huge difference does suggest that immigrants living in the Liberties had far higher educational expectations than did their Irish-born neighbours.

However, these findings should not be taken to carve too neat a distinction between immigrant families and those of the host population in comparatively deprived areas. Although immigrants in the WBCFN studies generally possess more educational and economic capital – and research in the Irish context suggests that individuals in low income households have significantly less opportunity to participate fully in education (Clancy, 1995; Lynch, 1999) – it cannot be assumed that comparatively poorer people do not value education. Although the findings of the WBCFN studies suggest that immigrants tend to have higher aspirations regarding their children's education, research in Ireland by Daly and Leonard (2002), which focused on a sample of poor indigenous families, found that such families also valued education to a high degree. Consequently, Daly and Leonard challenge the "cultural deficit" model of poverty, which pathologises working class culture and implies that low income groups pass on negative and socially-undesirable attitudes to their children (2002: 85).

THE FINDINGS IN CONTEXT

The findings on immigrant children in the above analysis of WBCFN data can be usefully considered alongside those of studies of the experiences of immigrant children in Irish schools. These notably include: (i) qualitative research undertaken by Devine (2005) amongst teachers working with immigrant children in deprived areas; (ii) McGorman and Sugrue's (2007) study which draws on data and interviews from all 25 of the primary schools in the Dublin 15 area (the North-West Dublin suburban area that in recent years has experienced the greatest overall increase in population and has come to have the highest concentration of immigrant pupils in the Republic of Ireland); and (iii) a recent study by Smyth et al. (2009). The latter drew on a postal survey of the principals of all 733 second-level schools in the Republic of Ireland and a sample of 1200 primary school principals selected to be representative of all primary schools in terms of size, location and disadvantaged status.

Devine's (2005) findings from research conducted in eight schools suggested that immigrant children were perceived by teachers to have positive dispositions towards schooling and education in general because immigrant parents were in the main highly educated:

> Positive accounts of migrant children's work, for example, were located in an assumption that such children generally came from middle-class backgrounds and as a result provided positive role models for Irish students, especially those in working-class schools (Devine, 2005: 64).

The inference was that parental human capital advantage translated into educational cultural capital advantage within deprived schools. Migrant children were depicted by teachers as having a potentially positive impact on some of the more "deficient" working-class students. Devine (ibid.) concluded that teacher interviewees often idealised migrant pupils, finding them "very education-orientated, very anxious for it" and noting "quite a contrast between them and our own kids" (p. 60–61). As such, in deprived areas some immigrants were depicted as role models for Irish children. Positive perceptions of newcomer children were rooted in the presumption that such children generally came from middle-class backgrounds and as a result provided positive role models for Irish students, "especially those in working-class schools" (ibid.: 60–61). Teachers, in Devine's analysis, perceived working-class students "in deficit terms" and their presumptions about migrant children were framed in terms of a middle-class cultural capital ideal (ibid.: 64).

Smyth et al.'s (2009) study, *Adapting to Diversity*, concluded that over-representation of "newcomers" (a term used to denote immigrant children in various education reports) within such disadvantaged settings was at once an obstacle to integration but also, possibly, a social inclusion boon:

> This suggests that some schools are dealing with, not only a larger proportion of newcomer students, but also considerable literacy, numeracy, behavioural

and attendance difficulties, and a high proportion of other disadvantaged groups like travellers, which could place a considerable burden on their resources. There is also a possibility that newcomer students may raise the standard and learning expectations in schools with a disadvantaged student intake (Smyth et al., 2009: 51).

Both Devine (op cit) and Smyth et al. (op cit.) described a "reference group" effect whereby teachers in disadvantaged schools made comparisons between newcomers (whose parents had higher educational levels and commitments to education) and Irish parents without such resources (ibid.: 175). Similarly, teachers interviewed in Dublin 15 as part of the study by McGorman and Sugrue (2007) highlighted the work ethic of many newcomer children who were committed to working hard to learn and to succeed. Some newcomers were perceived by teachers as a positive influence, notably in disadvantaged areas where it was felt that the arrival of such motivated high-achievers would serve as a good role model to Irish pupils (McGorman and Sugrue, 2007: 15).

Smyth et al. (2009) found that in 70 per cent of disadvantaged schools newcomers were perceived as being motivated above average (2009: 154). Yet, along with the McGorman and Sugrue (2007) study, they also highlighted considerable variation in terms of motivation for different immigrant groups, finding that children from Eastern European, Middle Eastern and Asian backgrounds were more motivated than children from African backgrounds. McGorman and Sugrue (2007) described the concerns of teachers in blunt terms:

Again and again, teachers in Junior schools pointed to the fact that many African children in the early years did not have the social skills to take part in class-groups of 29 children. This perceived lack of social skills, the teachers indicated, leads to considerable disruption. While teachers were somewhat reticent about 'naming' such concerns for fear of stereotyping particular ethnic groups, there was a strong sense also that remaining silent on the issue would allow it to fester below the surface, where it would be likely to become a throbbing racist sore (p. 67).

Dublin 15 teachers drew attention to cultural conflicts with African children and families about discipline. Interviewees referred to "some children exhibiting hugely disrespectful behaviour towards female members of staff" and, as one put it, "a general lack of respect of Nigerian and African boys towards teachers" (ibid.: 69). Somewhat similarly, an interviewee in Smyth et al.'s (2009) study stated: "There is a much higher number of behavioural problems with African newcomer boys in our school" (p. 67).

However, such perceptions of cultural conflict can obscure other factors that potentially affect the behaviour of children. In her study of English language support teachers, for example, Nowlan (2008) argued that bilingual students' linguistic abilities are not valued as cultural capital. Relatedly, Dublin 15 teachers identified frustrations amongst some children who "were bright and anxious to get on" but who were inhibited by their lack of English (McGorman and Sugrue 2007: 77).

Previously well-behaved children would enter "an angry phase" or "the silent phase" (op cit. p. 78). The Dublin 15 research, in common with Nowlan's (op cit.) research a year earlier, implied that the skills amongst teachers to address such issues were underdeveloped (McGorman and Sugrue, 2007). Nevertheless, whilst teachers seemed sensitive to a wide range of explanations of newcomer behavioural problems, a tendency to reduce these to a dominant cultural conflict narrative was evident. In particular, this tended to portray African children and families as deviant. In their study of Dublin 15 schools, for example, McGorman and Sugrue (op cit.) suggested that some of the comments of teachers about African children were "much too generalised", inferring some degree of stereotyping by teachers.

Strikingly, none of the children of African respondents in the 2007 and 2008 WBCFN studies (1% of families surveyed) were found to have 'serious difficulties' (Table 1), although this research did not examine Dublin 15. Nevertheless, it does suggest a need to question depictions of African children as disproportionately affected by behavioural problems. To some extent at least, the perceived behavioural problems of "newcomer" children cannot be explained by cultural factors. Racism and other negative experiences of the school system need to be taken into account also. Smyth et al. (2009) identified a tendency for non-white children to become socially-isolated within schools. As stated by one teacher in a disadvantaged school (that accepted referrals from social services, the Education Welfare Board and pupils who had been expelled from other schools) in Dublin 15: "The Eastern Europeans mix very well. The Africans tend to stay amongst themselves" (p. 85). Likewise, a teacher in another disadvantaged (and under-subscribed) school commented: "The Chinese in particular are a very close knit group that don't mingle with other students" (ibid.). In describing the "boys in our class from Africa", an Irish student interviewee similarly commented: "they don't get on well with other people like from Ireland or from different countries, they don't get on with that many people". Perhaps unsurprisingly, African pupils were more likely to report bullying than Eastern European pupils (ibid.: 184). As put by a teacher in the earlier study by Devine (2005: 63): "I would say that the non-nationals who are not black mix easier with the kids, if they have any kind of English at all they are accepted easier than the African kids".

According to Pierre Bourdieu (1985), cultural capital – manifested in the skills, norms, habits and dispositions that confirm social advantage upon individuals – is unequally distributed and contributes to the intergenerational reproduction of in-equalities. For Bourdieu, educational cultural capital is a form of intellectual capital that affects the life chances of individuals as it reproduces a specific social order and cultural hierarchies alongside material ones. Specifically in the case of education, Bourdieu (1999: 186) identifies a "hidden curriculum" loaded in favour of certain social groups and against others on the basis of class. Teachers emerge as key arbitrators in this. The values, norms and behaviour teachers respond to positively count as cultural capital advantage; conversely (and simplifying somewhat) cultural capital disadvantages are those dispositions that teachers tend to reject. In this sense, education is as much a battle for the hearts and minds of teachers as it is for those of pupils.

A recent analysis by Strand (2009) of the persistence of "ethnic gaps" in educational attainment in England emphasised the importance of socio-economic inequalities in explaining educational outcomes for different black and minority ethnic groups and, indeed, white pupils. Strand (2009: 4) cites findings that 29 per cent of black children in England are eligible for free school meals (a commonly used indicator of poverty) compared to just 14 per cent of white children. Similarly, McGorman and Sugrue (2007) note that the numbers of households in Dublin 15 in receipt of private rent supplement (again an indicator of poverty) rose from 1433 in 2002 to 2822 in 2006, almost doubling during a period when unemployment remained low for Ireland as a whole. Some 894 were "foreign nationals" in 2002 rising to 1910 in 2006. Of these 1910, some 61 per cent were African and 22 per cent were Eastern European. Hence, disproportionate risks of poverty amongst Africans in Ireland suggest that some African children face barriers to educational attainment that are better explained by socio-economic status (and possibly racism) than by presumed cultural capital deficits or by individual dispositions.

CHALLENGES

The WBCFN research drawn upon here consisted of efforts to measure individual-level child well-being. From a psychological perspective the SDQ measures evidence of conduct problems, emotional symptoms, hyperactivity, peer problems and anti-social behaviour. Child well-being (as revealed in parental perceptions) is assessed according to whether the child has 'no difficulties', 'some difficulties', or 'serious difficulties'. Likewise, the educational research examined above consisted mostly of efforts to measure the attitudes of teachers towards immigrant children. Devine's (2005) sociological analysis of such perceptions emphasises the importance of how teachers respond to children over and above the individual-level characteristics and dispositions of children; it emphasises the importance of cultural capital in how teachers respond to immigrant pupils. Significant epistemological differences here between both research approaches need to be acknowledged. Devine (2005), from a sociological perspective, finds that immigrant children in deprived areas are more likely to possess valued kinds of cultural capital than are the children of indigenous residents of deprived localities. However, to some extent, SDQ scores offer a proxy for educational cultural capital; in other words, what are measured (from a psychological perspective) are individual characteristics and dispositions understood (from a sociological perspective) to impede education, well-being and long-term life chance outcomes.

Bourdieu's (1999) cultural capital thesis endeavours to explain the workings of class inequality in fields such as education and employment. The OECD (2007) research cited at the beginning of this chapter draws attention to patterns of racialised class inequality (though it also emphasises the importance of linguistic cultural capital, i.e. being able to speak the host community language). The "social lift" hypothesis that high levels of migrant human and educational capital potentially translate to a form of cultural capital for the children of such migrants appears from all the studies cited here to hold for white migrant students but not for black students.

The 2006 census (CSO, 2006) identified a black or black African population of 53,318, of which Nigerians were the numerically largest group (16,677).[1] Some 41 per cent of Nigerian-born migrants were educated to degree level or higher compared to just over one quarter of Poles, 17 per cent of Lithuanians and 28 per cent of Chinese (CSO, 2007a: 109). However, this educational advantage is not reflected in the experiences of Nigerians in the labour market. Some clearly fared well compared even to white immigrant groups; 15 per cent of those in employment were listed in the "employers and managers" and "higher professional" groups compared to just 6 per cent of Poles and 5 per cent of Lithuanians. However, the 2006 census also identified male and female unemployment levels for Nigerians at 50 per cent and 70 per cent respectively (CSO, 2007b: 47). Moreover, the authors of a 2005 ESRI survey concluded that even after controlling for factors like education, age and length of stay, Black Africans experienced the most institutional racism as well as the most racism and discrimination in the work domain, in public places and in pubs and restaurants (McGinnity et al., 2006). Some 47.7 per cent of African respondents had third level education; nevertheless, the study found that these highly-educated respondents were significantly more likely than other respondents to experience discrimination in employment and public arenas (ibid.: vii). Such findings suggest that African educational and human capital does not translate into cultural capital to the same extent as has been found with equivalent whites. The nature and extent of educational barriers as experienced by their children therefore warrants serious consideration. Various studies suggest that cultural capital has, to some extent, become racialised; teacher interviewees, in turn, emphasise behavioural difficulties amongst black pupils. Further research on child well-being that focuses on black immigrant children is clearly needed to distinguish between prevalent racialised stereotypes and the distinct needs of such children.

NOTES

[1] Figure for number of citizens arrived at by subtracting number of Nigerian nationals (16,300) from number of Nigerian born (16,667) living in the Republic of Ireland. See Census 2006 Principal Demographic Results Tables 20 and 25 (CSO, 2006: 68, 73).

REFERENCES

Berry, J. W. (1997). Immigration, acculturation and adaptation. *Applied Psychology: An International Review*, *46*(1), 5–68.

Bourdieu, P. (1985). The social space and the genesis of groups. *Theory and Society*, *14*(6), 723–444.

Bourdieu, P., et al. (1999). *The weight of the world: Social suffering in contemporary society*. Cambridge: Polity Press.

Bradshaw, J., Hoelscher, P., & Richardson, D. (2007). An index of child well-being in the European Union. *Social Indicators Research*, *80*, 133–177.

Clancy, P. (1995). *Access to college: Patterns of continuity and change*. Dublin: Higher Education Authority.

CSO. (2006). *Census 2006 Principal demographic results*. Dublin: Stationery Office.

CSO. (2007a). *Census 2006 Volume 10 – Education and qualifications*. Dublin: Stationery Office.

CSO. (2007b). *Census 2006 Volume 8 – Occupations*. Dublin: Stationery Office.

Daly, M., & Leonard, M. (2002). *Against all odds: Family life on a low income in Ireland.* Dublin: Combat Poverty Agency.

Devine, D. (2005). Welcome to the Celtic Tiger? Teacher responses to immigration and increasing ethnic diversity in Irish schools. *International Studies in Sociology of Education, 15*(1), 49–70.

Directorate-General for Justice, Freedom and Security. (2007). *Handbook on integration for policy makers and practitioners.* EU Publications Office.

Duncan, G. J. (2005). *Income and child-well-being: The 2005 Geary lecture.* Dublin: Economic and Social Research Institute.

Fahey, T., & Fanning, B. (2010). Immigration and social spatial segregation in Dublin. *Urban Studies,* 1–18.

Gerard, A. B. (1994). *Parent-Child Relationship Inventory (PCRI): Manual.* Los Angeles: Western Psychological Services.

Helliwell, J. F. (2005, March 21). Well-being, social capital and public policy: What's new? Presented to the Royal Economic Society, Nottingham. Retrieved from http://www.gpiatlantic.org/conference/papers/helliwell.pdf

Hernandez, D., & Charney, E. (1998). *From generation to generation: The health and well-being of children in immigrant families.* Washington, DC: National Research Council.

Kamerman, S. B., Neuman, M., Waldfogel, J., & Brooks-Gunn, J. (2003). *Social policies, family types and child outcomes in selected OECD countries.* OECD Social Employment and Migration Working Papers No. 6. Available at http://www.childpolicyintl.org/publications/SOCIAL%20POLICIES,%20FAMILY%20TYPES,%20AND%20CHILD%20OUTCOMES%20IN%20SELECTED%20OECD%20COUNTRIES.pdf

Kawachi, I., Kennedy, B. P., Lochner, K., & Prothrow-Stith, D. (1997). Social capital, income inequality and morality. *American Journal of Public Health, 97*(9), 1491–1498.

Lindsay, G., Band, S., Cullen, M., & Cullen, S. (2008). *Parenting early intervention pathfinder evaluation: Additional study of the involvement of extended schools.* London: Department for Children, Schools and Families. Available at http://www.dcsf.gov.uk/research/data/uploadfiles/DCSF-RW036.pdf

Lynch, K. (1999). The status of children and young persons: Educational and related issues. In S. Healy & B. Reynolds (Eds.), *Social policy in Ireland: Principals, practice and problems* (pp. 321–353). Dublin: Oak Tree Press.

McGinnity, F., O'Connell, P. J., Quinn, E., & Williams, J. (2006). *Migrant's experience or racism and discrimination in Ireland: Results of a survey conducted by the Economic and Social Research Institute for the European Union Monitoring Centre on Racism and Xenophobia.* Dublin: ESRI.

McGorman, E., & Sugrue, C. (2007). *Intercultural education: Primary challenges in Dublin 15.* Dublin: Department of Education and Science.

Nowlan, E. (2008) Underneath the band-aid: Supporting bilingual students in Irish schools. *Irish Educational Studies, 27*(3), 253–266.

O'Boyle, N., & Fanning. B. (2009). Immigration, integration and the risks of social exclusion: The social policy case for disaggregated data in the Republic of Ireland. *Irish Geography, 42*(2), 145–164.

OECD. (2007). *International migration outlook.* Paris: Author.

Phinney, J. S., Horenczyk, G., Liebkind, K., & Vedder, P. (2001). Ethnic identity, immigration and well-being: An interactional perspective. *Journal of Social Issues, 57*(3), 493–510.

Shonkoff, J., & Phillips, D. (2000). *From neurons to neighbourhood: The science of early childhood development.* Washington, DC: National Academy Press.

Smyth, E., Darmody, M., McGinnity, F., & Byrne, D. (2009). *Adapting to diversity: Irish schools and newcomer students.* Economic and Social Research Institute Research Series No. 8.

Strand, S. (2009, January 4–7). *Do some schools narrow the gap? Differential school effectiveness by ethnicity, gender, poverty and prior attainment.* Paper presented at the International Congress for School Effectiveness and Improvement, Vancouver, Canada.

Straus, M., Hamby, S., Finkelhor, D., & Runyan, D. (1995). *Identification of child abuse with the parent-child conflict tactics scales (CTSPC): Development and psychometric data for a national sample of American parents.* Durham, NH: Family Research Laboratory, University of New Hampshire.

UNICEF. (2007). *Child poverty in perspective: An overview of child well-being in rich countries.* Innocenti Report Card 7. Florence: UNICEF Innocenti Research Centre.

UNICEF. (2009). *Children in immigrant families in eight affluent countries.* Innocenti Insight Series. Florence: UNICEF Innocenti Research Centre.

Woerner, W., Fleitlich-Bilyk, B., & Martinussen, R., et al. (2004). The strengths and difficulties questionnaire overseas: Evaluations and applications of the SDQ beyond Europe. *European Child Psychiatry, 13*(Suppl. 2), 1147–1154.

Youth in Mind. (n.d.). *Information for researchers and professionals about the strengths and difficulties questionnaire.* Available at http://www.sdqinfo.com/

Bryan Fanning
School of Applied Social Science
University College Dublin

Trutz Haase
Independent Social and Economic Consultant

Neil O'Boyle
School of Communications
Dublin City University

MICHAL MOLCHO, COLETTE KELLY
AND SAOIRSE NIC GABHAINN

11. IMMIGRANT CHILDREN IN IRELAND

Health and Social Wellbeing of First and Second Generation Immigrants

INTRODUCTION

The history of mankind is replete with stories of migration. People and tribes migrated in search for food and commodities, and people were sold for slavery. Such was the history of many peoples including the Irish. In the past decades, however, migration has changed to include more people than ever, involving millions of people and most countries (UN, 2002). In Europe, in 2006 alone, over 3.5 million people settled as new residents (Herm, 2008). While in some countries only 1% of the population are migrants, in others nearly 40% are reported to be migrants (Gushulak, Pace & Weekers, 2009). In Ireland in 2006, 15% of the overall population were foreign-born (Nolan & Maitre, 2008), placing Ireland among the countries with the largest proportion of immigrants in the EU (Gushulak, Pace & Weekers, 2009).

Immigration in modern Ireland is a relatively new phenomenon. After many years of emigration, a period of positive net migration was registered since the mid 1990s and for the first time since the 1970s, with immigration peaking in 2006 and 2007 (CSO, 2009). Although net negative migration was registered in 2009, it was primarily made-up of non-Irish nationals, and the proportion of non-Irish nationals in Ireland is still significant (CSO, 2009). Investigating the profile of immigrants in Ireland reveals that nearly half of the non-Irish nationals residing in the country are from the UK, with the rest coming from Central and Eastern Europe, the Americas, Asia and Africa. Many non-Irish nationals live in urban areas, primarily Dublin and Cork (CSO, 2009). Since immigration is relatively new to Ireland, only few studies investigated this phenomenon, focusing primarily on adult immigrants. Such studies investigated the demographics of the immigrant population and how they fare economically. Less is known on the experiences and integration of child immigrants in Ireland.

As with adults, children of immigrants leave their homeland and settle in a new country, often with different norms and values, and need to adapt to a sometimes markedly dissimilar culture and socioeconomic conditions, often facing discrimination and racism (Pantin et al., 2003; Berry, 1997; Ward, Bochner & Furnham, 2001). While the process of immigration is sometimes imposed on adult individuals, for children this is even more likely to be the case, as the decision to migrate is usually made by their parents or relatives, hence, the consequence of the immigration process

Darmody, Tyrrell, Song (eds.), The Changing Faces of Ireland: Exploring the Lives of Immigrant and Ethnic Minority Children, 183–201.

on children may be more acute. Additionally, children's integration is an important marker of the integration of the whole family in the new society; hence, studying the experiences of child immigrants is of importance.

In 2006, 6% of the child population (under 18) were non-Irish nationals (Hanafin et al., 2008), a proportion that is large enough to justify such investigation. As with adult immigrants, the largest portion of child immigrants in Ireland is from the UK (32%), with Poland, Nigeria and the US each accounting for approximately 8% of child immigrants (Hanafin et al., 2008). It is estimated that many of the child immigrants from the UK are of Irish descent, with families returning to Ireland after years or generations in the UK. As such, this group of immigrant children is potentially different from other immigrant groups and deserves special attention. This group may also be, at least in part, under-represented in the national figures as they may be reported in the census as Irish nationals even if they were born outside of the country. It is therefore important to consider the different definitions for immigration and the relevance of them to Ireland in particular.

Definitions

The United Nations defines 'migrants' as persons who have moved across international borders from their country of origin and taken up residence in another country (Van de Walle, 1982). For children, the definition is slightly different. While there are a variety of definitions employed, the two most common are first and second generation immigrants (The term '1.5[th] generation' immigrants is more recent). First generation child immigrants are children that were born outside of the country of residence (foreign-born); second-generation child immigrants are children for whom one or both of their parents were born outside the country of destination (residence), even if the children themselves were born in that country; 1.5[th] generation child immigrants are children who were born outside of the country of residence, but immigrated at a very young age. For the purpose of this chapter and given the emigration and immigration history of the Irish people, we examine the following groups: first generation immigrant children whose both parents were born in Ireland; first generation child immigrants for whom either parent was born outside of Ireland; and second generation immigrants.

Social-economic Circumstances

Studies of child immigrants have been mainly conducted in the US and Canada, with some studies from Europe (e.g., Stevens et al., 2003; Vollebergh et al., 2005; Storhmeier and Schmitt-Rodermund, 2008). These investigations have looked primarily at socio-demographic circumstances, involvement in risk behaviours, language fluency, school performance and mental health of immigrant children, compared to native children. Examinations of the living circumstances experienced by child immigrants have consistently shown that immigrant children are more likely to live in low-income households, less affluent families and in more crowded houses, are more exposed to food insecurity and less likely to have medical insurance (The Urban

Institute, 2006; Hernandez, Danton & Macartney., 2008; Vollebergh et al., 2005). These findings have been supported by those of Molcho et al. (2008) in their study of immigrant children in Ireland.

Mental Health

Unlike reports on the poor living conditions of immigrant children, studies on other aspects of the lives of immigrant children have yielded equivocal findings. In Italy, Vieno et al. (2009) reported that immigrant children experienced more psychosomatic symptoms and reported lower levels of life satisfaction, self-reported health, social integration, and higher levels of victimisation compared to their native peers. Studies of Turkish immigrant children, compared to their native peers in the Netherlands, found that Turkish immigrant children were more likely to report behavioural problems, both internalised and externalised, with depression as the leading problem. However, no differences were found between those immigrant children and their peers in Turkey in relation to mental and behavioural problems, although the immigrant group scored higher on a competence scale (Bengi-Arslan et al., 1997; Janssen et al., 2004). Studies of other immigrant groups in the Netherlands did not find differences in the mental health of immigrants when compared to their native peers (Vollebergh et al., 2005). Similarities in relation to mental health have also been reported in Canada (Ma, 2002), Australia (Davies and McKelvey, 1998), the US (Blake et al., 2001; Beiser at al., 2002) and Ireland (Molcho et al., 2008).

Risk Behaviours

Ambiguous evidence also exists in relation to involvement in risk behaviours, such as substance use, early sexual behaviour, fighting and bullying. Some authors have suggested that immigrant children, even those with low socioeconomic status, were less likely to smoke, drink alcohol, use drugs or engage in delinquent behaviours (Georgoades et al., 2006; Harris, 2004); while contradictory evidence emerged from other studies where immigrant children in Israel, the Netherlands and the US were more likely to be involved in such behaviour (Isralowitz & Slonim-Nevo, 2002; Bengi-Arslan et al., 1997; Pawliuk et al., 1996). In Ireland, Molcho et al. (2008) reported differences in involvement in risk behaviours between UK and non-UK immigrant children. While non-UK immigrant children were less likely to report involvement in risk behaviours compared to their native peers, this was not the case for UK immigrant children, who reported similar levels of involvement in risk behaviours to that of their native peers.

Language Fluency

Level of fluency in the language spoken in the country of residence is considered an important determinant of the lives of immigrants. Studies carried out in the US found that immigrant children are very likely to be fluent in English and become bilingual (Hernandez Danton & McCartney, 2008). However, about a quarter of child immigrants live in households with no one over the age of 13 who is fluent in English. These children may experience isolation from English speaking society, but are also frequently required to act as the primary intermediary between adult family members and professionals in various settings, a role that may expose them to more stress (Hernandez, Danton & McCartney, 2008). But here again, findings are not consistent. Some studies in the US have found that speaking the language of the country of residence predicts a greater likelihood of conduct problems and depressive symptoms (Gonzales et al., 2006), while others, again in the US, found that not speaking the language of the country of residence increases the risk for bullying victimisation (Yu et al., 2003).

Integration

Mental health status, involvement in risk behaviours and level of fluency in the language of the country of residence are all linked to integration. Being integrated may seem to be an appropriate goal for immigrant children, but evidence suggests that integration does not always work in favour of such children. Research among Lebanese immigrants in Canada revealed that immigrant children with strong Lebanese national identity reported fewer problems in daily life and were less likely to experience depression compared to Lebanese immigrant children who adopted a strong Canadian national identity (Gaudet, Clement & Deuzeman, 2005). Similarly, Russian immigrant girls in the US who reported higher levels of assimilation to the US culture were more likely to report sexual risk taking behaviours (Jeltova, Fish & Revenson, 2005). A more complex study that measured Turkish identity among immigrant children found that Turkish child immigrants with strong Turkish identity reported fewer behavioural problems in Sweden but not in the Netherlands (Vedder and Virta, 2005). The researchers explained these results with reference to the differences in immigration policies between the two countries of residence: while Swedish immigration policies encourage strengthening the ethnic roots of immigrants, policies in the Netherlands stress adaptation to Dutch language and culture.

Storhmeier and Schmitt-Rodermund (2008) argued that immigration in itself does not necessarily lead to adaptation problems. When such problems do exist, they appear to be moderated by levels of social cohesion, exposure to discrimination and exclusion, fluency in the language of the host country, the norms and expectations in the country of origin and in the host country and the actual process of adaptation. However, Molcho, Kelly & Nic Gabhainn (2010) found that even when controlling for different aspects of integration, immigrant children in Ireland report lower levels of life satisfaction, suggesting that, in fact, being an immigrant the act or process of immigration in itself can create pressures that are not moderated by level of integration. These findings deserve further investigation.

Using nationally representative data from the 2006 Irish Health Behaviour in School-Aged Children (HBSC) study, this chapter sets out to examine explanatory variables for the differences in health and social wellbeing between different immigrant groups, particularly examining language spoken at home and the differences between first and second generation immigrants. Given that some of the UK child immigrants could be from Irish families returning to Ireland, which can influence their sense of belonging and integration, UK immigrant children are analysed separately. We hypothesised that:

1. First and second generation immigrants will differ in their experiences of health and wellbeing;
2. Second generation immigrant children will experience higher levels of integration compared to first generation immigrant children;
3. Immigrant children who speak English at home will experience less social exclusion compared to children who do not speak English at home.

METHODS

Study Population and Procedures

A school-based anonymous survey was conducted during the spring of 2006, according to a common, cross-national, HBSC research protocol (Currie et al., 2008a). Primary and post-primary schools in Ireland were randomly selected using a two-stage sampling process designed to achieve a representative sample of school-going children aged 10–17 years. The sample was stratified by geographical region. A total of 10,334 school children were recruited from 215 schools, with a response rate of 63% at the school level and 83% at the student level. The current analyses are based on a sub-sample of self-identified immigrant children. Children were identified as immigrants if they were either born outside of Ireland or if both parents were born outside of Ireland. This paper presents a sub-sample of immigrants, with a total of 2,319 school children.

Measurement

Immigrant Status

Immigrant status was determined from three questions: 'Were you born in Ireland?'; with answer categories 'yes' or 'no'; 'In what country was your mother born?'; and 'In what country was your father born?'. The latter two questions were open-ended. Children that reported that they were born outside of the island of Ireland were categorised as first generation immigrants. First generation immigrant children were then divided into those whose both parents were born in Ireland (defined as returning emigrants) and those whose either one or both of their parents were born outside of Ireland (first generation immigrants). Children who reported that they were born in Ireland but either of their parents was born outside of the island of Ireland were categorised as second generation immigrants. Second generation immigrants were then dichotomised into those whose both parents were born in the UK, US or Canada (defined as UK/US immigrants) and those for whom either one or both of their parents were born outside the UK or US (defined as non UK/US immigrants).

Language Spoken at Home

Language of the family was measured using the question: 'What language do you speak at home?' This question was open-ended. Answers were categorised into 'English' vs. any other language.

Place of Residence

As was reported by the CSO (2009), many of the immigrants in Ireland live in urban settings. We therefore divided the study population to those living in urban area (city and town) vs. those living in rural settings (village and countryside).

Family Affluence Scale (FAS)

The Family Affluence Scale (Currie et al., 2008b) is an existing measure of material wealth that is based on four indicators of consumption / deprivation (vehicle owner-ship, bedroom sharing, holiday travel and computer ownership). Scores ranged from 0 to 7, with 0 representing the lowest family affluence and 7 representing the highest. The scores were combined into 3 categories as follows: low (0–3), medium (4–5), and high (6–7). The FAS shows good validity and yields lower non-response among children at all age groups compared to questions on parental occupation (Currie et al., 2008b).

Health and Wellbeing

Self-rated health was assessed by the question 'Would you say your health is …?' and the response options were categorized at 'excellent' (1), versus 'good' (2), 'fair' (3) or 'poor' (4). Self-reported happiness was measured by the question 'In general, how do you feel about your life at present?' and the responses were categorized at 'very happy', vs. 'quite happy', 'don't feel very happy' and 'not happy at all'. Children were also asked to rank themselves from 0 ('worst possible life') to 10 ('best possible life') on a life satisfaction ladder (Cantril, 1965). This scale was used to identify those with high life satisfaction (response >6).

Integration: School and Local area Perceptions

Using factor analysis, a statistical method that facilitates the identification of under-lying factors or dimensions from a larger number of questions, specific dimensions of school and local area were identified, and the following scales were constructed:

Student Relationships

Children were asked three questions about their relationships with other students in their class. Children were asked how much they agreed that students in their class are kind and helpful, that students in their class enjoy being together, and that students in their class accept them as they are. The response options for each of the questions were: 'strongly agree' (1); 'agree' (2); 'neither agree nor disagree' (3); 'disagree' (4); and 'strongly disagree' (5). The Cronbach alpha, examining the internal reliability of this scale, was 0.712.

Relationships with Teachers

Children were asked four questions about their relationships with teachers. Children were asked how much they agree that their teachers are interested in them; that their teachers encourage them to express their own views; that their teachers treat students fairly; and that they can get extra help from their teachers if they need it. The response options were 'strongly agree' (1); 'agree' (2); 'neither agree nor disagree' (3); 'disagree' (4); and 'strongly disagree' (5). The Cronbach alpha for this scale was 0.804.

General School Perceptions

Children were asked five questions about their general school perceptions. Children were asked how much they agree that the rules in the school are fair; that students are not treated too strictly; that school is a nice place to be; that they feel they belong at school; and that they feel safe at school. The response options were 'strongly agree' (1); 'agree' (2); 'neither agree nor disagree' (3); 'disagree' (4); and 'strongly disagree' (5). The Cronbach alpha for this scale was 0.787.

Perceptions of Local Area

Children were asked four questions about their local area. These comprised how often they feel that their local area is a good place to live in; that it is safe for young children to play outside; that there are good places to go to; and that they can ask for help from people in their local area. 'strongly agree' (1); 'agree' (2); 'neither agree nor disagree' (3); 'disagree' (4); and 'strongly disagree' (5). The Cronbach alpha for this scale was 0.674.

The responses on all of the scales were divided into tertiles indicating low, mid and high levels of positive perceptions towards each of the dimensions.

Data Analysis

In order to take into account potential socio-demographic differences between the immigrant population and the general population in terms of geographical location, or socio-demographic characteristics, the analyses controlled for gender, age, family affluence and place of residence (urban/rural). Descriptive analyses were used to describe the sample and the distribution of the measures, using the categorised variables. Analysis of Covariance (ANCOVA) was used to examine differences between groups on the constructed scales, while controlling for age, gender, family affluence and place of residence.

FINDINGS

Overall, 22.4% (n=2,319) of the children in the sample were immigrant children. Table 1 presents the characteristics of the immigrant population by their characteristics. About half of the immigrants were first generation immigrant (11.5%) and half second generation immigrants (10.9%). Of the overall sample, 8.1% of the

Table 1. Immigrant population by generation and language spoken at home (n=2,319)

		%
Total		22.4
First generation	All	11.5
	First generation	3.4
	Returning emigrants	8.1
Second generation	All	10.9
	UK/US	9.2
	Non UK/US	1.7
Language at home	English	20.2
	Other language	2.2

child immigrants were returning emigrants, and 3.4% were first generation immigrants. Of the second generation immigrants, the vast majority were UK/US immigrants (84.8%, n=957) and 15.2% (n=171) were non-UK/US immigrants. Of the immigrant child population, 90% of immigrant children spoke English at home, and only 10% reported that they speak a language other than English at home.

Immigrant Status

Table 2 presents the socio-economic characteristics of immigrant children by their immigration status. Second generation child immigrants were over represented in the younger age group while returning emigrants were over represented in the older age groups, suggesting that age differences exist between the groups. First generation immigrant children were over-represented in low affluent families while returning emigrants were over represented in mid-affluent families. Returning emigrants were also over represented in rural areas.

Table 3 presents the differences between the groups in self-reported health, life satisfaction, school and local area perceptions. The three immigrant groups were similar in the proportions reporting excellent health, however, the first generation immigrant children reported lower life satisfaction compared to the other two groups (p=0.055). First generation immigrants also reported poorer relationships with fellow students compared to second generation immigrants (p<0.001), and better relationships with teachers compared to the returning emigrants group (p<0.05). The three groups did not differ in their general school perceptions or in their perceptions of their local area. These analyses controlled for age, gender, family affluence and place of residence.

The differences that were found between the first generation, second generation immigrants and the returning emigrant group, together with the nature of immigration in Ireland, led us to divide the second generation immigrants into a UK/US group and a non-UK/US group. Children whose parents were from the UK, US or Canada were defined as the UK/US group, while children who have at least one parent who is not from the UK, US or Canada were defined as the non-UK/US immigrants.

Table 2. Socio-economic characteristics of immigrant children by immigration status

	Immigration status			
	First generation immigrants	Returning emigrants	Second generation immigrants	p-value
Gender (%)				
Boys	50.1	47.7	47.9	
Girls	49.9	52.3	52.1	
N	840	350	1,127	0.033
Age (%)				
10–11	12.2	8.4	15.6	
12–14	50.1	43.5	49.5	
15–17	37.7	48.1	34.9	
N	814	345	1,115	P<0.001
Family affluence scale (%)				
Low	25.5	16.1	22.9	
Mid	51.3	63.9	53.8	
High	23.2	20.0	23.3	
N	764	335	1,063	P<0.001
Place of residence (%)				
Urban	48.0	35.6	43.1	
Rural	52.0	64.4	56.9	
N	800	343	1,101	P<0.001

Table 3. Health, wellbeing and school perceptions among immigrant children,
by immigration status (n=2,319)

	Immigration status			
	First generation immigrants	Returning emigrants	Second generation immigrants	p-value
Excellent health (%)	33.7	33.7	31.3	
				0.511
High life satisfaction (%)	73.4	77.5	75.0	
				0.055
Student relationships (%)				
Low	32.4	27.0	25.0	
Mid	39.0	39.4	41.9	
High	28.6	33.6	33.1	
				P<0.001
General school perception (%)				
Low	29.7	29.4	26.7	
Mid	39.8	41.8	37.8	
High	30.5	28.8	35.5	
				0.125

Table 3. (Continued)

Relationships with teachers (%)				
Low	25.4	33.2	27.2	
Mid	34.4	31.8	33.4	
High	40.2	35.0	39.4	
				0.008
Perceptions of local area (%)				
Low	42.7	38.8	39.8	
Mid	30.6	32.2	32.5	
High	26.7	29.0	27.7	
				0.252

* Controlled for age, gender, family affluence and place of residence.

Table 4. Socio-economic characteristic of second generation immigrants, by origin

	Second generation immigrants		
	UK/US immigrants	Non UK/US immigrants	p-value
Gender (%)			
Boys	47.5	50.0	
Girls	52.5	50.0	
N	957	170	0.555
Age (%)			
10–11	15.0	19.2	
12–14	50.2	45.5	
15–17	34.8	35.3	
N	948	167	0.327
Family affluence scale (%)			
Low	22.0	27.8	
Mid	55.6	43.7	
High	22.4	28.5	
N	905	158	0.022
Place of residence (%)			
Urban	40.3	58.4	
Rural	59.7	41.6	
N	935	166	P<0.001

* Controlled for age, gender, family affluence and place of residence.

Table 4 presents the socio-economic characteristics of second generation immigrant children by their country of origin. Non-UK/US second generation child immigrants were younger compared to UK/US child immigrants. A U-shape relationship exists in relation to family affluence: non-UK/US second generation child immigrants were over represented in both low and high family affluence groups, and UK/US second generation child immigrants are over represented in the middle category of family affluence. Non-UK/US second generation child immigrants were also over represented in urban areas.

Table 5. Health, wellbeing and school perceptions among second generation immigrant children, by origin % (n=1,122)

	Second generation immigrants		
	UK/US immigrants	*Non UK/US immigrants*	*p-value*
Excellent health (%)	31.1	32.4	
			0.751
High life satisfaction (%)	76.1	69.0	
			0.047
Student relationships (%)			
Low	23.7	32.4	
Mid	43.4	33.5	
High	32.9	34.1	
			0.021
General school perception (%)			
Low	27.1	24.6	
Mid	38.2	35.7	
High	34.7	39.8	
			0.440
Relationships with teachers (%)			
Low	27.2	27.1	
Mid	33.8	31.2	
High	39.0	41.8	
			0.747
Perceptions of local area (%)			
Low	39.6	40.8	
Mid	32.7	32.0	
High	27.7	27.2	
			0.955

* Controlled for age, gender, family affluence and place of residence.

Table 5 presents the differences between the second generation immigrant children groups on the outcome variables. No statistically significant differences were found between the groups in relation to self-rated health. However, fewer non-UK/US second generation immigrant children reported high life satisfaction and more non-UK/US children reported poor relationships with students ($p<0.05$ for both). No other statistically significant differences were found in relation to school and local area perceptions. All analyses controlled for age, gender, family affluence and place of residence.

Language Spoken at Home

Another way of examining immigration is by considering the language spoken at home. Fluency in the language spoken in the country of destination is seen as an indicator for integration, while lack of fluency has been found to be associated with

*Table 6. Socio-economic characteristics of immigrant children,
by language spoken at home*

	Language spoken at home		
	English	Language other than English	p-value
Gender (%)			
Boys	48.3	50.0	
Girls	51.7	50.0	
N	2,068	228	0.618
Age (%)			
10–11	13.3	13.0	
12–14	48.6	50.9	
15–17	38.1	36.1	
N	2,039	216	0.806
FAS (%)			
Low	21.5	33.7	
Mid	55.4	47.1	
High	23.2	18.6	
N	1,320	141	P<0.001
Place of residence (%)			
Urban	41.4	62.7	
Rural	58.6	37.3	
N	2,014	212	P<0.001

* Controlled for age, gender, family affluence and place of residence.

*Table 7. Health, wellbeing and school perceptions among immigrant children,
by language spoken at home (n=2,281)*

	Language spoken at home		
	English	Language other than English	p-value
Excellent health (%)	31.8	38.8	
.			0.035
High life satisfaction (%)	74.7	76.5	
			0.560
Student relationships (%)			
Low	27.8	30.0	
Mid	40.5	39.2	
High	31.7	30.8	
.			0.789
General school perception (%)			
Low	28.6	22.6	
Mid	38.8	42.9	
High	32.6	34.5	
			0.148

Table 7. (Continued)

Relationships with teachers (%)		
Low	28.4	18.2
Mid	32.7	40.9
High	38.9	40.9
		0.003
Perceptions of local area (%)		
Low	40.6	41.2
Mid	31.5	33.6
High	27.9	25.1
		0.654

* Controlled for age, gender, family affluence and place of residence.

bullying, substance use and psychosocial problems (Gonsales et al., 2006; Yu et al., 2003). We therefore examined the differences between child immigrants who speak English at home and those who speak another language at home (both first and second generation immigrants).

Table 6 presents the socio-economic characteristics of child immigrants by language spoken at home. Both groups are similar in their age and gender distribution, but immigrants who do not speak English at home are more likely to report lower family affluence and to reside in urban locations.

Table 7 presents the differences in the outcome variables between immigrant children who speak English at home and immigrant children who do not speak English at home. Immigrant children who speak English were less likely to report excellent health and goof relationships with their teachers compared to those who speak language other than English at home (p<0.05 for both) but no other statistically significant differences were found after controlling for socio-demographic characteristics.

DISCUSSION

The purpose of this chapter was to examine the health, wellbeing and integration of child immigrants in Ireland. Our previous work (Molcho et al., 2008, Molcho, Kelly & Nic Gabhainn, 2010) indicated that child immigrants in Ireland are different from their peers and that UK/US immigrants fare poorly when compared to non-UK/US child immigrants in relation to life satisfaction and risk behaviours. We have also previously reported that non-UK child immigrants were less likely to report positive peer relationships compared to UK/US child immigrants. Last, we found that even after controlling for school perceptions as indicators of social capital, child immigrants reported lower life satisfaction. However, our previous work left gaps in the knowledge to date in relation to first and second generation immigrants, as well as gaps in relation to language spoken at home. This chapter aimed to fill these gaps.

The first finding in our study refers to the proportion of child immigrants in our survey. In our sample, 22.4% identified themselves as immigrants according to the standard international definition. Of them, the vast majority are children born outside of the country to Irish parents or are immigrants from the UK. These figures vary from the 6% of child immigrants, of which a third are from the UK, as reported by Hanafin et al. (2008). These differences can be explained by the differences in the definitions used. While we were focusing on immigrants as defined by country of birth and parental country of birth, the Central Statistics Office's figures are based on nationality. Thus, returning emigrants and their children will be defined as 'Irish nationals' by the Central Statistics Office but as 'immigrants' for the purpose of the current study. To overcome this issue, we have used a very conservative definition of returning emigrants – those who were born outside of Ireland for whom both parents were born in Ireland. According to this definition, slightly more than a third of the child immigrant population in this study were categorized as returning emigrants.

Our first and second hypotheses concerned the differences between first and second generation child immigrants in relation to health, wellbeing and integration in society. We hypothesised that second generation immigrants would differ from first generation immigrants in relation to health and wellbeing, and will perform better on indicators of integration in society. Our findings suggest that indeed, first generation immigrant children (but not returning emigrants) reported lower life satisfaction (similar to that reported by Vieno et al., 2009) and poorer relationships with fellow students compared to second generation child immigrants, suggesting that, indeed, second generation immigrants fare better than first generation child immigrants. Such findings were also reported by Portes and his colleagues (2009) in the US. However, it is worth noting that first generation child immigrants reported better relationships with teachers compared to returning emigrants. Among second generation child immigrants, fewer non-UK/US second generation immigrant children reported high life satisfaction and poor relationships with fellow students. While these were the only findings that were statistically significant, we also found, consistent with our hypotheses, that non-UK/US second generation children were more likely to report better relationships with teachers and better general school perceptions compare to UK/US second generation children. These findings are consistent with our previous findings (Molcho et al., 2008), and are in agreement in part with the work of Levels and Dronkers (2008).

Our third hypothesis was that immigrant children speaking English at home will experience less social exclusion compared to children who are speaking another language in their homes. Our analyses yielded only one significant difference between the groups – students who speak language other than English at home reported better relationships with their teachers (P<0.01). However, contrary to our hypothesis, we did find that immigrant children not speaking English at home were more likely to report excellent health, good relationships with teachers, and overall positive perceptions of school compare to child immigrants speaking English at home, even if not statistically significant. Investigating immigration in Ireland via language spoken at home may prove to be problematic, given that the vast majority of the children are from English-speaking countries. However, if we regard speaking a language other that English at home as a sign of 'disintegration' as was posited in extant literature (Hernandez, Danton & Macartney, 2008; Gonzales et al., 2006), our findings suggest no evidence to support that claim. It is possible that speaking the language of the country of origin in the home is not a sign of poor integration and is not the result of lack of fluency in the language of the country of residence, but rather a preference aimed at maintaining the original language, perhaps to allow better relationships with relatives in the country of origin. This interpretation can be supported by previous studies (Gaudet, Clement & Deuzeman, 2005) that have found that speaking the language of the country of origin could act as a protective factor and that this 'protective' effect can vary by the immigrant children's country of origin. While our findings do not support the third hypothesis, Bleakly and Chin (2008) argue that the speaking the language of the country of origin in the home is a predictor for poor outcomes and disintegration only when stemming from poor parental fluency in that language rather than from an informed decision to speak language of the country of origin.

Levels of integration in school and in the local area are important in adolescent lives. Sense of belonging to local area can assist in preservation of identity (Altman & Low, 1992). Sense of belonging to school and local areas can also assist in creating high-perceived levels of social capital. A high level of social capital, in turn, acts as a social strength, protecting individuals from involvement in antisocial behaviour and increasing wellbeing (Sampson & Groves, 1989; Bellair, 1997; Warner & Rountree, 1997). It is, therefore, very encouraging to learn that second generation immigrants and those not speaking English at home are showing signs of successful social integration through sense of belonging.

Limitations

The HBSC study provides a unique opportunity to gain understanding of the experiences of child immigrants, and more specifically, to address differences between first and second generations of child immigrants and between them and returning emigrants. Yet, there are some limitations to these data. First and foremost, the HBSC study is aimed at the general population and not at immigrants, resulting in a lack of specific questions that are relevant to this particular population sub-group. As a study that is aimed at the general population and with the goal of achieving a representative sample of school-going children in Ireland, it is likely that the sample is not representative of the child immigrant population in the country. Yet to date, however, it is the largest body of information on this vulnerable group. Additionally, the number of non-UK/US child immigrants in the sample does not allow us to stratify the analysis by country of origin, or to try to understand cultural differences between different groups of immigrants. Collapsing countries of origin in the way that has been necessary to conduct these analyses does not help us to understand of potential conflicts between country of residence and country of origin, and prevents us from making recommendations regarding specific ethnic minorities. The length of stay in the country can also be an indicator for integration. Indeed, the term '1.5th generation' immigrants was coined to address immigrants that arrived in a host country at a very young age. Unfortunately, the HBSC questionnaire did not ask about the age of entry, or family return, to Ireland and thus does not allow us to explore this important issue. It is also important to remember that this study is based on self-report data, and this can be vulnerable to social desirability bias.

Conclusions

Our findings indicate differences between the three immigrant groups. First generation immigrants report lower levels of social integration compared to returning emigrants and second generation immigrants, which could be explained by the fact that both returning emigrants and second generation immigrants have the potential for more social ties and higher social capital. Nevertheless, these patterns highlight the importance of distinguishing between immigrant groups, and need for definition of immigration that is more particular to the Irish context. While such a definition (of returning emigrants) may need to vary from the standard international definition, our findings clearly suggest that a variation is appropriate in Ireland. The need for a definition that takes into account the history of Ireland further illustrates the complexity of the migration phenomena. Indeed, it opens the door for more country-specific definitions, and indicates the need to be both flexible and cautious when studying the experiences of immigrants. Such vigilance is also required when comparing international data as was previously noted (Levels and Dronkers, 2008).

Across all studies, including our current findings, clear socio-economic disparities were evident. Immigrants tend to be less affluent (Molcho et al., 2008), and first generation child immigrants were particularly likely to be in less affluent families. While we controlled for such disparities in our analyses in order to identify group differences over and above socio-economic disparities, it is important to note that some of the differences between the immigrant groups are the result of such disparities.

Our third hypothesis was that immigrant children who speak English at home will experience less social exclusion compared to children who do not speak English at home. However, our findings did not support this, and in fact, contrary to past studies, the results (although not statistically significant) suggest that immigrant children who did not speak English at home were more likely to report excellent health, good relationships with teachers, and overall positive perceptions of school compare to child immigrants speaking English at home. The literature in the field had addressed the issues of bilingualism and its benefits. The advantages of bilingualism among immigrant children include the ability to benefit from the children's cultural heritage, and to maintain effective communication with parents, given that in immigrant families, the emergence of a language gap is a real possibility (Mouw, and Xie, 1999; Gaudet, Clement & Deuzeman, 2005). Hence, speaking language other than English at home could actually support integration rather than hinder it.

As Algan et al. (2010) pointed out, understanding the experiences and integration of immigrant children in society is important. Successful integration will translate to more positive attitudes of natives to immigrants and will result in more substantial contribution to the labour market and society at large. Poor integration, on the other hand, may lead to social and economic exclusion that could result in social unrest. Exploring the predictors of the integration of immigrants is a vital step in creating better opportunities for immigrants. The HBSC Ireland study provides a unique opportunity to study immigrant children. The large national sample provides a sufficient sub-sample of child immigrants that enables such analyses. Furthermore, the international aspects of the HBSC study, coupled with the large proportion of

UK immigrants, could provide further opportunities to investigate not only the experiences of child immigrants compared to their native peers in Ireland, but also compared to their peers in the UK, which would add another layer to our understanding of the experiences and adaptation of immigrant children in Ireland.

REFERENCES

Algan, Y., Dustmann, C., Glitz, A., & Manning, A. (2010). The economic situation of first and second-generation immigrants in France, Germany and the United Kingdom. *Economic Journal, 120*(542), F4–F30.

Altman, I., & Low, S. (1992). *Place attachment.* New York: Plenum.

Beiser, M., Hou, F., Hyman, I., et al. (2002). Poverty, family process and the mental health of immigrant children in Canada. *American Journal of Public Health, 92,* 220–227.

Bengi-Arslan, L., Verhulst, F. C., van der Ende, J., & Erol, N. (1997). Understanding childhood (problem) behaviour from a cultural perspective: Comparison of problem behaviour and competencies in Turkish immigrant, Turkish and Dutch children. *Social Psychiatry and Psychiatric Epidemiology, 32,* 477–484.

Bellair, P. E. (1997). Social interaction and community crime: Examining the importance of neighborhood networks. *Criminology, 35,* 677–703.

Berry, J. W. (1997). Immigration, acculturation, and adaptation. *Applied Psychology: An International Review, 46,* 5–68.

Blake, S. M., Ledsky, R., Goodenow, C., & O'Donnell, L. (2002). Recency of immigration, substance use, and sexual behavior among Massachusetts adolescents. *American Journal of Public Health, 91,* 794–798.

Bleakly, H., & Chin, A. (2008). What holds back the second generation? The intergenerational transmission of language human capital among immigrants. *Journal of Human Resources, 43*(2), 267–298.

Cantril, H. (1965). *The pattern of human concern.* New Brunswick, NJ: Rutgers University Press.

Central Statistics Office. (2009). *Population and migration estimates.* Dublin: Central Office of Statistics.

Coleman, J. S. (1988). Social capital in the creation of human capital. *American Journal of Sociology, 94,* s95–s121.

Currie, C., Nic Gabhainn, S., Godeau, E., Roberts, C., Smith, R., Currie, D., et al. (Eds.). (2008a). *Inequalities in young people's health: HBSC international report from the 2005/2006 survey.* Copenhagen: WHO.

Currie, C., Molcho, M., Boyce, W., Holstein, B., Torsheim, T., & Richter, M. (2008b). Researching health inequalities in adolescents: The development of the Health Behaviour in School-Aged Children (HBSC) family affluence scale. *Social Science & Medicine, 66*(6), 1429–1436.

Davies, L. C., & McKelvey, R. S. (1998) Emotional and behavioural problems and competencies among immigrant and non-immigrant adolescents. *Australian and New Zealand Journal of Psychiatry, 32,* 658–665.

Gaudet, S., Clement, R., & Deuzeman K. (2005). Daily hassles, ethnic identity and psychological adjustment among Lebanese-Canadians. *International Journal of Psychology, 40,* 157–168.

Georgiades, K., Boyle, M. H., Duku, E., & Racine, Y. (2006). Tobacco use among immigrant and non-immigrant adolescents: Individual and family level influences. *Journal of Adolescent Health, 38,* 443–447.

Gonzales, N. A., Deardorff, J., Formoso, D., Barr, A., & Barrera, M. (2006). Family mediators of the relation between acculturation and adolescent mental health. *Family Relations, 55,* 318–330.

Gushulak, B., Pace, P., & Weekers J. (2009). Migration and health of migrants. In *Poverty and social exclusion in the European region: Health systems respond.* Copenhagen: WHO Regional Office for Europe.

Hanafin, S., Brooks, A. M., Macken, A., Brady, G., McKeever, R., Judge, C., et al. (2008). *State of the nation's children: Ireland 2008.* Dublin: The Stationary Office.

Harris, K. M. (2004). The health status and risk behaviours of adolescents in immigrant families. In D. J. Henandex (Ed.), *Children of immigrants: Health, adjustment and public assistance*. Washington, DC: National Academy Press.

Helliwell, J. F., & Putnam, R. D. (2004). The social context of well-being. *Philosophical Transactions of the Royal Society of London, Series B, Biological Sciences, 359*, 1435–1446.

Herm, A. (2008). Recent migration trend: citizens of EU-27 Member states become ever more mobile while EU remains attractive to non-EU citizens. *Eurostat Statistics in focus, 98/2008*.

Hernandez, D. J., Denton, N. A., & Macartney, A. Z. (2008). *Children in immigrant families: Looking to America's future*. Social Policy report. Society for Research in Child Development. Fordham, NY: University City.

Isralowitz, R. E., & Slonim-Nevo V. (2002). Substance use patterns and problem behavior among immigrant and native-born juvenile offenders in Israel. *Addiction Research and Theory, 10*, 399–414.

Janssen, M. M. M., Verhulst, F. C., Benghi-Arslan, L., Erol, N., Salter, C. J., & Crijnen, A. A. M. (2004). Comparison of self-reported emotional and behavioral problems in Turkish immigrant, Dutch and Turkish adolescents. *Social Psychiatry and Psychiatric Epidemiology, 39*, 133–140.

Jeltova, I., Fish, M. C., & Revenson, T. A. (2005). Risky sexual behaviors in immigrant adolescent girls from the former Soviet Union: Role of natal and host culture. *Journal of School Psychology, 43*, 3–22.

Kawachi, I., Kennedy, B. P., & Glass, R. (1999). Social capital and self-rated health: A contextual analysis. *American Journal of Public Health, 89*, 1187–1193.

Kawachi, I., Kim, D., Coutts, A., & Subramanian, S. V. (2004). Commentary: Reconciling the three accounts of social capital. *International Journal of Epidemiology, 33*, 682–690.

Levels, M., & Dronkers, J. (2008). Educational performance of native and immigrant children from various countries of origin. *Ethnic and Racial Studies, 31*(8), 1404–1425.

Ma, X. (2002). The first ten years in Canada: A multi-level assessment of behavioural and emotional problems of immigrant children. *Canadian Public Policy, 28*, 395–418.

Molcho, M., Kelly, C., Gavin, A., & Nic Gabhainn, S. (2008). *Inequalities in health among school-aged children in Ireland*. Dublin: Department of Health and Children.

Molcho, M., Kelly, K., & Nic Gabhainn, S. (2010). Deficits in health and wellbeing among immigrant children in Ireland: The explanatory role of social capital. *Translocation: Migration and Social Change An Inter-Disciplinary Open Access E-Journal*. Retrieved from http://www.dcu.ie/imrstr/volume_6_issue_1/Molcho%20Kelly%20and%20NicGabhainn.pdf

Mouw, T., & Xie, Y. (1999). Bilingualism and the academic achievement of first-and second-generation Asian Americans: Accommodation with or without assimilation? *American Sociological Review, 64*(2), 232–252.

Nolan, B., Maitre, B. (2008). *A social portrait of communities in Ireland*. Dublin: The Office for Social Inclusion.

Pantin, H., Schwartz, S. J., Sullivan, S., Coatsworth, J. D., & Szapocznik, J. (2003). Parent-centered approach preventing substance abuse in Hispanic immigrant adolescents: An ecodevelopmental parent-centred approach. *Hispanic Journal of Behavioral Sciences, 25*, 469–500.

Pawliuk, N., Grizenko, N., Chan-Yip, A., Gantous, P., Matthew, J., & Nguyen, D. (1996). Acculturation style and psychological functioning in children and immigrants. *American Journal of Orthopsychiatry, 66*, 111–121.

Poortinga, W. (2006). Social relations or social capital? Individual and community health effects of bonding social capital. *Social Science & Medicine, 63*, 255–270.

Portes, A., Fernández-Kelly, P., & Haller, W. (2009). The adaptation of the immigrant second generation in America: A theoretical overview and recent evidence. *Journal of Ethnic and Migration Studies, 35*(7), 1077–1104.

Putnam, R. (1993). The prosperous community: Social capital and community life. *American Prospect, 4*(13), 35–42.

Sampson, R. J., & Groves, W. B. (1989). Community structure and crime: Testing social disorganization theory. *American Journal of Sociology, 94*, 774–802.

Stevens, G. W. J. M., Pels, T., Bengi-Arslan, L., Verhulst, F. C., Vollebergh, W. A. M., & Crijnen, A. A. M. (2003). Parent, teacher, and self-reported problem behaviour in the Netherlands. *Social Psychiatry and Psychiatric Epidemiology, 38*, 567–585.

Strohmeier, D., & Scmitt-Rodermind, E. (2008). Immigrant youth in European countries: The manifold challenges of adaptation. *European Journal of Developmental Psychology, 5*, 129–37.

United Nations. (2002). *International migration report 2002.* New York: Department of Economic and Social Affairs, Population Division.

The Urban Institute. (2006). *Children of immigrants: Fact and figures.* Washington, DC: Office of Public Affairs.

Vedder, P., & Virta, E. (2005). Language, ethnic identity, and the adaptation of Turkish immigrant youth in the Netherlands and Sweden. *International Journal of Intercultural Relations, 29*, 317–337.

Vieno, A., Santinello, M., Lenzi, M., Baldassari, D., & Mirandola, M. (2009). Health status in immigrants and native early adolescents in Italy. *Journal of Community Health, 34*, 181–187.

Vollebergh, W. A. M., Ten Have, M., Dekovic, M., Oosterwegel, A., Pels, T., De Winter, A., et al. (2005). Mental health in immigrant children in the Netherlands. *Social Psychiatry and Psychiatric Epidemiology, 40*, 489–496.

Van de Walle, E. (Ed.). (1982). *Multilingual demographic dictionary, English section* (2nd ed.). Paris: International Union for the Scientific Study of Population; New York: Department of Economic and Social Affairs, United Nations.

Ward, C., Bochner, S., & Furnham, A. (2001). *The psychology of culture shock* (2nd ed.). Hove: Routledge.

Warner, B. D., & Rountree, P. W. (1997). Local social ties in a community and crime model: Questioning the systemic nature of informal social control. *Social Problems, 44*(4), 520–536.

Yu, S. M., Huang, Z. J., Schwalberg, R. H., Overpeck, M., & Kogan, M. D. (2003). Acculturation and the health and well-being of US immigrant adolescents. *Journal of Adolescent Health, 33*, 479–488.

Michal Molcho, Colette Kelly and Saoirse Nic Gabhainn
Health Promotion Research Centre
School of Health Sciences
National University of Ireland Galway

DEIRDRE HORGAN, SHIRLEY MARTIN AND JACQUI O'RIORDAN

12. CHILD TRAFFICKING IN IRELAND

INTRODUCTION

This chapter examines the position of internationally trafficked children as a particularly invisible group of minority and migrant children in Ireland. In this regard we aim to assess Irish child protection policies and their contribution to the protection of children and young people who are trafficked into Ireland. The chapter begins with a discussion on the evidence of child trafficking in Ireland and the difficulties associated with research and data in this area. Then, we critically review recent legislative and policy developments in light of exploratory research we are conducting with childcare practitioners, immigration officials and NGOs working in this area. Moosa-Mitha (2007) discusses trafficked children's status as non-citizens as central to their experiences of injustice and exclusion in the destination country in which they reside. This seems to hold true in the Irish context where the European Commissioner for Human Rights (Hammarberg, 2008) has raised concerns about the inadequate measures of identification and poor level of care for separated children in Ireland placing these children at a high risk of being trafficked. We will explore evidence that these children experience differentiated rights based on their migration status in Ireland. Additionally, we will discuss children's agency and voice. In recognising children as active agents and meaning makers we will argue that policy development should be grounded in children's lived experiences. To conclude, we explore possibilities in the development of 'the protective environment' as a viable way forward in policy and practice, and one that minimises risk factors and maximises resilience among all actors.

RESEARCH METHODOLOGY AND DATA COLLECTION

Our discussion draws a number of different sources. In the first instance, it is informed by the outcomes of sixteen qualitative interviews undertaken between September 2009 and March 2010 with service providers and child protection agencies who come in contact with separated minors and/or child victims of trafficking. It is also informed through literature and policy developments in the areas of child trafficking and migration. With regard to our research, participants were professionals working in the area of child trafficking, including key Non-Governmental Organisations (NGOs) involved in the area of child trafficking, childcare professionals and immigration officials employed by statutory agencies. Interviews were also conducted with project workers in refugee support services and NGOs who have contact with separated children.

Darmody, Tyrrell, Song (eds.), The Changing Faces of Ireland: Exploring the Lives of Immigrant and Ethnic Minority Children, 203–219.

The interviews investigated the procedures with regard to the identification of and responses to children who have been victims of trafficking or are vulnerable to being trafficked. Themes addressed in the research interviews relevant to this chapter included a focus on causes of child trafficking, definitions and current policies and practices, as well as issues relating to agency and the rights of trafficked children. We were aware throughout the process of our ethical responsibilities in carrying out research on this sensitive topic. It is evident that people and organizations working in the field are themselves developing their understanding and responses to the challenges posed by child trafficking. In consideration of this, comments made by research participants have been made anonymous, and the research does not identify any individual person, organization or geographical area. In referring to the research participants in this chapter we have allocated numbers to participants according to the order of the interviews and in the text we differentiate between NGO and statutory agency participants. We have also attempted to highlight the issues arising within this process rather than engaging in critiques of specific agencies in order to further contribute to meeting the challenges posed by child trafficking.

DEFINITIONS AND CAUSES OF TRAFFICKING

Human trafficking relates to the movement of people for purposes of exploitation. It is bound up with power, servitude and slavery, and is a growing phenomenon in the contemporary global context. The majority of those who are at risk of being trafficked are women and children (Territo and Kirkham, 2010). Notwithstanding general agreement on this, how to define human trafficking is a contested issue in the literature and among our research participants. Indeed, it was one of the most contentious issues of debate in the drafting of the *UN Protocol to Prevent, Suppress and Punish, Trafficking in Persons, especially Women and Children 2000* (Raymond, 2002), more commonly known as the Palermo Protocol. In the drafting of this proto-col, much of the debate on definition centred on issues surrounding the presence, absence and presumptions of consent. The protocol itself, which Ireland recently ratified, was considered necessary in order to develop an updated transnational legal framework to combat the rise in trafficking in persons across the globe. The earlier 1949 *UN Convention for the Suppression of the Traffic in Persons and of the Exploitation of the Prostitution of Others*, was no longer considered effective in addressing the diverse ways in which international crime was developing in the area. Human trafficking is defined, then, within the Palermo Protocol (2000) as:

> "Trafficking in persons" shall mean the recruitment, transportation, transfer, harbouring or receipt of persons, by means of the threat or use of force or other forms of coercion, of abduction, of fraud, of deception, of the abuse of power or of a position of vulnerability or of the giving or receiving of payments or benefits to achieve the consent of a person having control over another person, for the purpose of exploitation. Exploitation shall include, at a minimum, the exploitation of the prostitution of others or other forms of sexual exploita-tion, forced labour or services, slavery or practices similar to slavery, servitude or the removal of organs. (Article, 2 sub-section 3, a)

It goes on to discount the concept of consent in relation to the trafficking in children, stating that 'the recruitment, transportation, transfer, harbouring or receipt of a child for the purpose of exploitation shall be considered "trafficking in persons" (Article, 2 sub-section 3, c) and defines 'children' as those who are under 18 years of age.

In the Irish context, the recently published *National Plan to Prevent & Combat Trafficking of Human Beings in Ireland: 2009–2012* (2009) uses this template in its definition of human trafficking. This definition is comprised of three components: an action, a means and exploitation.

[A]n action (the recruitment, transportation, transfer, harbouring or receipt of persons) must be carried out by a means (threat or use of force or other forms of coercion, abduction, fraud, deception abuse of power or of a position of vulnerability or of the giving or receiving of payments or benefits to achieve the consent of a person having control over another person) for the purposes of exploitation, for human trafficking to occur. (National Action Plan to Prevent & Combat Trafficking of Human Beings in Ireland, 2008, p. 8).

The Criminal Law Human Trafficking Act (CLHTA) 2008, section 1, the most recent legislative development in this area in Ireland, views exploitation arising from human trafficking in terms of labour exploitation, sexual exploitation, or exploitation consisting of the removal of one or more of the organs of a person. Under section 3, it creates specific offences as it pertains to trafficking of children, specifically in relation to issues of consent.

Notwithstanding attention to such definitions, many of those interviewed for this research highlighted the blurred distinctions that exist, in practice, in particular, between smuggling and trafficking. Such ambiguity is also evident in the literature, and the terms often intersect with conceptions of forced and voluntary migration, the latter which is associated with consent, but given constraints of emigration legislation, at times involving smuggling people across transit countries and into destination countries.

Another interesting aspect of the discourse on the definitions of child trafficking in Ireland is the concept of the movement of children within Ireland. Child trafficking has been identified both as an internal and national problem and as an international issue (ECPAT, 2009). In contrast, the Criminal Law Human Trafficking Act 2008, section 1, which primarily focuses on smuggling, recognises that trafficking can involve the movement of people into, within, and out of the state. This is a significant advance on the Illegal Immigrants Trafficking Act 2000, which only applied to people coming into the country. The more recent Irish legislation then is in agreement with the opinion of those working in the area, who argue that you do not have to cross a border to be defined as trafficked. For example, this broader definition of trafficking could include a child who is in Ireland and is taken from a care situation for the purposes of sexual or labour exploitation.

There is an ongoing debate as to what constitutes trafficking and smuggling in practice. There is an opinion among some of our research participants from statutory organisations that older children were more likely to be smuggled into the country as economic migrants rather than being considered vulnerable to being trafficked. This is contested largely by NGO participants in the research. The legal definition of child trafficking in the Criminal Law Human Trafficking Act 2008, does not consider the consent of child to being trafficked as relevant, whereas it is for adults. The presence of a motive for exploitation was considered central to understanding trafficking, whether such exploitation is noticed on arrival in the country or through having some knowledge of children's circumstances when they are living in the country. In such cases the emphasis is often placed on vulnerability to trafficking rather than defining it. This perspective is captured in the following quote:

> '[What] we're interested in is that there is a full understanding of how you make children vulnerable to trafficking and to traffickers...also concerned about the children who are coming into Ireland, potentially being labelled separated and very quickly being reunited with family. The lack of follow-up there is leaving those children vulnerable... so our definition is trying to capture all those vulnerabilities.' (Research Participant 8)

Furthermore, our attention is also drawn to issues related to children's own under-standing of their situations; depending on the specifics of their situations, they might not understand the terminology used, perceive themselves as being trafficked and might be under considerable pressure to make/continue contact with their traffickers (Joyce and Quinn, 2009). Effectively, these concerns move attention away from actually defining what is and is not trafficking, smuggling, differences in opinion on coercion, consent and so on, bringing the debate to focus more on the circumstances of children's lives.

EVIDENCE OF CHILD TRAFFICKING IN IRELAND

There is little reliable information on the number of children and young people[1] who are trafficked across and within EU borders, due to both the criminal and under-ground nature of human trafficking. The US Department of State's (2006) *Trafficking in Persons Report*[2] first named Ireland as a destination and transit country for human trafficking. The issue of Ireland as a transit country was highlighted by the research participants as being linked to the perception that there is an ease of entry at some of the Irish borders. In particular, the participants highlighted the lack of child protection staff and multi-disciplinary teams at the borders as a contributing factor to poor identification of separated or trafficked children.

Notwithstanding the difficulties in estimating trafficking, there is some limited evidence to show that child trafficking does occur in Ireland. This is evidenced mainly through concerns and reports related to missing migrant children and separated/unaccompanied minors entering the state. An issue which has been frequently mentioned in the literature and which was raised within our research more recently as evidence that there are incidences of child trafficking in Ireland is the number of foreign-born children who are missing from State-provided care in Ireland. There is concern that children are more likely to go missing when care arrangements are less strictly monitored, for instance at weekends or at night (Joyce and Quinn, 2009).

A total of 512 separated children went missing from State care between 2000 and 2010. (HSE in Smyth 2011).

While there is no evidence that *all* of these children have been trafficked (up to half are subsequently reunited with their families), it has been suggested by the US Dept of State (2009) and Non-Governmental Organisations (NGO) working in the area (Kennedy, 2008) that some of these children have been victims of child trafficking (van Turnhout, 2010). Some of these children have been found in involuntary servitude in brothels, restaurants, and in domestic service (US Dept. of State, 2009). Deputy Naughton in a Parliamentary Debate (2009) highlighted the case of Joy Imifidon, a seventeen year old Nigerian girl who was detained by the Irish Police when she was found in a brothel in County Kilkenny in 2008 and was charged with not having a passport or any other form of identification. At the time of her subsequent court appearance, both the police and the judge expressed concern that she was a victim of human trafficking. After being initially remanded in an Irish prison, she was then placed in the care of the Health Service Executive but had subsequently disappeared (Naughten, 2009, Parliamentary Debate). Furthermore, Joyce and Quinn (2009) point to a recent report on sex trafficking and prostitution that estimated that, of 102 women and girls who came to the attention of Irish authorities between 2007 and 2008 who could be viewed as victims of trafficking, eleven were children (Kelleher Associates et al., 2009). It is further argued that this very likely underestimates numbers of trafficked children. More recently, in a response to a claim made by the HSE that there was little or no evidence that children missing from their care had been trafficked, the Children's Rights Alliance, claimed to have knowledge of 25 cases of confirmed child trafficking for sexual or labour exploitation, five of whom had gone missing from HSE care (van Turnhout, 2010). The Irish Government recently published the first official report on Human Trafficking in Ireland and reported 68 incidents of human trafficking which came to the attention of the Irish police force (An Garda Siochana), including 17 minors, five of whom were separated children in HSE care (AHTU, 2010).

POLITICS OF TRAFFICKING AND CHILDHOOD

Anderson and Andrijasevic (2008) contend that current discourse on trafficking which focuses on the moral outrage and panic which trafficking elicits, and the focus on the criminal nature of trafficking, can lead to a situation where the systematic factors which can contribute to trafficking, such as state policies on migration and employment, can be ignored. They posit the following:

> Journalists, politicians and scholars are quick to depict migrant women in the sex industry as victims of abuse and violence, and traffickers as Mafia-like individuals and/or organisations that enslave women in prostitution ... Trafficking appears as an activity that takes place outside any social frameworks: it is criminal individuals that are responsible. (Anderson and Andrijasevic, 2008, p. 137)

The focus on the evils of the trafficker can serve to de-politicise the role of the state in anti-trafficking responses and interventions. Furthermore, the separation of issues of illegal migration and trafficking is problematic. Bastia (2005) demonstrates in her work on migration in South America that child trafficking follows already established patterns of human movement and migration and asserts that it is un-helpful to consider migration and trafficking as separate issues. She contends that the causes of trafficking are related to the factors that drive international migration such as political and economic crisis, decline of traditional industries, inadequate land distribution for sustainable agriculture, gender-based discrimination and the existence of race, class and ethnic inequalities. Our research revealed similar thinking on the structural and other causes of trafficking:

> Migration, globalisation, inequality, poverty, economic disparities are fuelling it (trafficking) and different immigration policies in different countries are building barriers and filtering immigrants. The filtering still allows immigration (into Ireland) of very vulnerable people. (Research Participant 3)

A key issue that needs to be explored is the role state-imposed migration controls play in increasing the vulnerability of migrants to exploitation and abuse (Anderson and Andrijasevic, 2008). In particular, Anderson and Andrijasevic (2008) are critical of the Palermo Protocol which focuses on prosecution and punishment of traffickers through strengthening state borders to prevent trafficking and smuggling, rather than providing human rights based protection for victims. The denial of citizenship rights and the current discourses which contribute to the social-construction of the victim of trafficking as passive and vulnerable deny the trafficked person any agency (Breuil, 2008).

> A highly political reality about the state's role in constructing vulnerability for non-citizens - a reality with potential political solutions - is obscured by calling on the states to protect the human rights of victims of trafficking. It is notable that there is no similar call by the state for the protection of the 'human rights' of 'illegal immigrants'. (Anderson and Andrijasevic, 2008, p. 142)

This situation, Anderson and Andrijasevic (2008) contend, 'reinforces the notion that one cannot engage with citizenship as a process, but only with citizenship as formal legal status administered by an omniscient state' (ibid, p. 143). The unsatisfactory levels of child protection support for unaccompanied minors and the critiques of this as outlined in the previous paragraphs could be seen as examples of the 'de-politicisation' of the anti-trafficking interventions in Ireland.

Further complexity when considering the issue of child trafficking is the influence of social construction of childhood itself. Breuil (2008) examines how implicit notions in the concepts of "children" who are often represented as dependant and innocent beings who should be protected and cared for by adults and "home" which is regarded as territorialised, unchangeable and safe, can oversimplify trafficked and migrating children's experiences. These social constructions are not necessarily untrue, but they are normative, and thus historically and culturally specific. Moreover, Breuil argues that these concepts may be adult-centred and inconsistent with children's own experiences. These images have become institutionalised and thus can often determine how we perceive and treat trafficked children. Breuil (2008) and Bastia (2005) also suggest that children experience varying degrees of powerlessness or control over their trafficking situations. The study of child trafficking might benefit from considering migration as less a physical movement from one place to another, but rather as a form of social movement within networks of unequally distributed power (Breuil, 2008, p. 232). More recent debates within child trafficking research and literature have included consideration of the immigration status of the trafficked child and critiques of the limited rights of the trafficked child, based on their lack of citizenship rights (Moosa-Mitha, 2007).

NATIONAL AND INTERNATIONAL LEGISLATION AND POLICY ON CHILD TRAFFICKING

Irish action in the field of human trafficking has gained considerable momentum in the last 5 years with the establishment of the Anti-human trafficking Unit in the Department of Justice, Equality and Law Reform in 2008; and the *Criminal Law (Human Trafficking) Act 2008* which creates separate offences of trafficking in children for the purpose of their labour, exploitation or the removal of their organs, and trafficking in children for the purpose of their sexual exploitation. Important steps have also been taken to address the discrepancy in emphasis between punitive and protection measures in policy with the *Immigration, Residence and Protection Bill (2010)*. This provides for the identification of victims of trafficking and establishes two new types of permits of residence specifically designed for victims of trafficking: the *Recovery and Reflection Permit* and the *Temporary Residence Permit* of six months that can be renewed on certain conditions. The publication by Government of the *National Action Plan to Prevent & Combat Trafficking of Human Beings in Ireland: 2009–2012* (NAP) proposes a child-sensitive approach in the development, implementation and assessment of anti-human trafficking policies and programmes.

Legislative and policy measures to address child trafficking intersect with issues of prohibition, punishment, criminalisation, protection and care. In Ireland the two key Departments/State agencies with responsibility in the area are the Department of Justice, Equality and Law Reform and the Health Service Executive (HSE). The Department of Justice Equality and Law Reform has responsibility for issues of migration, legislation, and compliance with international conventions, whereas the HSE, under the *Childcare Act, 1991* has responsibility for the care of trafficked children.

There is an onus on the Irish State to ensure that legal frameworks and policies reflect international legislation and internationally recognised best practice so that all children receive the care and protection they need. Indeed, it has been recognised that Ireland has made efforts in this regard (US Dept of State, 2009). Article 20 of the Convention on the Rights of the Child (1989) (CRC), of which Ireland is a signatory, states that children who are victims of trafficking are entitled to special protection measures both as victims and as children, in accordance with their specific rights and needs (Sillen and Beddoe, 2007, p. 38). While the Palermo Protocol (2000) provides a common definition of trafficking and gives children a special status, difficulties arise in relation to the lack of clear circumstances that can be classified as child trafficking, especially in view of the fact that key concepts such as "exploitation", "coercion", and "vulnerability" have been left undefined. Additional constraints inherent in the Protocol are that it is essentially a crime prevention instrument rather than a human rights instrument (Bastia, 2005; Anderson and Andrijasevic, 2008, p. 137) Also, it is rigid in the sense that it does not allow for more subtle forms of trafficking, including patronage as exists in South America (Bastia, 2005) or Roma children where their work flows from "normal" parental authority. The Irish government has recently ratified, the Council of Europe *Convention on Against Trafficking in Human Beings* (CoE Convention) in July 2010 which incorporates a National Referral Mechanism.

The national legislative context has focused on the prohibition of activity and the punishment of offenders in this area rather than providing special protection and a safe environment for children who are trafficked. For example the *Child Trafficking and Pornography Act, 1998,* the *Amendment Act, 2004* and the *Illegal Immigrants (Trafficking) Act, 2000* all focus on prohibition and punishment. The efforts to deter this type of criminal activity were reinforced with the introduction of the *Criminal Law (Human Trafficking) Act 2008.* The law goes beyond the recommendation of the Council of Europe *Convention on Action Against Trafficking in Human Beings (2005)* by removing the issue of consent in cases involving victims with mental disabilities. This should facilitate an increase in identification of victims of trafficking and subsequent prosecutions. In comparison to other jurisdictions, it provides more severe penalties for traffickers; and currently, Ireland is the only state in Europe that can imprison a trafficker for life.

Concerns have been raised by the European Commission on Human Rights about inadequate measures of identification of separated children in Ireland that may have directly contributed to the numbers of children who have gone missing, and that these children are at a high risk of being trafficked (Hammarberg, 2008). Research participants in this study were also critical of the reluctance to give official recognition to victims of trafficking as outlined by one research participant with reference to current immigration procedures.

> It's quite absurd in that if a child comes in [to Ireland] accompanied by an adult no questions are asked and that's quite bizarre because it's actually giving an open door to traffickers to actually come in with as many kids as they want. (Research Participant 4)

However, important steps are being taken to provide for the identification of victims of trafficking and to address the discrepancy in emphasis between punitive and protection approaches through the *Immigration, Residence and Protection Bill* (2010). This proposed legislation which has now gone through a number of amendments, allows immigration officers at the point of entry to require verification that adults accompanying children are in fact authorised to take responsibility for the child they are travelling with (Yonkova, 2008). It establishes two new types of permits of residence specifically designed for victims of trafficking who are identified: the *Recovery and Reflection Permit* and the *Temporary Residence Permit* of six months that can be issued and renewed on certain conditions. Aspects of the Bill have been heavily criticised for failing to meet the standards developed in the Council of Europe's *Convention on Action Against Trafficking in Human Beings* (2005). In particular, it fails to outline the entitlements guaranteed to suspected victims, such as accommodation, medical care and legal aid. The provisions of the Bill apply only to non-EU/European Economic Area (EEA) nationals. In relation to the *Immigration, Residence and Protection Bill* 2010, critisims made by, for example Brophy and McGonigle (2008) questioning whether the best interests of migrant children are paramount, were addressed to some extent in increasing the recovery and reflection period to 60 days and in making provision for an extension of this period for victims of child trafficking.

In our interviews, concerns were expressed by the NGO participants and some social workers about the that the temporary protection permit should not be linked to cooperation with authorities for a minor. The framework of the Bill places a lot of emphasis on prosecutions and does not allow for that period of recovery from possibly traumatic experiences, and there is a concern that the reflection period is used to carry out investigations.

Along with the above mentioned legislative measures, there have been a number of other policy developments in the area. Those initiated by the government include initiatives on anti-trafficking, including the establishment of an Anti-Human Trafficking Unit in the Department of Justice, Equality and Law Reform. This unit was founded in 2008 to co-ordinate the efforts in human trafficking at the national level. On establishment, the Anti-Human Trafficking Unit immediately assumed its role of a national point of reference with the establishment of a Non-Governmental and Governmental Roundtable Forum and Interdisciplinary Working Groups including a Child Trafficking Working Group. This latter group is now central in developing a co-ordinated response to child trafficking and in developing a protective environment for children which will be further discussed in this chapter. Furthermore, the *National Action Plan to Combat and Prevent Human Trafficking 2009–2012* was published in 2009 and includes twenty-five recommendations specifically on child trafficking. These recommendations are focused on reducing vulnerability, identification, protection, recovery and assistance of children, as well as residency and re-patriation of child victims of trafficking. It recognises children as particularly vulnerable and as a section of the population with particular needs, and states that the development of a protective environment is one of its fundamental goals. In 2008 the Unit also launched the *Blue Blindfold* campaign, which serves to raise public aware-ness of human trafficking in Ireland and is part of the European G6 Human Trafficking Initiative. The NGOs interviewed for this research were generally supportive of new initiatives, legislation and policy changes which have recently occurred. In particular, they expressed positive views on the work of the Anti-Human Trafficking Unit and the development of the recent national action plan on human trafficking.

CULTURE OF DISBELIEF AROUND CHILD TRAFFICKING
AND LACK OF PROSECUTIONS

A number of NGOs contended that despite recent policy and legislative developments in the area of child trafficking, there is reluctance on behalf of state agencies to acknowledge that child trafficking exists in Ireland. As previously discussed, there appear to be some tensions between the NGOs and statutory bodies in terms of consent and the child's ability to give consent to be smuggled, as well as the lack of prosecutions for child trafficking in Ireland to date, reflecting the very different structural positions from which they operate more generally.

> There have not been any victims of child trafficking identified in Ireland to date since the official identification procedure was introduced through the temporary administration measures in June 2008. We are still waiting to see the first victim of trafficking identified...which is surprising since identification of children should happen without a deep investigation given that the means of their recruitment are not relevant, The transportation, harbouring or receiving of children for the purposes of exploitation constitutes child trafficking, and the consent of the child is irrelevant. In these cases, children should be acknowledged and treated as victims of human trafficking as opposed to separated children. (Research Participant 3)

The legislation for child trafficking has rarely been tested with just one prosecution to date which occurred in March 2008 in Dublin Circuit Criminal Court.

> The accused admitted that in October 2005 he incited a named woman "to organise or knowingly facilitate the use of a child for the purpose of sexual exploitation", and was charged under the Child Trafficking and Pornography Act 1998. Judge Martin Nolan directed that his name be added to the register of sex offenders and remanded him on continuing bail for sentence at a later date. (Crowe, 2009, p. 52)

A statutory social worker discussed her concerns around child trafficking investigations and highlighted some of the reasons that active investigations did not always lead to convictions. These factors included a perceived lack of Gardaí experience in managing child trafficking cases, male Gardaí interviewing female teenagers and lack of trust. The social worker felt that a six month recovery and reflection period was inadequate for young people to get the support which they needed and longer reflection periods could perhaps facilitate investigations in the future. Also the social worker felt that, in her direct experience of such cases, there was a sense that the young person was not always believed.

Another limitation of relying on prosecution figures for child trafficking is that they do not include prosecutions of human trafficking outside of Ireland, which involved evidence collected in the Irish state. There was some criticism in our research of the US State Department's Annual Trafficking in Persons Reports for their focus on prosecutions as a measurement of success in combating human trafficking as these fail to take into account cross border cooperation in Europe related to Human Trafficking prosecutions. The recent Fusteac case provides an example of cross border police cooperation. In this particular case, three members of the same family were sentenced to seven years in prison in Romania. They were convicted of trafficking twenty-eight people, including one child, into Ireland in and around Enniscorthy, Co. Wexford for the purposes of labour exploitation. Evidence from the Irish Gardai on the exploitation of the trafficking victims in Wexford contributed to the prosecution of the Fusteac family. During the trial in Romania, many of the victims in the case refused to testify as they were still under threat from the traffickers, and it was reported that some of the witnesses had received death threats (O'Brien, 2009; Research Participant 12).

CONFLICTS BETWEEN MIGRATION POLICIES
AND CHILD PROTECTION POLICIES

Many of the research participants asserted that the responses to child trafficking in Ireland were focused on immigration rather than child protection. This was conveyed succinctly by one of the research participants who stated that 'the immigration lens which is used does not help and certainly children are viewed as victims of the illegal migration flow' (Research Participant 3). This is particularly evident when we look at the shortcomings of care arrangements for separated children in Ireland that operated until 2010. The majority of the separated children or unaccompanied minors who are missing in Ireland have gone missing from accommodation centres and hostels which were funded by the Irish State but were privately operated, and these types of accommodation appeared to be adding to the vulnerability of separated children. This accommodation has been subject to much criticism, and in particular, it has emerged that these centres were not subject to inspections by the Social Service Inspectorate and did not meet the legal minimum standards of care and safety for the residential care of children as required by the Child Care Act, 1991 (O'Brien, 2007; Hammarberg, 2008; OCO, 2009). The Irish state was interpreting these children's care needs in a functionary mode, primarily based on their migratory status and was disregarding their developmental, emotional and indeed educational needs and rights. This could be viewed as evidence that the Irish state did not acknowledge the vulnerabilities of such children to trafficking and that the state has made assumptions about their consent to be smuggled to Ireland.

The Ombudsman for Children and Young People, Emily Logan, has argued that the private hostel current accommodation in which separated chidren were largely accommodated are unsuitable for trafficked children because of lack of security and qualified staff (OCO, 2009). *The Implementation Plan of the Commission to Inquire into Child Abuse Report* (OMCYA, 2009) recommended the phasing out of the use of private hostels for separated children and the dispersal of these children and young people outside of Dublin; this process is now complete. However, some of the participants in this research have contended that the movement away from hostel accommodation and dispersal of separated children outside of Dublin has its own shortcomings.

> The argument is that in Dublin the young people are open to all sorts of risk, in particular drugs. Generally, however, these young people have not got into trouble or far less than Irish children of that age in care. Furthermore, they are equally at risk in Cork or Limerick. (Research Participant 5)

Other shortcomings of the dispersal policy for separated children highlighted by the research participants include the loss of specialised/experienced care staff, peer supports, religious supports, social networks, community based advocacy groups and opportunities for volunteering. Furthermore, it was argued that it would present difficulties in accessing refugee legal services and psychological services which are centralised in Dublin and Cork. It was suggested that the loss of these supports and services might present a serious risk of trafficking for some dispersed children and young people.

The NGO research participants were critical of the lack of access to the HSE National Operational Plan for separated children, which is referred to in the *National Plan to Prevent & Combat Trafficking of Human Beings in Ireland: 2009–2012*, as a central mechanism of improving the protection of potential victims of child trafficking. In the course of the research, none of the NGO participants had access to the plan or were aware of the contents of the plan. While the participants were supportive of the recent Protocols for Missing Children that have been established between the Gardaí and the HSE, there was a concern that these protocols were more appropriate for Irish born children who had absconded from care rather than the different needs of separated minors or trafficked children. The category of 'possibly at risk of trafficking' is not included in the new HSE and Gardaí protocols. There has also been a call from some of the NGOs for more inclusion by the HSE and Gardaí of the NGOs in cases where children are going missing particularly if an NGO has a prior relationship with the child.

PROTECTING AND PROMOTING THE VOICE AND THE AGENCY OF THE TRAFFICKED CHILD

Participants asserted that suspected victims of child trafficking were subject to multiple interviews with state agencies, for instance the Refugee Legal Service, the Gardaí, the Health Service Executive and Office of the Refugee Applications Commissioner. There was a concern that children have to recount their stories to multiple authority figures and that this process could be disempowering for the child.

> They are in a new country, they are very vulnerable, they have a story possibly in their head, they are not going to be telling you straight away. ...You have to go through it with Refugee Support Agency, and your social worker and possibly the Gardaí and all these different things they have to go through, and re-tell, and worrying they won't be believed. (Research Participant 1)

Some of the participants expressed concerns that suspected victims were being dealt with primarily under the criminal justice system rather than the child protection system. To ensure a child-sensitive approach as recommended in the National Action Plan, the research participants made the following suggestions. They recommended the use of multi-disciplinary teams including psychological supports at all ports of entry, robust development of child sensitive immigration and trafficking policies, and ensuring that children are aware of their rights to protection and assistance. Also, one of the participants suggested the use of child-friendly interview suites for children similar to the one employed by the Gardaí and the HSE in the investigation of sexual abuse. These views of the research participants area were echoed by Feijen (2008) who suggests that European countries adopt a child-sensitive entry management system in relation to immigration, and in particular, applications for asylum. An essential element of such proposals is the appointment of a legal representative and/or guardian as part of the reception process. The crucial role of *a Guardian ad Litem* for trafficked children is not fully acknowledged by the *National Action Plan* (NAP) or the IRP Bill 2010. The lack of a guardian *ad litem* (GAL) for separated children who would act as an advocate for the voice of the child during the asylum process is problematic and reflects a failure to recognize children's agency. The development of the guardian *ad litem* service would support the expression of children's voices and consideration of their experiences.

Research participants also emphasised that a broader understanding of guardianship was needed. In particular, some of the NGO participants commented on the role of independent guardians to provide an alternative support to the social work system in relation to knowledge gaps in trafficking and immigration legislation. The current immigration system can inhibit children from opening up about their situation, and there is a need for an independent voice outside of the statutory system of immigration and social work.

> [The] structures perhaps aren't the right ones…there is a need for the state to provide children, separated children, once they're in the care of the state, with a proper key worker, who will be able to develop a rapport with them that these things [the full complexity of children's journeys] can come out. (Research Participant 8)

Participants asserted that this guardianship role could provide an independent advocate, separate to the statutory social worker for the child.

> Children in care who have status are being given a GAL and surely these children who experience much more complex issues and are not just children in care, immigration, asylum, HSE care. [There] are lots of different areas of law coming together so more than anything they need a representative and that doesn't mean to say that they shouldn't have a social worker but they should have both a Social worker and GAL. And now they are likely to have neither and they are the most vulnerable and needy. (Research Participant 2)

Other forms of support identified by participants included peer support, schools and education supports, doctors and health services and religious organisations. These supports have provided positive relationships for some of the young people which the research participants had come in contact with and had allowed the young people access to social networks and provided advocacy support.

CONCLUDING COMMENTS

> The reality is this is a very tough process for anybody to go through. It's barely human centred, let alone child centred. So, for anybody to get over the

hurdles is very hard and for somebody who is terribly vulnerable and doesn't have the wherewithal...that becomes unbearably frustrating. (Research Participant 4)

This chapter discussed the position of trafficked children in Ireland in the context of recent policy developments. It examined current constructions and debates on trafficking identifying those children who are most at risk of being trafficked. Available evidence of child trafficking, in Ireland was outlined and the difficulties associated with data collection for this particular group of migrant children were highlighted. National law and International conventions were analysed in documenting the particular vulnerabilities of trafficked children in Ireland, who are primarily defined as migrants, and are not given the same degree of support and protection as other children in care. The participants interviewed for this research were generally supportive of new initiatives, legislation and policy changes, and in particular, the work of the Anti-Human Trafficking Unit. However, there is evidence that trafficked children experience differentiated rights based on their migration status in Ireland. There is a minimal use of guardians *ad litem*. Additionally, there are issues related to the current narrow interpretation of the role and further debate on the development of guardianship for children vulnerable to trafficking is required. There appears to be fundamental tension between child welfare/protection policies and migration policies, and the resulting interventions appear to contribute to the vulnerability and lack of agency of trafficked children and young people.

THE PROTECTIVE ENVIRONMENT AS A WAY FORWARD

In recognising children as active agents and meaning makers, we argue that policy development should be grounded in children's lived experiences. Because of the multiple chasms into which trafficked children fall, the value of this approach is even more important, where conventional child protection measures and assumptions about childhood have been shown to increase rather than decrease their vulnerability. A useful framework for understanding the responses required to protect trafficked children is the model of the Protective Environment which has been developed by UNICEF. The Protective Environment approach is a human-rights based model which recognises the agency and centrality of the individual child and acknowledges that child trafficking cannot be addressed in an isolated manner (O'Brien, 2008). Nationally and internationally, such a model is being promoted as a means of addressing child trafficking, and the Irish *National Action Plan to Prevent and Combat Trafficking of Human Beings in Ireland* (2009) states that the creation of a protective environment for children will be a key goal of the strategy. The *UN Protocol to Prevent, Suppress and Punish Trafficking in Persons, especially Women and Children* (2000) requires states to take measures to alleviate poverty, underdevelopment and lack of equal opportunity which lead to the vulnerability of persons, especially women and children to trafficking. The Protocol also points out that an important factor in the creation of an environment which is protective of all children is eliminating the demand for children as objects for sexual exploitation, or as a source of cheap labour, and suggests that this can be done through educational and social measures which reinforce the unacceptability of such practices (ibid, p. 168). Furthermore, the *Council of Europe Convention* (2005) obliges states to take specific measures to reduce children's vulnerability to trafficking by creating a protective environment for them.

The Protective Environment is a web of eight interconnected elements which influence the lives of children and the types of protections and risks which they may experience. These elements include government commitment, children's life-skills, attitudes, capacity, legislation and monitoring, media awareness and rehabilitation. While various aspects of the protective environment are currently in place in the Irish State, there are a number of areas which should be further addressed, such as children's life-skills, capacity, legislation and monitoring and rehabilitation.

Central to the construction of this protective environment, according to UNICEF (2005) guidelines, is the co-ordination of key agencies that are likely to come in contact with victims of child trafficking, including the police, border and immigration authorities, health, education and social welfare agencies and NGOs. Research partici-pants were critical of the current system where there is a lack of a multi-disciplinary ethos and as one participant contended the response of statutory agencies has been one of 'shifting responsibility'. We have discussed the weaknesses of legislation in this area which focuses on a punitive rather than a protective response to child trafficking. However, this will be ameliorated somewhat with the passage of the *Immigration, Residence and Protection Bill* (2010) into legislation.

UNICEF (2008) contends that all children should be able to access services for recovery and integration on a non-discriminatory and equal basis. However, as was already discussed, there appears to be some differences in the treatment of separated children seeking asylum and Irish born children in the care of the HSE. In this instance, the issue of residency status appears to influence the treatment of such vulnerable children and impact on their experience of the protective environment.

Kanics (2008) asserts that in developing this protective environment, the Irish government needs to focus on the issue of safe and secure accommodation and ensure that services are provided on a 'consensual and informed basis' which considers both the child's vulnerabilities and their rights (p. 397).

In relation to rehabilitation and recovery, Van de Glind and Kooijmans (2008) suggests that such responses should be "child-centred, and include individual needs assessments followed by tailor-made remedial action" (p. 163). While the limitations of the Palermo Protocol have been outlined in this chapter, the Protocol does provide a number of positive supports for the victims of trafficking. Moreover, it requires that in situations where a victim of trafficking wishes to be repatriated, the case should be facilitated in a manner that primarily ensures the victim's rights and safety. In regard to these commitments, Ireland has ratified the 2000 *Palermo Protocol on Trafficking* and signed but not yet ratified the Optional Protocol on the UN *Convention on the Rights of the Child* on the *Sale of Children, Child Prostitution and Child Pornography*.

The issue of child trafficking has been a problematic and relatively new area of policy and practice for the Irish state. While there has been much legislative and policy progress to-date, the Irish state has also struggled at times to respond to the challenge presented by this complex global and local phenomenon.

NOTES

[1] Within this Chapter we use the definition of the child as outlined in article 1 of the UNCRC as, 'every human being below the age of eighteen years unless, under the law applicable to the child, majority is attained earlier'.
[2] The US Department of State started monitoring Trafficking in Human Persons in 1994, and have produced yearly reports since then.

REFERENCES

Anderson, B., & Andrijasevic, R. (2008). Sex, slaves and citizens: The politics of anti-trafficking. *Soundings: A Journal of Politics and Culture, 40*.

Anti-Human Trafficking Unit, Department of Justice, Equality and Law Reform (2010). *Summary Report of Trafficking in Human Beings in Ireland for 2009*, Government Publications Office: Dublin.

Bastia, T. (2005). Child trafficking or teenage migration? Bolivian migrants in Argentina. *International Migration, 43*(4), 57–89.

Breuil, B. (2008). Precious children in a heartless world? The complexities of child trafficking in Marseille. *Children & Society, 229*(3), 223–234.

Brophy, G., & McGonigle, B. (2008, June). The immigration, residence and protection bill 2008 - Protecting children or traffickers? *The Researcher, 3*(2), 6–10.

Childcare Act. (1991). Dublin: Government Stationery Office.

Council of Europe. (2005, May 16). *Council of Europe convention on action against trafficking in human beings*. CETS 197. Retrieved March 25, 2010, from http://www.unhcr.org/refworld/docid/43fded544.html

Criminal Law Human Trafficking Act. (2008). Dublin: Government Stationery Office.

Crowe, O. (2009). *FRA thematic study on child trafficking*. Ireland: European Agency Fundamental Human Rights. Retrieved from http://fra.europa.eu/fraWebsite/attachments/Child-trafficking-09-country-ie.pdf

Department of Justice, Equality and Law Reform. (2009). *National action plan to combat and prevent human trafficking 2009–2012*. Dublin: Anti-Human Trafficking Unit.

ECPAT UK. (2009). *Child trafficking for sexual exploitation: Discussion paper*. Retrieved March 22, 2010, from http://www.ecpat.org.uk/downloads/Sexual%20Exploitation.pdf

European Commission. (2001). *Preventing and combating trafficking in women: A comprehensive European strategy*. Brussels: European Commission.

Feijen, L. (2008). The challenges of ensuring protection to unaccompanied and separated children in composite flows in Europe. *Refugee Survey Quarterly, 27*(4), 63–73.

Hammarberg, T. (2008). Report by the Commissioner for Human Rights, Mr. Thomas Hammarberg, on his visit to Ireland, 26–30 November 2007, Council of Europe. Retrieved June 21, 2009, from www.commissioner.coe.int

Immigration, Residence and Protection Bill. (2008). *Immigration, residence and protection bill*. Dublin: Government Stationery Office.

Joyce, C., & Quinn, E. (2009). *Policies on unaccompanied minors in Ireland*. Dublin: ESRI.

Kanics, J. (2008). Child trafficking and Ireland. *Studies, 97*(388), 387–402.

Kelleher Associates, in association with Monica O'Connor and Jane Pillinger. (2009). *Globalisation, sex trafficking and prostitution: The experiences of migrant women in Ireland.* Dublin: Immigrant Council of Ireland.

Kennedy, S., Sr. (2008, May 23). Concern that missing children 'trafficked'. *Irish Times.*

Moosa-Mitha, M. (2007). Citizenship rights in a globalising world. In L. Dominelli (Ed.), *Revitalising communities in a globalising world.* Aldershot: Ashgate.

Naughton, D. (2009). Daily debates/parliamentary debates, Ryan report on the commission to inquire into child abuse: Motion. Retrieved June 11, from http://debates.oireachtas.ie/DDebate.aspx?F=DAL 20090611.xml&Node=H5&Page=14

O'Brien, C. (2009, December 3). Three men jailed for trafficking into Ireland. *Irish Times.*

O'Brien, C. (2007, October 31). Child asylum hostels fail minimum standards. *Irish Times.*

O'Brien, K. (2008). Child protection, strategic interventions to combat child trafficking. In S. Martin, D. Horgan, & J. O'Riordan, (Eds.), *Combating child trafficking for labour and sexual exploitation.* Dublin: Original Writing.

Office of the Minister for Children and Youth Affairs. (2009). *Report of the commission to inquire into child abuse report implementation plan.* Dublin: Stationery Office.

Ombudsman for Children. (2009). *Separated children living in Ireland.* Dublin: Ombudsman for Children's Office.

Raymond J. G. (2002). The new UN trafficking protocol'. *Women's Studies International Forum, 25*(5), 491–502.

Separated Children in Europe Progamme/Save and Children. (2007). *Position paper on preventing and responding to trafficking of children in Europe.*

Sillen, J., & Beddoe, C. (2007). *Rights here, rights now: Recommendations for protecting trafficked children.* London: ECPAT UK and UNICEF.

Smyth, J. (2011, January 10). Eleven minors pursuing asylum go missing. *Irish Times*

Territo, L., & Kirkham, G. (2010). *International sex trafficking of women & children: Understanding the global epidemic.* Michigan: Looseleaf Law Publications.

UN protocol to prevent, suppress and punish trafficking in persons, especially women and children. (2000).

UNICEF. (2005). *Combating child trafficking, handbook for parliamentarians, no. 9.* New York: United Nations Children Fund.

UNICEF. (2008). *Child protection from violence, exploitation and abuse.* Retrieved from http://www.unicef.org/protection/index_environment.html

United Nations Convention on the Rights of the Child (UNCRC). (1989).

US Department of State. (2006). *Trafficking in persons report.* Washington, DC: Department of State.

US Department of State. (2009). *Trafficking in persons report.* Washington, DC: Department of State.

Van de Glind, H., & Kooijmans, J. (2008). Modern-Day child slavery. *Children and Society, 22*(3), 150–166.

van Turnhout, J. (2010). *Response to HSE statement that no missing child from HSE care has been trafficked.* Children's Rights Alliance.

Yonkva, N. (2008). Ireland on the road to ratification of council of Europe convention on action against trafficking in human beings. In S. Martin, D. Horgan, & J. O'Riordan (Eds.), *Combating child trafficking for labour and sexual exploitation.* Dublin: Original Writing.

Deirdre Horgan, Shirley Martin and Jacqui O'Riordan
School of Applied Social Studies
University College Cork

MUIREANN NÍ RAGHALLAIGH

13. RELATIONSHIPS WITH FAMILY, FRIENDS AND GOD

The Experiences of Unaccompanied Minors Living in Ireland

INTRODUCTION

In recent years researchers have begun to pay increasing attention to the circumstances of unaccompanied minors or separated children, who are defined as children and young people under the age of 18 who are "outside of their country of origin and separated from both parents, or their previous legal/customary primary caregiver" (*Separated Children in Europe Programme*, 2004: 2).[1] Records suggest that the first unaccompanied minor entered the Irish state in 1996. Since then, increasing numbers of professionals and service providers have come into contact with this population group. Within various disciplines practice wisdom suggests that these young people are faced with a host of challenges relating to their pre-migration experiences, their journeys from their countries of origin to Ireland, and their post-migration lives. Internationally, research findings lend evidence to these suggestions. They draw attention to experiences of oppressive circumstances and armed conflict prior to exile, abuse and exploitation en-route to Western Europe, the loss of culture and loved ones, and the challenges of the asylum and care systems whilst living in Ireland and other countries (Ayotte, 2000; Rea, 2001; Kohli and Mather, 2003; Thomas et al., 2004; Hopkins and Hill, 2006; Chase et al., 2008). Some authors have tended to focus on the vulnerability of these young people (Bean et al., 2007; Hodes et al., 2008; Rea, 2001) while others have highlighted their resilience (Robins and Rylands, unpublished data[2]; Wallin and Ahlström, 2005; Kohli, 2006a; Ní Raghallaigh and Gilligan, 2010).

In discussions of vulnerability and resilience within the wider body of literature on refugee studies, attention is often drawn to the risk associated with isolation and the strength that can be gleaned from social support and friendship networks. For example, in discussing the coping strategies of a sample of refugee youth in the United States, Miller et al. (2008) draw attention to the importance of a supportive parent with whom open communication is possible and the importance of supportive peers, particularly those of the same ethnic group. However, research in various countries has shown that refugees often suffer as a result of the loss of social networks and that they encounter difficulties in replacing these networks in the host country (e.g. Bennett and Detzner, 1997; McMichael and Manderson, 2004; Miller et al., 2002; Smyth and Whyte, 2005; Stanley, 2001; Vekic, 2003; Wade et al., 2005).

Darmody, Tyrrell, Song. (eds.), The Changing Faces of Ireland: Exploring the Lives of Immigrant and Ethnic Minority Children, 221–236.

Frequent reference is made in the literature to the myriad of losses, including the loss of relationships experienced by unaccompanied minors (Delaney, 2006; German, 2004). Whether these losses are as a result of death or separation, the social worlds of unaccompanied minors become seriously disrupted. Family and friends are left behind in their countries of origin. Although, at times, contact is maintained with loved ones, such contact is often infrequent and minimal in nature. Often, no contact is maintained at all (Ayotte, 2002). Unlike other refugee children, unaccompanied minors usually begin their new lives knowing nobody around them and are faced with the challenge of a complete recreation of their social networks. This can be a daunting task.

Yet, despite the obvious importance of these issues, within research little in-depth attention has been paid to the relationships that unaccompanied minors have. Several studies have made reference to unaccompanied minors being mutually supportive of each other (e.g. Goodman, 2004; Rousseau et al., 1998; Stanley, 2003; Summerfield, 2000). In general, however, research suggests that these young people experience loneliness and a lack of social support (McCrea, 2003). The views of unaccompanied minors have been elicited in studies by Hopkins and Hill (2006), Robins and Rylands (unpublished), Vekic (2003), and Wade et al. (2005), amongst others. These authors have highlighted the social isolation faced by many unaccompanied minors in different countries and the corresponding lack of social support that they experience. This chapter attempts to develop our understanding of the continuity and change experienced by these young people in the realm of relationships. Drawing on Ph.D. research undertaken with unaccompanied minors living in the Republic of Ireland, this chapter looks at the young people's narratives concerning family and friends in their countries of origin, the changes in their relationships since moving to Ireland, the role of friendships, and the comfort provided by a continuous relationship with God.

METHODOLOGY

In choosing a methodology for this study, particular attention was paid to the following: the fact that asylum seekers and refugees often find it difficult to trust those around them (Daniel and Knudsen, 1995; Robinson, 2002); that (potentially) the study involved sensitive or "deeply personal" (Lee and Renzetti, 1993: 6) topics; and that rather than seeking facts and causes of social phenomenon, the subjective experiences of unaccompanied young people were being explored. A qualitative methodology was adopted as it was deemed most appropriate in terms of these considerations. A decision was made to engage in participant observation in one of the hostels where unaccompanied minors live, primarily in order to attempt to build relationships with the young people, but secondarily in order to gain a deeper under-standing of their lives by spending some time in their place of residence. In addition, qualitative interviews with 32 young people took place, some of whom were residents of the hostel and some of whom lived elsewhere throughout Ireland. In general, the interviews were conducted in English. In instances where young people had limited English the author offered to have an interpreter present. However, this offer was only taken up by one young person. While this probably reflects the fact that most unaccompanied minors living in Ireland tend to speak English well, it may also be the case that some young people simply chose not to participate because of their limited English language abilities and the difficulties of communicating through an interpreter.

In arranging and conducting the interviews much attention was paid to ethical issues. Before interviewing the young people informed consent was obtained from the Health Service Executive (the statutory body responsible for their care) and from the young people themselves. During each interview every effort was made to ensure that the process did not cause harm to the participant. The specific strategies that were adopted included making efforts to put the participant at ease by engaging in small talk prior to the commencement of the interview; not asking the young person why he or she had come to Ireland but instead allowing him or her to chose whether or not to reveal this information; and displaying empathy and unconditional accept-ance throughout the process (Bertrand, 2000). At the end of each interview partici-pants were provided with a voucher as a token of appreciation.

The 32 interview participants included 14 males and 18 females. They ranged in aged from 14 to 19 years at the time of interview and consisted of 23 Christians and nine Muslims. The young people came from 13 different countries. However, in order to protect their identities, details of the specific countries of origin are not provided here. Instead, Table 1 below indicates the regions from which they came.[3]

The remainder of this chapter is based on the data which emerged from the inter-views. The findings are presented using direct quotations from the participants, privileging the voices of the individuals who took part.

Table 1. Regions of origin of interview participants

Region of origin	Number
Eastern Africa	14
Western Africa	13
Middle Africa	2
Southern Africa	1
Western Asia	1
Eastern Europe	1

FAMILY AND FRIENDS AT HOME: 'ORDINARY' LIVES

Initially, in the interviews with this study's participants, negative pictures of the past were painted: the young people narrated stories of poverty, conflict, and lack of opportunity, as well as other difficult experiences. However, with further exploration more positive descriptions also emerged. By deliberately *not* focusing on reasons for departure, this research allowed the participants to talk about what Kohli (2006b) has termed as the more "ordinary aspects of their past lives" (p. 715), many of which were positive in nature. An understanding of these circumstances is crucial if we are to seek to fully appreciate the previous experiences of these young people, the extent that their lives have changed as a result of leaving home, and the many strengths that they possess. Within descriptions of relationships with family members, friends and neighbours, we glean important insights into aspects of every day life prior to departure. This information is seldom present in the literature relating to unaccompanied minors or other forced migrant groups.

In describing their daily lives at home, some of the participants made frequent references to their parents and to other family members. However, others did not wish to talk about their families at all, choosing to be "silent" (Kohli, 2006b), as is often the case with unaccompanied minors. Of those who chose to speak openly, it was evident that some had been close to their parents and had positive memories of these relationships, whilst others had grown up in situations in which their parents were abusive or in circumstances where they did not have much contact with them. While occasionally the young people directly described how they felt about family members, more frequently it was through general conversations about everyday life that their feelings for their parents, siblings and extended family members became evident. The participants talked about eating meals with family members, going to religious services together, helping with household chores, listening to stories told by their parents, and playing and conversing with siblings and with friends. One boy, who seemed to have had a particularly close relationship with his mother before she was killed, described how they used to spend their time together:

> What kind of things we would … She would read me stories, she would, we would play games, cards … eh, we would cook ….

Descriptions like this one highlighted the multiple roles played by significant people in the pre-departure lives of the participants. Young people described how parents and other family members (siblings, grandparents, etc.) played with them, cooked meals for them, helped with homework, chatted, and listened to them when they had problems or worries. One boy described how his father often told him stories about the history of his country and about life before the war began. Also, parents and other older family members gave guidance and advice which helped to direct the behaviour of the participants. In particular, mothers were mentioned as people to whom the young people went when they needed help or support. In other cases, fathers got a particular mention. One girl, whose father's actions ultimately placed her life in danger, also recounted more 'ordinary' elements of her relationship with him. She talked about approaching him instead of her mother when she wanted something:

> Well … it seems strange, but … I seemed to get closer to my Dad than my Mum. When I was growing up. My Dad is very harsh. But … my Dad is harsh, my Mum is a disciplinaire. You understand. Why? … My Dad could beat me, like, once in six months. My Mum would beat me every day. […]⁴ So I tend to get closer to my… I seem to get comfortable with my Dad than with my Mum like. Most of the things, like, if I want anything, I usually goes to my Dad […]. I'm close to him. You know.

Elsewhere, some young people described close relationships with siblings. One boy, whose father had to leave his country when he was twelve, became very close to his older brother following his father's departure:

> The only person, can talk to me is my brother and the only person can talk to my brother, that's me. We understand each other very well, you know.

Actually, I love my brother more than my father and my mother. Because the time my father leave my country, you know, four years ago … four years ago, I was eleven … twelve, and my brother helped me a lot, you know.

As well as talking about time spent with family members in their countries of origin, the young people made frequent references to neighbours and friends. In describing the life left behind, many of the participants talked about the existence of a sense of community that had been a part of their home cultures. They talked about how people socialised informally by dropping in to see their friends whenever they wanted to do so. Some spoke about spending their evenings at home visiting neighbours. Companionship, and the support associated with it (Cohen and Wills, 1985), had usually been effortlessly available. Having a sense of community also meant that help was easy to find when needed. The young people talked about neighbours helping their families out in times of need. A male participant described how it was "normal" for him to drop into his friend's house for dinner, if he was hungry, or for his family to borrow money from their neighbours. Another participant mentioned how neighbours would come and "console you" or would give you a "kilo of milk" or other food items if needed. Thus, neighbours provided what Cutrona (2000) has termed "nurturant" and "instrumental" support.

In describing their friendships in their countries of origin, the young people often spoke about what they did when spending time with friends. While some 'extraordinary' events were mentioned - living on the streets with friends, fleeing to a friend's house when parents were murdered, playing football together in an area occupied by the military – a strong sense of 'ordinary' life with friends also was evident throughout their narratives. One girl described what she did at weekends:

Ehh, I have to go to my friend's place. Have a chat. Play around. Go back home. Just discuss about what happened on Friday in school [laughs].You know.

When asked about his friends, a male participant said the following:

You know, like they are friends, you meet them at school, like you, they help you with some homeworks if you need help, but, you know, I didn't need help with homework or anything like that. They would help, they would help other friends, so. Like, we would chat, laugh, play around.

Within narratives of friendship many of the participants depicted their parents or other caregivers as strict disciplinarians, who ensured that their behaviour was tightly controlled and that they were protected from 'Western influences' (for example drinking, smoking, and having boyfriends or girlfriends). However, whilst parents, caregivers, and society generally attempted to exert strong control on the lives of the young people, they were not always successful. Although some of the young people described not daring to disobey their parents for fear of the consequences, many described a type of "secret life" (Miller et al., 2008: 14) spent with siblings and friends. While Miller et al. (2008) use this concept to describe how young refugees negotiate life in exile, this current research suggests that such lives can often exist prior to exile. Within this 'secret life', the rules set down by family and the norms of society were broken. However, attempts were made to hide such behaviour from parents and from the community at large. For instance, many of the youngsters described how people of their age - including themselves, siblings or friends – often had girlfriends or boyfriends in secret. In relation to this, one girl's narrative suggested that secrecy represented a way of escaping from the"control" that parents tried to exert on their children. From her point of view this differed from her new life in Ireland:

> It's just different because your mother and your father controlling you and you can't go with some boy [...] And you can't go with some man. If they see you they can kill you, you know. And they can beat you. And if you are going with your boyfriend you have to go secret. You can't show them anybody, you know?

Disobeying rules and doing things in secret meant that many of the young people had memories of getting into trouble with their parents for things that they did with siblings or with friends. Amongst other things, they described instances when they stayed out later than they were allowed in the evening, when they went to the cinema even though children were not allowed to do so, when they were disrespectful towards teachers, and when they played in areas that their parents perceived to be dangerous because of conflict or other circumstances. The young people tended to describe these memories rather nostalgically despite the obvious discord that had been involved at the time. From the vantage point of their new worlds, where parents were absent, these instances were remembered fondly. This was evident from the animated way in which one Muslim boy described what he did on a Friday, when he had no school:

> When I woke up, I would be like, I had breakfast, watch about my Dad, and then if he's not in, I just go out with my friends [laughs]. And play football in, in the beach and come back to lunch … Then I'll go to sleep, then I'll woke up around three or three thirty. Then I'll go out and play football. Then sometimes if I came home around seven I will be in trouble because I'm late. I have to be home around six. Six pm. [...] Every Friday I was in trouble [laughs]... I [inaudible] I go to beach like. And if my Dad hears that I was in the beach or like if, if he, because he can see like, the sea sand in your sandals…

RELATIONSHIPS IN IRELAND: THE ABSENCE OF PARENTS AND THE IMPORTANCE OF FRIENDS

Within their descriptions of life in Ireland, the young people spoke of missing family members from home. These descriptions gave insight not only into the nature of their new life experience but also into how life had been previously. They talked about specific aspects of their relationships with people that they missed. These often involved 'ordinary' everyday interactions with particular individuals. They missed spending time with these people and chatting to them, they missed playing and eating together, and they missed benefiting from the advice, guidance, and support of family members. Many of the young people talked about missing food from home, and, particularly, their mothers' cooking. One boy spoke about the morning routines and interactions in his family home in his country of origin and how these differed from the mornings in the hostel where he now lived:

> It's not the same. [...] The difference is like, you ... Like, you know the way, like the, your mother tells you, like 'Good morning. Blah, blah, blah. Did you have nice dream, like, blah, blah, blah'. You know, that kind of stuff. Which, which Jane,[5] wouldn't ... I mean, which, you know Jane, on the staff? She wouldn't come and ask you how was your dream, blah blah blah blah. Which, is, like a difference. Your mother is your mother, you know like. If, nobody can fill that position.

In the absence of parents and family members, it was evident that their roles were often replaced – to a degree – by professionals, such as Health Service Executive social workers and project workers[6], teachers, hostel staff, care workers, or members of voluntary organisations. Indeed, many of the young people likened their social worker or project worker to their parents and expressed gratitude for the help that they received from them. However, they felt that these professionals could never adequately fill the role of parents. One female participant talked about her project worker. Although she knew that she could turn to her for advice and support, she stated that she didn't always "feel free to talk with her" because she knew that her project worker was listening to the problems of *all* the young people in the hostel. Instead, she longed to have someone of her own to talk to. Also, participants were aware that although professionals might genuinely care about them, they were being paid to be in this caring role. Their awareness of the limitations of these relationships echoes the concerns of a number of researchers regarding the danger of unaccompanied minors becoming dependent on professionals while remaining isolated from more informal supports (Stanley, 2001; Wade et al., 2005; Robins and Rylands, unpublished). One boy began by describing his social worker as "my first friend" and "like my parents", as someone he could talk to and the only person he could trust. However, upon reflection, the same participant acknowledged that the relationship was not a proper friendship:

> But, I can't say he's my friend. Just, because is just, you know, is like, ehh, is like, taking responsibility for me. So he's just like my guardian. That's it. But, I need a friend. [...] But if now I call my social worker, he'll tell me, 'oh wait until Monday'. Or 'I'll, I'll next week I'm not working'. You know? So that is work. So he is not a friend. He is just a guardian. [...] It's not a, it is not a relationship that one. It is just. I think it is a work thing. It's just work. [...]. He is getting paid. Like, a friend, a real friend, a friend, he, he or she, she, he can't be, nobody is paying to be my friend.

Often making such 'real' friends was not easy. Establishing relationships with Irish young people seemed particularly difficult. Several Irish studies on immigrant young people have highlighted the varying extent to which immigrant children and teenagers establish friendships with their Irish peers and the varying nature of these relationships (Gilligan et al., 2009; Smyth et al., 2009). Both of these studies have also suggested that establishing relationships with Irish young people might be more difficult for immigrant young people who have arrived at an older age, possibly because friendship groups within schools have already been well established. In relation to the study being discussed here, the majority of the 32 unaccompanied minor participants arrived in Ireland in their mid to late teens. Therefore, it is perhaps not surprising that few of them talked about friendships with Irish young people. Irish young people were perceived by many to be difficult to get to know and difficult to understand. One girl talked about not having the same "sense" of Irish people that she would have of people of her own ethnicity. She talked about knowing "how people act back home", but not having this knowledge in relation to Irish people. However, those who had made friendships with Irish people recognised the value of these friendships. It was evident that these friends played particular roles. One participant commented that he became friendly with Irish young people in order "to know much things and to really get how to speak English". Another participant, whose friends were mainly Irish, described in humorous terms how he learnt about the norms of behaviour at a school "social"[7]:

> But like ... Do you know the way people like at social here and everything like that, then they go, just come to you... 'do you want to shift[8] my friend?' and things like that [laughs]. The first time I went out and they were like 'do you want to shift my ...' My friend was like, ehm ... asking a girl. I was saying 'are you stupid? She wouldn't say yeah. Get real'. But he was like 'Ah no, no. That's the way we do it here'. I thought he was joking or something like that. I was seeing like deep shit in the jungle, like 'Wo!' [laughs].

Reflecting the findings of other research studies on unaccompanied minors in both the UK and in Ireland (Rea, 2001; Stanley, 2001; Vekic, 2003) the participants' main friendships in Ireland were with other unaccompanied minors or other immigrant young people. The majority of the participants lived in hostel accommodation for unaccompanied minors and cultivated friendships within these environments. Other research on asylum-seeking children has also pointed to the making of friendships within shared accommodation settings (Anderson, 2001; Ní Laoire et al., 2009), thus pointing to a crucially important but usually unacknowledged role played by the hostel and direct provision systems.

Although 'ordinary' aspects of life with friends – playing sports together, hanging out, chatting – were still evident in the participants' narratives within the Irish context, it seemed that, compared with friendships at home, friendships in Ireland also served new and multiple purposes. In the absence of family members and faced with multiple challenges, friendships often took on a new significance. To a large extent it appeared that peers facilitated the young people in their use of various coping strategies. The strategies identified through the research have been discussed in depth elsewhere (Ní Raghallaigh and Gilligan, 2010) and include, amongst others, the strategy of adjusting to life in Ireland by learning and changing, the strategy of maintaining continuity, and the strategy of seeking distraction. Peers facilitated adjustment to Irish society by helping the young people to learn new things or change their ways of behaving. The narratives suggested that, in particular, newly arrived unaccompanied minors were helped to orientate to Irish life by other un-accompanied minors who had been living in Ireland for longer. Those who had lived in the country for a period of time taught their peers about Irish culture and Irish people, about the asylum process, and about the practicalities of daily life. In addition, they provided support and encouragement. For example, one girl had a vivid memory of crying during her first meal at the hostel. Even the meal she was served - which she later learnt was spaghetti bolognaise - represented huge change in her life and had caused her stress and anxiety. She was provided with reassurance by the other young people who were present:

> [Laughs] They served me spaghetti bolognaise. I started crying [laughs]. I started crying because like … Ah … I remember it. I ate, I have ate spaghetti before but usually we grate it and we cook it with rice. And we mix it with rice. We don't eat it on its own like that. […] It's very long and coily. It's like … Oh my God. Then she gave me this cream … I think it's mayonnaise, but then I didn't know the name. And she gave me chips. I love chips. I was wondering, what's … you know the mayonnaise was in a cup in a small plate, and … What is this? Is it an ice cream? What am I supposed to do with it? [laughing] I was looking at, at other people eating chips with the mayonnaise. You know. Ah … but I was really crying. And there was this girl. She now came over and said 'What's wrong with you? Where are you from?' I say 'Nigeria'. 'I'm Nigerian too. You are all right … We are a lot of Nigerians here. You will be fine'. And she went to call about three or four girls.

In addition, some of the participants talked about being able to maintain some continuity in their lives, by conversing with other unaccompanied minors in their native language, by reminiscing about life at home, and by generally holding on to aspects of culture through interaction with peers (e.g. eating food and watching films from home, listening to music from home etc.). One girl – also from Nigeria – talked about time spent with her Nigerian friend in Ireland:

> I'd stay at one of my friends that has a baby. I would go to that place. Watch Nigerian movie because I like watching Nigerian movies. I would just be watching. Eating African food, do you know? Playing with the child. Discussing with the mother. Like that. I like it.

The narratives of the participants also suggested that friends – whether Irish or non Irish – served as sources of distraction from the many worries that they faced. The companionship of others meant that less time was spent thinking and worrying about problems in the past, the present, or the future. Other studies have also pointed to the use of distraction as a coping strategy (MacMullin and Loughry, 2000; Chase et al., 2008). Companionship also served as a buffer against loneliness. One girl, who had moved to private rented accommodation following her 18th birthday, talked about missing the companionship of those in the hostel. She spoke about feeling lonely and having too much time to think. She said that she was thinking of getting married partly because she was "afraid of being alone".

Yet, despite the many roles that friends played in the lives of the unaccompanied minors, relationships with peers were not without difficulties. Young people reported various problems when interacting with peers, including being excluded from friendship groups and being teased. In addition, the young people's descriptions suggested that their relationships with friends were largely characterised by a lack of trust. Although five of the participants said that they had no problems trusting people, all of the others reported difficulties in trusting those with whom they had contact in Ireland. Even though all of the young people talked about their friends, these friends were rarely people in whom they had complete trust. While some of the young people had experienced difficulties in trusting when at home also, many of them talked about having been able to trust previously but experiencing difficulties doing so now. Thus, for many, distrusting represented something new and seemed to form part of their strategy of coping with the challenges that they faced in Ireland (Ní Raghallaigh and Gilligan, 2010). One participant stated:

> For example, in school I don't have any, any friends who I can trust. I talk to them. I play with them. I don't trust them.

Such findings reflect the wider refugee literature where frequent reference has been made to the difficulties that asylum seekers and refugees have in trusting (e.g. Delaney, 2006; Eisenbruch, 1991; Hynes, 2009). While trust is widely viewed as a key component of relationships, with Mitchell (1990) asserting that "no major or enduring relationship can exist happily or comfortably without trust" (p. 849), this research draws attention to the very significant roles that relationships with friends can play even when trust is not present. The narratives of many of the participants suggested that trust was not perceived to be an essential ingredient in friendship.

RELATING TO GOD: A CONTINUING FRIENDSHIP

While the discussion thus far has suggested that, in general, the young people's relationships had changed immensely since their arrival in Ireland, almost all of the participants reported one relationship that had remained constant in their lives. This was their relationship with God. Of the 32 interview participants, 31 described God as being important in their lives. While the study had not set out to explore the significance of religious faith to the young people, this theme arose spontaneously within both the participant observation and the interview phase of the study. The study's flexible design then allowed this topic to be explored in more depth.

Anecdotal evidence suggests the importance played by religious faith and practice in the lives of asylum seekers and refugees generally. However, several authors have pointed to the scarcity of research on this topic (e.g. Ai et al., 2003; Goździak and Shandy, 2002.) In addition, or perhaps resulting from this lack of research, it seems that in a lot of professional practice settings the religious dimensions of people's lives (including asylum seekers) are often ignored, thus reflecting a "climate of discomfort" (Sahlein 2002: 381) that surrounds religion in various disciplines. Yet, within literature that deals with the issue of religion – either in depth or in passing – the evidence suggests that belief in God and religious practice serve many purposes for asylum seekers and refugees generally (McMichael, 2002; Smyth and Whyte, 2005; Thompson and Gurney, 2003) and, indeed, for unaccompanied minors specifically (Goodman, 2003; Robins and Rylands, unpublished; Wade et al., 2005). Within this current study, while attendance at religious services and participation in rituals served particular purposes (discussion of which is not possible here), the participants' relationships with God seemed especially important in providing them with a sense of both comfort and continuity as they adjusted to life in Ireland. In a context in which the participants were faced with many difficulties, including a huge sense of discontinuity both in the realm of relationships and in other realms, the comfort and continuity provided by faith were particularly important. The important role played by faith also can be found in the findings of McMichael (2002) in relation to refugee women in Australia.

The *Gallup International Millennium Survey* found that 97% of West African's view God as being very important in their personal lives (Corballo, 2000). The *World Values Survey* (Lippman and Keith, 2006) found similar results. While the unaccompanied minors participating in this research came from various countries, their narratives reflected the findings of Corballo (2000) and Lippman and Keith (2006). The importance of religious faith and belief in God in their countries of origin was emphasised and the participants narrated stories of attending churches and mosques at home, praying with family members, and relying on God for help and support. For example, one female participant stated:

> In Africa, like, everybody is hoping in God. They just, any, like everybody almost goes to church, every Sunday. It's not like, some people here, just say, they just go on Christmas and Easter. Where at home you just go to church because when you hear somebody testifying that 'I got this', 'Oh God gave me this', 'Oh I got school fees for my children', so you just, you'd be saying, 'oh where is that God that is giving you all that?' So you go to church and the ... the pastors, oohh, they are really lively. [...] They kind of encourage you... [...] encourage you to pray. They like preach about the hope that you are going to get things.

Having moved to Ireland, the young people spoke about God continuing to play an important role in their lives. Their narratives suggested that God acted as a friend, an advisor, a confidant, and as someone who provided for them and protected them. One participant talked about having known God in his country of origin and about the importance of continuing to appreciate him in Ireland. His words drew attention to the continuity within this relationship:

> It's like, I have been in problem [...] at home. I knew God since home. I appreciate anything he gave me. Food he gave me, clothes he gave me. You know I mean, yeah? I come back here, I don't have to forget about it. You know I mean, I still have to be straight what I was, you know I mean.

As well as feeling that they knew *God*, participants talked about the fact that God knew *them* well. This was particularly comforting for the young people in their current contexts, given the absence of parents, family members, and friends from home, and given that, frequently, they did not feel that people around them knew or understood them well. In addition, the participants voiced a sense of trust in God, something which – as noted above – was often absent from other relationships:

> The only, only, only friend [laughs] I trusted all the time, that's God. [...] I don't have any more friends ... I trusted more than God, I don't think so.

You know because, always God knows more than everybody. And God's gonna help you all the time. [...] God always gonna help.

Another participant talked about needing someone to talk to and being able to 'chat' to God. The comfort and emotional support provided by God is evident:

I believe that, like, there is a communication between, between me and God, you know. Like, trying to chat with God. [...] You know. That is the way. That is what I use, like, to try to talk to God. You know what I'm saying like. Try, because sometimes you need someone to talk to.

While God's presence seemed to take on a particular significance in the absence of other close trusting relationships and in the face of multiple challenges in Ireland, it is not being suggested that religion became important simply because of these factors. On the contrary, the participants' descriptions of everyday life in their countries of origin highlighted the importance attached to religious faith and practice within their home cultural communities and within their family backgrounds. Thus, while God provided comfort and emotional support to the young people as they adjusted to life in Ireland, this support did not emerge in a vacuum. Instead, as Pargament (1997) has suggested in relation to religious coping, religious faith was used because it was a key part of the young people's orienting system throughout their lives.

CONCLUSION

Adult Bosnian refugees interviewed by Miller et al. (2002) embedded their experiences of isolation "within a comparative temporal framework" (Miller et al., 2002: 344) by juxtaposing descriptions of their current isolation with narratives of the rich social networks that were available to them prior to migration. Although the participants in this study also compared the past with the present the results were somewhat different. Clearly, they really missed family members and friends from home. Indeed, most of these important individuals seemed to remain psychologically present despite their physical absence (Boss, 1999). Their presence was particularly evident within the narratives of the participants as they continually contrasted the past to the present. The participants' awareness that family members and friends were absent meant that they remained psychologically present to some degree. However, the young people's narratives relating to Ireland did not suggest that they were *isolated*, if we are to understand isolation as to mean being alone or solitary. Often, their descriptions suggested that they were surrounded by peers and constantly in the company of others. It seemed, however, that the characteristics of these friendships were different within the Irish context. They served important purposes, especially in relation to helping the participants to adjust to their lives in Ireland. However, there was little evidence of the existence of strong, trusting relationships. Instead, most of the participants talked about having difficulties trusting and about only trusting to a certain extent. Within this context the importance of their continuing friendship with God became even more significant. Faced with multiple challenges in adjusting to life in Ireland, God was depicted as a constant, trustworthy companion who had journeyed with them, who understood them intimately, and who would help them in whatever way help was needed.

The findings suggest a number of key points which must be taken into account by those who come into contact with unaccompanied minors. Firstly, creating simple dichotomies of 'home' and 'exile' are not helpful. Often, life at home is depicted in research and understood by professionals only in terms of its 'extraordinary' elements (Kohli, 2006b). In describing relationships that unaccompanied minors had with family members and friends in their countries of origin, this research suggests that a more nuanced understanding of life at home is needed. In working with this population group both the positive and negative experiences of life at home and of life in exile need to be considered, while always maintaining a sensitive approach and recognising that unaccompanied minors may not wish to talk about either the 'ordinary' or 'extraordinary' aspects of their pre-departure lives. Secondly, a more in-depth understanding of the relationships in the lives of unaccompanied minors needs to be developed. The crucially important roles played by peers – often those living in hostels with unaccompanied minors – need to be understood and appreciated for their value. Frequent reference has been made to the inadequate care provision available to unaccompanied minors in Ireland (Christie, 2002; Mooten, 2006). Until recently, most of these young people have lived in hostels instead of in approved residential or foster placements.[9] However, it cannot simply be concluded that un-accompanied minors should have the same care as Irish young people. Instead, an individualised approach to care planning is needed, whereby the needs and wishes of each young person are taken into account. In doing so, the positive aspects of hostel life (such as the invaluable peer support offered by other residents) need to be considered. In addition, the difficulties that unaccompanied minors experience in creating trusting relationships need to be taken into account, particularly when placing these young people in foster placements. Thirdly, professionals of all disciplines need to consider the potentially important role played by religious faith in the lives of unaccompanied minors. Otherwise, we will have an incomplete under-standing of how unaccompanied minors cope with the challenging experiences that they face.

ACKNOWLEDGEMENTS

The author would like to sincerely thank the young people who participated in the study and the HSE staff who facilitated it. The Ph.D. research on which this chapter was based was supervised by Professor Robbie Gilligan. The study was funded by the Office of the Minister for Children and Youth Affairs (formerly the National Children's Office) and by the Children's Research Centre and the School of Social Work and Social Policy, Trinity College Dublin.

NOTES

[1] In relation to the term 'unaccompanied minor' increasing attention has been paid to the fact that not all children who are separated from their parents or customary caregivers are 'unaccompanied' per se. For instance, some children may be living with extended family members, but may face similar risks to those encountered by unaccompanied refugee children. As a result, the use of the more inclusive term 'separated children' has been encouraged (e.g. UNHCR, 2004). However, as the

study being discussed in this chapter did not include unaccompanied children who were living with extended family members, the more specific term 'unaccompanied minor' will be used throughout.

[2] The research by Robins and Rylands is currently being published. The title of the research is "'A Child is a joy to the world' – The experience of unaccompanied minor mothers in Ireland: Supports, stressors, services." For further information the researchers can be contacted at leanne.robins@hse.ie or Jennifer.rylands@hse.ie.

[3] The regions used are those identified by the United Nations scheme of geographical regions.

[4] In quotations from the participants, square brackets indicate that some of the quotation was omitted, often because the material was not deemed relevant or was repetitive. Three dots indicate either that the participant did not complete the sentence or that there was a brief pause as he or she was thinking.

[5] 'Jane' is a pseudonym for one of the staff members in Valley Lodge, the hostel where the participant observation took place.

[6] In Ireland, the younger and most vulnerable unaccompanied minors are allocated a social worker. All of the hostels where unaccompanied minors live also have a project worker attached to them. Project workers often have a social care background, although not always.

[7] The word 'social' is used here to refer to a school disco.

[8] 'Shifting' is a word used by some Irish young people to refer to 'kissing'.

[9] At the time of writing hostels were being closed down and unaccompanied minors were being moved to approved residential homes and foster placements.

REFERENCES

Ai, A. L., Peterson, C., & Huang, B. (2003). The effect of religious-spiritual coping on positive attitudes of adult Muslim refugees from Kosovo and Bosnia. *The International Journal for the Psychology of Religion, 13*(1), 29–48.

Anderson, P. (2001). 'You don't belong here in Germany ...': On the social situation of refugee children in Germany. *Journal of Refugee Studies, 14*(2), 187–199.

Ayotte, W. (2000). *Separated children coming to Western Europe: Why they travel and how they arrive.* London: Save the Children.

Ayotte, W. (2002). *Separated children, exile and home-country links: The example of Somali children in the Nordic countries.* Copenhagen: Save the Children.

Bean, T. M., Eurelings-Bontekow, E., & Spinhoven, P. (2007). Course and predictors of mental health of unaccompanied refugee minors in the Netherlands: One year follow-up. *Social Science & Medicine, 64*, 1204–1215.

Bennett, J. A., & Detzner, D. F. (1997). Loneliness in cultural context: A look at the life-history narratives of older Southeast Asian refugee women. In A. Lieblich & R. Josselson (Eds.), *The narrative study of lives* (Vol. 5). London: Sage.

Bertrand, D. (2000). The autobiographical method of investigating the psychosocial wellness of refugees. In F. L. Ahearn, Jr. (Ed.), *Psychosocial wellness of refugees. Issues in qualitative and quantitative research.* Studies in Forced Migration (Vol. 7). Oxford: Berghahn Books.

Boss, P. (1999). *Ambiguous loss: Learning to live with unresolved grief.* London: Harvard University Press.

Carballo, M. (2000). Religion in the world at the end of the millennium. In Gallup International (Ed.), *Gallup international millennium survey.* Retrieved from http://www.gallup-international.com/Content Files/millennium15.asp

Chase, E., Knight, A., & Statham, J. (2008). *The emotional well-being of young people seeking asylum in the UK.* London: British Association for Adoption and Fostering.

Christie, A. (2002). Responses of the social work profession to unaccompanied children seeking asylum in the Republic of Ireland. *European Journal of Social Work, 5*, 187–198.

Cohen, S., & Wills, T. A. (1985). Social support, stress, and the buffering hypothesis. *Psychological Bulletin, 98*, 310–357.

Corbett, M. (2008). Hidden children: The story of state care for separated children. *Working Notes, 59,* 18–24.

Cutrona, C. E. (2000). Social support principles for strengthening families: Messages from the USA. In J. Canavan, P. Dolan & J. Pinkerton (Eds.), *Family support: Direction from diversity.* London: Jessica Kingsley Publications.

Daniel, E. V., & Knudsen, J. (Eds.). (1995). *Mistrusting refugees.* London: University of California Press.

Delaney, D. (2006). The asylum process and psychological needs of unaccompanied asylum seeking children in Ireland. *Studies – An Irish Quarterly Review, 95*(Spring), 2006.

Eisenbruch, M. (1991). From post-traumatic stress disorder to cultural bereavement: Diagnosis of Southeast Asian refugees. *Social Sciences and Medicine, 33*(6), 673–680.

German, M. (2004). Enabling reconnection: Educational psychologists supporting unaccompanied, separated, asylum-seeker/refugee children. *Educational and Child Psychology, 21,* 6–28.

Gilligan, R., Curry, P., McGrath, J., Murphy, D., Ni Raghallaigh, M., Rogers, M., et al. (2010). *In the front line of integration: Young people managing migration to Ireland.* Dublin: The Children's Research Centre, Trinity College.

Goodman, J. H. (2004). Coping with trauma and hardship among unaccompanied refugee youths from Sudan. *Qualitative Health Research, 14,* 1177–1196.

Goździak, E. M., & Shandy, D. J. (2002). Editorial introduction: Religion and spirituality in forced migration. *Journal of Refugee Studies, 15*(2), 129–135.

Hodes, M., Jagdev, D., Chandra, N., & Cunniff, A. (2008). Risk and resilience for psychological distress amongst unaccompanied asylum seeking adolescents. *Journal of Child Psychology and Psychiatry, 49,* 723–732.

Hopkins, P., & Hill, M. (2006). *'This is a good place to live and think about the future … ': The needs and experiences of unaccompanied asylum seeking children in Scotland.* Glasgow: Scottish Refugee Council.

Hynes, P. (2009). Contemporary compulsory dispersal and the absence of space for the restoration of trust. *Journal of Refugee Studies, 22,* 97–121.

Kohli, R., & Mather, R. (2003). Promoting psychosocial well-being in unaccompanied asylum seeking young people in the UK. *Child and Family Social Work, 8*(3), 201–212.

Kohli, R. (2006a). The comfort of strangers: Social work practice with unaccompanied asylum seeking children and young people in the UK. *Child and Family Social Work, 11,* 1–10.

Kohli, R. K. S. (2006b). The sound of silence: Listening to what unaccompanied asylum-seeking children say and do not say. *British Journal of Social Work, 36,* 707–721. Oxford: Oxford University Press.

Lee, R. M., & Renzetti, C. M. (1993). The problems of researching sensitive topics: An overview and introduction. In C. M. Renzetti & R. M. Lee (Eds.), *Researching sensitive topics.* London: Sage Publications.

Lippman, L. H., & Keith, J. D. (2006). The demographics of spirituality among youth: International perspectives. In E. C. Roehlkepartain, P. E. King, L. Wagener & P. L. Benson (Eds.), *The handbook of spiritual development in childhood and adolescence.* London: Sage Publications.

MacMullin, C., & Loughry, M. (2000). A child-centred approach to investigating refugee children's concerns. In F. L. Ahearn, Jr. (Ed.), *Psychosocial wellness in refugees: Issues in qualitative and quantitative research.* Oxford: Berghahn Books.

McCrea, N. (2003). *Steps towards inclusion: Developing youth work with separated children.* Dublin: Youth Action against Racism and Discrimination.

McMichael, C. (2002). 'Everywhere is Allah's place': Islam and the everyday life of Somali women in Melbourne, Australia. *Journal of Refugee Studies, 15*(2), 171–188.

McMichael, C., & Manderson, L. (2004). Somali women and well-being: Social networks and social capital among immigrant women in Australia. *Human Organization, 63*(1), 88–99.

Miller, K. E., Worthington, G. J., Muzurovic, J., Tipping, S., & Goldman, A. (2002). Bosnian refugees and the stressors of exile: A narrative study. *American Journal of Orthopsychiatry, 72*(3), 341–354.

Miller, K., Kushner, H., McCall, J., Martell, Z., & Kulkarni, M. (2008). Growing up in exile: Psychosocial challenges facing refugee youth in the United States. In J. Hart (Ed.), *Years of conflict: Adolescence, political violence and displacement.* London: Berghahn Press.

Mitchell, S. E. (1990). Development or restoration of trust in interpersonal relationships during adolescence and beyond. *Adolescence, 25*(100), 847–854.

Mooten, N. (2006). *Making separated children visible: The need for a child-centred approach*. Dublin: Irish Refugee Council.

Ní Laoire, C., Bushin, N., Carpena-Méndez, F., & White, A. (2009). *Tell me about yourself: Migrant children's experiences of moving to and living in Ireland*. Cork, Ireland: University College Cork.

Ní Raghallaigh, M., & Gilligan, R. (2010). Active survival in the lives of unaccompanied minors: coping strategies, resilience, and the relevance of religion. *Child and Family Social Work. Child and Family Social Work, 15*(2), 226–237

Pargament, K. I. (1997). *The psychology of religion and coping: Theory, research, practice*. London: Guilford Press.

Rea, A. (2001). *Psychological needs, social support and estimates of psychological distress among unaccompanied refugee minors in Ireland*. Unpublished doctoral dissertation, Queens University, Belfast.

Robinson, V. (2002). 'Doing research' with refugees and asylum seekers. *Swansea Geographer, 37*, 61–67.

Rousseau, C., Said, T. M., Gagné, M. J., & Bibeau, G. (1998). Resilience in unaccompanied minors from the north of Somalia. *Psychoanalytic Review, 85*(4), 615–637.

Sahlein, J. (2002). When religion enters the dialogue: A guide for practitioners. *Clinical Social Work Journal, 30*(4), 381–401.

Separated Children in Europe Programme (SCEP). (2004). *Statement of good practice* (3rd ed.). Geneva: Save the Children & UNHCR.

Smyth, E., Darmody, M., McGinnity, F., & Byrne, D. (2009). *Adapting to diversity: Irish schools and newcomer students*. Dublin: The Economic and Social Research Institute.

Smyth, K., & Whyte, J. (2005). *Making a new life in Ireland: Lone refugee and asylum-seeking mothers and their children*. Dublin: Children's Research Centre, Trinity College.

Stanley, K. (2001). *Cold comfort: Young separated refugees in England*. London: Save the Children.

Summerfield, D. (2000). Childhood, war, refugeedom and 'trauma': Three core questions for mental health professionals. *Transcultural Psychiatry, 37*(3), 417–433.

Thomas, S., Thomas, S., Nafees, B., & Bhugra D. (2004). 'I was running away from death': The pre-flight experiences of unaccompanied asylum seeking children in the UK. *Child: Care, Health and Development, 30*, 113–122.

Thompson, N. E., & Gurney, A. G. (Eds.). (2003). 'He is everything': Religion's role in the lives of immigrant youth. In *New Directions for Youth Development*, Issue 100. Wiley Publications.

Vekic, K. (2003). *Unsettled hope: Unaccompanied minors in Ireland: From understanding to response*. Dublin: The Centre for Education Services, Marino Institute.

Wade, J., Mitchell, F., & Baylis, G. (2005). *Unaccompanied asylum seeking children: The response of social work services*. London: British Association for Adoption and Fostering.

Wallin, A. M., & Ahlström, G. I. (2005). Unaccompanied young adult refugees in Sweden, experiences of their life situation and well-being: A qualitative follow-up study. *Ethnicity and Health, 10*, 129–144.

Muireann Ní Raghallaigh
School of Applied Social Science
University College Dublin

CORONA JOYCE AND EMMA QUINN

14. POLICY RESPONSES TO UNACCOMPANIED MINORS IN IRELAND

INTRODUCTION

An "unaccompanied minor" is defined as a person below the age of eighteen who arrives in a country "…unaccompanied by an adult who is responsible for them whether by law or custom".[1] They may also be referred to as separated children although in the current research this term is taken to refer to a broader group.[2] Available data indicate that the number of unaccompanied minors arriving in Ireland increased significantly during the 1990s and peaked in 2001 before falling off quite steadily. This trend is in line with general non-EU immigration to the Republic of Ireland. While the number of unaccompanied minors referred to the Health Service Executive (HSE)[3] has declined in recent years, they are still a significant group with very specific and critical needs as demonstrated later on in the chapter. This chapter provides an overview of the number of unaccompanied minors who have arrived in Ireland in recent years and explores why such potentially high-risk migration takes place. This is followed by a discussion of the response of the Irish State. Furthermore, it will be shown that State policy has evolved in a piecemeal manner, with a high level of discretion still in evidence at local level, particularly regarding HSE care provision. The particular issues of age assessment, asylum, legal immigration status and return of unaccompanied minors will be discussed in the subsequent section. The chapter also touches upon a conflict between an unaccompanied minor as a protection applicant or person of otherwise undefined legal (immigration) status, versus a minor who should invoke the 'best interests' of the child principle. This chapter specifically focuses on the experience and expertise of service providers, while many of the existing studies in the area consist of primary research with unaccompanied minors.[4]

METHODOLOGY

This chapter draws on the findings of the Irish contribution to a European Migration Network study into existing policies on unaccompanied minors (Joyce and Quinn, 2009).[5] The aim of the original study was to present information on the numbers of unaccompanied minors and current policies and practices on reception, integration and return of unaccompanied minors. The EU-wide study was intended to provide an overview of provision in the area across Member States, to highlight presenting issues and challenges as well as instances of best practice with a view to assisting

Darmody, Tyrrell, Song (eds.), The Changing Faces of Ireland: Exploring the Lives of Immigrant and Ethnic Minority Children, 237–252.

policy formation at national and EU level. Of note, the *Stockholm Programme* was adopted by the European Parliament in December 2009 and defined the priorities of the European Union (EU) in the areas of freedom, security and justice (JLS) issues from 2010 to 2014. Of particular relevance, the Programme saw the European Council call upon the European Commission to give 'special attention' to children in 'particularly vulnerable situations' including: "...children that are victims of sexual exploitation and abuse as well as children that are victims of trafficking and unaccompanied minors in the context of immigration policy." (Council of the European Union, 2009).

Particular recognition is provided to minors within the asylum system and it is requested that 'priority' be given to the reception and international protection needs of unaccompanied minors. The Stockholm Programme recognised the challenges for Member States when dealing with this group and identified areas requiring 'particular attention' as those of:

> ...the exchange of information and best practice, minor's smuggling, co-operation with countries of origin, the question of age assessment, identification and family tracing, and the need to pay particular attention to unaccompanied minors in the context of the fight against human trafficking (*Ibid.*).

In Ireland no national policy for unaccompanied minors is currently in operation, and relatively little printed policy information exists. Desk research for the study was therefore supplemented with a number of interviews with key State, Inter-Governmental Organisations (IGO) and Non-Governmental Organisations (NGO) actors in the field including: the Anti-Human Trafficking Unit (AHTU), Department of Justice, Equality and Law Reform; the Garda National Immigration Bureau (GNIB); HSE Crisis Intervention Service; International Organization for Migration (IOM) Dublin; Irish Naturalisation and Immigration Service (INIS), Department of Justice, Equality and Law Reform; Irish Refugee Council (IRC); the Office of the Refugee Applications Commissioner (ORAC); and the Refugee Legal Service (RLS). Front line services are provided to unaccompanied minors by Health Service Executive (HSE) social work teams. As will be discussed below the approach adopted by social work teams can vary widely and in order to investigate such regional variations interviews were conducted with the Liberty House Social Work Team in Cork, HSE South; the Social Work Team, HSE Wexford; and the dedicated Social Work Team for Separated Children Seeking Asylum, HSE Dublin South.[6]

One of the most significant challenges to researching unaccompanied minors in Ireland is the lack of accurate, national-level statistics. The limited statistics that exist are confined to specific geographical HSE areas and cannot be aggregated to the national level because (a) not all HSE social work teams collect data on un-accompanied minors, (b) there is no agreed standard on exactly which data to collect, and (c) there is no way of safeguarding against double counting of minors who move from the care of one social work team to another. Even within one social work team double-counting of individual minors who move care placements can be a problem.

Most unaccompanied minors in Ireland fall under the care of the HSE Dublin Social Work Team for Separated Children Seeking Asylum, hereafter referred to as the HSE Dublin Social Work Team for Separated Children.[7] Statistics collected by this team will be the main source of quantitative data used in this chapter. The Office of the Refugee Applications Commissioner (ORAC) also maintains detailed data on unaccompanied minor asylum applicants and these data will be discussed below.[8]

OVERVIEW IN NUMBERS OF UNACCOMPANIED MINORS IN IRELAND

The number of unaccompanied minors referred to the HSE Dublin Social Work Team for Separated Children during the period 2000 to 2008 is shown in Table 1. In 2001 the number of minors referred peaked at 1,085 and has declined steadily since. Although these data relate to referrals to the HSE Dublin Social Work Team for Separated Children only, other social work teams consulted in Cork and Wexford related a similar trend at a much lower level. As discussed above a total, national count of unaccompanied minors in Ireland does not exist.

Between 2004 and 2008 Nigerian nationals accounted for between 49–60 per cent of unaccompanied minors referred to the Dublin Social Work Team for Separated Children. The gender breakdown of the minors is quite even throughout the period. This is unusual in an international context: UNHCR data indicate that in most

Table 1. Referrals to HSE Dublin social work team for separated children 2000–2008

	2000	2001	2002	2003	2004	2005	2006	2007	2008	Total
Total Referrals	520	1,085	863	789	617	643	516	336	319	5,688

Source: HSE Dublin Social Work Team for Separated Children.

Table 2. Top five nationalities of unaccompanied minors referred to HSE Dublin social work team for separated children 2004–2008

2004	%	2005	%	2006	%	2007	%	2008	%
Nigeria	59.9	Nigeria	59.0	Nigeria	51.8	Nigeria	50.5	Nigeria	48.5
Romania	6.7	Romania	10.1	Romania	13.2	China	6.9	China	6.0
DR Congo	3.5	Somalia	5.9	Somalia	6.8	Ghana	5.3	Zimbabwe	6.0
Moldova	3.2	DR Congo	2.8	Guinea	2.5	Somalia	5.3	DR Congo	5.7
Somalia	3.0	Moldova	2.2	China	2.3	Camer-oon	2.8	Malawi	2.7
Other	23.6	Other	20.0	Other	23.3	Other	29.3	Other	31.3
Total	100.0	Total	100.0	Total	100.0	Total	100.0	Total	100.0

* This table is indicative only. The annual totals of the disaggregated nationality data do not exactly match the data on total referrals. This is because nationality data were not available for all referred minors. Furthermore, in some years minors were "double counted" in the HSE records.

Source: HSE Dublin Social Work Team for Separated Children.

European countries unaccompanied minors tend to be predominantly male (UNHCR, 2007). In 2004, 63 per cent of unaccompanied minors referred to the HSE Dublin Social Work Team for Separated Children were under 14 years old and 37 per cent were aged 14–17 years. The balance steadily shifted and in 2008, 57 per cent of un-accompanied minors referred were aged 14–17 years, while 44 per cent were aged 13 years and under.

WHY DO UNACCOMPANIED MINORS TRAVEL TO IRELAND?

There are many reasons why children undertake or are sent on such potentially dangerous journeys alone. Social workers indicated that children in poor health, often with chronic illnesses such as sickle cell anaemia or Hepatitis B, may be sent to Ireland by their parents in order to receive medical attention. Minors may also be sent in order to access educational opportunities not available to them in their home countries. Some are trafficked into the country to enter forced labour or prostitution. Accessing reliable data on trafficking is a huge problem, partly because the crime is so hard to prove. A recently published report on sex trafficking and prostitution (kelleherassociates et al., 2009) indicated that over a 21-month period between 2007 and 2008, 102 women and girls presented at Irish services who may be considered victims of trafficking using the definition set out in the UN Palermo Trafficking Protocol.[9] Of these, 11 were children at the time they were trafficked.

Substantial numbers of unaccompanied minors in Ireland claim asylum. Between 2002 and 2008, approximately 2–3 per cent of the total applications for asylum to the Office of the Refugee Applications Commissioner (ORAC) per year have been made by unaccompanied minors. Table 3 shows the number of asylum applicants who were unaccompanied minors at the time of their application. There is an incentive for unaccompanied minors to apply for asylum on or after arrival in Ireland to regularise their status; if they do not do so they do not technically have an immigra-tion status. The issue is particularly pertinent for minors who are about to turn 18 and this problem is explored further below.

There is an important distinction to be made between minors who arrive un-accompanied but who have family resident in Ireland and those who arrive alone and have no family in the State. Figures from the HSE Dublin Social Work Team for Separated Children indicate that between 2002 and 2007 one-half to two-thirds of unaccompanied minors were reunited with family members after referral to the service. In 2008, just under half of minors referred to the service were reunited with

Table 3. Asylum applications made by unaccompanied minors 2002–2008

	2002	2003	2004	2005	2006	2007	2008
Asylum applications made by UAMs	288	271	128	131	131	94	98
Total asylum applications	11,634	7,900	4,766	4,323	4,314	3,985	3,866
UAMs as % of total asylum applications	2.5	3.4	2.7	3.0	3.0	2.4	2.5

Source: Office of the Refugee Applications Commissioner.

family. Some children may then proceed to claim asylum after they have joined their family.

It is possible that recent policy developments around citizenship have influenced the flow of unaccompanied minors. In 2000, 21 per cent of unaccompanied minors referred to the Dublin service were subsequently reunited with family. This proportion grew steadily and peaked at 69 per cent in 2005. In January 2005 there was a very significant change in relation to non-Irish nationals and Irish citizenship. Prior to the enactment of the *Irish Nationality and Citizenship Act, 2004* which commenced in 2005, Ireland granted citizenship to everyone born on the territory. Non-Irish parents of Irish-born children could apply for residency based on the Irish citizenship of their child, up to January 2003 when the processing of such claims was suspended. This provision led to concerns that immigrants were travelling to Ireland and having children in order to gain residency in Ireland. It is possible that during this period older siblings of Irish-born children travelled to join parents in Ireland. After a referendum in 2004 and a subsequent Constitutional amendment, changes in citizenship provisions were enacted which mean that any person born in Ireland after 1 January 2005 to non-Irish parents would not be automatically entitled to be an Irish citizen unless one of the parents was lawfully resident in Ireland for at least three out of the four years preceding the child's birth. In January 2005, the families of Irish-born children were invited to apply for permission to remain in Ireland under the *Irish Born Child 2005 Scheme* (IBC/05).[10] Almost 18,000 applications were submitted under the Scheme and of these almost 16,700 were approved. During 2007 arrangements were put in place for the processing of applications for renewal under the IBC/05 Scheme and 14,117 renewals had been granted by year-end 2008 (Joyce, 2009). Applicants under the IBC/05 Scheme were asked to sign a declaration which stated that they understood that, if they were granted residency, this would not give them any entitlement to reunification with any other family members residing outside of the country. This was widely (and incorrectly) interpreted as a ban on family reunification applications made by parents resident here under the IBC/05 Scheme. NGOs have commented that this confusion probably led to large numbers of older siblings being brought into the country by informal channels, and as unaccompanied minors in some cases.

EXISTING STATE PROVISION FOR UNACCOMPANIED MINORS IN IRELAND

On Arrival to Ireland

Every minor who presents at an Irish border must be admitted to the State; the best interests of the child must always take precedence. Under the *UN Convention on the Rights of the Child* (1989) the State is obliged to provide all unaccompanied minors with the same level of treatment as national or resident minors. An unaccompanied minor:

> …shall be accorded the same protection as any other child permanently or temporarily deprived of his or her family environment for any reason, as set forth in the present Convention (Article 22, UN Convention on the Rights of the Child (1989)).

There is no dedicated domestic instrument dealing with unaccompanied minors in Ireland. The two Acts that are most relevant here are the *Refugee Act, 1996* and the *Child Care Act, 1991*. The *Refugee Act, 1996* states that in cases where it appears that a minor presenting at the border or within the State is alone or in the company of an adult with whom the Immigration Officer is not satisfied has a genuine relationship with the child, the Immigration Officer must contact the HSE as soon as possible and thereafter, the provisions of the *Child Care Act, 1991* apply, meaning that the HSE assumes responsibility for that child. The *Child Care Act* places an obligation on the HSE to have regard to the principle that it is generally in the child's best interests to be with his or her own family. The Act is wide-ranging and makes no specific reference to unaccompanied minors.

While the official position is that unaccompanied minors are not to be refused permission to enter the State, some NGOs have stated concern that on occasion unaccompanied minors are turned away at the border due to an age dispute. The Garda National Immigration Bureau (GNIB) refutes such claims arguing that while mistakes may be made when a child first presents with an Immigration Officer (such as age-assessing minors as adults), such errors are resolved by working with the relevant social work teams and do not result in the refusal of entry of an unaccompanied minor to the State.

Age assessments take place at the border, at point of reception and by ORAC if an unaccompanied minor applies for asylum. At the border, age assessment interviews are conducted by Immigration Officers with an interpreter present or available over the phone. Basic questions are asked on topics such as school and the reason for travel while taking account of the maturity of the person.

In cases where an Immigration Officer has concerns that a minor is being brought into Ireland or met by an adult who is not a family member or carer, the Immigration Officer conducts interviews with the adult and child to ascertain whether a genuine relationship exists. If it is suspected that the minor has been smuggled or trafficked into Ireland or other types of criminality have been exposed, the Gardaí may invoke an Emergency Care Order under Section 12 of the *Child Care Act* and the child will be removed to a place of safety.

While all parties agree that it would be preferable for a social worker to attend all interviews involving minors at the border in practice resources do not yet exist for such a presence. Photographing and/or fingerprinting of minors is not standard practice at the border, although the GNIB are now taking photos and fingerprinting in cases of unaccompanied minors who present and are identified as being at high risk of going missing or being re-trafficked.

Reception, Care Placements and Social Work Supports

The HSE has defined its role regarding unaccompanied minors via the *Refugee Act, 1996* (as amended) and *Child Care Act, 1991* and stated that its main responsibilities are as follows:
− To assist in the decision as to whether it is in the best interests of the child to make an application for asylum,

- If it is decided that the child should seek asylum to support them through the application process,
- To provide for the immediate and ongoing needs and welfare of the child through appropriate placement and links with health, psychological, social and educational services.[11]

Responsibility for the welfare of all children considered to be 'at risk' in the country (regardless of nationality) is delegated by the HSE to HSE Administrative Areas, which in turn, administer local Community Care Areas on an operational level.[12] In practice, this has resulted in each Administrative Area seeking legal advice and applying their own decision on how best to apply the *Child Care Act, 1991* to the care of unaccompanied minors. This decision is based on an assessment of which application of the Act best suits the local situation in terms of current practice and available resources, especially child placements. The minors must be referred to the social work team operational in the geographical area in which they present. Service provision to unaccompanied minors who arrive in Ireland therefore depends very much on where children are found or make themselves known to the authorities.

The three social work teams interviewed for this research apply different sections of the *Child Care Act, 1991*. In Cork, the Liberty Street Social Work Team mainly applies Section 5 of the Act and provides services to unaccompanied minors on par with out-of-home Irish minors. In the greater Dublin area the dedicated HSE Dublin Social Work Team for Separated Children take unaccompanied minors into voluntary care under Section 4 of the Act while in Wexford social work team invokes several parts of the *Child Care Act, 1991* depending on the exact circumstances and nature of the case. For example, if the child is over 16 years they are usually treated as out-of-home minors. If they are under 16 years, they are usually taken fully into care under Section 13 (Emergency care order), followed by Section 17 and 18 (Interim Care Order and Care Order).

Such variations in the local social work teams' approach to the care of unaccompanied minors are a consequence of each team trying to match existing resources to the local situation. This inconsistency in approach impacts negatively on data gathering and information sharing. These implications are discussed further in the conclusions to this chapter.

The standard of placement available to unaccompanied minors has been criticised by NGOs and child rights organisations, in particular the lack of equity with that provided to Irish out-of-home minors. The type of care placement depends on the age and perceived vulnerability of the child. In the Dublin region the accommodation situation is improving.[13] Minors under 12 years old are always placed in foster homes. Minors between 12 and 16 years are, or will be (new centres are opening), housed in residential units where each residential unit can house 6 young people. There are also 6 hostels: 3 hostels for males aged between 16 and 18 years and 2 for females aged between 16 and 18 years. There will also be one for mothers (aged 16–18 years) with babies. Care workers are not on site in these hostels and the social work team provides services on a Monday to Friday office hour basis.

The *Child Care Act, 1991* does not provide for the enforcement of various regulations for children residing in hostels which are contracted to private entities by the HSE. In practice this means that there is no legislative provision for the inspection of environment and accommodation against the standard for Children's Residential Centres for unaccompanied minors in hostels which are managed by private service providers.[14] Research conducted by the Ombudsman for Children's Office found that 7 of the 9 accommodation centres for unaccompanied minors in Dublin were provided by non-statutory service providers and not subject to independent inspection (Ombudsman for Children's Office, 2009). The Irish Refugee Council (among other parties) has drawn repeated attention to the inadequacy of available care placements and the possible link between poorly staffed facilities and children going missing from care (Mooten, 2006; Barnardos, 2009).

In the period January 2000 to May 2009, 486 unaccompanied minors went missing from State care. Of these, 61 have been accounted for. While it is likely that some of the missing minors may simply have reunited with family either in Ireland or elsewhere, others may have been trafficked into forced labour or prostitution. Social workers interviewed stated that certain patterns have been observed in the disappearance of children. In Cork, Romanian children and in Wexford, Romanian and Moldovan children have been deemed to be at risk of disappearing, while in recent years numbers of Chinese minors have disappeared from Dublin care placements. Several of those interviewed for this research expressed the belief that traffickers were aware of the locations of hostels used to house unaccompanied minors and whether they were staffed appropriately by qualified childcare workers. Social workers consulted for the study stressed the importance of having trained professionals on site in order to try to gain the trust of vulnerable minors.[15]

In the *Implementation Plan of the Report of the Commission to Inquire into Child Abuse, 2009* the Irish government announced a 99-point plan to strengthen the child protection system including the cessation of separately run hostels for unaccompanied minors. By December 2010, all unaccompanied minors are to be accommodated in mainstream care 'on a par with other children in the care system'. It is undertaken that in the interim period the HSE will inspect and register residential centres and hostels where unaccompanied minors are placed. The *National Action Plan to Prevent and Combat Trafficking of Human Beings in Ireland 2009–2012* stated that the HSE is currently developing a Plan to mainstream the services provided to separated children and "...the practice of accommodating children in hostels will be brought to an end as alternative arrangements become available. The main focus of the Plan is to place children in families and local communities throughout the State."[16]

Perhaps linked to a disparity in application of the *Child Care Act, 1991* and available resources, regional disparities in the level of available social work supports is also in evidence. For example in the Dublin region only the most vulnerable unaccompanied minors (such as suspected victims of trafficking and mothers with infants) are guaranteed a dedicated social worker, whereas in Cork all unaccompanied minors are allocated a social worker. However, within Dublin unaccompanied minors who present at night or during the weekend are referred to the Out-of-Hours Social Work Team which is part of the Crisis Intervention Service (CIS).[17] This service does not exist outside of Dublin and how children are dealt with varies greatly. In Cork unaccompanied children who are not deemed to be at high risk are referred directly to emergency hostel accommodation. In other parts of the country, for example Wexford, children may be sent to local hospitals and are referred to the local social work team when the office reopens.

The importance of adequate out-of-hours support was repeatedly stressed in the course of this research due to the fact that children quite often go missing from care at the weekends or at night when social work supports are at their weakest. In cases of suspected trafficking, a child may not yet realise that he or she has been trafficked and may have either placed their trust in the trafficker or be afraid to disobey. It was reported by the Anti-Human Trafficking Unit, among other bodies, that there are indications that traffickers or smugglers deliberately bring children in at those times when social work supports are low though this is not possible to verify based on information currently available.[18]

In 2008, 46 per cent of unaccompanied minors referred to the Dublin Social Work Team for Separated Children were subsequently reunited with family members in Ireland. All social work teams conduct a series of checks to verify the relationship of the minor to the alleged family members before allowing reunification. Documents such as birth certificates and photographs are routinely requested. Crosschecks may also be made with ORAC's records where asylum applicants are asked to list their children and/or family members upon completion of their initial questionnaire. Social work teams may also undertake verification checks with the GNIB, local Gardaí, Community Welfare Officers, Public Health Nurses and social workers in the local area of residence of the family member if different to the area where the child presented. The Dublin Social Work Team for Separated Children routinely uses DNA testing of the minor and family member but this is not standard practice in all parts of the country. Reunification will proceed only if the social worker is satisfied that it is in the minor's best interests.

All social workers interviewed expressed concern about the fact that they have in-sufficient resources to conduct follow-up checks on family reunifications. The history of separation between the child and their family members/guardians, together with their relocation to another country, means that there is a potential for substantial relationship difficulties upon reunification. The potential for follow up is even less likely in cases where families relocate to a different Community Care Area (CCA) due to a potential breakdown in communication between CCAs and restricted resources.

Guardianship for unaccompanied minors is provided for under section 26 of the *Child Care Act, 1991* where provision for the appointment of a *guardian ad litem* under certain circumstances is outlined. This is not, however, common practice in any of the HSE Regions interviewed. A *guardian ad litem* is an independent representative appointed by the court to both ensure that the views of the child are heard by the court and to advise the court on the best interests of the child. Guardians may be appointed by judges for the purposes of appeals or court order applications but it is uncommon. This practice has been criticised by many NGOs, including the Irish Refugee Council (2008) and Barnardos (2008) who have called for the insertion of provision for appointment of a *guardian ad litem* for all unaccompanied minors in the *Immigration, Residence and Protection Bill, 2008*.[19] The Department of Justice,

Equality and Law Reform (2009) has stated that under the *Child Care Act, 1991* the HSE project and/or social worker involved must regard the "welfare of the child as the first and paramount consideration" which therefore mitigates the need for a *guardian ad litem*. Others have questioned whether the HSE has a conflict of interest in taking on such a role.[20]

AGE ASSESSMENT

Age assessment is a difficult and cross-cutting issue. Adults may state that they are aged less than 18 years in order to be allowed leave to land and to benefit from the special protections available to children. Conversely, young people aged under 18 years may hold identity documents which suggest that they are adults, thus enabling them to cross borders without arousing suspicion. Criticism of the age assessment process centres on a lack of consistent, standardised testing by bodies in conjunction with a formalised appeals process.[21] All of those interviewed for this study have stated that the nature of age assessment is not a precise matter, with a potential for a margin of error several years in each direction particularly in cases of minors close to 18 years. In Ireland, interviews (by social workers, Immigration Officers and ORAC officials) and age assessment tools are used to assess age. There is no current written policy regarding age assessment determination and consequently variation exists in how different actors undertake such assessment. Several NGOs, including the Irish Refugee Council, have called for the adoption of a clear policy on age assessment in line with best international practice in order to limit the amount of discretion used by individual officers (Irish Refugee Council, 2008).

Social work teams assess an unaccompanied minor's age when a minor enters State care by using a social work assessment tool. ORAC also assesses the age of an unaccompanied minor applying for asylum via a specific interview for such a purpose. In cases of age dispute, the asylum applicant has the right to a review of his or her age assessment by a more senior officer in ORAC. In practice there is a large degree of consensus between ORAC and the HSE on age assessment and an inter-agency decision is taken regarding disputed age status decisions. If the authorities cannot agree on a precise age, the final benefit of the doubt is given to the individual concerned but social workers and ORAC officials expressed concern that there is thus potential for adults to be housed alongside children in hostel accommodation. A lack of clarity regarding the process exists, in particular with regard to age reassessments of persons claiming to be under the age of 18 and placed in adult accommodation centres.

A related issue is that of detention. Officially, a minor should not be detained in Ireland unless they commit a crime. NGOs have reported cases in which minors have arrived without the necessary documentation and were detained as adults, sometimes for several weeks, without an age assessment interview or having been age assessed as being over 18 years. In response to these claims, the Garda National Immigration Bureau (GNIB) argue that, in some cases, the person initially claims to be an adult or is holding documents identifying them as an adult and this may be why they do not receive an age assessment interview until they identify themselves as a minor.

CLAIMING ASYLUM AS AN UNACCOMPANIED MINOR

Between 2002 and 2008, 1,141 unaccompanied minors have applied for asylum in Ireland (Table 4). During this same timeframe, 312 unaccompanied minors were granted asylum in Ireland at first instance.

Table 4. Unaccompanied minors granted asylum in Ireland at first instance 2002–2008

	2002	2003	2004	2005	2006	2007	2008
Asylum applications made by UAMs	288	271	128	131	131	94	98
UAMs Granted Asylum (by year of recommendation)	93	38	58	56	30	24	13

Source: Office of the Refugee Applications Commissioner.

During the course of interviews for this research, both social workers and NGOs expressed concern regarding the appropriateness of the asylum system as a whole for an unaccompanied minor. It was felt that the system is adult-oriented, involving legalistic language and has the potential to re-traumatise the minors involved. ORAC has stated that it recognises that some minors may manifest their fears in ways that are different to adults, and they may not be able to fully elucidate the reasons why they left their country of origin. In the examination of these claims, it may therefore be necessary to have greater regard to certain objective factors such as country of origin information, and to determine, based upon these factors, whether a minor may be presumed to have a well-founded fear of persecution. Specific procedures for working with minors under 14 years were introduced by ORAC in 2003. Unaccompanied minors in Ireland also have the right to apply for subsidiary protection or leave to remain in the State although no data exist in the public domain regarding the number of such claims made or their respective outcomes.

LEGAL STATUS OF UNACCOMPANIED MINORS AND AGED-OUT MINORS

In most cases unaccompanied minors have no immigration or legal status beyond being a minor 'in care' unless they have applied for or have been granted refugee status. As a result they often exist in an ambiguous legal status when they turn 18 years old. With regard to minors who were in the care of the HSE, the *Child Care Act, 1991* states that the HSE's responsibility towards them changes from 'shall' to 'may' upon turning 18 years. In some instances the way in which a minor has been processed under the *Child Care Act, 1991* can influence the ease or otherwise of their transition into adulthood in terms of State supports available. For example, a child registered as an out-of-home minor may progress more smoothly to being an out-of-home adult and benefit from additional support than a minor taken in under voluntary care.

Unaccompanied minors who have applied for protection are, upon turning 18 years, transferred from the care of the HSE to the direct provision accommodation system for adult asylum seekers, administered by the Reception and Integration Agency (RIA). Social workers consulted for this research argue that such direct provision centres can be unsuitable and stress the vulnerability of these young adults. Since the beginning of 2009, RIA has implemented a new policy of targeted dispersal of aged-out unaccompanied minors. Aged-out minor asylum applicants are now housed in one of five direct provision centres in Cork, Limerick, Sligo, Galway or Athlone. RIA states that the centres were selected because they are family centres and are close to education facilities and other supports such as youth networks.

RETURN OF UNACCOMPANIED MINORS

Unaccompanied minors may be transferred from Ireland under the Dublin Regulation to another EU country, including instances in which another family member may have submitted an asylum application. Given the difficulties in conducting family social work assessments in separate countries, DNA testing of alleged family members is routinely used in such cases. Unaccompanied minor transfers under the Regulation do not take place in cases where the social work team is either unable to establish contact with the referring body in the country of transfer or the standard of care in the receiving country is not deemed to be of an adequate standard. Between 2004 and July 2009, 7 unaccompanied minors have been transferred from Ireland under the Dublin Regulation.[22]

While no legislative prohibition to the deportation of unaccompanied minors exists, in practice no such deportations take place. Unaccompanied minors who "age-out" at 18 years may however be subject to a deportation order with regard to their country of origin

Unaccompanied minors in the care of the HSE are, in cases, offered the possibility of returning voluntarily to their country of origin under the IOM-run Voluntary Assisted Return and Reintegration Programme (VARRP). All decisions regarding return are taken by a social worker (and Judge when relevant) and according to the principles of the best interests of the child. Specific HSE return procedures vary according to the relevant care team and particular case, but generally include extensive family assessment in the country of origin and agreement regarding monitoring of the unaccompanied minor post-return. Post-return monitoring of the minor may be in the form of weekly or monthly telephone conversations with the minor and their family over a specified period of time, home visits to the family etc. Monitoring is however, dependent on the capacity of the IOM local office to carry out these activities. Between 2002 and 2008, 21 unaccompanied minor returns have taken place via IOM Dublin to 8 countries. Difficulties in verifying family information provided by the unaccompanied minor can often contribute to the low numbers of returns.

CONCLUSIONS

The current research highlights a number of issues and problems regarding the provision of services to unaccompanied minors in Ireland. The regional nature of service provision to this group in Ireland means that the experience of individual children depends on which part of the country they present at. Outside of the greater

Dublin area, services for such minors are at varying levels of development and influenced by the number of unaccompanied minors presenting, the work load of the responsible team and the available resources. There is also no official national forum for information sharing between social work teams on their experience of working with unaccompanied minors.[23] Standardised national data do not exist.

In a related vein, there is no national register of unaccompanied minors and this compromises the Gardaí or HSE's ability to trace a minor who goes missing in one part of the country and reappears in the services of another social work team or indeed in another country. Overall, minors may be afraid to reveal their true identity, age or route of travel or may have been instructed not to. Fingerprinting of minors at the border is not routine and its possible introduction has raised concerns regarding the 'criminalisation' of minors. The amount of identifying information on unaccompanied minors stored by each social work team varies greatly according to region and perceived vulnerability of the minor.[24]

The devolved nature of care provision to this group and the many stakeholders involved has the effect that no individual actor, body or agency may be ultimately held accountable for the type and quality of reception and care of unaccompanied minors. Time and resource pressures mean that sufficient social work supports are not in place, for example for minors housed in hostels or to follow up on minors reunited with family in the State or to provide supports to aged-out minors. The absence of a national Out-of-Hours social work service is a presenting issue for both unaccompanied minors and other vulnerable groups in Ireland. Outside Dublin, un-accompanied minors who present between the hours of 5 pm and 9 am may be accommodated in an ad hoc manner. These children are recognised as being at high risk of going missing and are poorly protected from traffickers.

An unaccompanied minor who presents in Ireland, whether at a border or inland, automatically falls under the protection of the *Child Care Act, 1991*. This means that the HSE assumes responsibility for the promotion of the welfare of that child. However, in the vast majority of the cases concerning unaccompanied minors, the minor has no official immigration status and, therefore, no defined independent right to be in the country. This lack of legal status places individual minors in a very ambiguous position. When an unaccompanied minor turns 18 years old the *Child Care Act, 1991* states that the HSE's responsibility towards them then becomes discretionary. The regional nature of service provision to unaccompanied minors has the effect that minors may have very different experiences reaching the age of majority dependent upon the application of the *Child Care Act, 1991* by the local responsible team. In cases, social workers may recommend that unaccompanied minors make an asylum claim when nearing 18 years simply to regularise their status in order that they can access adult supports.

During the course of this research, the commitment of many individual social workers and others working with unaccompanied minors was evident, often in the context of limited resources and structural difficulties. There is a need for a targeted national-level policy for the care of unaccompanied minors in Ireland. It is reported that the HSE is developing an operational plan for this group but further information could not be found for the current research. In the absence of sufficient follow-up services, further research in the area (e.g. regarding reunified families; undertaking of a pilot exercise to collate local-level data on a centralised basis) may elucidate the situation of unaccompanied minors in Ireland. A formalised development of information-sharing channels between social work teams is also recommended.

NOTES

1. Temporary Protection Directive (Council Directive 2001/55/EC).
2. The European Migration Network (EMN) glossary (available at http://www.emn.europa.eu) defines a 'separated child' as a child under 18 years of age who is outside their country of origin and separated from both parents or their previous legal/customary primary caregiver. Some may be totally alone while others may be living with extended family members. All such children are separated children and entitled to international protection under a broad range of international and regional instruments. This definition covers both Third-Country National and EU National children, while unaccompanied minors can refer only to Third-Country Nationals.
3. The Health Service Executive (HSE) was established in January 2005 as the single national body responsible for meeting Ireland's health and social care needs, including social work services.
4. E.g. Ombudsman for Children's Office (2009).
5. The synthesis report of 22 EU member states' studies on this subject may be found at http://www.emn.europa.eu.
6. All terminology and referenced authority names were correct at time of publication of initial research.
7. This dedicated team was established in 2002 in order to provide services to an increasing number of unaccompanied minors arriving in Ireland. All referrals are non-EU nationals.
8. Figures lower than 10 cannot be published in order to protect the identity of those concerned.
9. Under the UN Palermo Trafficking Protocol, the 'consent' of the victim to the intended exploitation is irrelevant, provided that the trafficker has used threats, force, coercion, abduction, fraud, or deception, the abuse of power of a position or payments or benefits to achieve the consent of a victim. Significantly, where minors are concerned, consent to exploitation can never be present regardless of what methods are used. In the case of minors, the overall element of consent is also not relevant given the age of the victim.
10. A post-referendum Constitutional amendment in 2004 saw the enactment of the *Irish Nationality and Citizenship Act 2004*, which commenced in January 2005 and stipulated the grounds by which citizenship of children born on the island of Ireland may be granted. In January 2005 the Department of Justice, Equality and Law Reform moved to clarify the position of the non-Irish national parents of Irish-born children who had applied for residency on the basis of their Irish child but had had their claims suspended in 2003, and invited such persons to apply under the Irish Born Child 2005 Scheme (IBC/05). This was a special scheme under which non-Irish national parents of Irish children could apply for permission to remain in the State. Almost 18,000 applications were submitted under the 2005 Scheme, with 16,693 applications approved. An arrangement for renewal of leave to remain for the non-Irish national parents of Irish born children granted leave to remain under the IBC/05 Scheme occurred in 2007, with a further renewal arrangement put in place in 2010.
11. HSE *Services for Separated Children Seeking Asylum*. Available at http://www.hse.ie/eng/Find_a_Service/Children_and_Family_Services/Child_Welfare_and_Protection/Services_for_Separated_Children_Seeking_Asylum/
12. HSE West; HSE South; HSE Dublin North East; and HSE Dublin Mid Leinster.
13. As of January 2010 professionally qualified care staff have been placed in all remaining hostels within the Dublin Area. All remaining hostel accommodation is intended to close by December 2010.
14. See Conroy (2004) *Trafficking in Unaccompanied Minors* for further discussion on this topic.
15. A *Joint Protocol on Children Missing from Care* was signed by the Garda Síochána and the Health Service Executive in April 2009. This Protocol set out the roles and responsibilities of various agencies dealing with missing children and defines the course of action which should be taken by both organisations in cases where a missing child report is made (An Garda Síochána and the Health Service Executive, 2009).

[16] During 2010 the process of reception of unaccompanied minors within the Dublin Area changed both in terms of a move to a short-term assessment model (up to six weeks) and a policy of dispersal of young people to care placements (predominantly foster care placements) throughout Ireland. Once effected, these foster care placements place the unaccompanied minor under the care of the local care area. Regarding unaccompanied minors coming to the notice of service providers at first instance in places outside Dublin, a similar level of support through accommodation and social work/child care leader contact continues as previously.

[17] The Out-of-Hours Team provides a service between 6.00 pm. to 6.00 am, 365 nights of the year and also from 9.00 am to 5.00 pm each Saturday, Sunday and Bank Holiday.

[18] Ireland's response to the issue of trafficking has been criticised, most recently in the US State Department Trafficking in Persons Report 2008. However there have recently been significant administrative and legislative developments in relation to trafficking which impact on children trafficked into Ireland. A new Anti-Human Trafficking Unit produced a *National Action Plan to Prevent and Combat Human Trafficking* in June 2009. Furthermore the *Criminal Law (Human Trafficking) Act, 2008* creates an offence punishable by up to life imprisonment to traffic a child for the purpose of the child's sexual exploitation and seeks to give effect to the criminal law elements of the *Council Framework Decision of 2002 on Combating Trafficking in Human Beings; the UN Protocol to Prevent, Suppress and Punish Trafficking in Persons, Especially Women and Children; and the Council of Europe Convention on Action against Trafficking in Human Beings.*

[19] The *Immigration, Residence and Protection Bill, 2008* was withdrawn in 2010, with the *Immigration, Residence and Protection Bill,* 2010 launched in June 2010, incorporating many amendments to the 2008 Bill which had arisen during the legislative process.

[20] The Irish Refugee Council and University College Cork held a conference on "Guardianship and Migrant Children" in 2007. Some of the presentations may be viewed at http://ns3.ucc.ie/en/ccjhr/NewsandEventsArchive/bodytext,64751,en.html.

[21] See Ombudsman for Children's Office (2009) for further discussion on this topic.

[22] Ireland partakes in the Dublin Regulation regarding determination the Member State responsible for examining an asylum application. There are specific provisions for unaccompanied minors seeking asylum within the European Union, and reunification with family members legally present in another Member State highlighted as best practice if at all possible. Under the Humanitarian Clause, if the asylum seeking unaccompanied minor has a relative(s) in another Member State who may take care of them, Member States shall if possible reunite them if determined to be in the minor's best interests. A family member definition for unaccompanied minors is that of 'the father, mother or guardian when the applicant or refugee is a minor and unmarried'. In the absence of a family member, the Member State responsible for hearing an unaccompanied minor application for asylum shall be that where the minor has lodged their application for asylum.

[23] IOM Dublin coordinates a small working group on unaccompanied minors under the UAM Voluntary Assisted Return and Reintegration Programme (VARRP) which in the past has gathered social workers from Dublin, Cork and Galway at regular intervals to share experiences on UAMs, mainly in the context of return and reintegration.

[24] The *Immigration, Residence and Protection Bill, 2008* contains provisions for the registration of 'foreign national children' in the State. In general, at present, only those aged 16 years or over are required to register with the GNIB. However, the existing Section 38 of the Bill relates only to foreign nationals who receive a residence permit or make a protection application and would not include separated children who did not submit an application for protection.

REFERENCES

An Garda Siochana and the Health Service Executive. (2009). *Children missing from care: A joint protocol between An Garda Ssíochána and the Health Service Executive.*

Conroy, P. (2004). *Trafficking in unaccompanied minors.* Dublin: International Organization for Migration, Dublin.

Council of the European Union. (2009). *The stockholm programme. An open and secure Europe serving and protecting the citizens.* Swedish Presidency of the European Union. available at http://www.se2009.eu/polopoly_fs/1.26419!menu/standard/file/Klar_Stockholmsprogram.pdf

Barnardos. (2008). *Barnardos' submission to the joint committee on justice, equality, defence and women's rights: Immigration, residency and protection bill 2008.* Dublin: Barnardos.

Department of Justice, Equality and Law Reform. (2009). *National action plan to prevent and combat trafficking of human beings in Ireland 2009–2012.* Dublin: Department of Justice, Equality and Law Reform. Available at http://www.justice.ie/en/JELR/Final%20National%20Action%20Plan2.pdf/Files/Final%20National%20Action%20Plan2.pdf

Department of State (U.S.). (2009). *Trafficking in persons report 2008.* Available at http://www.state.gov/documents/organization/105655.pdf

Joyce, C. (2009). *Annual policy report on migration and asylum 2008: Ireland.* Dublin: The Economic and Social Research Institute.

Immigrant Council of Ireland. (2007). *Submission to the national action plan to prevent and combat human trafficking.* Available at http://www.immigrantcouncil.ie

Irish Refugee Council. (2008). *Ensuring protection for separated children: The Irish refugee council's submission on provisions of the immigration, residence and protection bill 2008 related to the protection of separated children.* Dublin: Irish Refugee Council. Available at http://www.irishrefugeecouncil.ie

Kelleherassociates, O'Connor, M., & Pillinger, J. (2009). *Globalisation, sex trafficking and prostitution: The experiences of migrant women in Ireland.* Dublin: Immigrant Council of Ireland.

Mooten, N. (2006). *Making separated children visible. The need for a child-centred approach.* Dublin: Irish Refugee Council.

Ombudsman for Children's Office (2009). *Separated children living in Ireland.* Dublin: Author. Available at http://www.oco.ie/assets/files/SeparatedChildrenProjectReport.pdf

UNHCR. (2009). *UNHCR statistical yearbook 2008.* Geneva: UNHCR. Available at http://www.unhcr.org/

Corona Joyce and Emma Quinn
The Economic and Social Research Institute
Dublin, Ireland

MERIKE DARMODY, NAOMI TYRRELL AND STEVE SONG

CONCLUSION

Immigrant and Ethnic Minority Children in Ireland:
New Challenges and New Opportunities

INTRODUCTION

There is a general consensus among researchers that due to increased globalization, migration is likely to remain an important feature of European societies for the foreseeable future (Heckmann 2009). While a number of policy documents address the issue of adult migration and integration, less attention has been paid to the experiences of immigrant children. Some of the areas that are yet to be fully explored include: the reasons for child migration, the experiences of migrant children, the effects of immigration policies on children, the consequences of adult migration for children who are left behind, and children's rights that are affected by a wider migration processes (Farrow, 2007). A growing number of authors acknowledge that while all immigrant children require some time to adapt to their situation in a new country, sometimes including a new culture and language, the experiences of children in the receiving country may vary according to their countries of origin - while some may 'acclimatise' with a relative ease, others may experience abuse and exploitation (Shuteriqi, 2007). In addition, many immigrant children may have resided in a number of countries, making their experiences particularly fractured (Niessen and Huddleston, 2009).

While considering migration trends in Europe, it is important to acknowledge that migrants in Europe are not a homogenous group, and the reasons behind their migration may differ greatly. While some are migrant workers, moving to a new country to improve their economic circumstances, others flee as refugees or asylum seekers fleeing from persecution or from war-torn countries. As with adult immigrants, it is possible to differentiate between different types of immigrant children: children of migrant workers, children arriving during the family reunification process, unaccompanied minors and asylum-seekers (de Wenden, 2007, Ní Laoire et al., 2009). These children often have markedly different experiences of the immigration and integration processes. In particular, separated children may find the migration experience challenging as they are lacking family support (Touzenis, 2007, Charles, 2009). As we discuss in the Introduction of this volume, it is important to understand that issues associated with immigration and integration are not only important for the individuals involved in the process but also for social cohesion in the receiving societies (European Commission, 2009; Heckmann, 2008). Continuing, and in some case increasing, immigration flows point to the need for receiving societies to adapt to new social realities; hence making immigration is a high political priority (European Commission, 2009).

While interest in immigrant children, and children in immigrant families, has grown in countries that have long histories of immigration (see Coe et al., forthcoming; Crawley, 2009; Crul and Vermeulen, 2003; Karsten, 2009; OECD, 2009; Penn and Lambert, 2009) over recent years, research is slowly starting to emerge in 'new' immigration countries. As exemplified in the chapters of this book, Ireland has experienced a sharp increase in the number of immigrants arriving from a number of different countries over the last 15 years. As outlined in the Introduction, the aim of this book was to contribute to the growing body of work focused on immigrant children in Ireland. As we have seen, Ireland is a particularly interesting country to focus on because of the extent, pace and heterogeneity of recent immigration (Darmody et al., forthcoming). In the following sections of this chapter we discuss some of the challenges and opportunities associated with the transformed social fabric of Ireland with a particular reference to immigrant and ethnic minority children.

NEW COUNTRY: NEW CHALLENGES AND NEW OPPORTUNITIES

It is generally recognised that immigrant children face many challenges when moving to a new country (European Commission, 2008). One of the greatest issues is proficiency in a language of the receiving country (Niessen and Huddleston, 2009). Previous research indicates that low levels of proficiency is likely to become a barrier for parents and children alike when accessing information about the education system of the country, and is likely to impede children's chances for successful social and academic integration (see Smyth, et al., 2009). In addition, while most policy documents focussing on immigrant children acknowledge the importance of acquiring the language of the host country (see European Commission (EC) Green Paper, 2008), a growing number of authors acknowledge the importance of maintaining heritage languages, especially from a human capital perspective (Niessen and Huddleston, 2009).

The Green Paper (2008) also highlights the importance of maintaining and learning heritage languages. It recognises that heritage language is 'valuable for the cultural capital and the self confidence of children of migrants, and it may also represent a key asset for their future employability (ibid, p. 10). The European Commission (2009) notes that linguistic diversity must be seen as having an asset to the society. In her chapter, Francesca La Morgia (Chapter 2) argues that as a result of migration, many children are growing up in Ireland speaking two or more languages. While this constitutes a positive change for the country, the process of understanding and valuing linguistic diversity and multilingualism generates the need for new policies, projects and initiatives that allow children to develop linguistic skills in English, Irish and the other languages spoken in their homes.

On the related issue of language and immigration, Rory McDaid (Chapter 3) examines the feelings, experiences and understandings of minority language children in the Irish primary education system with regard to language learning. The chapter focuses on two particular areas: the importance of learning English and the importance of maintaining, and developing, children's own first languages. Language is closely connected to an individual's identity. How young Poles in Ireland construct their identities through the patterns of language use at home and at school is discussed in the chapter by Niamh Nestor and Vera Regan (Chapter 4). The experiences of immigrant children in Ireland are also discussed by Angela Veale and Emily Kennedy (Chapter 5), focussing in particular on Indian young people's participation in immigration processes and their negotiation of transnational identities. What emerges from all four chapters is the fact that heritage languages receive little attention in schools in Ireland because of the focus on bringing the new arrivals 'up to speed' in the language of instruction (usually English). The European Commission (2009) emphasises that linguistic diversity must be seen as being an asset to societies. Considering the diversity of first languages spoken by immigrant and ethnic minority children, they suggest the involvement of communities, diasporas and of the countries of origin in providing tuition. They also call for increased teacher education in dealing with multicultural and multilingual classes. In 2007, the Department of Education and Skills increased the number of language support teachers in schools in Ireland. Unfortunately, recent government spending cuts have resulted in reduced provision in this area. The processes of understanding and valuing linguistic diversity and multilingualism in Ireland generates the need for new policies, projects and initiatives that allow children to develop linguistic skills in English, Irish and the other languages spoken in their homes.

Language is an important issue with regard to immigrant parents' links with schools. The EC Green Paper (2008) suggests that learning the new country's language is vital to immigrant children's educational success and that language is a barrier between immigrant families and schools. There is general consensus that parental involvement in schools is important for information to flow between the home and the school (Turney and Kao, 2009). It also has been found to have important implications for children's academic and behavioural outcomes (Becker and Epstein, 1982). In this book, Merike Darmody and Selina McCoy (Chapter 10) argue that parental involvement can be limited due to a number of factors acting as barriers: proficiency in the language of the receiving country, limited knowledge of educational system and school processes, and differences arising from cultural backgrounds. Being proficient in the language of the receiving country, parents can become more actively involved and greater involvement may translate into increased academic success for their children, in line with international research (Jeynes, 2003). In order to assist immigrant parents, the EC (2009) recommend that they are provided with accessible information on the education system of the country of residence and offered other types of assistance to enable them to become equal partners in their children's education. For this to happen, the report recommends the involvement of community mediators and the devising of programmes specially targeted towards immigrant parents. Similarly, the Education, Audiovisual and Culture Executive Agency (EACEA) (2009) outlines three methods of promoting communication between schools and immigrant families: publication of written information on the school system in the language of origin of immigrant families; the use of interpreters in various situations in the school life; and the appointment of resource persons (such as mediators) to be specifically responsible for liaising between immigrant pupils, their families, and schools. In Ireland, to date, the DES provides information on the education system in a number of different languages on its website. An additional resource that has the potential to be developed further in helping immigrant parents and children is the Home School Community Liaison Scheme that provides a bridge between schools and parents. In recent years, the Pathways to Parental Leadership toolkit[1] is being developed by in Ireland. The toolkit is aimed at helping immigrant parents to become more involved in their children's school lives.

Considering recent immigration trends have changed the social composition of many schools across Europe, an increasing importance has been attached to the need to develop intercultural education in schools that would benefit all children. Batelaan and Coomans (1999) argue that intercultural education should be promoted, in order to foster tolerance, understanding and respect between individuals as well as groups of people of different backgrounds. The United Nations Convention on the Rights of the Child states that "the education of the child shall be directed to the development of the child's personality, talents and mental and physical abilities to their fullest potential" (Article. 29a). However, as it is often seen in Ireland, newly arrived ethnic minority groups are given different status, resulting in inequality and discrimination between groups. Batelaan and Cooms (1999) argue that it is not possible to deal with issues of diversity without dealing with issues of inequality. Dympna Devine (Chapter 6) discusses the experiences of migrant children in Irish schools. She touches upon the dynamics of power and control in their relations with others that was influenced by perceptions of, and attitudes towards, cultural and ethnic difference. In his chapter, Karl Kitching (Chapter 7) examines some of the key issues facing certain ethnic minority and/or marginalised young people in schools in Ireland. He incorporates critiques of social exclusion in Ireland and challenges how social and educational exclusion have been framed discursively in official policy. In trying to overcome inequality in schools in Ireland, the pertinence of intercultural educational approaches are highlighted by Niamh Nestor and Vera Regan (Chapter 4), with regard to Polish children in Ireland; Audrey Byran (Chapter 8), who examines ethnic minority students' perceptions of curricular knowledge about their ethnic identities and their experiences of engaging with, and negotiating, this knowledge in learning contexts; and Emer Smyth and Merike Darmody (Chapter 9), in the context of provision of religious education in Irish schools What these chapters have in common is their acknowledgement that despite the provision of intercultural education guidelines for primary and secondary schools in Ireland, intercultural education approaches are still in their infancy. It is hoped that the recently published Intercultural Education Strategy (DES, 2010) will provide a framework for further positive policy changes in Irish schools.

It is important to acknowledge, as Michal Molcho, Colette Kelly and Saoirse Nic Gabhainn (Chapter 12) remind us, that immigrant children are different to adults in that the processes of immigration are more likely to be imposed on them rather than be their active decision. However, as with adults, immigrant children leave their homeland and settle in a new country, often with different norms and values, and need to adapt to a sometimes markedly different culture and socio-economic conditions, often facing discrimination and racism. Therefore immigration can have a marked affect on children's health and well-being, as the chapter by Bryan Fanning, Trutz Haase and Neil O'Boyle (Chapter 11) and Chapter 12 discuss. Related to children's well-being, authors in this book also have reflected upon the situations and experiences of immigrant children in Ireland who are particularly vulnerable and at risk. Deirdre Horgan, Shirley Martin and Jacqui O'Riordan (Chapter 13) examine the position of internationally trafficked children as a particularly invisible group of ethnic minority and immigrant children in Ireland and assess the successes and failures of policies that have been put in place for their protection. The chapter by Muireann Ní Raghallaigh (Chapter 14) points out that unaccompanied minors or separated children are faced with a host of challenges, relating to their pre-migration experiences, their journeys from their countries of origin to Ireland, and their post-migration lives. Following on from this, Corona Joyce and Emma Quinn (Chapter 15) critique state policy that is focused on this group of children in Ireland, discussing the increased numbers of unaccompanied minors and analysing the motivations for their immigration. They highlight the issue of age assessments, as well as discussing the numbers of unaccompanied minors currently missing from state care.

MOVING FORWARD

It is important to note that immigrant children and their families have a lot of positive attributes to offer the societies of their new countries and that their resources may well be insufficiently used. This book has discussed a number of key issues facing immigrant and ethnic minority children in Ireland today. As we pointed out in the book's Introduction, the empirical material and/or critique presented in the chapters contribute to a growing body or research in this area. The issues that the authors examine are not exhaustive and we hope that the book will prompt further research into, and discussion of, the experiences of immigrant and ethnic minority children in Ireland. Most of these children are of school-going age, hence many of the chapters have discuss the experiences of immigrant children in the context of education and schooling. The presence of significant numbers of these children has substantial implications for education systems of receiving countries such as Ireland (Byrne et al., 2010) and international research has highlighted the crucial role of schools in the 'integration' of children and young people into the new society (Gitlin et al., 2003). Immigrant children spend a large part of their day in schools, where they encounter students and teachers from the majority culture and learn to adjust to a new institutional environment (Darmody et al., forthcoming). The EC Green Paper (2008) suggests ways in which education policies may tackle some of the challenges posed by immigration. Key issues include: improving equity in education for all children, accommodating increased cultural and linguistic diversity, building intercultural skills, adapting teaching skills to new social realities, and forging links with immigrant families and communities. In Ireland, one way forward would be establishing intercultural and multilingual approaches in schools, and acknowledging that the presence of immigrant children has a positive effect on society as a whole because it increases cultural and linguistic diversity, raises awareness of different cultures and favours international contacts (see EC 2009). We feel that a whole school approach with strong support by schools' leaderships is crucial to ensuring successful inclusion of immigrant children in Irish society.

Immigration has benefited Ireland economically and has provided cultural diversity. Research has shown that immigrant children often are hard-working, motivated, and have high educational and career aspirations (Ní Laoire et al., 2009; Smyth et al., 2009). Therefore immigrant children should be considered to be positive assets to society in Ireland and considering that many immigrant families have made Ireland their home, it is vital to ensure that ethnic minority children have equal opportunities during their school years and beyond.

NOTES

[1]   Immigrant Council of Ireland in association with EPIM (European Programme for Integration and Migration, 2008–2011, see also http://www.ucd.ie/education/recentresearchactivitiesstaff/funded researchawards/.

REFERENCES

Byrne, D., McGinnity, F., Smyth, E., & Darmody, M. (2010). Immigration and school composition in Ireland. *Irish Educational Studies*, *29*(3), 271–288.

Central Statistics Office. (2008). *Non-Irish nationals living in Ireland*. Dublin: Stationery Office.

Charles, K. (2009). *Separated children living in Ireland, a report of the Ombudsman for Children's Office*. Dublin: Ombudsman for Children's Office.

Coe, C., Reynolds, R., Boehm, D. A., Meredith Hess, J., & Rae-Espinoza, H. (Eds.). (forthcoming). *Everyday ruptures: Children, youth, and migration in global perspective*. Tennessee, TN: Vanderbilt Press.

Crawley, H. (2009) The Situation of Children in Immigrant Families in the United Kingdom, *Innocenti Working Paper* No. 2009–18, Florence: UNICEF Innocenti Research Centre

Crul, M., & Vermeulen, H. (2003). The second generation in Europe. *International Migration Review*, *37*(4), 965–986.

Darmody, M., Smyth, E., Byrne, D., & McGinnity, F. (forthcoming). New school, new system: The experiences of immigrant students in Irish schools. In *Migration, minorities, and learning – Understanding cultural and social differences in education*.

Department of Education and Skills and the Office of the Minister for Integration. (2010). *Intercultural education strategy, 2010–2015*. Retrieved September 16, 2010, from http://www.education.ie/servlet/blobservlet/mig_intercultural_education_strategy.pdf

Devine, D. (2005). Welcome to the Celtic Tiger? – Teacher responses to immigration and increasing ethnic diversity in Irish schools. *International Studies in Sociology of Education*, *15*, 49–71.

Devine, D., & Kelly, M. (2006). I just don't want to get picked on by anybody': Dynamics of inclusion and exclusion in a newly multi-ethnic Irish primary school, *Children & Society*, *20*, 128–139.

Devine, D., Kenny, M., & MacNeela, E. (2004). Experiencing racism in the primary school - Children's perspectives. In J. Deegan, D. Devine, & A. Lodge (Eds.), *Primary voices-equality, diversity and childhood in Irish primary schools*. Dublin: Institute of Public Administration.

de Wenden, C. (2007, March 20–21). Child migration: A global perspective. In S. Swärd & L. Bruun (Eds.), *Conference report: Focus on children in migration - From a European research and method perspective*. Warsaw, Poland. Organised by Save the Children Sweden, Separated Children in Europe Programme and European Network of Masters in Children's Rights.

European Commission. (2008a). *Education and migration, strategies for integrating migrant children in European schools and societies*. A synthesis of research findings for policy makers, NESSE/European Commission.

European Commission. (2008b). *Green paper: Migration and mobility: Challenges and opportunities for EU education systems*. Brussels: Author.

European Commission. (2009). *Commission staff working document. Results of the consultation on the education of children from a migrant background*.

Eurydice. (2004). *Integrating immigrant children into schools in Europe*. Retrieved October 12, 2007, from http://www.eurydice.org/ressources/eurydice/pdf/catalogue_2003/catalogue_2003_EN.pdf

O'Connell Davidson, J. & Farrow, C. (2007). *Child Migration and the Construction of Vulnerability*, Stockholm: Save the Children Sweden, available at http://shop.rb.se/Product/Product.aspx?ItemId= 2967801

Hammarberg, T. (2007, March 20–21). The rights of children in migration must be defended. In S. Swärd & L. Bruun (Eds.), *Conference report: Focus on children in migration - From a European research and method perspective*. Warsaw, Poland. Organised by Save the Children Sweden, Separated Children in Europe Programme and European Network of Masters in Children's Rights.

Heckmann, F. (2009). *Education and migration, strategies for integrating migrant children in European schools and societies*. Brussels: European Commission. Available online.

Jeynes, W. (2003). A meta-analysis: The effects of parental involvement on minority children's academic achievement. *Education & Urban Society, 35*(2), 202–218.

Karsten, S. (2009). *The labour market integration of immigrants: School segregation*. Brussels: OECD.

Ní Laoire, C., Bushin, N., Carpena-Mendez, F., & White, A. (2009). *Tell me about yourself: Migrant children's experiences of moving to and living in Ireland*. Cork, Ireland: University College Cork.

Niessen, J., & Huddleston, T. (2009). *Handbook on integration for policy-makers and practitioners*. Brussels: European Commission.

OECD. (2009). *OECD reviews of migrant education: Closing the gap for immigrant students, policies, practice and performance*. Paris: Author.

Smyth, E., Darmody, M., McGinnity, F., & Byrne, D. (2009). *Adapting to diversity: Irish schools and newcomer students*. Dublin: ESRI.

Penn, R., & Lambert, P. (2009). *Children of international migrants in Europe: Comparative perspectives*. Basingstoke: Palgrave Macmillan.

Shuteriqi, M. (2007, March 20–21). Children in migration: Who are they and how can we assist? In S. Swärd & L. Bruun (Eds.), *Conference report: Focus on children in migration - From a European research and method perspective*. Warsaw, Poland. Organised by Save the Children Sweden, Separated Children in Europe Programme and European Network of Masters in Children's Rights.

Touzenis, K. (2007, March 20–21). The international protection of migrant children – Is it adequate? In S. Swärd & L. Bruun (Eds.), *Conference report: Focus on children in migration – From a European research and method perspective*. Warsaw, Poland. Organised by Save the Children Sweden, Separated Children in Europe Programme and European Network of Masters in Children's Rights.

Merike Darmody
Economic and Social Research Institute
Dublin

Naomi Tyrrell
School of Geography, Earth and Environmental Sciences
University of Plymouth

Steve Song
George Fox University
Oregon

BIOGRAPHICAL NOTES OF BOOK AUTHORS

Melíosa Bracken works as a researcher at the School of Education, University College Dublin. Her interests lie in the interface between formal and non-formal education, particularly in the areas of development education, adult education, adult literacy and community education. She is currently working on a major qualitative study with Dr Audrey Bryan exploring how notions of development issues, ideas and images are constructed, communicated and understood in Irish post-primary schools.

Dr Audrey Bryan teaches sociology in St. Patrick's College, Drumcondra. Her research publications include work on interculturalism, development studies, citizenship education, and sexuality, gender and schooling. Her current research involves an analysis of the cultural politics of teacher education reform in Sub-Saharan Africa and a study of representations of international development in Irish schools.

Dr Merike Darmody is a Research Officer at the Economic and Social Research Institute (ESRI) in the Republic of Ireland. She mainly works in the area of education but is also interested in broader issues of the relationship between an individual and society. Her more recent work includes a study focusing on the integration of immigrant students in Irish primary and secondary schools and a European comparative study on the provision of religious education in a multicultural society with a special focus on primary schools.

Dr Dympna Devine is a Senior Lecturer in the School of Education, UCD and General Editor of Irish Educational Studies. Her work spans the fields of Childhood Studies, Ethnic/migrant studies and professional development of teachers. In recent years she has specialised on the impact of immigration on schooling in Ireland and has engaged in wide ranging research on the experiences and practices of parents, teachers, school leaders and the role of the State in this area. Her specialist focus has been on processes of adaptation and dynamics of inclusion/exclusion in migrant children's everyday lives in schools. Her recent book 'Immigration and schooling in Ireland - making a difference' (Manchester University Press) is due to be published in spring.

Professor Bryan Fanning lectures in the School of Applied Social Science at University College Dublin (UCD). He is also co-director of the Migration and Citizenship Research Initiative (MCRI) at UCD. He is the author of Racism and Social Change in the Republic of Ireland (2002), Immigration and Social Change in the Republic of Ireland (2007) and most recently, New Guests of the Irish Nation (2009).

Trutz Haase is an independent Social and Economic Consultant and has worked for a number of Irish Government Departments, Local Authorities and non-governmental agencies. In his work as a consultant, Mr. Haase has been responsible for the design and implementation of monitoring and evaluation frameworks for government programmes aimed at alleviating poverty, as well as developing resource allocation models to target social expenditure on the basis of objective need criteria. He is best known for his work on the development of an Irish Index of Relative Affluence and Deprivation.

Dr Deirdre Horgan is a Lecturer in Social Policy at the School of Applied Social Studies at UCC since 1991. She is currently Deputy Director of the BA (Early Childhood Studies) a multi-disciplinary degree. She also teaches on the Social Science and Social Work degrees in the Department. Her primary research interests include child care policy, children's rights and citizenship, childhood & global diversity, early years care and education, child protection, family support, and personal social services. She is a member of the Child Migration and Social Policy research group in the School.

Corona Joyce is Policy Officer at the Irish National Contact Point of the European Migration Network at the Economic and Social Research Institute (ESRI) in the Republic of Ireland. She researches policy in the fields of migration and asylum in both national and EU contexts including involvement in tracking of activities under the European Pact on Immigration and Asylum and the Stockholm Programme in Ireland. Her more recent work includes an overview report of migration and asylum policy development and an analysis of Ireland's migration and asylum statistical data trends.

Dr Colette Kelly is a Senior Researcher in the Health Promotion Research Centre, National University of Ireland Galway, Ireland. Colette is the project manager for the Health Behaviour in School-aged Children (HBSC) survey in Ireland and her particular research expertise is the dietary behaviours of young people and the factors influencing their food choice.

Dr Karl Kitching is a Lecturer in the School of Education, University College Cork, and previously worked as a primary school teacher in Blanchardstown, Dublin. His current and forthcoming publications focus on the ways in which new migrant students are considered acceptable or unacceptable in educational settings, particularly in terms of racism, class and gender inequalities. His next research project aims to analyse children and family experiences and media representations of First Holy Communion in Ireland.

Francesca La Morgia is teaching fellow in Psycholinguistics at the University of Reading. She has also taught linguistics at University College Dublin and Dublin City University. Her main research interests are child language development and child bilingualism. She is the founder of the information and consultancy service Bilingual Forum Ireland, which was awarded the European Award for Languages – The Language Label in 2009.

Dr Shirley Martin is a Lecturer in Social Policy at the School of Applied Social Studies at UCC since 2004. She is a member of the BA Early Childhood Studies team and contributes to the Masters in Social Policy. She is a member of the Child Migration and Social Policy research group in the School. As well as child migration, her other main research interest is in the well-being of children and her research relates to key areas of children's lives including early years care and education and educational disadvantage.

Dr Selina McCoy is a Senior Research Officer at the Economic and Social Research Institute (ESRI) in the Republic of Ireland. She has published extensively on equality in Irish education, with a particular focus on second level student experience and higher education access. Most recently she has examined higher education retention, the costs associated with college participation and the role of school level processes in shaping higher education entry.

Dr Rory McDaid is a Research Fellow in the Children's Research Centre, Trinity College. He completed his Doctorate in Education while working as a language support teacher in St. Gabriel's National School in Dublin 7, Ireland and as a Research Associate in the Special Education Department, St. Patrick's College, Drumcondra, Dublin 9, Ireland. His teaching and research interests include minority ethnic and minority language children, inclusive education, commercialism in Irish schools and participatory action research.

Dr Michal Molcho is a Lecturer in the School for Health Sciences and a senior researcher in the Health Promotion Research Centre (HPRC) in the National University of Ireland Galway, and she is the Deputy PI of the Health Behaviour in School-Aged Children (HBSC) in Ireland. She focuses mainly in adolescents health and violence and injury prevention, but more recently her work is focusing on the health and well-being of child-immigrants.

Niamh Nestor is a PhD candidate at the School of Languages and Literatures at University College Dublin, Ireland. Her PhD research has been funded by the Irish Research Council for the Humanities and Social Sciences and forms part of a joint project between Trinity College Dublin and University College Dublin. The research focuses on a group of young Poles living in Ireland and explores issues of language variation and identity. Niamh is also working with Professor Vera Regan on a project on language identity and migration which is funded by the Irish Research Council for the Humanities and Social Sciences.

Dr Saoirse Nic Gabhainn is Director of the Health Promotion Research Centre at the National University of Ireland Galway, Ireland. Her work is focused on health and well-being among young people with a particular interest in risk-taking behaviours and youth involvement in the research process. Currently directing the fourth round of the Health Behaviour in School-aged Children (HBSC) study in Ireland, she is also involved in studies on school health education and promotion.

Dr Muireann Ní Raghallaigh is a Lecturer in Social Work in the School of Applied Social Science in University College Dublin, Republic of Ireland. Muireann previously worked as a social worker with unaccompanied asylum seeking children. She is interested in the experiences of asylum seekers, refugees and other migrants living in Ireland and in the coping strategies that they use. She is also interested in culturally competent social work practice and in international development issues.

Dr Neil O'Boyle lectures in the School of Communications, Dublin City University (DCU), where he is also director of the International Media, Interculturalism and Migration research cluster. He is a member of the MCRI and was formerly the lead researcher on the IRCHSS theme-funded project 'Immigration and Social Change in the Republic of Ireland'.

Dr Jacqui O'Riordan joined the school of Applied Social Studies, UCC in 2006 as part of the BA Early Childhood Studies team and is a member of the Child Migration and Social Policy research group in the School. She also lectures in sociology, women's studies and adult education settings and worked as an independent researcher in Ireland and Tanzania. Her work with the Higher Education Equality Unit gained her extensive experience in a range of equality concerns. Her research interests focus on a range of issues concerning equality and diversity in local and global contexts, with a particular interest in the intersection between lives and livelihoods, childhood and global diversity, women's studies and gender.

Emma Quinn is National Coordinator of the Irish National Contact Point of the European Migration Network located within the Economic and Social Research Institute (ESRI) in the Republic of Ireland. She also has a particular research interest in the experiences of discrimination among migrants, integration monitoring, and the impact of migration on the Irish labour market. Recent publications have investigated Irish economic migration policy development and the assisted return of migrants from Ireland.

Prof. Vera Regan is Associate Professor of Sociolinguistics at School of Languages and Literatures at University College Dublin. Her research and publications focus on sociolinguistic approaches to second language acquisition. She is currently President of the Association of French Language Studies and has been President of the European Association for Second Language Research. She is currently Principal Investigator for a project on language identity and migration funded by the Irish Research Council for the Humanities and Social Sciences. http://www.ucd.ie/sllf/Staff/Regan_Vera_profile.html

Prof. Emer Smyth is a Research Professor and program coordinator of Education Research at the ESRI. Her areas of interest include education, school to work transitions, and women's employment. She has a strong interest in comparative research on education and labor market issues. Currently she is a co-coordinator of a study that explores the transmission of religious beliefs and values through the education system and the family across different EU country contexts.

Dr Steve Song is an Assistant Professor of Education at George Fox University, located near Portland, Oregon. Prior to his current professorship, he was a post-doctoral research fellow at the Geary Institute, University College Dublin. In addition to his work in Ireland and other parts of Europe, Dr Song has examined immigrant student adaptations in the United States through his involvement in the Harvard Immigration Project, and in South Korea as a visiting research scholar at Korea University. His research interest includes immigration, race, ethnicity, comparative education, and international education policy.

Dr Naomi Tyrrell (née Bushin) is a Lecturer in Human Geography at the University of Plymouth, UK. She researches children's experiences of migration in European contexts and was a postdoctoral researcher on the Marie Curie Migrant Children Project at University College Cork, Ireland. She has recently published papers on aspects of child migration in *Area, Children's Geographies* and *Population, Space and Place*. Her current research project focuses on the impact of scientific mobility on the children of mobile scientists in Europe.

Dr Angela Veale is a Lecturer in Applied Psychology, University College Cork, Ireland. Her research interests include children and young people in post-conflict contexts, refugee and asylum seeker children and families and transnational migration. Her recent research has included participatory action research on the social reintegration of young mothers formerly associated with armed groups in Liberia, Sierra Leone & Northern Uganda and is presently co-partner in a NORFACE project on child-rearing and wellbeing in transnational families.

Lightning Source UK Ltd.
Milton Keynes UK
173651UK00001B/17/P